DATE DUE FOR R

Alexander
Bestuzhev-Marlinsky
and
Russian Byronism

Lewis Bagby

Alexander Bestuzhev-Marlinsky and Russian Byronism

The Pennsylvania State University Press
University Park, Pennsylvania

Library of Congress Cataloging-in-Publication Data

Bagby, Lewis, 1944–
    Alexander Bestuzhev-Marlinsky and Russian Byronism / Lewis Bagby.

        p.   cm.
    Includes bibliographical references and index.
    ISBN 0-271-01336-2 (alk. paper)
    1. Marlinskiĭ, A. (Aleksandr), 1797–1837.   2. Authors,
Russian—19th century—Biography.   3. Romanticism—Russia.
4. Byron, George Gordon, Baron, 1788–1824—Influence.
I. Title.
PG3321.B45Z59   1995
891.73′3—dc20   10004606010
    [B]   93-47591
                                                                                                CIP

Published by The Pennsylvania State University Press,
University Park, PA 16802-1003

It is the policy of The Pennsylvania State University Press to use acid-free paper for
the first printing of all clothbound books. Publications on uncoated stock satisfy the
minimum requirements of American National Standard for Information Sciences—
Permanence of Paper for Printed Library Materials, ANSI Z39.48–1984.

Contents

This book is dedicated to

my parents, Dorothy and Grover

my wife, Donna

and our sons, David and Ryan

Preface and Acknowledgments

In Russia of the 1820s and 1830s Alexander Bestuzhev (pseudonym Marlinsky) was a compelling life model for writers and readers; in Russia of the 1850s and 1860s he was emulated by political activists. He was also the most popular writer of ultraromantic prose fiction for the Russian reading public, and his life and literature had remarkable influence on the young Tolstoy and Turgenev. Because his aesthetics have remained important to the way Russians think about culture, develop life roles based on literary texts, and construct heroic self-images, the effect of his example is tangible in socialist realism as well. In this book I attempt to reestablish Bestuzhev's position in Russian cultural history while at the same time introducing a forgotten literary icon to an audience not familiar with him. I also attempt to recover, if not restore, the criteria of assessment lost in the shift from the romantic to the realist eras, because it is only by the standards of the early nineteenth century that Bestuzhev-Marlinsky's accomplishments in life and letters can be evaluated objectively and fairly.

Chapter 1 introduces the reader to the historical setting, describes Bestuzhev's family, and locates Bestuzhev himself within the fashionable trends of early European romanticism. Chapters 2 through 5 describe and analyze Bestuzhev's entry into the literary arena as a quasi-Byronic figure and his self-conscious development into a full-blown Byronic literary persona intricately connected to his military career, the literary polemics of his day, fiction writing, and political activism. The next three chapters investigate his involvement in the Decembrist Revolt (1825), reinterpret the significance of that event in his life and in Russian culture, and indicate how severely the revolt and its aftermath challenged his

Byronic self-conception during the years of his Siberian exile. The final two chapters present Bestuzhev's exile in the Caucasus, where he fought against its indigenous peoples, established himself as a premier literary figure (more popular than Alexander Pushkin) under the pseudonym Marlinsky, and met a rather mysterious end. I take a chronological, historical approach to Bestuzhev's literary life in the tradition of the Russian biographical genre *trudy i dni* (life and works), operating inductively from primary sources to restore and maintain the system of values and organizational principles under which Bestuzhev and his generation operated. Through extensive documentation of the behavioral codes of the era gathered from Bestuzhev's letters, diaries, critical essays, and fictional tales, I view him and his generation (including Tsar Nicholas I) from within the system of motives, intentions, and desires belonging to their period.

This approach permits me to reread Bestuzhev's life and literary identity and the Decembrist Revolt, a subject long monopolized and politicized by Soviet-era scholarship. These two elements coalesce in the themes of carnival rebirth and heroic death, which I see as driving impulses behind the impact of the Decembrist Revolt and behind Bestuzhev's life, his career, his reception by a growing readership, and his rejection by subsequent generations as well.

In sum, in this study I hope to unify our understanding of the mysteries surrounding Bestuzhev's identity, disappearance, and ill-treatment since the height of his popularity. My main contributions to this project are an appreciation of a specific example of Byronism in Russia and an analysis of disparate cultural phenomena (political revolt, literary polemics, military service, political exile, artistic creativity, identity formation) from the perspective of what might be called the romantic carnivalesque, the cultural representation of ritualized forms of life, death, and rebirth in the early nineteenth century.

A study that has taken the better part of the past fifteen years has necessarily required the assistance, had the support, and tried the patience of many people and institutions. In many respects, my curiosity about Bestuzhev began when I was a graduate student of Donald Fanger's at Stanford University. His presentation of Bestuzhev as a representative of popular literature against which the accomplishments of Gogol and Pushkin could be measured first piqued my interest. John Mersereau Jr., whose seminar on Russian romantic prose at the University of Michigan introduced me in an authentic way to Bestuzhev's work, guided me into the unique features of the long and unjustly discredited romantic prose movement in Russia. His direction of my Formalist-oriented dissertation on Bestuzhev's prose practices formed the nexus of my original interest in ultraromanticism as a cultural phenomenon. This book represents a resurgence of my interest, which came in the late 1970s on the basis of the work of Yury Lotman and Lauren Leighton, who helped me see how very much the life-text Bestuzhev built was connected to an aesthetic text. This study attempts to describe that connection.

I have been assisted by many research libraries over the years, including those at the University of Michigan, Ohio State University (with thanks to Frank Silbajoris), Princeton University (with thanks to Victor Brombert), the University of Edmonton, the Slavic Library in Helsinki, and the Saltykov-Shchedrin Library in St. Petersburg. Support for work in those libraries has come from a variety of sources, most consistently from the University of Wyoming's College of Arts and Sciences, the Offices for Academic Affairs and Research, and the Department of Modern and Classical Languages. For their assistance I am indebted to Dean Oliver Walter, Provost Albert Karnig, Vice-President Derek Hodgson, and department heads Ian Adams, Lowell Bangerter, and Klaus Hanson. Funding has also come from the National Endowment for the Humanities (Travel Grants and Summer Seminars for College Instructors). I would like to express my appreciation to the editors of *Russian Literature* and *The Slavic and East European Journal* for their permission to use materials from articles that appeared on their pages in the 1980s. Permission to reprint the SEEJ article has been granted by AATSEEL of the U.S., Inc.

The most gratifying aspect of the project has been collaborating with colleagues whose invaluable comments, suggestions, disputations, and corrections have helped clarify my thoughts and prose. For suggestions of a semantic and stylistic nature, I have my father, Grover C. Bagby, to thank with a son's deepest love and respect. To John Mersereau, Jr., I owe a sincere debt of gratitude for his twenty years of continued encouragement and learned cautions. Lauren Leighton has proven the most diligent critic of my ideas; his enthusiastic support and careful attention to detail have been very useful in the evolution of the research and writing. Irina Paperno's interest in the study goes back to 1978 when I first outlined the argument to her in Leningrad, and she gave much valued advice. It was she who suggested I work with Philip Winsor, senior editor at Penn State Press, who helped the project through the vicissitudes of production. I most gratefully acknowledge Pavel Sigalov, my colleague and friend in the Russian Program at the University of Wyoming, who has urged me to complete the project against the rigors of extensive teaching and administrative obligations. His assistance on matters pertinent to the stylistic and linguistic details of Bestuzhev's prose has been of the highest professional caliber. Neil Cornwell read with great sensitivity and acumen the original draft submitted to his care and analyzed the penultimate draft with an eye toward the presentation of the argument. My friends Tilly Warnock, John Warnock, and Eric Nye, who are professors of English, read early chapters and made helpful comments about the book's content, organization, and appeal to an audience of humanist readers.

The copies of Nicholas Bestuzhev's portraits of himself and his brothers come thanks to the efforts of Ms. Ospovit of the Pushkin Museum in St. Petersburg. The Mikhail Lermontov drawings of scenes from Alexander Bestuzhev's "Ammalat-bek" appear from the archives of the Pushkin House, St. Petersburg. Igor Nemirovsky and Natalya Speranskaya delivered the materials from both institutions in a timely and helpful fashion, and I am grateful to them for their dedicated work on behalf of this project. Professor Lauren Leighton deserves my gratitude here, too, for allowing me to use a copy in his possession of Alexander Bestuzhev's self-portrait from the period of the Caucasian exile.

To my wife, Donna, and our sons, David and Ryan, I owe the most. Their unswerving belief in this project over the years has buoyed me greatly and helped bring it to fruition. I can never repay them for their love, patience, and encouragement. Donna's hours of labor over the loose and baggy early drafts made the dream of completing it a reality.

In many respects the book is not my own, but the issue of an extensive and supportive community; responsibility for the result, however, is mine.

Transliteration

In the footnotes, parenthetical citations, and bibliography I employ a slightly modified version of the Library of Congress system of Russian transliteration, but in the body of the text I use a system that is easier to read for those who know no Russian. First names are anglicized when they correspond to widely recognized forms in English. When an individual of Russian origin is well known in the West under a conventional form, that orthography is used.

People take for gospel all I say, and go away continually with false impressions. *Mais n'importe*! it will render the statements of my future biographers more amusing; as I flatter myself I shall have more than one. Indeed, the more the merrier, say I. One will represent me as a sort of sublime misanthrope, with moments of kind feeling. This, *par exemple,* is my favorite *role*. Another will portray me as a modern Don Juan; and a third . . . will, it is to be hoped, if only for opposition sake, represent me as an *amiable,* ill-used gentleman, "more sinned against than sinning." Now, if I know myself, I should say, that I have no character at all. . . . But, joking apart, what I think of myself is, that I am so changeable, being everything by turns and nothing long—I am such a strange melange of good and evil, that it would be difficult to describe me.

 —*Byron: A Biography* by Leslie A. Marchand, citing
   Lady Blessington, citing George Gordon Byron

Introduction

Literature is a good friend but an evil master.
—Bestuzhev-Marlinsky

In early-nineteenth-century Russia, the narratives of Alexander Alexan-drovich Bestuzhev-Marlinsky (1797–1837) literally moved men to ac-tion, catalyzing life choices by literary example. They captured the imagi-nation of not only his generation but the next. In his memoirs Ivan Turgenev (1818–83) insisted that Bestuzhev-Marlinsky's heroes were to be met everywhere in society, young men conversing in "marlinisms," a special metaphoric and flamboyant language coined from Bestuzhev's pen name Marlinsky to describe the style he innovated in Russian letters. According to Turgenev, these "marlinist" poseurs appeared haughty and insolent, alternately pulling sorrowful and belligerent faces, and lived their short days and long nights, "with storms in their souls and fire in their blood."[1] He himself was moved to youthful excess by Bestuzhev-Marlinsky's fiction and in a letter to Leo Tolstoy (1828–1910) confessed that he would "kiss Marlinsky's name on journal covers."[2] Tolstoy went even further, journeying south from Great Russia to the Caucasus, a land Bestuzhev-Marlinsky had popularized in his stories, in quest of the archetypal romantic hero within.

Bestuzhev-Marlinsky was arguably the most advanced writer of prose in the 1820s and demonstrably the most popular writer in Russia in the 1830s. He was an individual in whom Russian culture was condensed with incredible richness. We need only survey his life, examine his work, and review his mysterious death to see that he represents the challenges and dilemmas of his time and bears dramatic witness to the desires and imperfections of mankind.

It is my purpose to restore him to cultural history in a manner that befits his accomplishments. So frequently is his importance attested in the documents of the great Russian writers and in the life patterns of the forgotten readers of his time that his contribution to that culture deserves an accounting. An assessment of his legacy must also address the reasons for his having been neglected since then, for only when this issue is put in historical perspective is an objective picture of his place in Russian romanticism possible.

In the second decade of the nineteenth century, Bestuzhev-Marlinsky dedicated himself to a new and radical behavioral model only recently acquired from the West, specifically from Lord Byron (1788–1824), whose works were known to the Russian public in French and Russian translations. A repository of ambiguity, social masks, intentional inconsistency, and ironic play with an unsuspecting audience, Byronism in Russia accounts for some of Bestuzhev-Marlinsky's historic inaccessibility. When Bestuzhev-Marlinsky donned a Byronic mask, Russian society was alternately horrified and delighted. There was, however, an important difference between Byron's reception in the West and the Byronic character's apprehension in Russian culture. Byron in his time represented an enigma to his audience; he challenged conventional social and literary norms in a manner that would not submit to simplistic interpreta-

1. "Stuk . . . stuk . . . stuk," in *Polnoe sobranie sochinenii i pisem v 30 tomakh* (Moscow, 1978), 8:228. The line "with storms in their souls" is taken from Bestuzhev's tale, "Lieutenant Belozor" (1831). Turgenev attests that in the 1830s Bestuzhev was more popular than even Pushkin.
2. *Perepiska I. S. Turgeneva*, ed. K. I. Tiun'kin (Moscow, 1980), 2:118.

tion. Russian Byronism, however, was perceived against the background of the cultural model already supplied from England. Consequently, Bestuzhev-Marlinsky was seen as a comprehensible phenomenon. His many stories and tales of adventure were treated as clues to his substantive identity. His literary heroes were so thoroughly fused with the persona he projected in everyday life, that for the Russian readers from 1820 to 1850 there was no enigmatic self lurking behind a mask; Bestuzhev-Marlinsky's literary identity, social persona, and authentic self were assumed to be one and the same.

Because of his readers' assumptions, Bestuzhev-Marlinsky found it possible to encode more than literary texts; he created stories of himself in daily life to meet the expectations created by those texts. In effect, he wrote both his fiction and his life. In addition to his literary efforts (which won the Grand Dowager's favor in the 1820s), he was a military officer whose exemplary behavior promised to bring him into the service of Tsar Alexander I (1801–25). But after his participation in the first Russian revolution, the Decembrist Revolt of 1825, which challenged the succession of Nicholas I (1825–55) to the throne, Bestuzhev-Marlinsky was stripped of his noble status and exiled first to Siberia and then to the Caucasus. Temporarily forgotten by his public, his fate was kept secret until his death in 1837 when it was announced that the exiled Alexander Alexandrovich Bestuzhev had authored many popular tales of the 1830s under the pseudonym Marlinsky. His works were immediately published in a multivolume set that sold out within weeks of its issue. His political activism became a model for later generations of revolutionaries, and his martyrdom in exile inspired legends about him after he disappeared. Successive generations of readers have assumed that the mask was the man and interpreted Bestuzhev-Marlinsky's persona as an authentic representation of his self.

The memoirist P. S. Shchukin, who visited Bestuzhev-Marlinsky when he was living in exile in the far north of Siberia, confessed, "I gazed upon him with altogether different eyes [than earlier in my life]. I virtually reread his stories [while listening to what he had to say] and I attempted to catch in his character features of the heroes he had introduced on the stage [of his art]."[3] Society and the individual colluded to form an identity by reinforcing the generation and reception of the persona. The

3. "A. Bestuzhev-Marlinskii v Iakutske," in *Pisateli-dekabristy v vospominaniiakh sovremennikov*, ed. V. Vatsuro et al. (Moscow, 1980), 2:140–47.

authorial projection in life as well as in letters coupled with public response (which confirmed the projection in every detail) to structure the unique nature of aesthetics in early-nineteenth-century Russia.

Nicholas Karamzin (1766–1826) is the acknowledged father of the sentimental tale in Russian letters. His first publications, appearing in print before Bestuzhev-Marlinsky was born, projected a narrator, hero, and authorial persona in confluence with one another. It was Karamzin's prose that most influenced Bestuzhev-Marlinsky's development of a personal voice three decades later. To Karamzin's prose model must be added those of Vasily Zhukovsky (1782–1856) and Konstantin Batyushkov (1787–1855). Although meager in their production of fiction, together with Karamzin they established the norm for sentimental prose at the turn of the century. Vasily Narezhny (1780–1825), who preceded Bestuzhev-Marlinsky as well, represented an opposite pole. Working from the tradition of the didactic adventure novel of the eighteenth century, Narezhny enlivened his *Gil Blas* imitations with a coarse, vernacular Russian that contrasted with the sensitivity and musicality of the Karamzin school's salon language. By the 1820s, however, the voices of these initiators of a modern prose fiction in Russia had, for the most part, fallen silent. Karamzin turned from belles lettres in order to complete his *History of the Russian State* (*Istoriia Gosudarstva Rossiiskogo*, 1818); Batyushkov was overcome by mental illness, which lasted until his death; Zhukovsky continued to make only a minor contribution to prose fiction.

Bestuzhev-Marlinsky was one of a small group of prose writers in the early 1820s. He is acknowledged to be the prime bearer of the Karamzinian tradition and at the same time to have advanced Russian prose beyond the limitations imposed on it by that tradition. Orest Somov (1783–1833), Fyodor Glinka (1786–1880), Nicholas Grech (1800–1858), and Nicholas Bestuzhev (1791–1855) all made contributions of a disparate kind to the travelogue, which revitalized the cloying sentimentalist prose. Unlike Bestuzhev-Marlinsky's, Somov's prose inclined toward the metonymic rather than the metaphoric. Glinka's military accounts developed the literary language in the direction of a virile and direct form of address, but his historical tales maintained the Karamzinian affective style. Grech entertained a matter-of-fact discourse in his narrator, and his style was metonymic. Bestuzhev-Marlinsky's brother Nicholas opened the literary language to naval vocabulary and used an analytic style more representative of eighteenth-century rationalism than nineteenth-century romanticism.

In romantic excess, Bestuzhev-Marlinsky surpassed all of his contemporaries. His prose is saturated with metaphors, flights of fancy, and the "marlinism" (the peculiar and witty style of his characters' and narrators' speech). It distinguishes itself from that of his peers in the early 1820s by its adherence to the theatricality of the Byronic pose and the techniques of *L'École frenetique* associated with early Victor Hugo. Almost single-handedly Bestuzhev-Marlinsky revived the historical tale, a genre which had lost its efficacy through the sentimentalist restrictions placed upon it. He reinvigorated it through his ultraromantic style, the symmetry of his period, a dashing bravado in relation to the utterance, and a reliance on new models of discourse encountered in French and English literature. Although Wilhelm Küchelbecker's (1797–1846) characters and plots echo many of Bestuzhev-Marlinsky's Livonian tales, his style has an ease and a sense of effortlessness that Bestuzhev-Marlinsky rarely achieved. Bestuzhev-Marlinsky's goals were entirely different. Where his contemporaries used restraint and natural expression to form their discourse, Bestuzhev-Marlinsky inclined toward the extreme, the improbable, and the self-aggrandizing.

The marlinism in Bestuzhev-Marlinsky's prose (as in his criticism and letters) is distinguished by several stylistic features, all of which he activated in art and in life. Many derive from the sentimentalist's stylistic arsenal: sound repetition, alliteration, assonance, symmetry, isocolon, anaphora, epithet inversion, rhythm, and parallel construction. These techniques occur as linear phenomena, elaborated in time as the syntagma moves forward, as any given utterance develops from beginning to end (whether edited or not). The syntagma is not developed out of a dialogic relationship to what has been uttered, by questioning what has been committed to the page. Rather the initial word or words condition what follows, structuring a rhythmic sound repetition based on the initial segment of the utterance. To these sentimentalist techniques Bestuzhev added other linear features: ellipsis, aphoristic sententiousness, unmotivated shifts (for example, from high to low speech), verb strings, and three constantly recurring rhetorical devices—paregmenon, polyptoton, and antithesis.

In exile Bestuzhev-Marlinsky was separated from the literary milieu, which was expanding in every conceivable direction: new authors, genres, and language. The late 1820s brought a variety of new story types, including the supernatural tale (and its parody), the frame tale (à la Washington Irving), the physiological sketch, the society tale, story cycles, the picaresque novel, the tale of merchant life, and the historical novel. Authors developed interests in merchants and peasants and sprinkled (or saturated) their narratives with phrases of the lower classes: proverbs, idioms, folk locutions, as well as the vernacular. The expansion of the literary language brought about by Mikhail Pogodin (1800–1875), Nicholas Polevoy (1796–1846), Faddei Bulgarin (1789–1859), Alexei Perovsky-Pogorelsky (1787–1836), Mikhail Zagoskin (1790–1852), and Orest Somov surely caused Bestuzhev-Marlinsky to consider what future contribution he might make to the development of Russian prose.

When Bestuzhev-Marlinsky entered the prose arena for a second time (under the pseudonym Marlinsky), he quickly established his place among writers, who included people familiar to him from the 1820s like Vladimir Odoyevsky (1803–69) or his friend Alexander Pushkin (1799–1837), but new writers as well: Nikolai Gogol (1809–52), Ivan Lazhechnikov (1792–1869), Nicholas Pavlov (1803–64), Osip Senkovsky (1800–1858), Alexander Veltman (1800–1870). These authors won the interest of a growing readership through a variety of styles peculiar to each. Gogol's innovations hardly require mention here except to say he represented the greatest challenge to Bestuzhev-Marlinsky's preeminence. Lazhechnikov and Zagoskin engaged in a genre that remained beyond Bestuzhev's grasp—the historical novel. For their roughly hewn achievement they were duly rewarded by critical acclaim and wide popularity. Odoyevsky's philosophical prose also remained beyond Bestuzhev-Marlinsky; his bent toward German idealism left Bestuzhev-Marlinsky as cold and uncomprehending as when he read *Faust*. Veltman and Senkovsky, however, afforded Bestuzhev-Marlinsky hours of enjoyment, but he was quick to note their deficiencies, which, interestingly, he shared—a penchant for long periods, effusiveness, and an unabated irony and wittiness that sometimes submerges the substance of the narrative.

As the competition increased, Bestuzhev-Marlinsky persisted in his well-developed style of the 1820s. Although the consistency eventually marked him as an easy target for the next generation of writers, his extreme romantic style, narrators, characters, plots, and exotic settings made him the author of the decade, Gogol notwithstanding. The marlinism is the most salient element that binds his work together, from literary criticism to personal letters, and from anecdote to historical fiction. Early-nineteenth-century Russian poets sought a special stamp by which even their unsigned work could be recognized. Bestuzhev's was the marlinism, his trademark in fiction and in society. He prepared his audience to read his literary texts and his life-text as one and the same, thereby fulfilling the period's expectation that art and life are most meaningful when they coincide. Bestuzhev-Marlinsky's witty narrators were taken for the author himself. The confusion of Bestuzhev's personality with his Marlinsky persona began very early in his career.

Bestuzhev-Marlinsky's writings also became a textbook from which students learned how to view reality. A. L. Zisserman, who participated in the Caucasian wars and distinguished himself there, published his memoirs in the 1870s in which he attests to the deep penetration of the literary model into his personal life. Drawing a direct line between his reading of Bestuzhev-Marlinsky's Caucasian tales and his own life, Zisserman bears witness to the psychological impact of Bestuzhev-Marlinsky's model:

> When I was seventeen and yet living in the provinces I chanced to read some of Marlinsky's stories for the first time. I cannot begin to describe with what enthusiasm I praised his "Ammalat-bek," "Mulla Nur," and sundry sketches of the Caucasus. Suffice it to say that this reading gave birth in me to the thought that I should give everything up and fly to the Caucasus, to that enchanted land, with its awesome natural surroundings, its warrior inhabitants, marvelous women, poetic sky, high mountains eternally covered in snow, and other such charms which entirely entranced the imagination of a seventeen-year-old mind, not to mention of a child who since birth had shown an inclination toward experiences and emotions very much stronger than the usual schoolboy fancies.[4]

Zisserman's remarks depict traditional romantic literary values, particularly self-absorption to the extent of needing to mythologize the self in quasi-hagiographical terms. It took a major turn in Russian culture to extract Russian youth and Russian letters from Bestuzhev-Marlinsky's compelling grip.

---

4. "Otryvki iz moikh vospominanii," *Russkii vestnik* 5 (1876): 52.

By the 1830s Russian criticism had begun to move away from the dynamic and flamboyant conception of self and the world. Since Bestuzhev-Marlinsky was the most popular writer of fiction at the time, it was quite natural that he should come under attack. Vissarion Belinsky (1811–48) represented the first prominent voice advancing a new relationship between literature and reality. He thought literature was meant to serve the public by educating its audience about social, economic, and political life and to serve reality by depicting it adequately. Belinsky opposed the Bestuzhevan tendency to replace reality with fantasy and to advocate personal desire over social good. For him Bestuzhev-Marlinsky's example constituted an outworn and even dangerous phenomenon in Russian cultural history. Aiming his barbs directly, Belinsky challenged Russia's readership in 1834: "We have very few authors who have written as much as Mr. Marlinsky, but this abundance springs not from the largess of talent, not from a surplus of [authentic] creative energy, but from habit, simply from doing the same thing over and over again. . . . He has talent, but not a great talent, for it is weakened by his eternal compulsion to be witty."[5] No one, perhaps, more than Bestuzhev realized his limitations as a writer, but unlike Belinsky, he appreciated his own real accomplishments: "I am far from being an egotist, but just as far from self-abasement. I know my worth in the world of Russian letters, even though I have attained my value by chance, through the lack of prose writers in contemporary literature. Thus, I still feel that I have services to perform for our native language."[6] This balanced view became all the more rare with each passing decade of the nineteenth century.

At this historical juncture, with the rise of the age of realism, both Bestuzhev-Marlinsky's life and fiction began to be measured by criteria that did not belong to his time. What had once elicited enthusiastic responses from young Turgenev and Tolstoy was now seen as excess. Bestuzhev-Marlinsky's fiction was dismissed outright because it did not hold to a new set of values. In the middle of the nineteenth century Tolstoy reflected Belinsky's reorientation when he concluded that romantic fiction clouded the minds of naive readers (as he had been in his youth) and created expectations in life that could not be fulfilled. To

5. *Polnoe sobranie sochinenii* (Moscow, 1953), 1:84–85.
6. "Pis'ma Aleksandra Aleksandrovicha Bestuzheva k N. A. i K. A. Polevym, pisannye v 1831–1837 godakh," *Russkii vestnik* 3 (1861): 323.

assert his own definition of reality, in his early fiction Tolstoy assailed Bestuzhev-Marlinsky's prose. If Bestuzhev-Marlinsky presumed that art produces as well as reproduces reality, Tolstoy promulgated the contrary notion, that life informs fiction. Tolstoy satirized Bestuzhev-Marlinsky's dual texts—both the fiction that proffered its audience models for daily life and the author himself, whose biography reinforced the fiction.

In "The Raid" ("Nabeg," 1853) Tolstoy's narrator re-creates the Bestuzhev-Marlinsky code of behavior only to expose its artificiality:

> A couple of hundred yards ahead of the infantry rode some Tatar horsemen. With them, riding on a large white horse and dressed in Caucasian costume, was a tall, handsome officer. Throughout the regiment he had a reputation for reckless courage and for not hesitating to tell anyone what he thought of him. His soft, black Oriental boots were trimmed with gold braid as was his black tunic under which he wore a yellow silk Circassian shirt. The tall sheepskin hat on his head was pushed back carelessly. A powder flask and a pistol were fastened to silver straps across his chest and back. Another pistol and a silver-mounted dagger hung from his belt next to a saber in a red leather sheath. A rifle in a black holster was slung over his shoulder. From his dress, his style of riding, all his movements, it was obvious that he wanted to look like a Tatar. He was even saying something to the Tatars in a language I couldn't understand. But then, judging by the bewildered, amused looks they exchanged with one another, I guessed they couldn't understand him either.
>
> He was one of those dashing, wild young officers who attempt to model themselves on the heroes of Lermontov and Marlinsky. These officers see the Caucasus only through the prism of romance, and in everything they are guided solely by the instincts and tastes of their models.[7]

Tolstoy's assault on the Bestuzhev-Marlinsky canon reflected a broad cultural movement in the second half of the nineteenth century to reassess romantic art. Both his and Belinsky's renderings of Bestuzhev-

7. "The Raid," in *The Cossacks and the Raid,* trans. Andrew MacAndrew (New York, 1961), 190–91.

Marlinsky, however, represent the mechanism by which cultural systems evolve, not the objectivity of a culture to describe itself.

Since the end of the nineteenth century the rejection of Bestuzhev-Marlinsky's persona and fiction has been balanced by critics seeking to reestablish his contribution. Nevertheless, these critics persist in the notion that the persona was the man. Turn-of-the-century criticism sought the roots of Bestuzhev-Marlinsky's fiction in the European romantic tradition. N. Kozmin's *Sketches on the History of Russian Romanticism* (*Ocherki iz istorii romantizma*, 1903), A. N. Pypin's *History of Russian Literature* (*Istoriia russkoi literatury*, 1903), and I. I. Zamotin's *Romanticism of the 1820s in Russian Literature* (*Romantizm dvadtsatykh godov XIX stoletiia v russkoi literature*, 1911) made important contributions to our appreciation of the foreign influences on Bestuzhev's work, for example, Irving, Hoffman, Radcliffe, Scott, and Byron. These same critics, however, cite the words of Bestuzhev-Marlinsky's protagonists as representative of the author's own utterances about himself. In their writings it is not unusual to find a passage from a Bestuzhev-Marlinsky story juxtaposed with a passage from one of his personal letters. If there is reason to make such a reading (and there surely is), it does not lie in the simplistic linkage of Bestuzhev's mask with his personality. The two must be differentiated.

In response to this approach, Soviet criticism inclined in two general directions, one reacting strongly to the deficiencies of the earlier tradition and the other honing and reshaping it. Russian Formalist critics disconnected life from letters and proceeded to examine Bestuzhev's art as a discrete system. In an article titled "The Early Marlinsky" ("Rannii Marlinskii," 1920s), N. Kovarsky, a young student of Yury Tynianov and Boris Eikhenbaum, focused on the development of Bestuzhev-Marlinsky's style and on the evolution of the historical genre in his hands. Yet the linkage of literature to life that so dominated the early nineteenth century was viewed as tangential, rather than integral to the text, its generation, and its reception. The Formalist approach could neither account for Bestuzhev-Marlinsky's popularity nor measure his cultural significance save in the narrowest terms.

For historical and political reasons, the Formalist approach to Bestuzhev-Marlinsky's work ceased soon after it was initiated and was replaced by a branch of Soviet criticism that foregrounded Bestuzhev-Marlinsky, rather than his work. The voices of his heroes were again made to speak for the author, but this time with a significant change. These critics focused on the ideological content of the protagonists' and narrators' tirades and monologues. In Soviet criticism of this type we learn of Bestuzhev's attitude toward the people, revolution, and bourgeois society. A. G. Tseitlin's *Russian Literature of the First Half of the Nineteenth Century* (*Russkaia literatura pervoi poloviny XIX veka*, 1940) and B. S. Meilakh's "The Literary and Aesthetic Program of the Decembrists" ("Literaturno-esteticheskaia programma dekabristov," 1958) are two of a very large group of monographs and essays that used this approach. This form of ideological criticism culminated in S. Golubov's *Bestuzhev-Marlinsky* (*Bestuzhev-Marlinskii*, 1960), a fictional biography that made no attempt to distinguish the author from his fiction or his literary persona, and A. P. Sharupich's two book-length studies of Bestuzhev-Marlinsky's fiction. The first, *The Decembrist Alexander Bestuzhev: Questions of Worldview and Creativity* (*Dekabrist Bestuzhev-Marlinskii: Voprosy mirovozzreniia i tvorchestva*, 1962), attempts to consider Bestuzhev-Marlinsky's prose at a philosophical level, which it hardly contains, and the second, *Alexander Bestuzhev's Romanticism* (*Romantizm Aleksandra Bestuzheva*, 1964), treats the quintessential aspects of Bestuzhev-Marlinsky's extreme form of romanticism.

S. G. Isakov, writing from Tartu in the 1960s, presented a historical approach to Bestuzhev's art as it addressed Livonia and the Baltic region. His studies focus on the historical veracity of Bestuzhev-Marlinsky's work, its political orientation toward Decembrist themes, and the author's importance to early-nineteenth-century prose development. The central issue of Bestuzhev-Marlinsky as simultaneously literary, political, and social phenomenon is considered tangential, which is surprising given the early theoretical formulations of the Tartu school of semioticians. Nevertheless, Isakov's studies encapsulate concisely Bestuzhev-Marlinsky's contribution to historical prose of the early 1820s. More characteristic of the Tartu school in the 1960s, Kh. D. Leyemets's dissertation on Russian romantic prose of the 1820s and 1830s offers a more thorough examination of the formal attributes of Bestuzhev-Marlinsky's prose. Leyemets's article, "Toward the Question of the Semantic Structure of the Metaphoric Epithet in Russian Prose at the Beginning of the Nineteenth Century (on the basis of Marlinsky's Works)" ("K voprosu o semanticheskoi strukture metaforicheskogo epiteta v russkoi proze nachala XIX v. [na materiale proizvedenii A. Marlinskogo]," 1971), suggests how strongly the Formalist school continued to operate in some corners of the Soviet Union.

More recent Soviet scholarship also turned to a formal examination of Bestuzhev-Marlinsky's texts. E. M. Pulkhritudova in her "Literary Theory in Decembrist Romanticism in the 1830s" ("Literaturnaia teoriia dekabristskogo romantizma v 30-e gody XIX veka," 1968) respects the difference between aesthetic and biographical information and attempts to survey Bestuzhev-Marlinsky's development as a writer from the 1820s to the 1830s. She brings a thematic focus to her work and touches on topics of universal appeal, such as Bestuzhev-Marlinsky's understanding of man. Kanunova's *Aesthetics of the Russian Romantic Tale (A. A. Bestuzhev-Marlinsky and the Romantic Literati of the 1820s and 1830s)* (*Estetika russkoi romanticheskoi povesti [A. A. Bestuzhev-Marlinskii i romantiki-belletristy 20–30-kh godov XIX v.*, 1973) advances Pulkhritudova's work significantly. Her study is psychological and treats the theme of personal identity in Bestuzhev-Marlinsky's fiction. Her scrutiny of his rough drafts allows us to observe Bestuzhev-Marlinsky's writing process and his editing practices.

Bestuzhev-Marlinsky criticism has also brought national questions to the fore, spawning a series of works devoted in part or wholly to Bestuzhev-Marlinsky's presentation of Siberia and the Caucasus in his fiction. A. V. Popov's *The Decembrist Writers in the Caucasus (Dekabristy-Literatory na Kavkaze,* 1963), based on an earlier study, *Russian Writers in the Caucasus (Russkie pisateli na Kavkaze,* 1949), treats Bestuzhev-Marlinsky's contribution to Russian society's understanding of the Caucasus from an ethnographic perspective. Similarly, V. Shaduri's *Decembrist Literature and Georgian Society (Dekabristskaia literatura i gruzinskaia obshchestvennost',* 1958) describes the authenticity with which Bestuzhev-Marlinsky presented Georgian culture to the Russian reading public in the 1830s. R. Yu. Yusufov's *Dagestan and Russian Literature at the End of the Eighteenth and First Half of the Nineteenth Centuries (Dagestanskaia i russkaia literatura kontsa XVIII i pervoi poloviny XIX vv.,* 1964) includes a chapter on Bestuzhev-Marlinsky's "Dagestan Theme." Yu. S. Postnov's *Siberia in Decembrist Poetry (Sibir'v poezii dekabristov,* 1976) picks up on the regional theme, too, but since Bestuzhev-Marlinsky's creativity inclined more toward prose genres, the chapter on his Siberian poetry is necessarily scanty. All of these studies have their beginnings in the brief study of Bestuzhev-Marlinsky in Siberia by G. V. Prokhorov. His "A. A. Bestuzhev in Yakutsk" ("A. A. Bestuzhev v Iakutske," 1926) and V. Vasil'ev's "The Decembrist A. A. Bestuzhev-Marlinsky as a Writer and Ethnographer" ("Dekabrist A. A. Bestuzhev-

Marlinskii kak pisatel'-etnograf," 1926) formed the basis for extracting historical and ethnographic information from Bestuzhev-Marlinsky's fiction and letters. Indeed, since that time virtually every decade has produced a study along these lines, including V. Vasil'ev's own *Bestuzhev-Marlinsky in the Caucasus* (*Bestuzhev-Marlinskii na Kavkaze*, 1939). Ismorphic to the reading of Bestuzhev's persona as the man, these critical studies extract what is considered fact from his fiction.

Outside the Soviet Union scholarly interest in Bestuzhev-Marlinsky has been limited. Lauren Leighton's *Alexander Bestuzhev-Marlinsky* is the second complete survey in the West, the only one in English. It was preceded by H. V. Chmielewski's book-length study, *Alexander Bestuzhev-Marlinsky* (*Aleksandr Bestuzhev-Marlinskii*, 1966); Janusz Henzel's comprehensive study of Bestuzhev-Marlinsky's early prose fiction, *The Prose of Alexander Bestuzhev-Marlinsky in the Petersburg Period* (*Proza Aleksandra Biestużewa-Marlinskiego w okresie Petersburgskim*, 1967); and Dominique Barlesi's "The Function and Language of the Dramatis Personae of Bestuzhev-Marlinsky's Historical Fiction" ("Fonction et Langue de Personnages dans les Nouvelles Historiques de Bestuzev-Marlinskij," 1973), which takes a structuralist approach to character types in the fiction. Leighton's concise introduction to Bestuzhev-Marlinsky's life, literary criticism (in which the study excels), tales, and poems presents an overview of Bestuzhev-Marlinsky criticism since 1834 and steers an objective scholarly course through the myriad problems attending Bestuzhev-Marlinsky research. While thoroughly cataloguing Bestuzhev-Marlinsky's contribution to the early nineteenth century, like Chmielewski and Henzel, Leighton does not penetrate the Byronic guise under which all the author's writings are subsumed.

In effect, Bestuzhev-Marlinsky has slipped through all the critical nets thrown into his waters. Kanunova's attentiveness to the question of personal identity in Bestuzhev-Marlinsky's fiction comes close to broaching the topic from as fresh a perspective as has been written since N. Kotliarevsky's *The Decembrists Prince A. I. Odoyevsky and A. A. Bestuzhev-Marlinsky: Their Life and Literary Activity* (*Dekabristy Kn. A. I. Odoevskii i A. A. Bestuzhev-Marlinskii: ikh zhizn' i literaturnaia deiatel' nost'*, 1907). Kotliarevsky's penchant to disbelieve the Bestuzhev-Marlinsky persona is as often comic as it is instructive, but his excessive disdain for romantic speech and gesture creates an imbalance in his study, which militates against an objective understanding of Bestuzhev-Marlinsky's contribution. Kotliarevsky, however, can be credited with suggesting covertly that Bestuzhev is not Marlinsky, an idea that I have taken as the thesis of this book. Kanunova must be given credit, too, for raising the theme of identity in a compelling manner that revisits Kotliarevsky's point, albeit from a different perspective.

A psychological portrait must in some manner accommodate the distinction between the man and the dashing, heroic idea of himself he presented to the public. Since critics, like Bestuzhev-Marlinsky's contemporaries, have read his fiction as a coded diary and have viewed his behavior and speech in everyday life as a guide to his literature, the question is not whether Bestuzhev-Marlinsky resembled his heroes, but how he created this effect. It is quite remarkable that Bestuzhev-Marlinsky has managed to convince his readership for over a century that his art represents his person. But we must now ask ourselves what the equation of biography and literature meant both in his life and in his writing. If we are to address them so that both Bestuzhev-Marlinsky and his art might be viewed clearly, a precise idea of the internal conflicts the author experienced must first be extracted from his texts and developed into a coherent picture of the man who fostered such a compelling persona. Only then may we begin to appreciate why he went about convincing himself and the world that he was a living example of what he wrote.

Guided by contemporary literary theory, we may begin to unravel the texts Bestuzhev-Marlinsky created—those printed onto the page, those encoded into his life, and the critical literature about him, which mixes the two together. From this perspective it is possible to view Bestuzhev's equation of self to art as a form of communication in which each component is assigned a distinct value and a discrete function. Such an approach recommends itself by allowing us to separate Bestuzhev-Marlinsky's personality from his persona.

As we examine Bestuzhev-Marlinsky's many words, both fictional and otherwise, study the accounts memoirists and diarists have left that depict him, peruse government documents of the Decembrist Revolt, scrutinize the record of his interrogation, and survey letters and recollections of members of his family, a dialogue between Bestuzhev's heroic persona and his private personality emerges. We shall refer to the authentic self as "Bestuzhev," and to the heroic persona he projected in daily life and in fiction as "Marlinsky." The separation of Bestuzhev from

Marlinsky is of utmost importance to an objective rendering both of his contribution to Russian culture and of his humanity.

For Bestuzhev the pseudonym Marlinsky operated first as a disguise, then as a secret literary code, and finally as a container into which he attempted to pour his whole identity. Bestuzhev originally had taken the name Marlinsky in 1817 when he was stationed near Peterhof, the tsar's summer palace, at Marli. By 1819 he was using the name to mask his well-known identity and biases from his opponents in the literary polemics of the day. He rarely used it, but it attests very early in his career to a recourse to disguise, albeit superficial. Later, in exile, Bestuzhev was allowed to publish only under the condition that he assume a pen name. Again he selected Marlinsky, this time as a code, the import of which was to disclose his identity to, not hide his identity from, a public that had lost contact with him. Throughout his life, the heroic persona, which was so compelling to him for the problems it ostensibly solved, constituted a disguise and a code that allowed him alternately to conceal and reveal himself to the world about him. In exile the romantic persona Bestuzhev projected in his fiction and nonfictional writings took on the exclusive name Marlinsky. "Marlinsky," as heroic self-idea, became the repository of the identity Bestuzhev conceived for himself and propagated at every turn in life and in letters.

Unlike the persona, an authentic personality represents something immanent, it is the whole human being seeking to find him or herself in the process of representing that self in the material world. Its actual representation, deceptive or true, is inevitably a partial presentation of self, for it is virtually impossible to be everything one is at all times in every gesture, word, act, and thought. Human beings are reduced by sheer materiality to personae. Bestuzhev, from this perspective, is no different from anyone else. During Bestuzhev's early adult years, however, the persona took on the distinct forms that create differences between people.

The persona, acquired from the period's confluence of life and art, and with Bestuzhev's psychologically profound dedication toward its heroic manifestations, seemed to be an adequate means for fully expressing his personality. The dynamic changes wrought in the years immediately following the Napoleonic wars forged new ideas of identity that influenced Bestuzhev directly. The epoch's concern with the search for identity appealed to young minds in their quest for a unique sense of self.

The heroic persona supplied an aestheticized form of personality as fluid and vital as the times in which Bestuzhev came to maturity. The idea of self in the early 1820s proved adequate to reality.

The Decembrist Revolt, the interrogation, and the years of exile severely challenged the persona's integrity. It had to be either dismissed out of hand or altered to permit a wider range of human characteristics and to suit new circumstances. Introspection and analytic skill were required to render the persona anew, skills that Bestuzhev did not possess, a point he actively argued with his brother Nicholas. Consequently, the next stage in the development of Bestuzhev's persona, for dismissing it was out of the question, represented an imaginative continuation of the basic heroic outline, but with distinct Byronic characteristics affixed to it— weariness of life; impatience with human imperfections; a keen sense of one's superiority and consequent isolation from the herd; a consciousness of life's transience; a combative, confident and assertive grasp of one's right to define reality, and with it a glorification of the ego and its authority in such matters; and the idea of death as the consummate act of the heroic will. Bestuzhev wove these features into his view of himself and the world and encoded them onto the pages of his fiction.

Having reached this stage in the evolution of the romantic persona, Bestuzhev began to interpret the whole of world history and the evolution of art in similar terms—as the product of the romantic spirit. For example, in his defense of his publisher Nicholas Polevoy's novel, *The Oath on the Tomb of the Lord* (*Kliatva pri grobe gospodnem*), Bestuzhev asserted that the history of Western literature beginning with the early Christians is romantic. This is a grandiose claim that has been examined from two distinct perspectives. First, it reproduces arguments made in the West that advanced romanticism as a complete philosophical system. Bestuzhev was hardly a theoretician, for he lacked the essential skills by which discursive logic posits its thesis and argues its validity. Consequently, his turn toward philosophy and history must be explained from another perspective. This raises the second point: Bestuzhev's attempt to comprehend both history and contemporary life and art have been attributed to the Marlinsky persona and its inclination to aggrandize itself through dramatic utterance and bold gestures, in this instance, the positing of extreme propositions. But this interpretation treats Bestuzhev's motivation at the surface level. A third possibility incorporates the utterances of the persona and simultaneously the speaker's motivation for making them. More specifically, in viewing Bestuzhev's self-serving and grandiose claims for romanticism as an expression of personal desire and human need, we obtain a view of the man separate from his persona.

Bestuzhev's humanistic portrait has at its base a most compelling theme. Just as his whole personality has eluded capture in the critical literature, he, too, may have been unaware of his complete self. Studying his words and behavior for inconsistencies, for structural clues into the workings of his mind, and for coherent (but unconsciously encoded) symbolic information, we may extract from the fiction and the biography the outline of a thoroughly human identity that is at once heroic and common, unique and average, daring and fearful. With Bestuzhev's unwitting aid we are guided into the privacy of an authentic personality, into the enigmatic life of an elusive self he apparently could neither admit to nor totally suppress in his creations. From this portrait it is but one step to an understanding of Belinsky's, Tolstoy's, and later generations' apprehension of the man, and then to a rectification of his place in Russian culture.

In this study I begin with a description of Bestuzhev's early life, his family, and his initial endeavors to invent himself à la Byron. I pay particular attention to the quality of his mind and his reading habits. I discuss romanticism, as it stormed Russia in the second decade of the nineteenth century, with a focus on Bestuzhev's earliest attempts at poetry, his more successful literary criticism, and his fiction. I examine these genres to determine the psychological force that motivated him to turn toward an extreme representation of romanticism in letters and in life. I discuss in detail Bestuzhev's part in the Decembrist Revolt and the unconscious recesses of his psyche brought forward by it. His behavior during the interrogation and afterward represents one of the first opportunities by which we may scrutinize the effectiveness with which his social persona ("Marlinsky") operated in reality. I examine Bestuzhev's exile to Yakutsk in northern Siberia, where his self-idea was challenged severely, and then to the Caucasus where he experienced two divergent movements: personal disintegration and simultaneously a deeper projection of his self-idea in society. It was his Caucasus fiction that conditioned generations of readers either to reject his fiction outright or to accept him and his art as manifestations of Byronism. I conclude my analysis by discussing Bestuzhev's theatrical death and the impact it made on his reception.

Bestuzhev-Marlinsky's place in Russian cultural history is advanced in this study, but in the final analysis Bestuzhev's humanity motivates it. In these chapters I attempt to introduce a new Bestuzhev, to describe the world in which he lived, to elucidate the norms by which he wrote and acted, and to illuminate how he influenced the aestheticization of his rise and fall in Russian culture. In the vast web that entangles life and letters, Bestuzhev's biography and art are exemplary if only because they make such wonderful witness to the chance discoveries, revelations, joys, sorrows, triumphs, and utterly dismal failures that, despite our loftiest intentions, make up our lives. He strove with all his talent and enthusiasm to overcome the frailties and imperfections of being human. Bestuzhev's dilemma—the endless search for a unified self and persona—belongs to us all.

1
Cultural and Personal Context

For God's sake, don't remember me for my
stories!
—Bestuzhev-Marlinsky

Historical Setting

The period into which Alexander Alexandrovich Bestuzhev was born on
October 23, 1797, may be characterized as a time of conflict between
Enlightenment ideas and harsh, medieval social conditions. The tension
was manifest in various strata of Russian society, but it had entered into
the very marrow of the young educated nobility. Bestuzhev was one of
these men whose dreams, behavior, and writings testify to the human
drive to find order in the chaos of an era in which spiritual, intellectual,
and political authority was being challenged.

Since the reign of Peter the Great (1682–1725), Russia had been
adopting science, technology, language, and social customs from the
West. The Russian Orthodox Church with its traditional view of God

and authority lost significant ground as education, economics, medicine, dynastic, and intellectual life were placed in the control of government and private agencies. The shift in emphasis from the sacred to the secular can be measured in material signs (documents, social forms, the arts), but Russian secularization ultimately was, as Eugene Lampert put it, a "manifestation of a struggle which man has been waging with himself, the world and with God throughout history, and its arena is closely and constantly related to the deepest questions which can move the heart and mind of man."[1] The displacement of spiritual problems onto the social and political world became significant to Bestuzhev's generation, for it allowed these noblemen to posit eternal questions in their own language rather than in the dogmatic utterances of an emasculated Church. Spiritual concerns about man's existence were translated into a political language, giving birth to social ethics.

Literature played a significant role in formulating and disseminating social and ethical issues in Russia. Even before Bestuzhev's time, Empress Catherine II (1762–96) had encouraged and written for satiric journals critical of Russian political and social conditions and of those backward noblemen who refused to support progressive social programs. But in time literature began to advance liberal ideas counter to the interests of the throne. As the journals proved less satiric and more directly critical, Catherine terminated her support. With revolution in America and France, her rule turned conservative and repressive. In 1790 Alexander Radishchev (1749–1802) wrote his sensational *Journey from St. Petersburg to Moscow* (*Puteshestvie iz Peterburga v Moskvu*) in which the barbaric horrors of Russian rural life were chronicled. When Catherine suppressed the book and exiled Radishchev to Siberia, Russia quite suddenly had its first literary martyr. Tsar Paul I pardoned Radishchev in 1797 when Radishchev returned to Russia. Fearing that social change would never be realized, he killed himself a year after Paul I's assassination by palace aides. Radishchev's fusion of poet with political radical and of word with deed took root at a deep emotional level in the hearts of many of the educated Russian nobility who were dedicated to altering the course of Russia's future. The symbolic contest for power and authority between tsar and poet continued under Alexander I, and for two decades writers suffered strict censorship.

The tsar, traditionally viewed in Eastern Orthodox tradition as the

---

1. *Studies in Rebellion* (London, 1957), 15.

prime bearer of the faith and of the heavenly order on earth, lost authority as God and Church lost ground. As John G. Garrard explains it: "By the reign of Alexander I (1801) the upper echelons of the nobility had become truly enlightened and European in more than name only: they were beginning to leave their rulers behind."[2] The Romanov dynasty had begun to prove its ineffectiveness at modernization by the end of Catherine the Great's reign, but its shortcomings were even more apparent in the sorry rule of her son Paul I (1796–1801). Although Catherine's grandson Alexander I (1801–25) assumed the throne with the promise of progress on his lips, he abandoned plans for change as power, mystical inclinations, and wary councilors took control of his thinking.

Liberals who had hopes for individual improvement began to realize that social programs instituted by the government affected only the lives of the privileged class. A select few were allowed to develop their talents and intellect; the rest were consigned to live and die in feudal conditions. Unfair distribution of land and inhuman treatment of the serfs and peasants were obvious reminders of the backwardness of Russian society. In 1826, representing his generation's liberal voice, Bestuzhev wrote to Tsar Nicholas I (1825–55), Alexander I's successor: "The beginning of the reign of Emperor Alexander was marked with bright hopes for Russia's prosperity. The gentry had recuperated, the merchant class did not object to giving credit, the army served without making trouble, scholars studied what they wished, all spoke what they thought, and everyone expected better days. Unfortunately, circumstances prevented the realization of these hopes, which aged without their fulfillment."[3] Enlightenment ideas had provided the educated elite with a belief in the efficacy of the individual as the author of self, society, and history. The persona of the romantic poet was of particular importance, for it wedded literary and sociopolitical domains in exciting new ways. Bolstered by faith in an evolving self, the men of Bestuzhev's generation attempted changes that the crown and Church were unwilling to make. They tried to turn their vision into action using not just the pen but the sword.

Unlike the liberals of the preceding generation, whose thinking had inclined toward an idealized past or an undefined future, Bestuzhev's generation focused on the present and how society might be altered. Using letters, essays, and fiction to outwit the censor, they wrote about

2. *The Eighteenth Century in Russia* (Oxford, 1973), 21.
3. *Readings in Russian Civilization* (Chicago, 1969), 2:299.

Russia's past in order to examine contemporary social and political programs. This generation's right wing (like the radicals of their parents' time) believed in a constitutional monarchy. The left wing was committed to revolution, regicide, and the formation of a republic. Like other forms of violence, regicide had been an established part of Russian life, but it was experienced anew in Bestuzhev's time when Paul I was murdered in 1801. The assassination stirred up a public already agitated by a new social awareness. A group of officers and writers, including Bestuzhev, believing they carried the conscience of the nation on their shoulders, formed the Northern and Southern Societies and on December 14, 1825, attempted to overthrow Nicholas I. The unsuccessful insurrection now bears a poetic label taken from that fateful month—the Decembrist Revolt. Its tragic aftermath had a profound effect on Bestuzhev and his generation.

After the revolt Bestuzhev explained to Tsar Nicholas I: "The government itself spoke such words as 'Liberty, Emancipation!' It had itself sown the idea of abuses resulting from the unlimited power of Napoleon, and the appeal of the Russian Monarch resounded on the banks of the Rhine and the Seine" (ibid., 299). Referring to the tsar's role in vanquishing Napoleon, restoring peace to Europe, and instituting democratic forms of government there, Bestuzhev cited Alexander I's unwillingness to relinquish similar power to his own people upon his return from Europe. As a result, Bestuzhev asserted, "the military men began to talk: 'Did we free Europe in order to be ourselves placed in chains? Did we grant a constitution to France in order that we dare not even talk about it [in Russia], and did we buy at the price of our blood priority among nations in order that we might be humiliated at home?' . . . Inspired by such a situation in Russia and seeing the elements ready for change, we decided to bring about a *coup d'etat*" (299).

The Decembrists had previously conspired to kill Tsar Alexander I, but he had foiled their plans by dying unexpectedly while traveling in southern Russia. Upon his death most loyal citizens, government officials, officers, and soldiery had sworn an oath to Constantine, whom they considered quite logically the new tsar. For fear of reprisal Nicholas was reluctant to announce that his brother Constantine had secretly abdicated.

During the weeks of confusion in the royal family over succession, the Secret Society met and plotted to institute a constitutional form of government. On December 14, the day Nicholas I finally resolved to take power, these men led three thousand soldiers to Senate Square to swear their allegiance to Constantine. Utilizing his rhetorical gifts to inflame passions, Alexander Bestuzhev inspired the regiment considered most prestigious yet least likely to support the cause. It was the first group to appear that day. Through a show of numbers, the Decembrists hoped to intimidate the Senate into granting their demands, but several disasters undermined their plans. First, the Senate had already taken an oath of allegiance to Nicholas; second, Prince Sergei Trubetskoy, who was to assume temporary control of the provisional government, lost heart and hid all day at his brother-in-law's apartment; third, spies had forewarned the tsar about the revolt; and finally, many regiments did not arrive in time to assist in the insurrection. The Decembrists held their position on Senate Square surrounded by troops loyal to the crown.

The first day of Nicholas I's reign was filled with troubled negotiations, the promise of complete amnesty if the insurgents would return to their barracks, murder of a governmental envoy, raucous laughter among the troops, a festive crowd supportive of the revolutionaries, comic spills on slippery ice, and rude remarks aimed at the tsar, his loyal regiments, and even at the metropolitan, who attempted to negotiate with the rebels. By nightfall tragedy struck. Fearful of mob violence and anxious lest sympathetic regiments join the Decembrists, Nicholas gave the order to fire on the revolutionaries and the crowd. All were dispersed, except the seriously wounded and the dead. Before the first rays of dawn, nameless workers had cleansed the blood from the square, cobblestone by cobblestone, resurfaced the damaged building facades, which had been peppered with shot, and slipped dead and nearly dead bodies under the ice of the Neva River. In short order the conspirators were arrested, interrogated, and several months later sentenced to death or exile, bringing Russia's first modern revolt to a catastrophic halt.

Bestuzhev turned himself into the authorities on the morning of December 15. He took the trouble to dress for the occasion in the ritual decoration of a society dandy. This calculated theatrical act was followed by an abject confession in which Bestuzhev told the tsar absolutely everything, including Decembrist plans of regicide. He spent the remainder of his life in exile in Siberia and then in the Caucasus where he fought the mountain natives as a common soldier. As a reward for confessing so openly and freely, Tsar Nicholas I secretly allowed Bestuzhev to publish in exile under his pseudonym Marlinsky (from Marli at Peterhof where Bestuzhev had been stationed in 1817). He was the only Decembrist allowed to do so, but the privilege carried restrictions.

From the day of his arrest on December 15, 1825, to the day of his death on June 7, 1837, Bestuzhev's every official move was controlled by Nicholas I.[4] Threatened, but perhaps even attracted by the power of the writer in society, Nicholas I tirelessly followed his life in exile. Despite this persecution, Bestuzhev transformed the ideological program of the Secret Society into a heroic quest for a meaningful existence in a troubled exile. Both the political and personal aspirations belonged to Bestuzhev's time, but for him they had their immediate roots in his family upbringing.

Father and Sons

Bestuzhev's father Alexander Fedoseyevich (1761–1810) was of ancient noble lineage, but the family had fallen on hard times in the eighteenth century. This problem was compounded when he took a wife below his station from the merchant class. In the context of the Enlightenment belief in equality, the marriage created pride in the eight children, for it represented the transference of belief into behavior, but the social stigma drove each of the Bestuzhev children to bring honor to the family name, which was derived from *bestuzh,* an Old Russian adjective denoting "without shame."

The Bestuzhev children were raised in a home regulated morally and intellectually by their father, the repository of family authority. Their mother, Praskovya Mikhailovna Bestuzheva (1776–1846), loved and respected by all her children, influenced their rearing emotionally rather than intellectually. Parental attentiveness engendered a peculiar and rare kind of security. One of the sons, Mikhail, wrote "our parents' love, their concern and open caresses did not spoil us for they did not indulge our faults and weaknesses. We were given freedom to choose not to transgress the line of [acceptable behavior]."[5] It was a very tightly knit

4. Virtually all biographers of the Decembrists develop the theme of Nicholas's control over them. See, for example, Glynn Barratt, *The Rebel on the Bridge* (Athens, Ohio, 1975), 91, 102, 103, 108, 131.

5. M. A. Bestuzhev, "Detstvo i iunost' A. A. Bestuzheva (Marlinskogo): 1797–1818," in *Pisateli-dekabristy v vospominaniiakh sovremennikov,* ed. V. Vatsuro et al. (Moscow, 1980), 122.

family, which remained in close contact, even after the sons' participation in the Decembrist Revolt when emotional and financial resources became severely strained.

Alexander Fedoseyevich Bestuzhev was known as an enlightened gentleman, officer, and writer. Mikhail recalls that his father, a retired artillery officer under Catherine the Great, was a "fully educated man, given by inclination to science, the Enlightenment, and service to the homeland" (ibid., 121). He became well known at Court, in the Academy of Sciences, in societies dedicated to the fine arts, and in literary circles. With Ivan Pnin (1773–1805), an influential Enlightenment writer and one-time president of the Free Society of Lovers of Literature, Science, and Art, he published the *St. Petersburg Journal* during Paul I's brief reign. It propagated Enlightenment ideas in philosophy, politics, education, and social thought. His vast library and those of his friends were open to his male children. When the 1804 statute on censorship released former restrictions on reading material, the Bestuzhevs had access to the current ideas in Europe "on philosophy, political ideas, political economy, and technology."[6] The Bestuzhev children were also exposed to the latest in European literature in the original and in Russian or French translations. Their home was visited by many important figures in the sciences, arts, and letters.

In his memoirs Mikhail states that their father expected them to be educated on the model he himself had designed and published in 1798. This study, "On Upbringing" ("O vospitanii"), begins with a credo: "Upbringing is a science by means of which children are educated and taught in such a manner as to become useful and pleasant people within the family and for the homeland and in order that they might obtain for themselves complete well-being."[7] For Alexander Fedoseyevich Bestuzhev it was imperative that his children be adept in the sciences, technology, the arts, social theory, politics, philosophy, military tactics, military machinery, history, and leadership. He "stressed the development of a proper moral sense and high-mindedness as essential qualities of the defender of the fatherland" and proposed a "well-rounded and technically sophisticated general education for the officer" (Raeff, 149–50).

6. Marc Raeff, *Imperial Russia, 1682–1825: The Coming of Age of Modern Russia* (New York, 1971), 151.

7. "O vospitanii," in *Russkie prosvetiteli (ot Radishcheva do dekabristov)* (Moscow, 1966), 1:83.

These ideas particularly influenced his oldest children, Nicholas, Elena, Alexander, and Mikhail.[8]

The father had high expectations of performance. Punishment for transgression came in the form of a reprimand that included withholding affection. The tradition-bound technique had a predictable effect. Mikhail quotes his oldest brother Nicholas: "[Father would say] 'you are not worthy of my friendship; I withdraw from you. Live as you wish, but by yourself.' These simple words, spoken without malice, quietly but firmly, worked their effect on me to the extent that I reformed immediately" (M. A. Bestuzhev, 122). Nicholas observed that his younger brother Alexander also responded to this form of discipline.

Nicholas (1791–1855) became a military officer as well as an accomplished writer both of fiction and of scientific treatises. He was also an inventor of machines for farming and transportation and an ethnographer of several Siberian tribes. After his years of penal servitude for participation in the Decembrist Revolt, he lived as a gentleman farmer in Siberia with his brother Mikhail and his family. In the 1840s, after the death of his mother and brothers, Alexander, Peter, and Pavel, his sisters moved to join him in Selinginsk.

Elena (1792–1879) assumed many traditional male roles in a period in Russian history when a feminist ideology was not yet formed. She ran the family businesses and domestic affairs at home while all her brothers served their sentences. As the hub of the nearly broken family wheel for twenty years, she carried the family's practical burdens and offered primary care to her mother, sisters, and younger brothers all their lives. She cared for her mentally deranged brother Peter on his return to Petersburg from the war in the Caucasus. From contracts to book jackets, she handled all the practical details of publishing Bestuzhev's stories while he was in exile; she saw to the printing of the complete editions of his work after his death. When Nicholas and Mikhail beseeched the women to unite the remaining members of the family in their place of exile, it was Elena who sold the family estate and arranged the transfer of all their belongings so that they might live together.

Mikhail (1799–1858) was the family archivist, and with his sister

8. Olga (1793/4–1889) and Maria (1793/4–1889) are shadowy figures in the Bestuzhev history. Their father's influence on them seems to have been much less significant than their mother's. This circumstance reflects contemporary social models, of course, but is also due to the early demise of Alexander Fedoseyevich.

Elena collected and organized the family papers for publication. He was of great assistance to the historian Mikhail Semevsky, who took an interest in the Bestuzhev family in the 1860s and had their letters published for the first time (adjacent to the works of Dostoyevsky and Tolstoy). He was the only one of the siblings to marry, but his children died before reaching adulthood.

Alexander (1797–1837), the most Dionysian personality of the family, delighted his younger siblings with his imaginative projects. Mikhail attests to Alexander's primacy in aesthetic matters. Nicholas clearly deferred to Alexander in the realm of imagination, apparently with no small degree of condescension,[9] but the father encouraged the carefree play of his son's mind, even to the extent of taking part in the dramas and fantasies that Alexander initiated.[10] Perhaps seeing that his older brother with his practical bent could not be surpassed in technology, economics, and philosophy, Alexander was inclined to dismiss these areas, concentrating instead on the expressive domains—as a child in games, as an adult in letters.

It is in Mikhail's memoirs that Bestuzhev's youthful escapades are documented. Once his quick-wittedness saved a friend from drowning during a game of robbers enacted on the river at the family dacha. Significant, of course, is Bestuzhev's heroic act. Important, too, is that the German literary source for the game of brigands he so often played was in his father's library. Mikhail recalls that Bestuzhev was allowed to enter the library whenever he pleased. In fact, only he and Nicholas were permitted to use the key to the library shelves to select reading material without their father's supervision. Fiction appears to have been Bestuzhev's preference.

Young Bestuzhev wrote dramas based on romantic models in which central roles were assigned to a hero, heroine, villain, coward, and joker (or trickster), the latter inserted for comic relief. No small amount of energy was expended on these projects, and Mikhail attests to their popularity among the family and friends who attended them. Bestuzhev saw to the construction of theaters for his performance and to the creation of the scenery and puppets necessary to staging his compositions. During the

9. Alexander attempted in his mature years to convince brother Nicholas that his style, his mode of expression, and his imagination were not such bad characteristics after all, and that they were consistent with his impulsiveness as a child.

10. M. K. Azadovskii, ed., *Vospominaniia Bestuzhevykh* (Moscow, 1951), 213.

performance of his play "The Enchanted Forest," he spontaneously averted disaster when the younger children forgot their lines, stage props failed, and puppets refused to operate: "The traitor (a real sweet-tooth and regular scoundrel) is tempted by the forbidden apple in the Enchanted Forest, and he attempts to pick it. But just as he approached the apple tree the lines to his arms broke and instead of picking the apple his hands fell motionless. We all cried out in despair, but brother Alexander did not lose his senses. He swung the tricksters out onto the stage and began to improvise so effectively that he continued the movement of the drama even to the extent of improving upon the original" (ibid., 128). This spontaneity became a trademark of his fiction.

Mikhail remarks that his brother had "a strange habit of youth—he would read lying down—as he did in his adult years. Furthermore, he composed lying down, either having awakened from a sleep or just before falling asleep" (ibid., 120). The habit associates Bestuzhev's work with a state much beloved in romanticism—sleep—and its relationship to the unconscious.

Bestuzhev was consumed by the activity of creating stories: "With pen in hand [Alexander] would distance himself completely from his surroundings: music, speech, song, or dance could not lure him away [from his writing]. It would quite frequently happen, sometimes on purpose and sometimes unwittingly, that we would cast a shadow over the edge of [Alexander's] writing table. Only then would he respond, reacting instinctively to the fact that there was no more room to write. He would pick himself up and move from his corner to another without even noticing the laughter his obliviousness to us roused" (ibid.). These details in Mikhail's account are highly suggestive of Bestuzhev's absorption in fantasy to the exclusion of his surroundings, of reality.

Not all Bestuzhev's time, however, could be devoted to escape. At the age of nine he was enrolled in the Cadet Corps of Engineers as specified in his father's plans. He had hoped to follow in his older brother's footsteps, eventually moving from the Corps of Engineers to a naval career, but his temperament and intellectual skills, particularly in mathematics, were not adequate. He transferred into the Guard Officer Corps where he excelled and was advanced to adjutant in 1822, serving under the illustrious General Augustine Betancourt. Soon afterward Bestuzhev became adjutant to Duke Wurtemburg, whose wife was related to the empress, and he was introduced at Court.

With Alexander Fedoseyevich Bestuzhev's premature death in 1810, his family lost the domestic head through whom behavior, speech, education, and the formation of an identity were regulated. Nicholas, Elena, and Mikhail had apparently reached sufficient maturity to maintain a stable course in their lives. The father's death, however, appears to have been most deeply unsettling for thirteen-year-old Alexander and his younger siblings, Olga, Maria, Peter, and Pavel. With God the Father in the form of the Church, the tsar-father, and now their own father ravaged by the mysterious, violent workings of time, the younger children were left to an internalized set of controls. It is difficult to calculate in concrete terms the extent of Bestuzhev's loss, but there is indirect evidence to suggest that from this critical moment his inner life was overtaken by a fascination with death.

The Brothers Bestuzhev

There is little direct information available about Bestuzhev's life from his father's death to 1817, but those years seem to have been important for the formation of his identity in his father's absence. His schooling finished, Bestuzhev was admitted into the crack Light Dragoon Regiment, which was noted for its officers' flamboyant and hedonistic style. Bestuzhev excelled: "His enthusiasm and wit quickly won him attention, and he was marked by his superiors as a popular leader of soldiers and promising staff officer."[11] As though by a natural process, he rose to a position of prominence by adopting and then perfecting the egocentric and dashing style of his military cohorts. Later, in 1823 he would become enmeshed in the ascetic behavioral code of the Decembrist. Between these two extremes Bestuzhev eventually established his own particular identity.

Bestuzhev's dragoon behavior was the theme of a letter written to him in 1817 by his brother Nicholas. The two were cut from quite different cloth. Bestuzhev did not invent tools and conveyances as did Nicholas. Bestuzhev invented fiction. Nicholas was an empiricist with classicist leanings, much like their father, Bestuzhev an irrationalist with romantic proclivities. The disparity between them was dramatically represented in Nicholas's every remark. Urging Bestuzhev to avoid

11. Lauren Leighton, *Alexander Bestuzhev-Marlinsky* (New York, 1976), 14.

Fig. 1.   Alexander A. Bestuzhev (1797–1837), gouache by Nicholas Bestuzhev, 1823–24

the dragoon behavioral model in life, Nicholas recommended an alternative: "No matter what you assert, [no matter] what you say to convince me that you have already learned to think well, I cannot believe you in the least as long as your sphere of action is [limited to life in the military]. Only more reason sharpens reason. A fiery imagina-

Fig. 2.   Nicholas A. Bestuzhev (1791–1855), gouache self-portrait, 1814–15

tion [like yours] is not helpful at all, especially when it allows wit to take the place of common sense."[12]

Nicholas discussed two issues that impeded establishment of an identity of substance. First, he mentioned the officer's preference for wit

12. M. K. Azadovskii, *Pamiati dekabristov* (Leningrad, 1926), 1:9.

over reason, imagination over critical analysis, and said this placed
Bestuzhev in the camp of the frivolous gentleman and bawdy officer,
whose facile, playful speech Nicholas saw as preventing genuine feelings
and thoughts by promoting a flaccidity of judgment.[13] Second, Nicholas's introductory statement firmly addressed the dilemma twenty-year-
old Bestuzhev would face: the perception of self in adequate terms. For
Nicholas, the transcendence of a narrow frame of reference was the first
requirement of a sufficient self-understanding. The military life Bestuzhev was leading hardly afforded the broad perspective from which he
might assess the officers' values. In advising Bestuzhev to acquire a
critical distance from the behavioral norms of society, Nicholas urged
Bestuzhev to operate outside the deterministic model his group foisted
upon him.

Nicholas saw the source of Bestuzhev's and his fellows' behavior,
remarking: "If one cannot be a Hero or a Phoenix, then let him be a
human being" (Azadovskii, *Pamiati dekabristov*, 12). Both the mythological phoenix and literature's romantic hero were fabrications. Consequently, Nicholas felt they should be treated with caution and reserved
for fantasy, not carried into life as a facet of one's quest for identity or as
a goal toward which one might aspire. To clarify his perspective for
Bestuzhev, Nicholas deepened his argument psychologically:

> If you want, I will prove the accuracy of my description. I can
> prove that you have grown accustomed merely to a manner of
> thinking, but not to profound thought. The two are entirely
> distinct. The first belongs to the poet, the second to us
> prosaists—we live, after all, in a prosaic world. Dreams alone
> comprise poetry. But all that is visible is prosaic. You say that
> you await a decent rank. But this is all fantasy. You philosophize
> over the issue [of your career] beautifully, but then at the same
> time you say that you shall find glory and fame in high society.
> What is all this balderdash? If you're after riches, then a military
> life will not do, for an officer comes off poorly if he is avari-
> cious. And if it's glory you want, a hired hand [a military offi-
> cer] never finds it. (9–10)

13. Iurii Lotman, "Dekabrist v povsednevnoi zhizni (Bytovoe povedenie kak istoriko-
psikhologicheskaia kategoriia)," in *Literaturnoe nasledie dekabristov* (Leningrad, 1975),
35–36.

Nicholas could neither tolerate his brother's blind obeisance to the officers' behavioral code nor his insistence on its correctness. He attacked the moral underpinnings of a barracks existence:

> The complex of ideas and morals represented by one's fellows (and even their career status) works on our character, perniciously altering the course of thoughts, inclinations, and habits and, in a word, changing our identities entirely, particularly in the tender years which are now yours. I am not saying this in order to convince you that you have a soft character that someone else can alter into any shape he might want. People of strong character and in possession of a sound sense [of self] often give over to the example provided by those with whom they live. You are, for example, beginning to think already about dueling, seeing, apparently, true honor in bullying others and in others bullying you. You assume, quite obviously, that self-respect is to be derived in no other manner than in bullying someone. I, however, think that a healthy reason must necessarily guide us in all circumstances [in life]. It is not one's calling that tells us how to behave, but reason which must always govern our calling. Reason alone must be the rule by which we measure all our actions. (Ibid., 12–13)

The goal of dominance, which motivates dueling, Nicholas asserted, was not guided by reason but by shallow ego drives founded on a need for display rather than on an authentic sense of self:

> The contemporary *militaire* is governed by the following rules: lacking the wherewithal to surpass others by means of substantive personal characteristics, and incapable of achieving a measure of excellence through requisite intellectual development, the officer gains the attention of others of his ilk by means of a pseudo-courageousness more properly called obstinacy. One cannot get close to [the military heroic type], for he fears he might reveal his weaknesses; the slightest indication of weakness he counts an offense; indeed, it is an offense to such a person if his deficiencies are seen at all; therefore he loves [to keep his distance], to shine at balls or on parade rather than appear in friendly and intimate society, for in the first he can show up momentarily in a good light, but in the other he undergoes a most trying test. (Ibid., 13)

The military officer's persona formation was greatly informed by self-deceit and manipulation. As a consequence, according to Nicholas, he was to be abhorred: "Accustomed to his own narrow opinions, the officer considers his attitude correct and just. He thus acquires a peculiar form of thought. The ceaseless march of his thoughts, always one and the same, comprises and expresses his personality. The military man in society is more prone to set himself apart as superior than he is to distinguish himself as moral" (ibid.).

Nicholas would not have his brother imitate superficial people immersed in glitter and violence or unquestioned heroic literary models. He would rather have Bestuzhev think deeply and carefully about what is indeed lasting in life:

> Everyone, before becoming a soldier, is first and foremost a human being. And when he quits military service he must also remain a human being. It follows, therefore, that the rights and behavior of each one of us must be everywhere and at all times one and the same, at least to the extent that one does not alter his basic character structure. But in order that one's behavior remain the same, it is necessary that it be governed by those principles and rules generally accepted by man and not simply by those which a small part of society [the military] selects for itself. Don't think, Alexander, that a company of twenty or thirty young frivolous men, each acting in accordance with his own set of rules, represents the type of society I am speaking about. Each officer, either earlier or later, will recognize his error and will surely mend his ways. But would it not be better to mend them earlier? (Ibid.)

The concerns expressed in Nicholas's letter (supported by evidence that his brother's analytic skills were not sufficient to permit his entry into a naval academy) imply that Bestuzhev's thoughts were characterized by free association, the domination of fantasy and desire, obeisance to a code belonging to a narrow professional group, and a lack of intellectual discipline and rigor. Apropos, Nicholas concluded his letter with a final word of advice: "Only be more discriminating in your thinking. I do not say this so that you become more self-conscious about what you say, but so that your thoughts might be more ordered and logically connected" (ibid., 14). Nicholas's analysis of the officer's life and its pernicious influence on young minds is an insightful description of early-nineteenth-century forces that influenced Bestuzhev's personality development. He objected vociferously to the choices his brother made in directing his life. But in the years between Bestuzhev's receipt of the letter and his induction into the Secret Society, there is much to suggest that he did not follow Nicholas's counsel.

Nicholas had reason to denounce dueling, which was in vogue among the gentry. Dueling offered Alexander a shortcut to prestige, power, and fame. In Mikhail's memoir, it is recorded that Bestuzhev fought in three duels and participated in others as second. The first duel occurred when Bestuzhev was in the Light Dragoon Guards, that is, at the time Nicholas wrote to convince him he should not participate in this violent social ritual.

The first duel resulted from Bestuzhev's lifelong propensity to ridicule with pen and ink. In his youth he had been chastised for drawing caricatures of his teachers and fellow students (Vatsuro, 124). As an adult this propensity almost cost him his life. Mikhail related the story: "He had drawn caricatures of the entire society of officers as birds and animals. Everyone, upon recognizing himself, laughed heartily, except one who, seeing himself represented in the image of an Indian cock, took offense at the joke. So they fired at each other" (124).

Mikhail did not give details of the second duel, but mentioned its frivolous cause: "[The contest] was provoked by dancing" (ibid., 135). In the social norms of the time, the typical nobleman went to balls, played cards, gambled, and had affairs. His hedonism was based upon an egocentric cult of freedom, that is, on the notion that personal freedom could be won by challenging the previous generation's definition of irresponsible behavior (Lotman, 55–61). Both the nobleman and young officer were passionate in a carnal sense, but they thought of themselves as good citizens, liberal thinkers, and believers in freedom and personal happiness. Life for them was a carnival holiday. For the nobleman it was a ball or a dance; for the officer it was an orgy or a drunken spree (51–55). For the young radical, on the other hand, life was serious. He did not attend the club or the salon unless it was to advance his political ideas. He was not an epicure, but a stoic. He, too, was passionate, not carnally but ideologically. Consequently, life for him was not a carnival but service, not an orgy but private study. Significantly, these men attended balls, not to be entertained but to protest the vacuousness of social ritual. They went to *not* dance. In a theatrical gesture that guaranteed that they would be not only noticed, but viewed as odd and mysterious, they left their spurs on (62–63). For Bestuzhev to have been willing to risk his life over such a trifle as a dance, he must have immersed himself in ritualized forms of comportment that favored dying as a hero over living out one's days as a mere human being.

The third duel was precipitated by outright conflict. It took place in the early 1820s when Bestuzhev was in Duke Wurtemburg's service. Mikhail reported that the duel involved a member of the duke's retinue with whom Bestuzhev was in competition for the duke's favor. The rival took offense at something Bestuzhev said, so they fought a duel over it.

One of the compelling features of dueling was that it enabled the principals to conceive of their lives as scripted. The aesthetic aspects of dueling were experienced as a validation of the personal. By dueling they invested humdrum daily existence with the excitement of fiction and dissolved the distinction between poetry and prose. Dueling, therefore, represented a symbolic means toward understanding the larger social code under which Bestuzhev and his peers operated. The danger and drama of the duel were organized narratively: the introduction of the principals (their prior relationship); the complication (events precipitating the conflict); the elaboration of pre-duel rituals (confrontation with the fundamental question of life and death); the specification of the conflict in ritualized spatial terms (measurement of the barriers separating the antagonists) followed by specifications in ritualized temporal terms (drawing lots to determine the firing order); the crisis; and the denouement. As in Bestuzhev's childhood drama "The Enchanted Forest," the duel mixed the roles of villain, hero, and death-cheating trickster. One man's hero was the rival's enemy; those who survived beat death. This is the stuff from which myths could be fashioned.

The Diary of a Superfluous Man

Bestuzhev's dedication to military social models that entailed display in high society and behavior that presented the self in an advantageous light can be found on the pages of the sketchy diary he kept from 1823 to 1824, a period that includes both his introduction to the Secret Society and his advancement in the service. Diaries held an ambiguous position for romantics in Russia at this time. Young people like Bestuzhev apparently felt that their behavior, their personal letters, and their literature were text enough to present themselves to posterity. The diary was viewed with suspicion as Alexander Pushkin (1799–1837) suggested to Prince Peter Vyazemsky (1792–1878): "Why do you regret the loss of Byron's notes? The devil with them! Thank God they are lost. He made his confession in his verses, in spite of himself, carried away with the rapture of poetry. In cool prose he would have lied and acted crafty, now trying to sparkle with sincerity, now bedaubing his enemies. He would have been caught in the act, just as Rousseau was caught in the act—and spite and slander would have triumphed."[14] If people were to keep diaries, then, they would need to avoid self-aggrandizement.

Bestuzhev's Moscow journal is sketchy. It is precisely this quality which suggests that for Bestuzhev it was a device meant to trigger memory at some later date. The information is coded: the details recorded represent personal and social events, both ideological and psychological. The diary does not record the analytic qualities of Bestuzhev's mind, but documents rather his continued immersion in the behavior of officer life while a member of the antipodal Decembrist organization, the Northern Society.

As a social phenomenon, the serious Decembrist was a curiosity whose theatrical behavior differed from that of his peers. For him the link between word and deed was inflexible, whereas for society's gentleman words led to more words, all equally empty, in a round of idle chatter. For the Decembrist, language initiated action—whether at a ball or on Senate Square. The bon mot, when it was utilized, had a political purpose. The Decembrist behaved consistently but unconventionally in pursuit of his political goals. He expressed political opinions and made critical, even abusive judgments of society. Because he acted with flagrant disregard of salon etiquette, his actions were deemed improper. He threw himself into absurd situations in which his pride and abruptness set him apart and marked him as different if not something of a spectacle. He thought his every act should symbolize his political beliefs. As a consequence he memorized Brutus's monologues from Shakespeare and Don Riego's from Schiller. The Secret Society represented Bestuzhev's opportunity to develop the substantive characteristics his brother Nicho-

14. *The Letters of Alexander Pushkin,* ed. J. Thomas Shaw (Madison, Wis, 1967), 263. Pushkin's remarks also show the orientation toward a manufactured image of self presentable to the public. Byron's base and petty sides, Pushkin considers, should not be encoded but publicly suppressed (and individually repressed).

las valued. Contact with an aggressively analytic political ideology might control Bestuzhev's spontaneity and bravado, which could endanger the Secret Society's very existence.

Bestuzhev began his diary during a visit to Moscow on official business. Each entry reveals his preoccupation with social norms and behavioral models as well as the mundane details of his life: "Day Three. The Hall of Congresses. No mirrors anywhere. Cavaliers don't dance. The ladies are masked. Acquaintance with Prince Vyazemsky and with Davydov. . . . Invitations. . . ." (Azadovskii, *Pamiati dekabristov,* 56). Bestuzhev became friends with Prince Vyazemsky, one of the leading romantic poets of the day, and they established a personal relationship to supplement their professional, literary one. Vyazemsky assisted Bestuzhev in procuring manuscripts for the literary journal, *The Polar Star,* he began publishing with Kondraty Ryleyev (1795–1826) in 1823, and also gave Bestuzhev an entrée into radical groups to recruit new members for the Secret Society.

Denis Davydov (1784–1839) represented the archetypal romantic hero for many young men of Bestuzhev's generation. The commingling of a literary life and a heroic persona made him a most sought after personality. Davydov was the model of Tolstoy's Denisov in *War and Peace;* he was renowned for having acquitted himself in a triumphant manner during the Napoleonic Wars. He was also known for his "hussar" poems, which glorified the military life, the hedonistic impulses of officer society, and the bravado of the military man. Bestuzhev once confessed to Prince Vyazemsky that he loved "the Davydov life."[15] Davydov was a living example that ideals could be attained both in print and in reality.

Bestuzhev's mention of the Hall of Congresses, particularly its lack of mirrors, suggests his orientation toward the outward presentation of himself. To assess his reflection in society and project a consistent persona, Bestuzhev needed mirrors. It is not coincidental that mirrors played such an important role in the romantic period and its literature, for it was there that the persona (and in the Gothic tradition, the hidden self) was reflected. The mirror held the potential for self-revelation, on the one hand, and for self-observation of a superficial kind, on the other. The remark about "ladies in masks" reinforces this notion, emphasizing

---

15. "Pis'ma Aleksandra Bestuzheva k P. A. Viazemskomu (1823–1825)," in *Literaturnoe nasledstvo: Dekabristy-literatory,* ed. V. V. Vinogradov (Moscow, 1954), 60:208.

a persona that implies a "real" identity behind it. Indeed, most persistent in his diary are references to those conventions which directed the way individuals presented themselves in society, the persona, or what brother Nicholas called derisively the *militaire:* "I was at a ball at Bagration's in ordinary shoes!—Costumes." "Dinner at Tolstoy's. Friendly companionship. . . . —A ball at Fedorov's. Davydov's bon mot about feet and heads" (Azadovskii, *Pamiati dekabristov,* 57). Bestuzhev's orientation was toward masks, mirrors, clothes, fashion, poses, and wit.

Ostensibly, Bestuzhev had gone to Moscow on military business, but many of the contacts he mentions in his diary suggest engagement in sub-rosa political activity. The political agenda Bestuzhev carried with him to Moscow was connected to the cavaliers who appeared at balls specifically in order not to dance. Bestuzhev's St. Petersburg branch of the Secret Society had not yet begun to affect this specific manifestation of protest.

On his return to St. Petersburg, Bestuzhev decided to keep up his diary. He continued to use the shorthand structure of jottings developed in Moscow. Back in his normal daily routine, Bestuzhev's diary records in striking detail the days and nights of the epicurean "Davydov life." "Wednesday, January 2. The duke sent for me to tell him to whom he should give his theater tickets. I ate at the Titovs'. In the evening I had ten stout lads over. We laughed, drank our fill and parted satisfied with ourselves" (ibid., 59–60).

Even in the pitch of revolutionary activity, which called forth an ascetic code for some Decembrists, Bestuzhev recorded a never ending round of dissolute behavior: "Monday, January 7. The day passes like a shadow without a trace." "Tuesday, January 8. I don't recall anything." "Sunday, February 17. Went at one o'clock with Mukhanov to Akulov's where everyone was already gathering for a *partie de plaisir.* A pile of women. A race. A ride. Dinner. Dances. Nonsense and bother. The day is killed, but melancholy is not. I was going to go to a masquerade but thought better of it" (ibid., 63–64). "January 7. I was at a wonderful ball in the evening at the Bergins'. The theater was superb, many beautiful young girls were in attendance. I danced a great deal, but left with an empty head" (60). "Thursday, January 10. . . . In the evening I was until midnight at Akulov's. I danced, but my heart did not bounce to the music *because W. was not there*" (60). "Sunday, January 27. I ate the noon meal at home and then jested all day long with the ladies. I lied a great deal" (62). By January 28, "W." is replaced: "In the evening I was at a ball at Muddleton's—I saw M. She is a prize, but I did not speak or dance with her—it was very depressing. I didn't sleep all the rest of the night and got up with a heart of lead" (62). Unlike the Moscow cavaliers who kept their spurs on, Bestuzhev enjoyed the dance.

On the other hand, Bestuzhev wished to project a Decembrist image to those who would be receptive. In a letter of 1824 to Prince Vyazemsky, Bestuzhev wrote: "My work is in studying and reading English prose. I myself am writing nothing. . . . Boredom leadens me. People don't appeal to me. Society has lost its charm. I vegetate and hardly live. Pity me, dear Prince" ("Pis'ma," 218).

At alternate moments in his life, Bestuzhev wound his way back and forth between socially determined forms and Decembrist counterforms. He was both playful and serious, depending on whether he was with the officers or with radicals, with the aristocrats or with the plebeians. It was a complex scheme. With Kondraty Ryleyev Bestuzhev was the ascetic; with the publishers Nicholas Grech and Faddei Bulgarin he was the businessman; with the writer and publisher Nicholas Polevoy, he was the deeply committed liberal plebeian; with the popular poet Anton Delvig (1798–1821) and the liberal prince Sergei Trubetskoy, he was the aristocrat. Out of what appears to have been a compelling need to be liked and to win attention, Bestuzhev functioned in a wide variety of groups, within a broad series of behavioral possibilities. As a result, his position was dramatically ambiguous. He was an outsider and an insider depending on his audience. He adapted to his environment, accommodated himself to dominant beliefs, obeyed mutually conflicting behavioral codes, and subscribed to different speech genres, all of which recalls again the dramatis personae of "The Enchanted Forest."

From a psychological perspective it is revealing that Bestuzhev's diary gives us little direct information about his identity, his experiences and feelings, or the process by which he acquired a heroic persona. We must look to his poetry, criticism, and prose for a reflection of the man as he understood himself. The diary leaves us with sketches of his models, an idea of his daily round, and a sense of the social and historical forces that shaped his life, but no analysis or reflection. At the age of twenty-seven Alexander Bestuzhev had not acquired the traits Nicholas encouraged him to develop in order to become a substantive individual.

2

Bestuzhev and Romantic Praxis

[Glinka] belongs to that rare group of writers
whose biographies best serve as forward and
commentary to their art.
—Bestuzhev-Marlinsky

Entering the Literary Arena

Bestuzhev made his first forays into literary society in 1818. Assessments
of his success are usually based on his fiction, criticism, political songs,
and publication venture, *The Polar Star*.[1] Little mention is ever made of
his poetry or his first attempt to open a literary journal with his brother

1. Lauren Leighton's *Alexander Bestuzhev-Marlinsky* is the only book-length study in English. Neil B. Landsman treats Bestuzhev's work from a Decembrist perspective in "Decembrist Romanticism: A. A. Bestuzhev-Marlinsky," in *Problems of Russian Romanticism*, ed. Robert Reid (Hants, 1986), 64–95. See also, Dmitrij Cizevskij, *The Romantic Period*, vol. 1 of *History of Nineteenth-Century Russian Literature*, trans. Richard Noel Porter (Nashville, Tenn., 1974), 100–104, and William Edward Brown, *A History of Russian Literature of the Romantic Period* (Ann Arbor, Mich., 1986), 2:119–218.

Mikhail. From 1818 until 1822 Bestuzhev's literary endeavors were almost exclusively confined to criticism and minor attempts at poetry. This period preceded his correspondence with Alexander Pushkin and his introduction to Kondraty Ryleyev, Prince Peter Vyazemsky, and other secondary figures of early-nineteenth-century Russian literature. Without a proper literary milieu, Bestuzhev's career could hardly advance in the direction he hoped.

At the age of twenty-two Bestuzhev petitioned the Petersburg Education Bureau to introduce a journal containing Russian and foreign literature, criticism, and all branches of civic and military science. In response to the proposal, the censors Timkovskoy, Yatsenkov, Zon, and Spada wrote Sergei Uvarov, head of the Bureau, "In order to effect such grandiose plans, what is required is an equally extensive knowledge in each field, not to mention practical experience in such matters, in order to guide the editor's choices in selecting material suitable for publication, especially material connected with government affairs. By virtue of Bestuzhev's youth, the Committee can neither recommend nor refuse this request."[2] Although the censors thought the journal too broadly conceived, the range of subject matter indicated Bestuzhev's interests were extensive. However, in 1818 there was still a wide gap between his ambitions and his abilities.

The committee of censors felt the issue of youth was particularly important, reminding Uvarov that in recent years young people had started journals only to have their enthusiasm flag within a few months, whereupon the venture would fold. The committee thought this worked a deceit on the public, which paid yearly subscriptions in advance for issues it would never receive. To protect readers' interests, they felt it best to place the matter on hold.[3]

The censors also based their decision on the merits of the application. They listed the subjects Bestuzhev had studied as a cadet: Latin, French, German, geography, history, rhetoric, poetry, logic, philosophy, natural science, physics, mechanics, chemistry, higher mathematics, astronomy,

2. "Popytka brat'ev A. A. i M. A. Bestuzhevykh izdavat' zhurnal, 1818–1923," *Russkaia starina* 8 (1900): 392.

3. Uvarov concurred with the committee's assessment and forwarded its recommendation to Alexander Golitsyn, the minister of the Department of Religion and Education. Golitsyn sent the matter to committee, where it was again decided not to decide, but to await reconsideration under more favorable circumstances, to wit, a literary record of distinction on Bestuzhev's part. Within four years Bestuzhev won permission to publish *The Polar Star*.

statistics, political economy, law, architecture, artillery, and fortification. They went on to note that despite Bestuzhev's education, his proposal contained three spelling errors within only ten lines, "indicating, if anything, at least an inattentiveness and carelessness" unbefitting an editor ("Popytka brat'ev," 392). To make matters worse, two articles Bestuzhev submitted with his application as samples of his work were not received well: "[They] attest only to Bestuzhev's aptitude for performing school exercises. His translations of articles on Estonian and Latvian peasantry are not distinguished by stylistic clarity or correct usage of the language" (392). This testimony to Bestuzhev's callowness not only reinforces his brother Nicholas's perspective, but also suggests that Bestuzhev's ultraromantic style was well established by this time, at least sufficiently well established to dismay an older generation.

Curiously, Bestuzhev did not advance this style in his early verse, which, according to William E. Brown, "occupies a very minor place among the younger modernists of the romantic school" (Brown, 2:119). This is not inconsequential, for the first decades of the century presented Russian verse at the summit of its achievement—its Golden Age. People who were interested in entering the literary world were virtually obliged to establish their qualifications in rhyme and meter. Success in this domain was no small feat, for the budding poet had to meet the expectations of a small but refined readership that included "Russia's first romantic poet: Vasily Andreevich Zhukovsky" (1:185), who introduced the folkloric and mystical German brand of romanticism to Russia in exquisite musical form; Konstantin Batyushkov, the premier early romantic poet of light verse; Denis Davydov (1784–1839), Bestuzhev's model for the conjunction of literature and life at its most heroic; Alexander Pushkin, during his brief Byronic phase; and sundry secondary poets, critics, and writers with whom Bestuzhev became familiar through literary societies and polemics—Alexander Voyeikov (1779–1839), Nicholas Gnedich (1784–1833), Fyodor Glinka, Pavel Katenin (1792–1853), Orest Somov (1793–1833), Vladimir Rayevsky (1795–1872), and Alexander Odoyevsky (1802–39). Across vast differences in poetic practice, from those heeding the call of Western models to those wishing to develop native Russian language, style, and syntax, there were nevertheless points of connection between them.[4]

Taken as a whole, the poetry of the early nineteenth century advanced

4. Iurii Tynianov, *Pushkin i ego sovremenniki* (Moscow, 1960), 27–30.

two major themes, the definition of personal identity and the formulation of a distinct national character in the arts.[5] Civic verse and the more intimate elegiac verse forms embodied these twin themes.[6] In addition, the text was approached from two angles (Lotman, 27). First, the poem was treated as a qualitatively greater or lesser representation of the culture's striving for adequacy in the expression of emotion and thought. Here the word was crucial, viewed as a signal that conditioned a particular kind of reading for those in command of the code (Ginzburg, 10–11). Civic verse, for example, was marked by a set of related lexical features ("freedom," "law," "citizen," "tyrant," "chains," "dagger"). The revolutionary's voice was audible to those familiar with the genre even when these nouns were dispersed widely over a poem. The elegy also contained words of an emotional coloring that conditioned the text's reading. For instance, the related nouns "tears," "dreams," "youth," "death," "joy," "love," "sorrow" were read as ideas related to the poet's and hero's personae.

Second, the poem was viewed from the privileged perspective of those who knew the poet and the details of his biography and even his daily life. Uniqueness of personality was considered the key aid to the reader's interpretation of the poem. The poet's private life as a rule was not mentioned in literary texts, but it was of great interest to certain readers, whether fellow members of a society, friends, family members, or social acquaintances. The biographical element followed the poet's verse like its shadow, individual poems being read with the writer's social persona (assumed to be equivalent to an authentic identity) in mind.

Once Russian culture of the early nineteenth century established a link between writer and text, it became possible for the poet to manipulate that relationship. Play with the public's perception of personal life led quite naturally to the notion of self as another order of text. Masks were donned as a matter of course, sometimes ironically, sometimes in jest, or even sometimes to hide one's identity from a member of an opposition group. Many writers practiced this ruse. The poet Alexander Voyeikov continually affected different identities and used many pseudonyms, sometimes of deceased poets, sometimes of his own fabrication (Lotman, 33–34). Orest Somov used a variety of pen names, as did Wilhelm

5. Iu. M. Lotman, ed., *Poety 1790–1820* (Leningrad, 1971), 7.
6. Lidiia Ginzburg, ed., *Poety 1820 i 30ikh godov* (Leningrad, 1972), 6.

Küchelbecker.[7] Self-reliance and self-allusion were quite common in their verse and prose. Deciphering the poet behind his code was something of an intellectual game, and the author's style was the conduit to his identity.

Bestuzhev resorted to this practice as well. He drew his pen name Marlinsky from the location of his military quarters adjacent to Peterhof, the tsar's summer palace, at Marli. He first used the pseudonym in 1819 to mask his identity from his opponents in the polemical debates of the day. The selection of the name from a location proximate to the sovereign's residence also suggests Bestuzhev's aspiration for fame and glory, both of which naturally emanate from the top of the political hierarchy. Marlinsky is not "far" spatially (and in terms of desire) from the tsar and his power.

These aspects of the poetic world grew out of literary societies and clubs where writers met to read poetry and discuss poetics. The fruits of their many labors were published in journals specifically attached to individual groups. Polemics were a matter of course, not only between independent societies, but within them as well. These literary societies, however, lacked a center. Groups quickly merged and dissolved; some of the most important figures in literature joined them, others did not; and of those who joined the societies, many entered more than one at a time, including some apparently representing opposing camps (Brown, 1:164–65; Mersereau, 14–15). Wilhelm Küchelbecker and Bestuzhev were on different sides in the literary polemics of the early 1820s, but they momentarily became political allies on the day of the Decembrist Revolt. Orest Somov and Bestuzhev at first differed substantively in their orientation toward the new literature, but by 1823 they lived as neighbors and, together with Ryleyev, collaborated on the publication of *The Polar Star* (Mersereau, 15–21). Pushkin and Bestuzhev kept an active correspondence in the early 1820s, and both argued for the creation of a new literature in Russia. But Pushkin later came to see deficiencies in Bestuzhev's ultraromantic style and urged him to moderate it. Opponents in one context, friends in another, co-conspirators in yet a third—these were the conditions out of which individuals developed a unique style in pursuit of national and personal identity.

Competition in the literary arena, recourse to disguises, mutability of

7. John Mersereau, Jr., mentions Somov's pseudonyms in *Orest Somov: Russian Fiction Between Romanticism and Realism* (Ann Arbor, Mich., 1989), 15, 26.

relationships, and the changeability of allegiances distinguish the literary world Bestuzhev entered through his meager verse. Bestuzhev's poetry was unusual in this milieu in that his first attempts did not address any of the predominant themes of poetic culture. For this and for aesthetic reasons, it is the rare anthology of Russian romantic poetry that includes him. His verse has been relegated to a minor position in special anthologies of Decembrist poetry where he is thoroughly outdone by Kondraty Ryleyev and Wilhelm Küchelbecker. Apart from questions of literary quality, however, Bestuzhev's poetry provides insights into his character.

A Poetics of Forgetting

Bestuzhev's first poetic publication was a translation of the French secondary poet Jean-François de La Harpe's (1739–1803) translation of the sixteenth-century Portuguese poet Luiz Vaz de Camões (c. 1524–80). Typical of Bestuzhev's acquisition of art forms and subject matter from the West, he gave his readers not an original outpouring, but a representation of a representation of authentic speech. The subject matter of the poem is traditional. It is titled "The Spirit of Storm" ("Dukh buri") and presents in eighteenth-century allegorical verse form a personification of violent weather. Storm speaks and moves, and because of its threatening aspect represents dark forces at work in the world. This theme is close to the romantic's heart for it permits the artist to present the hero on the same plane as natural phenomena.

The verse is quite wooden, a point made by Lauren Leighton in the sole article on the prosodic features of Bestuzhev's verse.[8] Leighton writes, "Marlinsky differs from his contemporaries in his metric practice in that no other poet of his time made such a literal and unimaginative use of syllabo-accentual versification techniques in his early poetry" (310). Nevertheless, the poem's prosodic features serve as a guide to the secret heart of the text. Each rhyme of the poem is grammatically exact over the thirty-six lines of the poem save in three couplets. Two are worthy of attention. The first, which appears in the poem's initial two lines, refers to a ship put out into the uncharted sea by a brave captain

---

8. Lauren Leighton, "Bestuzhev-Marlinsky as a Lyric Poet," *Slavonic and East European Review* 42 (July 1969): 308–22.

who is seeking "fame and glory." The poem presents the captain with a single aspiration, that is, within a narrow definition of the hero. It also avoids any development of a lyrical interior, effectively shutting off the captain's emotional experience from the reader. This places the work in a position counter to the dominant trends toward lyricism and civicism in Russian verse of the time. In the poem's first rhyme, the noun "ships," so often associated with the romantic poet's self, rhymes with the verb "sailed" (*korabli / tekli*). This subject and verb nearly encapsulate the entirety of the plot. It may not be coincidental that the year in which the poem appeared (1818) brought the advent of Bestuzhev's literary career as poet and critic. Into the stormy debates of the decade Bestuzhev set sail on a metaphorical journey that could make or break his career.

On the captain's trip the Spirit of Storm is encountered; it destroys all on board. The poem's theme, therefore, strongly links the hero's quest with death.[9] The idea of life's journey and the image of the grave are embedded in the other nongrammatical rhyme in the text. Representing Storm's voice, the stanza in question reads:

Nay. Be afraid! Your soul is filled with vanity.
Melinda will carry you to the rushing waves,
Which fate has in the distance hidden;
Other sorry tribes will follow you,
But again the open country [expanse]
Will become for all new arrivals an enormous grave.

[Нет, трепещи! Твой дух корыстолюбьем полн,
До быстрых пренесет тебя Мелинда волн,
Которые вотще судьба вдали сокрыла;
Тебе последуют несчетны племена,
Но вновь открытая страна
Всем будет пришлецам обширная могила.][10]

The hero-adventurer reaches his goal at death. This is the earliest indication in Bestuzhev's writing of an orientation toward the theme of demise.

Interesting in this poem are conflicting tendencies of the age—the adoption of an abstract classical subject and its incorporation into the

9. Bestuzhev was as yet unfamiliar with Byron's poetry in the original and perhaps he was not as informed as he soon would be about the connection between the two in Byron's work.
10. *Sochineniia v dvukh tomakh*, ed. N. N. Maslin (Moscow, 1958), 2:463.

work of the romantic school with its focus on the hero; the presentation of the captain as an abstraction devoid of an interior versus the new propensity to overindulge the subject's emotional life; the rigidity and monotony of the verse form against the romantic's inclination toward formal experimentation (and the sense of freedom it brings). Bestuzhev's first published poem falls into the former, classical side of the equation and does not indicate how much he would soon swing toward the opposite pole. Yet the seed was there for the growth of the hero in his quest even in death. Bestuzhev failed, however, to resolve the question of the hero's immortalization. He immortalized instead the process of literary evolution (from the Greeks to Camões to La Harpe to Bestuzhev) rather than the hero of his poem (who remains an unnamed silhouette).

Another poem of 1818, "To K——" ("K K——"), addresses a minor poet and friend, Alexander Krenitsyn, who had despaired at being demoted to the ranks for protesting mistreatment by his superiors.

Is it worthy of you, young charge of the Muse,
to be tormented by the sorrow of sonorous tears,
to bow your brow to boredom?
Having lived to the age of fifteen years,
Forgetful of the eagle's flight,
You've frozen yourself within your fate!
Can a poet really be so faint of heart?

True, it is not in our power
To be happy in this vale.
But it is possible to suffer less
in the chains of a useless sorrow.
Believe me in this, my dear friend,
It is possible to reforge
the lead of a leaden fate.

The Winds do not howl forever on the plains.
Winged Perun[11] does not work for all time
at the granite chain of the Caucasus mountains.
So why by your will must you suffer like Prometheus,
or trample the lily of joy,
or darken your gaze with grief?

11. The Slavic god of thunder.

Yet, of course, who has avoided deep sorrow?
Nothing against it can stand,
neither youth nor gray hair,
neither station nor birth.
Everywhere complaint suffuses it,
and goblets of great feasting
stream over with the sighs of the tsar.

[Тебе ли, муз питомец юный,
Томить печалыю звучны струны,
Чело под скукою клонить?
Прожив три люстра с половиной,
Полет забывши соколиной,
Оледенить себя судьбиной!
Поэту ль малодушным быть?

Бесспорно, что не в нашей воле
Быть счастливым в сей юдоле;
Но можно менее страдать
В оковах грусти бесполезной;
Поверь мне в этом, друг любезной:
Возможно жезл судьбы железной
Терпением перековать.

Не вечно ветр в долинах воет,
Не век перун крылатый роет
Гранитну цепь Кавказских гор;
Почто же волею своею
Страдать, подобно Прометею,
Топтать веселия лилею,
Печалью свой туманить взор?

Конечно, кто избег кручины!
От ней ни юность, ни седины,
Ни сан, ни род не защитят—
Везде ее проникнут жалы,
И часто пиршества бокалы
Вздыханья царские струят.]

(*Sochineniia*, 2:464–65)

The poem draws toward an end with a reminder that life is a fleeting joy, its pleasures always momentary. Then, in a dramatic turn, Bestuzhev concludes in an anacreontic vein:

> Let your boredom go with the winds
> and rush along the familiar path now with a cup of
>   golden nectar
> now with the sportive crowd of Graces
> and in happiness sing of happiness!

> [А скуку на ветер пускай,
> То с чашей нектара златою,
> То граций с резвою толпою.
> Спеши знакомою тропою,
> И в счастье счастье воспевай!]

(465)

Bestuzhev utilized iambic tetrameters, which conform to the period's norm of a weakened third stress. The occurrence of pyrrhic feet in the second position is also commonly encountered in tetrameters of this epoch, but it rarely occurs on the first foot. Since Bestuzhev usually fulfills metric patterns completely, discovery of an initial pyrrhic foot is of consequence: "And life irretrievable flies away" [A nevozvratna zhizn'—letit). This formal break in the rhythmic pattern occurs as a consequence of the qualifer. Leighton comments on Bestuzhev's awkward use of the short-form adjective to qualify nouns: "The young Zhukovsky resorted to the practice in his first poems and quickly abandoned it, again except for stylistic effect. More comparable to Marlinsky would be Pushkin or Yazykov, and it can be found that they both used it in very early poems and then quickly abandoned it. Marlinsky, on the other hand, employed it for more than a decade with no other apparent intent than to force agreement between syntax and meter" (Leighton, "Lyric Poet," 312). It may be psychologically important that the deformation of the poetic norm occurs in the poem when the matter concerns death.

If death is a central problem for the hero, particularly the inexperienced one, then it must be resolved in some manner, even if only by projecting the problem onto another (Krenitsyn). A partial solution, however, can be found in the poem where we find another initial pyrrhic foot: "Friend! Make peace with yourself" [Drug, primiris' s samim soboiu]. It was common at that time to assume that the greatest peace would come through self-knowledge, but the Epicurean style, represented by the military verse of Denis Davydov and the officer's club, took the injunction "Know Thyself" as a call to convivial celebration. For Bestuzhev, in his early twenties, reconciliation with mortality did not come through wisdom but from wine.

In an untitled song written between 1818 and 1819, the theme of death occurs more directly. Bestuzhev's narrator describes a young warrior standing beside a river at sunset thinking of his beloved and his homeland. The song is steeped in sentimentalist images but adds the language of the warrior-hero-poet archetype to them:

> A beauteous youth by his camp stands,
> Bows down beside the river, kneels,
> Clear eyes take in the waters,
> He leans upon his bow of steel.
>
> His flowing hair in waves
> Is plied by a gentle evening wind,
> Sunlight from the west grows dim
> Upon his crimson shield.
> He sings. . . .
>
> [Близ стана юноша прекрасный
> Стоял, склонившись над рекой,
> На воды взор вперивши ясный,
> На лук опершися стальной.
>
> Его волнистыми власами
> Вечерний ветерок играл,
> Свет солнца с запада лучами
> В щите багряном погасал.
> Он пел. . . .]
> (*Sochineniia*, 2:474)

For the warrior, the impending battle presents two possibilities. He may survive to return home, where he might then fulfill his twin aspirations of love for a woman and dedication to his homeland. Then again, he may fall in battle, winning in their place a hero's immortality. At the moment in the song when the warrior voices this second possibility, the grammatical rhyme that governs the piece breaks down:[12]

> Perhaps tomorrow in battle's thrall
> a fateful arrow will to me wed;
> Fighting others, I too may fall
> into the dust on bodies dead.

> [Но, может, завтра ж роковая
> Меня в сраженье ждет стрела,
> Паду и сам, других сражая,
> Во прах на мертвые тела.][13]
>   (*Sochineniia*, 2:475)

In each of these early poetic works by Bestuzhev, grammatical rhyme is consistently abandoned when the issue concerns death, mortality, and the ephemerality of existence. It is as though poetic form tells a tale behind the tale. Object focus broadens to encompass the subject. If Bestuzhev simultaneously confronted and avoided death in these poems, he stayed within the fictionalized vantage point of an other—the cameo captain, the fifteen-year-old Krenitsyn, or the warrior in the twilight. The heroes, therefore, represent psychological projections. Broken form suggests the poet's anxiety, unconscious though it may be.

Although this last point must remain conjectural for the moment, it is given some credence in another of Bestuzhev's early poems, "Dream's Domicile" ("Obitel' sna," 1820), an imitation of Ovid. In this work repression is investigated indirectly through the phenomenon of sleep. The poet envisages oneiric existence in physical terms. The interior landscape of dreaming is associated with enclosures (caves and empty vaults) and distant lands:

> At the entrance to the Kimmerian mountains a bleak
>   cliff
> Has fashioned a chamber from a dark vault,

12. "Arrow" (*strela*, a nominative feminine singular) rhymes with "dead bodies" (*tela*, an accusative neuter plural).

13. The final two lines cited here became a facet of the reading of Bestuzhev's mythological self in Russian culture upon his death. He fell defending his comrades in battle [Padu i sam, drugikh srazhaia], thus effecting a linkage between his art and his life.

Where, in the depths of the moss grown caves,
Untroubled Sleep sleeps there in a desert silence.

[В горах Киммерии в чертог его над входом
Скала угрюмая сложилась мрачным сводом,
Где, мхом увенчанных пещер во глубине,
Беспечный дремлет сон в пустынной тишине.]
(Ibid., 475–76)

In the cave, where the unconscious (sleep) is kept at rest, a drama of inaction unfolds against the background of the outside world (waking):

A dubious dawn in mists forlorn
Weakly pours its pale glimmer around . . .
There the rooster has never awakened the dawn,
Nor arisen to the howls of the hounds
Or the prophetic bird's sonorous sound.
. . . .
No steed's stormy fall, nor wolf's cry down the
     centuries,
No horn's clarion call, nor man's song,
Nor the breeze which passes, whistling in the crag's
     caves,
Trouble the peace of this speechless desert.
Everywhere deathliness. . . .

[Лишь с влажным сумраком сомнительный рассвет
В туманах бледное мерцание лиет.
Там петел никогда не пробуждал денницы
И никогда лай псов и голос вещей птицы,
. . . .
Ни коней ржание, ни вой волков, от века,
Ни бранный звук трубы, ни песни человека,
Ни мимолетный ветр, свистя в ущельях скал,
Немой пустыни сей покоя не смущал.
Повсюду мертвенность. . . .]
(476)

The world cannot reach within the cave to stir the sleeping giant, for, as Bestuzhev developed the notion, the rightful condition of the unconscious is silence. He delivered a double sign of this idea when he wrote that this god "beneath a wreath of poppies / forever delights in an unbroken dream" [pod makovym ventsom / Vek naslazhdaetsia nenarushimym snom] (ibid.). Thus the personification of Dream dreams, never awakened by what it dreams, lulled by the opiate scent of the poppies. The inner life remains doubly unconscious, or thoroughly forgetful of itself. Sleep sleeps, inhaling the scent that guarantees permanent sleep. Bestuzhev makes a connection between the god of sleep and the frivolous, epicurean persona of literary and officer societies:[14]

> And there, in the quiet of the chambers unknown to the
>   heavens
> Under ancient curtains, in the shade of a double veil,
> Lying on his bed embroidered in luxury,
> indulging a languorous laziness in the folds of many
>   pillows,
> the silent god of sleep beneath a wreath of poppies
> forever delights in an unbroken dream.

> [Но там, в тиши палат, безвестных для небес,
> На ложе, роскошью изобретенном, лежа,
> И томну лень свою в зыбях пуховых нежа,
> Сна молчаливый бог, под маковым венцом
> Век наслаждается ненарушимым сном.]

The connection between a social type and a psychological condition is direct. The oneiric god adopts their pose.

In personal letters during this period Bestuzhev belabored his addressees with a similar image of himself. To his sisters he once wrote, "My life is a bore. Everything is a bore. I am of the certain belief that there is no joy on this mortal coil after eighteen years of age."[15] To his mother: "Laziness has gripped me for quite some time now, dear mother. Forgive me . . . but I do nothing. . . . This damned inactivity has put its root in me deep. I spend most of my time at Bulgarin's dacha. I sleep and lie

---

14. The Arzamas society, for example, extolled languor, lassitude, and laziness.
15. M. K. Azadovskii, *Pamiati dekabristov,* 1:47.

about." (51–52). Bestuzhev invested this image with its romantic correlative, the epicure: "Boredom and lifelessness rule me. Nothing in particular is going on which might impress me and my days come and go one like the other. I see our brothers rarely. I am usually alone and seized by laziness. I wander about the garden and philosophize. Before dinner I am a Stoic. During the meal a real epicure. I am a Democritus more in image than at heart" (53). To Vyazemsky Bestuzhev wrote, "It is clearly my fate, dearest Prince, to begin each of my letters to you with excuses for my idleness. . . . Boredom leadens me."[16]

It is the connection of this self-image with sleep that is of particular interest. Two of the three nongrammatical rhymes in the poem allude to unconsciousness and its source. Lines 11 and 12 join the "walls" (*stenakh*) of the cave to "fear" (*strakh*). This rhymed pair produces a notion of the material inscribed on the walls of Dream's domicile. Although no specific information can be gleaned from the cave's interior, the reaction to that content may be posited from the rhyme—fear. What more youthful rationale for unconscious anxiety can there be than this?

If we examine the breaks in the formal design Bestuzhev imposed on his minor poetic output, we find a nexus of ideas associated with the hero: his narrowly conceived identity; the conception of life as a journey; a struggle with boredom and despair in society compensated by hedonistic activity; and an overarching propensity to project and/or repress thanatos. Bestuzhev's "school translations" are deficient for their rigidities, lapses, and inconsistencies, faults rarely to be met in the verse of Pushkin and his "pleiad."[17] These poems also lack that special feature which distinguishes the genre during the first decades of the nineteenth century—the unique, individual style by which the reader might identify the poet. The absence of an individual stamp is striking and seems to be connected to Bestuzhev's inability to fashion his thoughts in verse form.

By 1824, however, Bestuzhev reached a temporary solution to the dilemma of poetic technique and the theme of heroism. "Mikhail Tverskoy" ("Mikhail Tverskoi," in *Sobraniia*, 2:477–78),[18] adapted

16. "Pis'ma Aleksandra Bestuzheva k P. A. Viazemskomu (1823–1825)," 217–18.
17. Not that Pushkin's work is without fault; see A.D.P. Briggs, "Fallibility and Perfection in the Works of Alexander Pushkin," 25–48.
18. Reminiscent of Byron's "Prisoner of Chillon," "Mikhail Tverskoy" is set against the following political background. The Tver Principality was particularly powerful during the thirteenth century. Since it was less accessible to Tatar raids than other principalities, it grew in population, independence, and thus political power. In the 1260s Yaroslav Yaroslavich at-

from the historical sources when Bestuzhev was intensely involved in conspiratorial activities, asserts the fundamental importance of a heroic persona faced with moral decisions that entail ultimate sacrifice. The poem is of interest for the parallels it establishes with historical fact—within a year of its writing Bestuzhev himself was faced with moral decisions that entailed ultimate sacrifice—in the Decembrist Revolt.

Projecting psychological material onto the social and political planes, in "Mikhail Tverskoy" Bestuzhev turned again to the image of the enclosure, this time the dungeon, converting it into a dual symbol of release and death. Symbolically, the poem asserts that the interior holds regenerative powers. Bestuzhev interpreted those forces from the perspective of a revolutionary ideology. Liberation comes through political action rather than introspection.

Mikhail Tverskoy meets with his father, the tsar, in the latter's cell prior to the father's execution at the hands of the Tatars. The father exacts a promise that Mikhail shall not avenge his death. At the spectacle of their tsar's demise, the masses are incited to riot. Against his oath, Mikhail rallies the people to revolt: "And those defeated by their servants / were made slaves" [I porazhennye slugami / Oni ikh sdelali rabami] (ibid., 2:478). Although Tverskoy's subjugation of the tyrant is a heroic act, it is nonetheless accomplished against the word given his tsar-father. Bestuzhev thus dramatized the power of the heroic persona to surmount all obstacles to bring freedom and autonomy to the homeland. Through the equation of the search for a national identity with that of personal identity, the poem links the victory over tyranny with the acquisition of a permanent, historically validated, personality.

There are parallels, therefore, between the poetic text and Bestuzhev's personal life-text, but not of the sort usually conceived in the literature. Rather than a mere elaboration of Bestuzhev's political beliefs, the poem enacts a personal drama. Bestuzhev's father, like Mikhail Tverskoy's, would hardly have sanctioned his son's participation in a revolt against the sovereign, and as an enlightened and rational gentleman of the eighteenth century, his example and command were sacrosanct. To go

---

tempted a unification of its several regions, a policy continued by Mikhail Tverskoy, who ruled from 1285 to 1318, and who occupied the key Vladimir throne as early as 1305. The Golden Horde, worried lest Tver's power supersede that of the Horde's ally Moscow, determined to punish its princes. In 1318 Khan Uzbek put Mikhail Tverskoy to death and then his successor Dmitry as well.

against him might certainly provoke guilt, unless conscience were assuaged by a larger historical calling, the greater good of the people. The poem links ideology, father, tsar, and death, and as a consequence animates both personal and political information: the assassination of Paul I, the plans to murder Alexander I under discussion in 1824, and the death of Bestuzhev's father. These factors indicate the psychological import of the text.

Within the symbolics of the poem, the father's command to his son uttered in the dark enclosure again brings forth the idea of the unconscious. The father image is crucial here, for it speaks to the hero from out of the ultimate cave, the final darkness—death. All the subtle cultural and personal forces operating on early-nineteenth-century society and on Bestuzhev's identity are focused at this moment in the poem. "Mikhail Tverskoy" is a deeply personal record of Bestuzhev's development toward heroics, political action, guilt, historical atonement, and mythologization.

Questions concerning the heroic persona emerge. Certainly the literary and historical model represented in "Mikhail Tverskoy" expressed Bestuzhev's hope. But would the warrior-poet Bestuzhev perform as bravely in reality as Mikhail Tverskoy does in Bestuzhev's fiction? Is the heroic persona in fact prepared to overthrow the tyrant, or will he cower before authority? Will a heroic self-image sacrifice itself for a political cause larger than the self and accept death gladly? The quest for an authentic identity broadens into a full range of human potentials, from cowardly acts to heroic deeds. In Bestuzhev's text, however, these potentials represent desired and feared qualities, but they are not analyzed or examined.

There is reason to conclude that these questions were rooted deeply in Bestuzhev. In effect they constitute the message that Dream does not awaken to read within its cave. Such material can cause projection, repression, and anxiety, but it also holds the key to psychological well-being. Like the uninterrupted dream in "Dream's Domicile," Bestuzhev's unconscious slept and obscured all doubts about the emerging Marlinsky persona and its right to transgress any father's law. But then, the unconscious is usually asleep in youth. The drama is in its awakening.

3

Literary Criticism

Shishkov is as dumb as a post; Everyone
laughs at this fool.
                    —Bestuzhev-Marlinsky

Polemics: Pen as Sword

From 1818 to 1825 Bestuzhev published over forty articles, including
book reviews, feuilletons, translations, ethnographic studies, satires,
historical treatises, archeological studies, short commentaries on public
affairs, and letters to the editors of various journals.[1] He made his
biggest impact when he entered the renowned battle of the ballad in
1819, four years after its inception. He belonged to the ultraromantic

---

1. Lauren Leighton, *Alexander Bestuzhev-Marlinsky*, 53 (henceforth *ABM* when cited parenthetically in text or notes), and N. Kotliarevskii, *Dekabristy Kn. V. F. Odoevskii i A. A. Bestuzhev-Marlinskii: Ikh zhizn' i literaturnaia deiatel'nost'* (St. Petersburg, 1907), 296. Leighton delivers a thorough and concise account of Bestuzhev's contribution in these genres (*ABM*, 37–66).

wing of romanticism, which supported and eventually surpassed Karamzin's reforms of Lomonosov's high, middle, and low styles of the literary language. These "young innovators"[2] (Karamzinians) generalized the middle style of Lomonosov's scheme, revamped his generic hierarchy, and introduced gallicisms into literary Russian, all of which reflected current salon usage of the upper classes. The opposition, the "young archaists" (Kateninites), attempted to include the vernacular style in literary language. This group was identified with the conservative Admiral Alexander Shiskov, whose pronouncements on political and literary matters dumbfounded Bestuzhev's camp.

Debate between the two factions was heated, but it played an important role in the formation of the romantic and national literatures of Russia. The most immediate focus of the argument related to language innovation and the concept *narodnost'* (nationality). Because national feeling is so closely connected to the national language, the development of a Russian identity was a major theme of these debates on language. The discussions reflected more unity across opposing sides than the participants had anticipated. As early as the late 1820s the "young archaist" Wilhelm Küchelbecker declared that the debaters were all romantics squabbling over stylistic details.[3] The "young innovator" Prince Peter Vyazemsky made very much the same assessment in the second half of the nineteenth century. But at the time the writers and critics saw the polemics as very important. The ferocity of the debate underscored a crucial feature of the era—its combativeness and the sense of self that issued from the competition.

When Bestuzhev entered the literary debate, precisely in this spirit, critical genres were not yet formulated. Feuilletons, letters to the editor, personal letters (which were decidedly literary and therefore distinguished from private epistles to a specific addressee), lengthy formal articles that treated the development of Russian literature, translations of European literary criticism, anonymous notes, verse satires, public addresses, epigrams, and charades in verse comprised the open market of genres available to the critic.

The ballads that fanned the debate for decades were two translations of Burgher's "Lenore" by Vasily Zhukovsky in 1808 (under the title "Ludmila") and by Pavel Katenin (1792–1853) in 1815 (under the title

2. Iurii Tynianov, "Arkhaisty i Pushkin," in *Arkhaisty i novatory* (Munich, 1967), 87–227.

3. Lauren Leighton, *Russian Romanticism: Two Essays* (The Hague, 1975), 57.

"Olga"). They represented two distinct approaches to the development of a native ballad tradition and to the formation of a national literary language. Zhukovsky's attempt was influenced by German romantic-mystical tendencies and adhered to Karamzin's middle style, but Katenin utilized common speech to russify his translation. Bestuzhev's vitriolic criticism heated the tempers of his future literary collaborator, Orest Somov, his fellow Decembrist conspirator, Wilhelm Küchelbecker, and his colleague and envied acquaintance, Alexander Pushkin.

In the early 1820s, *The Son of the Fatherland* (*Syn otechestva*), a literary almanac, published Katenin's epic "The Lay of the First Russian Campaign under the Command of Prince Galitsky, Mstislav Mstislavich the Brave against the Tatars on the River Kalka" ("Pesn' o pervom srazhenii russkikh s tatarami na reke Kalke pod predvoditel'stvom kniazia Galitskogo, Mstislava Mstislavicha Khrabrogo"). It elicited a great deal of discussion, in the center of which was Bestuzhev's attack cast in the form of a dramatic dialogue. The narrator enters a bookstore and finds an older gentleman leafing through journals. From his looks the narrator assumes the older man to be an opponent of "modern ideas." Curiosity leads him to speak to the man, who announces (in concert with Bestuzhev) "we have yet no Russian literary criticism."[4] In the end, the up-to-date gentleman, rather than the narrator, speaks for Bestuzhev. This conceit allowed Bestuzhev the opportunity to play with identity, authoritative judgment, and reader expectation. It also permitted shifting voices, points of view, tones, and emotional registers, techniques useful to a budding prose fictionalist.

There are two striking features of Bestuzhev's feuilleton, a rigorous attention to details of language, and the density of its metaphors.[5] The plethora of figures of speech in Bestuzhev's article dramatized his criteria for judgment, disparaged contemporary literature, and developed a public awareness of his peculiar style (the marlinism). Bestuzhev's abundant figures of speech came to signal his presence even when writing under the pen name Marlinsky. He used this pseudonym for the first time during these debates (Leighton, *ABM*, 42). In the voice of the older

---

4. Not only criticism, but Russian literature was presumed not to exist either (Donald Fanger, *The Creation of Nikolai Gogol* [Cambridge, Mass., 1984], 24–29).

5. For purposes of comparison, Wilhelm Küchelbecker wrote an article, part of which was dedicated to an analysis of Katenin's ballad. It employed one quarter the number of metaphors of Bestuzhev's article. See "Vzgliad na tekushchuiu slovesnost'," in *Literaturno-kriticheskie raboty dekabristov*, ed. L. G. Frizman (Moscow, 1978), 171–86.

gentleman, Bestuzhev criticized the Katenin poem on aesthetic grounds, attacking him for stylistic *faux pas*, grammatical errors, lapses in taste, blunders in diction, and historical inaccuracy.

Bestuzhev made a strong case in his analysis of Katenin's stylistic errors. In his use of metaphors, however, Bestuzhev's essential ideas of a national literature and a literary self were presented in narrow terms. Speaking of the excessive attention to drama in the critical literature, he said that "criticism must not be a misfunctioning compass needle that always points in one direction." He maintained that criticism is like a microscope. Elsewhere he spoke of "journalistic ballast," which need not be constituted of "contraband" but of legitimate cargo. Zoological and botanical images also appear: "In order to protect the tender shoots of the blooming tree of our language, we must pluck caterpillars from it." In defense of his harsh treatment of the ballad, he stated that "sharpness in criticism is as necessary an element as an alloy for minting coins." These biological and metallurgical metaphors were intended to create an illusion of analytic rigor, to give the argument scientific credibility.

Bestuzhev also resorted to mundane figures of speech (the shop, foodstuffs, and dry goods) in order to deflate and ridicule Katenin and his verse: "Lyrical verse must not be Milyutin's Shop [well known in St. Petersburg at the time], where pineapples and oysters lie side by side on the counter." In another deflating metaphor he said: "[Katenin's] poem is written without purpose, without a beginning or end, without the colors of the historical moment and without the flowers (I will not say mushrooms) of real literature." Wit replaced analysis, as Bestuzhev relied on the strength of *bon mot* to overcome more rational discourse. Utilizing wit to halt serious debate, he elaborated his point of view on Katenin's poetry: "Music without poetry lacks a soul, and poetry without music is dull" [Muzyka bez poezii bezdushna, no poeziia bez muzyki—skuchna]. Bestuzhev became known for his marlinisms, word play used to make a point and disarm counterargument by eliciting laughter or delight.

Bestuzhev's stylistic techniques and their effects were dramatic and self-aggrandizing. The egotism of his stance was prominent in his early criticism, as he advertised himself as a heroic poet. Under his microscope the specimen (Katenin's poem) was obscured by the shadow of the observer. Bestuzhev's criticism did have substance, but it paled in the light redirected to illuminate the narrator's persona, which readers assumed represented the author. Metaphors not only call attention to the argument advanced by the gentleman in the bookstore, but also reveal the rhetorical structure of the dispute. Introducing the reader to the creative consciousness behind the work, Bestuzhev's critic states that "the public . . . is a fair lady; it loves to be taken by the arm" and led to understand what good literature is. The metaphor works a dual effect. It encapsulates a sentimentalist point of view (with its canonical orientation toward the female reader), and displays Bestuzhev, the real-life dandy who owns it. The persona project, constructed on the basis of Bestuzhev's understanding of his readers, is the ultimate purpose of the trope in his criticism. It advertised Bestuzhev's idea of himself and implanted this persona in his audience's mind.

Bestuzhev's critic claims that he is delighted with the heroic theme of national identity Katenin chose for his epic poem. He is displeased, however, with its execution. The old gentleman states that an author may reduce the quality of his vision by his own aesthetic and conceptual inadequacies. In comparison with the elevated and solemn language of the chronicle from which Katenin received his tale, the critic finds the hero's dying words too prosaic. Furthermore, he thinks Katenin's lexicon deflates the poem's tragic moment by using the verb "to make merry" (*veselit'sia*) at the tale's climax—the death of the hero. Bestuzhev's negative reaction to this moment in Katenin's poem was based on stylistic problems, but it pointed to the most crucial element in the poem for Bestuzhev—the hero's glory realized in a selfless, sacrificial death. For Bestuzhev the connection between the hero and his martyrdom was profound, and any diminution in the hero's image at such a critical moment was bound to offend him. Bestuzhev's emotional response focuses attention on another issue of the times—the relationship of literature to life. As Bestuzhev crafted a literary persona imbued with the values of romantic heroism, the presentation of self was all-important. Heroism could ultimately be assessed only against the protagonist's confrontation with death, in his willingness to sacrifice himself for a higher cause, and through the performance of this final act of magnanimity.

Bestuzhev did not argue by syllogistic reasoning but by emotional appeal, witticisms, metaphoric flourishes, and the weight of the library he commanded. He was victorious in raw combative terms. Leighton argues that "the battle of the ballad was elaborated in a major confrontation between Katenin and Bestuzhev over the Russian language and the theory of genre" (*Russian Romanticism*, 20). What is most remarkable about this debate, however, is that Bestuzhev was so effective he drove Katenin from literary practice (at least until the end of the decade). Clearly, the arena of literary debate belonged to the warrior-poet and guardian of the native tongue and *narodnost'*.

Selected Passages from Correspondence with a Friend

Bestuzhev displayed the combative features of literary life in his letters to Prince Peter Vyazemsky, with whom he maintained an extensive correspondence after their meeting in Moscow in 1823. Bestuzhev's letters are remarkable for their openness. Other than occasional references to himself as an idler, Bestuzhev avoided clichés, which gives his letters a tone of authority appropriate to a newly confident personality in command of its beliefs and aspirations. Bestuzhev discussed the St. Petersburg literary scene—meetings, dinners, and arguments within the Society of Lovers of Russian Literature. These documents provide the context in which his criticism and art developed.

In keeping with social behavioral patterns of the times, the club members displayed a dual attitude toward literature, at once playful and serious, epicurean and ascetic: "March 21, 1823. There will be a public meeting of the society and I have been asked to write something amusing. I am hard pressed to do it. It is difficult to be funny on demand. I would like to write something like my 'Evening at a Bivouac' ["Vecher na bivuake," an anecdotal piece which appeared in *The Polar Star* in 1823], but I don't think I can manage it."[6] In May Bestuzhev informed Vyazemsky in detail about the meeting:

> Forgive me, my dearest Prince among all other princes known to me, for not writing to you for so long. The reason for this has been the public meeting of our Society. I have awaited its conclusion in order to report to you about its success. I begin forthwith not from Leda's eggs, nor from the eggs of this past Holy Week, but almost from there. I begin with the preparatory organizational meetings which turned out to be quite stormy.
>
> I must tell you, Prince, that our Society has, God knows why,

6. "Pis'ma Aleksandra Bestuzheva k P. A. Viazemskomu (1823–1825)," 200.

several factions. [Nicholas] Gnedich, who has been relieved of his duties as Vice President, is the silver-plated catch spring of the first faction. Through [Anton] Delvig and [Peter] Pletnyov he is spreading rumors as through a sieve. These rumors turn into rank poison after passing through [Alexander] Voyeikov's viper mouth. As a consequence of the rumors, [Fyodor] Glinka became greatly dissatisfied with [Nicholas] Grech and at the Society itself which, he concludes, seeks to remove him [from the Presidency]. The second group is composed of the completely tasteless. Its titular head is Tsertelev, and its tail (there is no body) is Boris Fedorov [a government informer], and two or three other snakes. There are some censorial, better yet, police partizani, namely Voronov. The rest are represented by the good intentioned vociferous ones, the half-vocal faint-hearted, and the speechless. The number of these last, predictably, is the largest. (203–4).

Bestuzhev's wit renders a lively and sarcastic picture of the society. His judgment of others signals his competitiveness in literary activity. His clever digs call attention to himself and attempt to elevate his own image before Vyazemsky. He continued giving details of the debate:

At first there were arguments whether or not to name a day for public readings. Some thought we should not, because they have written nothing [to read]. Others weren't sure whether the remaining members of the group would write anything worthwhile. But since each of those called upon do indeed wish to be among the select group of readers, the majority decided to set a date. Then there followed a selection process by which we identified the works to be read. I suggested, among others, your sketch from the biography of our respected poet I. I. Dmitriyev, but since your manuscript is still with the censor, it cannot presently be read in public. At our last reading I suggested to the Society that we exclude from our readings Tsertelev's commentary to Derzhavin's odes. It is pure nonsense where, besides the words "beautiful," "inimitable," and "glorious," the only enlightened thought was the name of the great poet himself. But not to show prejudice I agreed to exclude my "Second Evening at a Bivouac" ["Vtoroi vecher na bivuake"]. Tsertelev objected, made a great row, defended the beauty of his work, taking umbrage at our selection procedure, saying that now it is too late to set a date for the reading. But I proved the opposite point. Grech took a vote, and it was approved nineteen to four.

The meeting took place on May twenty-second in the evening at Madame Derzhavin's. There was a great crowd. Stars, feathers, and sultans were aglow. The readings began at 7:30. Grech presented a speech on the purpose of the Society and its philosophy as an introduction and concluded by expressing the Society's gratitude to the President, who could not attend due to an illness. (Imagine, Prince, that this expression of gratitude toward Glinka found its detractors in the Society). The left, no the right, faction was victorious. Even though Glinka did not attend out of caprice, the Society nonetheless owes him its gratitude for his labor and sanguineness. For his rare moral stature we owe him our respect. Gnedich wasn't in attendance either. (Ibid., 204)

The public was not privy to the society's internal difficulties and did not know that Glinka and Gnedich were involved in a divisive competition. Their absence from the meeting was a dramatic indication of how seriously literary differences were taken.

Bestuzhev completed his description of the literary evening with a brief synopsis that captures the flavor of the public reading and of the divisions within the society:

[Faddei] Bulgarin's essay was engaging. We do not, however, have the ability to adequately assess historical fiction. [V. I.] Tumansky was applauded warmly, which he deserved. His verse is sonorous and picturesque. Everyone liked Kornilovich's verse, which my brother [Mikhail] read very well. Ryleyev's "The Exile" was replete with noble sentiment and rare elevated thought. It was received with heartfelt enthusiasm. Nikitin read your [biographical] piece [on Ivan Dmitriyev]. Everyone liked it and not only because it was simply stated, but because they love [Dmitriyev]. They applauded you. I read Pushkin's short poem "Farewell to Life." Pushkin is everywhere just who he always is. Lobanov's translation from "Phaedra" was good, but Boris Fedorov was quite foul. He is a plagiarist and reads verse in an exceedingly offensive manner. I just don't know why his work was accepted, especially since there was such opposition to it. To conclude the evening, Izmailov made everyone laugh, but this was more because of his bulk than for his verse. In general, the public was very well satisfied and everything went splendidly. [The public] is already asking for another evening like this one. (Ibid.)

Although it would be incorrect to call the society's evening of readings a Saturnalia (in the proper sense of a folk celebration and spectacle), Bestuzhev did describe a carnival spirit: the Society topples the high and elevates the low through false praise and mocking adoration; they subvert authority and hierarchy, and put language, often base language, to use in pursuit of all these ends. As in the medieval tradition, jesters (such as Tsertelev) emerge. Offense is compounded by counteroffense in the earthy and expressive verbal genres of the market place and holiday mummery. Resigning his high position as president, Glinka refuses to attend further meetings. Although he sincerely appreciated Glinka's many contributions, Grech's gratitude toward Glinka is suffused with an irony that scarcely masks his pleasure at Glinka's departure. Derision and laughter mingle with respect and honor. Izmailov's bulk overtakes his text and becomes a higher order of text.

This carnival spirit is more obvious in another letter to Vyazemsky written several months before the Decembrist Revolt:

There were some literary comedies here lately that almost made us die of laughter. Bulgarin, drunk, made up and kissed Del'vig and Fyodorov just like it was Holy Monday. Everyone's petty little peeve came to light and each spoke his dissatisfaction aloud. It all took place at Nikitin's. Lobanov, for example, admitted that he is angry with everyone for not praising his work. He asked Cheslavsky's forgiveness for lambasting his translation of "Phaedra," and so forth and so on. I spent the holidays here very wildly. Bacchus's outpourings were constant and strong. I thought I had been reborn and was living out our Moscow life once again. Remember our Herculean feats, dear Prince? True, I remember with pleasure the violent storm in which we whirled. I wished to fall again into [the storm] with you. (Ibid., 228)

The laughter, street emotions, breaches of decorum, shouts, arguments, and comic outpourings at Nikitin's, together with allusions to debauches, madcap feats of drinking and womanizing with Vyazemsky, speak with a voice of Dionysian passion.

Outside this enchanted sphere, however, there lurked a world of doubts, fears, and challenges. Bestuzhev's letters also reveal the oppressiveness of the real world and the disillusionments to be met in daily life. As a writer in the 1820s, Bestuzhev was continually engaged in the task of creating an audience by simultaneously entertaining and educating them. In January 1824, indicating the magnitude of the challenge, Bestuzhev responded to news that Vyazemsky was planning to publish his own literary journal: "I have heard that you and Denis Vasiliyevich [Davydov] are to issue a publication on the order of a literary almanac. Let me know what kind it is to be, and when it will come out. I wish you in advance every success. But remember, you must shake up [*rastatarit'*] Moscow and teach it again about taste and literariness" (ibid., 211). His remarks allude to the problems he had been encountering as editor of *The Polar Star* and, as one of its main contributors, in ascertaining the nature of the new reader whose taste he was trying to develop. This frustration brought moments of disillusionment: "Give me, Prince, your opinion of my *Polar Star* for the year. Whose opinion is more useful to me than yours? Let me know what you think. Local society's opinion is mixed. The ladies (as I expected) do not praise the new issue because the prose in it is not to their taste. The men, however, have taken to it and claim it is more exciting than last year's issue" (210).[7]

No literary almanac had been as successful as *The Polar Star*, and its financial returns were unprecedented for publisher, editors, and contributors alike. The jealous response of Bestuzhev's competitors caused him no small degree of distress: "If you can believe it, there are people whom we considered the most unbiased in society who nonetheless envy our latest success (that is, our profits) and by what they say they clearly wish to erase *The Polar Star* from society's horizon" ("Pis'ma," 210). Bestuzhev thought former supporters of the almanac were undermining it in an attempt to reduce sales.

Bestuzhev succumbed to the competitive urge as much as his rivals.

7. The second issue of *The Polar Star* had a decided military, Davydov-esque thrust in its prose entries (penned by Alexander, his brother Nicholas, Bulgarin, Zhukovsky, and one of his future publishers in the 1830s, Senkovsky). Bestuzhev rightly predicted that it would not appeal to his female readership, which was more interested in sentimental tales. The sexual differentiation of the audience constituted a dilemma for the writer, and it was Bestuzhev's wish to bring the two together. But much to his disappointment the task proved beyond him.

Responding to the news that Vyazemsky planned to open his almanac in Moscow, he offered advice, which Vyazemsky hardly needed, about the sorry state of the arts in Russia and the difficult lot of being a publisher. He began his letter (June 1824) in a paternalistic vein, presupposing in each utterance his own superiority, the unique character of his own success with *The Polar Star*, Vyazemsky's inability to surmount the obstacles that he had overcome, and the general vacuousness of Russian society—in short, striking a thoroughgoing Byronic pose:

> Your idea, dear Prince, of putting together a society that will publish literature belongs to the dreams of poets and not to the prosaic truth of our daily lives. Your idea bestows honor upon you. But, Prince, perhaps only your heart alone among all your friends and comrades has not grown old in the icy cold of egotism, has not dried up from being manipulative and calculating. Just look about you and whom will you find to be a cheerful helper? They may be able to help you, but they will not want to. Others may want to help, but will not be able to because they lack resources, money and more money. It's senseless to depend on sales—you have always erred on this score, Prince, imagining that books actually are read and sold by us Russians. And do not forget how you shall be met by the censors and ministries of government. No! No! "We see golden dreams / but ourselves die of hunger." (Ibid., 220)

Bestuzhev posed as a font of wisdom before an author quite clearly his superior and dispensed insincere words of encouragement with utter confidence in his ability to do so. He was clearly convinced of his authority in such matters. With Ryleyev he had quickly and successfully become the most outstanding publisher of the day, a writer of fiction to be counted among the leaders of the new generation, a sensational and effective critic, and a *militaire* who cut a dashing figure in society and at Court. But it is clear that Vyazemsky's publication represented a threat. The success of *The Polar Star* had already produced rival almanacs, the success of which reduced Bestuzhev's subscriptions and eventually led to its closure in 1825.[8] The covert message of the letter was to discourage

---

8. In the fall of 1824 A. F. Voeikov published thirty-five lines of an error-ridden edition of Pushkin's "Robber Brothers," lines already contracted to Bestuzhev and Ryleyev for *The Polar*

Vyazemsky from publishing another almanac. Bestuzhev competed with his friends and opponents alike.

Bestuzhev's First "Glance"

The literati viewed competition in the literary arena as a form of combat. Aesthetic causes were construed as personal programs, and in this fusion of literature and biography, personal offense was frequently taken over matters of style. The bombastics of the Bestuzhev and Katenin debate raged for years and at one point threatened their lives. But temperate minds cooled the angry, impassioned opponents and a duel was averted (Kotliarevskii, 431n.152). Alexander Pushkin was a bemused witness of these events and kept an active correspondence with both parties. Although he was generous to Bestuzhev, he was more favorably disposed to Katenin, who argued reasonably and with a finely honed aesthetic sensitivity. Bestuzhev impressed Pushkin with his wit, but not with the substance of his argument.

Pushkin cautioned Bestuzhev to beware of his publicist tendencies and tried to keep him at the job of careful analysis. He discouraged Bestuzhev from making declarations without argument and from rendering subjective judgments without concrete evidence to support his claims. Despairing that Bestuzhev would ever respond to his prodding, Pushkin wrote to Gnedich (the translator of a very readable edition of *The Iliad* who had first waged battle with Katenin on the ballad) that it would be amusing to force another duel between Bestuzhev and Katenin.[9] He suggested that such a confrontation would be eminently more interesting than the dull art and even duller criticism Bestuzhev and others were creating at the time. In response to Bestuzhev's first review "A Glance at Ancient and Modern Literature in Russia" ("Vzgliad na staruiu i novuiu slovesnost' v Rossii"), published in the inaugural issue

---

Star. He writes to Vyazemsky, "I write to unburden my soul which is now so distraught by man's baseness. . . . They are printing verse contracted to *The Polar Star.* . . . They have even convinced Baratynsky [1800–1844, metaphysical poet of early Russian romanticism] to take the work back he sold us long ago. . . . In a word, they are making literature into a regular flea market" (ibid., 223).

9. Aleksandr S. Pushkin, *Sobranie sochinenii,* ed. D. D. Blagoi et al. (Moscow, 1962), 9:41.

of *The Polar Star* (1823), Pushkin expressed distaste for Bestuzhev's
florid style and publicist tendencies. He wrote Prince Vyazemsky, "I have
read your poems in *The Polar Star.* They are charming. But for God's
sake don't forget about prose. Only you and Karamzin have mastered
that genre. . . . Bestuzhev's [review] article about our [literary] brother-
hood is frighteningly juvenile [*moloda*]. [This is especially pernicious]
for everything we print [on Russian literature] has an effect on sacred
Rus' " (Pushkin, 9:61).[10]

If Bestuzhev's articles were immature, they nonetheless initiated a
tradition in literary criticism for which he must be given credit. Leighton
argues that

> the importance of [Bestuzhev's] position should not be underesti-
> mated, for it signifies that Bestuzhev is honored as the intellectual
> ancestor of such major critics and philosophers as Vissarion
> Belinsky (1811–48), Alexander Herzen (1811–70), Nikolai Nek-
> rasov (1821–78), Nikolai Chernyshevsky (1828–89) and Nikolai
> Dobrolyubov (1836–61). He is no less than a pioneer of the
> cultural trend that leads to the Civicism of the later nineteenth
> century and to Positivism, Utilitarianism, Nihilism, Populism,
> and Socialist Realism. For this reason the three politically ori-
> ented "Glances" at Russian literature which prefaced the annual
> issues of *The Polar Star* and served as its editorial manifesto are
> treated [in Soviet criticism] as Bestuzhev's central contribution to
> Romantic criticism. (*ABM,* 37)

Bestuzhev did make a major contribution to the creation of an authentic
Russian literary criticism in the 1820s and consequently had to be reck-
oned with by later generations (such as Vissarion Belinsky in the 1830s).

Bestuzhev's articles cannot be considered *literary* criticism in the sense
we have come to understand the term. Pushkin had similar reservations,
which he expressed in a letter to Bestuzhev:

> Permit me to be the first to overstep the bounds of propriety[11] and
> heartily thank you for *The Polar Star,* for your letters, for the

---

10. See also Kotliarevskii, 397.
11. Pushkin uses the familiar "thou" form of address and thereby initiates a more intimate
address between the two; hence his mentioning "propriety."

article on literature, for [your story "Roman and Olga"] and especially for the [military anecdote] "An Evening at a Bivouac." All of this is marked with your stamp, i.e., with your intelligence and marvelous liveliness. We might argue at our leisure about the "Glance." I confess that there is no one that I so much like to argue with as you and Vyazemsky. You two alone can rouse me to heated debate. (Pushkin, 9:67)[12]

Pushkin refrained from attacking Bestuzhev's article as he had in his letter to Vyazemsky, but he did not let Bestuzhev off the hook completely: "For the time being I will complain to you only about one thing. How could you forget Radishchev in an article on Russian literature? Just whom are you going to remember then? The failure to mention him is unforgivable and I did not expect it of you" (Pushkin, 9:67).

Bestuzhev's "Glance at Ancient and Modern Literature in Russia" was polemical in that it continued the debate with the Kateninites. Consequently, his detractors aimed words less kind than Pushkin's at it. An anonymous critic stated that "the enumeration of authors without a definition of their relative significance" renders the "Glance" empty of content. "Its exterior form of expression secrets an inner vacuousness" (Kotliarevskii, 320). Another critic wrote that "Bestuzhev expresses himself concisely and strongly, but unevenly. There is great wit in him which often appears to be refined. He loves word play with a passion, and in his adorned phrases one frequently encounters something either too immature or too fanciful" (320).

In the journal *The Herald of Europe* (*Vestnik Evropy*), Bestuzhev was taken to task for his style and wit, both of which diminished matters of substance. The reviewer could not forgive Bestuzhev's own museum of linguistic curiosities. Bestuzhev's description of language as "broken, bright, ruptured, fluid, injudicious, unbounded, melodious, decisive, picturesque, stubborn, at home in society, boiling over with ideas, heartfelt, heavy, elusive, abrupt, complicated, intricate, fluent, rusty, and so forth" was inadequate (ibid., 320–21). His figurative speech outraged many, and his marlinisms were rejected outright by critics from several quarters.

For writers who were not opposed to salon language and its figurative speech, Bestuzhev's article was unacceptable on different grounds. The "Glance" was considered a disgrace to the image of the author and critic it

12. See also J. Thomas Shaw, ed., *The Letters of Pushkin*, 113–14, with corrections.

projected. Bestuzhev was perceived as too condescending, sarcastic, and egocentric. Karamzin took umbrage in a letter to Ivan Dmitriyev (1760–1837): "The review of Russian literature is written as if in ridicule, although the author is not without talent it would seem" (ibid., 321). Izmailov, whose rotund form had impressed Bestuzhev more than his art, wrote "with what bias and illogic in its rendering of our latest writers and with what a foolish language is it all described by the hand of this temporary visitor to our Parnassus" (321). Both supporters and opponents were dissatisfied with Bestuzhev's advertisement of his persona at the expense of the topic under discussion and with his flamboyant style, which emphasized subject rather than object. He inverted critical principles (subjectivism and impressionism outranked logic and analysis).

Bestuzhev did not feel obliged to answer his critics immediately, and when he finally did, his response was emotional rather than measured: "I foresaw [in writing my 'Glance'] that the older generation would cry out against my unheard of temerity for writing what I thought at such a [young] age."[13] Bestuzhev attacked the characters of his critics instead of responding to the substance of their arguments. Following the competitive code, which dominated his apprehension of literary relationships, he suggested that his detractors were jealous of his success at such a young age. Bestuzhev was apparently unwilling to face threats to his persona and his authority. He characteristically refused to examine the writing on the wall even when it was accessible to him at a conscious level. Denial appears to have been a strong component of his personality. In fairness to Bestuzhev, however, there was ample cause for jealousy—the success of *The Polar Star*. That he and Ryleyev made a profit of 23,000 rubles (a sum unheard of before this time in publishing)[14] brought them notoriety that others envied. Furthermore, their almanac

became a model of refined taste. All the most significant writers, poets and novelists contributed to it, and presented at least in the first volume fine examples of their art. . . . In less than a week over six hundred copies were sold and in three weeks all copies [1500] were sold out. This was a singular example in Russian

13. "Otvet na kritiku 'Polarnoi zvezdy', pomeshchennuii v 4, 5, 6, i 7 nomerakh *Russkogo invalida* 1823 goda," in Frizman, 56.

14. For comparative information, see Gary Marker, *Publishing, Printing and the Origins of Intellectual Life in Russia, 1700–1800* (Princeton, N.J., 1985), 103–35.

literature at the time (with the exception of [Karamzin's] *History of the Russian State*) of a success that not another book or journal had ever enjoyed. The editors had the great fortune of delivering a copy of *The Polar Star* to the Grand Empress herself and received the greatest attention [in society and at Court] from it. K. F. Ryleyev received two diamond signet-rings and A. A. Bestuzhev a gold snuff box of the most excellent hand work as well as a diamond ring. (Kotliarevskii, 303–4)

Bestuzhev's "Glance" is a remarkable work not for its content as much as for its style and what it indicated about his thought. N. Kotliarevsky maintains that Bestuzhev employed no analytic language in his "Glance" not because it was uncommon for romantics to use it, but because Bestuzhev did not command it. As a consequence,

Bestuzhev collected various literary curiosities which made their way onto the pages of the Russian journals. He informed his public that he already had in his possession a whole museum of rarities—Tatar and Vargangian phrases, Gordian thoughts, philosophical bubbles, outworn similes—all of them freaks of common sense. "Just imagine what I have gathered: jumping spiders, for example, and bent-knee snakes, doves and ducks with teeth, stentorian corks, blood-thirsty death-caps," Bestuzhev wrote. And he of course never imagined that in time this list of curiosities would be filled with his own *faux pas*. (Ibid., 300)

The Language of an Adequate Self

Bestuzhev's "Glance at Ancient and Modern Literature in Russia" is well over five thousand words long and represents a concerted effort to discuss all of Russian literature from its beginnings in the eleventh century to 1823. Perhaps it was audacious for a twenty-six-year-old to have undertaken such a task, but "Glance" became a landmark in Russian literary criticism because it appeared just as Russian culture was demanding a historical description of its verbal arts. Bestuzhev did not argue his claims but presented a panorama of Russian literature in metaphoric terms. It is—at the very least—a remarkable compendium of figures of speech.

There are over one hundred figures in "Glance." They constitute a conscious element of the discourse, for these figures are no spontaneous flow of metaphors and similes (as we find in his poetry and fiction), but an extended series of clichés culled from European works that Bestuzhev was reading and translating at the time. His description of Mikhail Lomonosov (1711–65) and Gavril Derzhavin (1743–1816) indicates this propensity: "Like the northern lights from the shores of the Arctic Sea the genius of Lomonosov illumined our midnight sky. . . . And finally to the glory of our people and the [eighteenth] century, Derzhavin appeared. This lyricist and philosopher divined the art of telling the tsars the very truth, and he discovered the secret means of uplifting souls. His word is swift, untouchable, like lightning, and it is rich like nature itself" (ibid., 313).[15] The same images are utilized in Bestuzhev's descriptions of his great contemporaries Nicholas Karamzin, Vasily Zhukovsky, and Konstantin Batyushkov: "Karamzin flashed on the horizon of prose like a rainbow after the deluge";[16] "There is a time in life when a flood of incomprehensible feelings overwhelms our breast; the soul thirsts to pour itself forth but cannot find a way to express itself; in Zhukovsky's verse as though through a dream we meet our visions personified, like old friends, and resurrect the past" (530); "Batyushkov's poetry is like a steep waterfall now flying in a measured fashion, then suddenly spraying aloft in a gentle breeze" (531). In "Glance," the figures of speech come in such rapid succession that the object is gradually obliterated and the subject is thrust into the foreground.

Bestuzhev's style was meant to instruct his readership on how to approach him and his texts through "word and deed" (ibid., 525), that is, in literature and in life. In his description of Nicholas Glinka's (1786–1880) compositions, Bestuzhev stated that the work, "illuminates his bright soul. He [belongs] to that rare group of writers whose biographies best serve as foreword and commentary to their art" (532). Bestuzhev had Lord Byron (1788–1824) in mind, of course. Byron's example was considered emblematic, the archetypal plot Bestuzhev-Marlinsky would

---

15. Mikhail Vasilievich Lomonosov was the most outstanding practitioner of science and letters in the eighteenth century. Gavril Romanovich Derzhavin (1743–1816) was a poet, statesman, and soldier, the greatest poet of the late eighteenth century.

16. *Sochineniia v dvukh tomakh*, 2:527.

impose upon his life and letters. Bestuzhev's commentary to Vyazemsky on Byron's death is instructive:

> We have lost a brother, Prince, in Lord Byron. Mankind has lost its defender and literature its Homer of ideas. Now one may cry out in the words of the Bible, "Whither hast thou gone, radiant Lucifer!" "Death has torn this golden star from the sky." And some great despairing echo of his fall resounded in the hearts of all kindred spirits.
>
> I could not believe the news, nor did I wish to. I thought it a newspaper death, the fabrication of journalists. But it is the truth, the horrible truth. He died, but what an envious death it was. He died for Greece, if not for the Greeks who have again washed themselves in the bloody font of their former shame. [Byron] bestowed on mankind great truths through his great and amazing gifts. But in the nobility of his spirit [he has set] an example for all exalted poets. And yet this giant was beset by calumny, and envy drove him from his homeland. Both poisoned the air [he breathed]. History will list him among those few people who were not taken with a predilection for Self, but who acted for the good of mankind. ("Pis'ma," 219)[17]

Bestuzhev's remarks, like these, were often glaringly self-serving. But it was not always notables whom Bestuzhev cited for self-glorification: "To the honor of the military calling it must be stated that young officers much more than any other group really [pursue knowledge and] study" (*Sochineniia*, 2:539). Like Glinka and Byron, Bestuzhev's life was to represent a running commentary on his art. His writing, at the same time, was meant to elaborate the self-idea he wished to bear into life.

The hero-warrior-poet nexus is apparent elsewhere in "Glance." In speaking of "The Lay of the Host of Igor" (a twelfth-century epic that holds a unique position in East Slavic letters), Bestuzhev remarked that "the unnamed bard breathed a fighting Russian spirit into the young Russian language" (ibid., 523). The emphasis on combativeness and linguistic reform should not be overlooked. When describing Derzhavin, Bestuzhev noted that he was capable of "criticizing the Russian tsars,"

---

17. Bestuzhev's judgment is in extreme error, the result of his desire to mask his own ego purposes.

something close to the Decembrist heart. Bestuzhev also called Derzhavin the Russian Pindar (526). The young romantics saw in the Greek poet the consummate warrior-bard whose elevated verse preserved for later generations the glorious and daring deeds of the past. Bestuzhev and his friends memorized Pindar's verse, learning the language of a heroic stance through his aestheticized discourse. These authors and their literature were models for Bestuzhev's generation in terms of behavior and the conception of self in heroic terms.

If it has been common to decipher Bestuzhev's proud sense of himself in his "Glance" (for he scarcely hid it), the confession of personal desire has gone unnoticed. The concluding paragraph of "Glance" represents perhaps the most remarkable display of a young writer's longing:

Man is by nature more enamored of himself than of glory. The poet, the romantic, the scientist all work in the quiet of the study to pluck the fruit of self-knowledge from [the tree of] mankind. But when he sees his labor withering on the bookstore shelf, [experiences] the great silence which meets him in good society, where not a one would suspect him to be a man of talent, when indeed instead of rewards he receives naught but reproach, can he be expected to exchange the poppies of the present for an uncertain laurel wreath of an uncertain future?

The most important reason [for the poor state in which Russian literature finds itself] is the way our native language is driven from society as well as the indifference of the fair sex to everything written in Russian. What then can perfect if not simply serve the benevolent gaze of our Russian beauties? What prosaic heart does it not inspire with its poetry? But one smile from a lady, dear and enlightened, would reward all one's efforts, one's sacrifices. We do not experience such charms, and it is for you, my lovely female compatriots, that the muses are grieved, for you yourselves!

But let us take heart. The public's taste, like an underground stream, seeks to reach yet higher. The new generation is beginning to feel the charm of its native language and to express its strength in it. Time, without our witness, sows enlightenment, and the fog which now obliterates the field of Russian literature, while troubling its course, will nonetheless deliver the sheaves of firmness and promises a rich harvest. (Ibid., 539)

Unlike Pushkin, who disavowed recognition as a motive force in art, Bestuzhev sought it, not in the distant future, but in the present. He desired the acceptance and attention of women, whom he attempted to manipulate to do his bidding. Pushkin responded to this notion, claiming it was outdated and incapable of illuminating the problem of the arts in Russia: "Kornilovich is a fine fellow and shows much promise. But why does he write 'for the indulgent attention of the gracious lady NN' and await 'the encouraging smile of the fair sex' before continuing his interesting work? All this is old and unnecessary" (Shaw, 151). Bestuzhev, however, was very much interested in the response of the female reader. Fictional plots could work as entrées into real relationships. Flowery speech, condescension, and wit opened doors.

Although Bestuzhev's readers interpreted his stylistic novelty as a reflection of his uniqueness, Pushkin grew dissatisfied with this element of Bestuzhev's writing. Where Bestuzhev praised a now virtually unknown lyricist Vasily Petrov (1736–99) for his "inflamed and daring turns of speech and quickly captured dramatic scenes" (*Sochineniia*, 2:525), Pushkin could only recoil. Although he chided Bestuzhev for his "rapid tales" with their sudden twists of fate based on foreign models, Bestuzhev was not about to abandon a style synonymous with his name. It was part and parcel of his natural inclination toward metaphor and aphorism, which were also essential components in the art of recruiting a readership.

Bestuzhev praised Ivan Dmitriyev (1796–1837), calling him sufficiently "playful and witty" to be "a model" for other poets (ibid., 526). Because playfulness and wittiness are also invariant features of his own prose, Bestuzhev indicated how his readers should approach his writing. In defending Prince Vyazemsky, Bestuzhev denied that there was any egocentric motive behind his technique: "[Vyazemsky] has been scolded for an extravagant wittiness, but this [feature of his poetry] derives not from a base desire to amaze the reader with his intelligence, but from a lack of this desire altogether" (532). Bestuzhev wished to fend off accusations about his egocentric style leveled by authoritative literati such as Karamzin. Just as stylistic bombastics defined the area of contact between Bestuzhev's persona and his audience (his public reception), it also delineated the area of contact between Bestuzhev's self and his persona (his own reception of his self-idea).

There were dangers inherent in penning a subject-oriented prose. There were occasions when Bestuzhev's projections onto the ostensible object of description backfired, particularly his negative assessments of other writers. He wrote that Glinka's "prose is direct, mellifluous and well shaped, although a bit too fecund" (ibid., 532) in an article that was criticized as being condescending and egotistical, as well as too fecund. When Bestuzhev criticized contemporary Russian culture for its inability to produce and encourage writers, he unwittingly condemned himself for the excesses he found in the "frivolous" poets of his day: "No one dedicates himself to the profitless and silverless trade of the writer; and if one does write, it is not in earnest, but only in jest" (538–39). This is precisely the criticism Karamzin and Izmailov leveled at Bestuzhev's "Glance."

Bestuzhev wrote three criticial reviews of Russian literature between 1823 and 1825. The style of all three "Glances" reveals his use of language to represent self.[18] Together with his many figures of speech, his marlinisms were of great importance. The term was coined in the 1840s to refer to a special type of speech characteristic of Bestuzhev's discourse. Given the polemical combativeness of the period, his opponents produced a pejorative variant, *bestuzhevshchina*,[19] based on his surname.

The marlinism was primarily a euphonic linguistic structure containing parallelisms and balanced structures that often utilize paregmenon. The marlinist utterance was cast for sound effect in conformity with rules of grammar, but not necessarily those of reason or logic. In effect, if the sentence was grammatic, euphonious, and compact, then, no matter what its content, Bestuzhev considered it sufficient. From Bestuzhev's first "Glance" the following false generalization is representative: "Our wealthy are not well-educated, and our well-educated are not wealthy" [Nashi bogachi ne slishkom ucheny, a uchenye vovse ne bogaty] (*Sochineniia*, 2:539). Content has been sacrificed to an overextended wit.

Examples of this type of utterance abound in the third "Glance." "It is said that in order to comprehend something one must feel everything;

---

18. "A Glance at Modern and Ancient Russian Literature" (1823), "A Glance at Russian Literature for 1823" ("Vzgliad na russkuiu slovesnost' v techenie 1823 goda," 1824), and "A Glance at Russian Literature for 1824 and the Beginning of 1825" ("Vzgliad na russkuiu slovesnost' v techenie 1824 i nachale 1825 godov," 1825), in Bestuzhev-Marlinskii, *Sochineniia*, 2:521–58.

19. The suffix *-shchina* connotes a critical evaluation of a social phenomenon. *Bestuzhevshchina*, for example, is derogatory (as with *oblomovshchina*). On other occasions the suffix remains neutral, as in *barshchina* (quitrent).

but is it not necessary to feel everything in order to comprehend everything?" [Govoriat: chtoby vse vyrazit', nadobno vse chuvstvovat'; no razve ne nadobno vsego chuvstvovat', chtoby vse ponimat'?] (ibid., 548). The marlinism shuffles subjects, predicates, and objects. It appears meaningful, but it is merely linguistic play, a substitution for thought.

There are occasions when Bestuzhev's marlinisms are predicated on strict numerical values, usually two or three: "Personalities and situations may pass, but peoples and conditions remain forever" [Litsa i sluchainosti prokhodiat, no narody i stikhi ostaiutsia vechno] (ibid., 549). Binary (compound) subjects constitute the parallel elements of the utterance, which also contains marked prosodic features (the first, fifth and ninth syllables are accented, with a weak stress on the eleventh). Bestuzhev strove for pithiness: "Grief is the embryo of thought, isolation is its crucible" [Skorb' est' zarodysh myslei, uedinenie—ikh gornilo] (549). Although paregmenon came from the venerable traditions of antiquity, it too can be found in the sequential and horizontal movement of Bestuzhev's thought. For example, Bestuzhev wrote that the first chapter of Pushkin's *Eugene Onegin* was "an alluring, animated picture of our inanimate society" [zamanchivaia odushevlennaia kartina neodushevlennogo nashego sveta] (553). The word Bestuzhev committed to the page elicited a related word—an antonym, the same root in another word, an inversion, or a negation. Two or three nouns might be duplicated by an equal number, or the negative prefix might be added to the first word. In each instance spontaneous speech leads to a linguistically related utterance. Thought and critical analysis are transcribed as pleasing rhythms and word play. For Bestuzhev writing concerned opinions rather than ideas, any one of which has a legitimacy determined by the expressive means available to the writer: "Each has his weight of words, each his own opinion" [U vsiakogo svoi ves slov, u kazhdogo svoe mnenie] (556).

Bestuzhev's storehouse of linguistic forms limited his ability both to express ideas and to subject them to critical analysis. Consequently, his arguments can be turned on him. When he assaulted a rival almanac *The Moscow Telegraph* (*Moskovskii telegraf*), his criticism could have been applied to his own writing: "[*The Telegraph* is marked by] an uneven style, self-assurance in its judgments, a sharp tone in its assessments [of writers], subjectivism, and everywhere the temerity to teach" (ibid., 557). And of another journal, *Mnemosyne*, Bestuzhev implicated himself unwittingly when asserting that the journal displayed a "passion for theory that the authors disprove in their very practice" (555). It is as though Bestuzhev unconsciously placed himself in contact with his own deficiencies, which served only as projections rather than as moments of self-illumination. The marlinism contained the seed of its own destruction.

Bestuzhev's second and third "Glances" reflect the degree to which his writing was left open to attack. Kotliarevsky maintains that the second comprehensive article on Russian literature, "A Glance at Russian Literature for 1823," was "more serious than the first and its tone more austere." But he is critical of this second "Glance," stating that it too proves the "inconsistency of [Bestuzhev's] critical tastes and faculties" (Kotliarevskii, 323). Lauren Leighton holds a contrary opinion, and sees a serious attempt on Bestuzhev's part to advance the argument concerning foreign borrowings, particularly gallicisms: "In his expression of distaste for French calques and his stress on patriotism Bestuzhev was in no way supporting either the Shishkovite or the Kateninite positions, and his remarks are well in keeping with Karamzinian esthetics. His objection was not to the use of French as a model for Russian, but to the extent—and even more—to the nature of that use. His objections were to servile imitation of foreign models without concern for the native condition of the Russian language, and he made his objections even more clear in his third article" (ABM, 47). Leighton's argument appreciates the kernel of Bestuzhev's idea; Kotliarevsky's remains sensitive to Bestuzhev's rhetoric. The second "Glance" is indeed very much concerned with imitation and originality, but only in reference to gallicisms. In keeping his remarks focused on French calques (which he had occasion to use, but only in the measured proportion he recommended in this "Glance"), Bestuzhev obscured the extent to which his own writing was influenced by anglicisms. Small wonder Pushkin addressed Bestuzhev as "my dear Walter [Scott]."

Vyazemsky took exception to the second "Glance," scoring Bestuzhev's indiscriminate focus: "You are not free [to speak spontaneously] and you have consequently been caught in tangential matters of secondary concern. And who [among us] should be most independent if not we writers? Independence [of thought and speech] is the power we must serve in truth and in faith. Without it there can be no salvation for the writer. Without it everything, the mind, the heart and even one's inkwell, will dry up" (Kotliarevskii, 323). Vyazemsky, a perceptive reader of Bestuzhev as well as Pushkin, found behind the bombastic exegesis something false. Bestuzhev's discussion of imitation and originality was a cover (for his own anglomania) and derivative at the same time. In other words, his call for an original literature was itself imitative, based entirely on European models. Like Pushkin and Nicholas Bestuzhev, Vyazemsky criticized Bestuzhev's subjectivity. The consequences of that subjectivity were damaging—an inability to render a well-reasoned and internally consistent argument.

Bestuzhev may have inadvertently touched on the source of this deficiency. In the concluding paragraph of the second "Glance" he used the image of sleep to indicate deep, unknown forces latent in a Russian culture yet to be awakened. Interestingly, his description of the Russian language resembles his description of the unconscious in his poem "Dream's Domicile": "Our language can be compared to a lovely sleeping child. He mumbles in his sleep some harmonious sounds or sighs over something unknown, but a ray of thought rarely can be discerned on his brows. This child, mind you, is not Hercules, who even as a babe in his crib smothered a serpent. Shall our child sleep into eternity?" (*Sochineniia*, 2:546). Many themes meet in this image, as it draws into close configuration a powerful hero, a powerless child, and an anxiety that the state of unconsciousness shall persist, that the child shall never awaken. Bestuzhev's third "Glance" developed this image further, again as a projection onto Russian culture rather than as a point of conscious self-understanding: "We are like children who test their strength on toys only to break them open where we might gaze inside with curiosity" (548). From Bestuzhev's perspective the image of the curious child represents the inferior status of the arts in Russia, but it delivers another enclosure (also associated with sleep and the unconscious in "Dream's Domicile"). In this figure, Bestuzhev suggests that knowledge of hidden content results from the destruction of the pleasing object. Awakening is a breaking into the suppressed or unknown, but it brings a new understanding of how things really work.

In the "Glances" we observe Bestuzhev's desires at many different levels. First, he would like to create an authentic and original Russian literary criticism; he did not accomplish this, but he contributed greatly to its development. Second, he wished to make a name for himself through his writing; at this he was successful. And finally, he seems to have wanted to gain access to the secret resources of his interior life, his drives, motives, and aspirations; yet "the silent god of sleep [slept] beneath a wreath of poppies / forever delight[ed] in an undisturbed dream."

4

Prose and the
Projected Persona

Bulgarin does not have the time to put the
finishing touches on his work.
                            —Bestuzhev-Marlinsky

Aesthetic Inheritance

Bestuzhev began writing fictional anecdotes and travelogues when Russian prose was in a woeful state. In his critical articles he had attacked the fiction produced by imitators of the sentimental school and by authors who continued to write adventure novels. In the 1820s he set out to redefine the norm and make his own mark on Russian prose. After Bestuzhev's death, Vissarion Belinsky (1811–48) grudgingly admitted that Bestuzhev's prose had been important to the development of Russian literature: "In order not to say too much, I will say that Mr. Marlinsky was our first teller of tales, he was the creator, or more properly speaking, the instigator of our Russian prose tale."[1] The praise for

1. Vissarion Belinskii, *Polnoe sobranie sochinenii*, 1:272.

Bestuzhev was faint but significant, because it came from the pen of a critic who had taken him to task throughout the 1830s.

By the turn of the century the adventure novel, which had dominated the middle eighteenth century, had become an "enormous, multi-volume novel with its focus on plot swollen to extraordinary dimensions. It was not a large form, strictly speaking, but a 'colossal' one."[2] In these novels episodes were strung together until the author felt the hero, heroine, and reader were sufficiently edified in moral terms to bring the narrative to a close. As the adventure novel began to involve love intrigues, the number of lyrical moments increased, and the number of adventures declined (22). As the device of the personalized narrator became more prevalent, entertaining events virtually disappeared, leaving in their stead letters and impassioned monologues. Despite this change in focus, the monumental scale remained. The novel's size was matched by elaborate sentences marked by "subordinate clauses, one after another" that were "logically imprecise due to the abundance of copulative conjunctions" (24). The speech of the characters was also convoluted, as in Fyodor Emin's "Letters of Ernest and Doravra" (1766):

> Doravra, kindest Doravra, what do these changes mean? You are distressed with me! Ah! I am beginning to feel the consequences of my audacity! But you, composite of all that is pleasant, why are you troubled? If I forgot about decorum, if I said what courtesy forbids you to hear, when I could not guess at the most worthy signs of esteem which by the customs of your land are due your nobility and your beautiful personage, then for my vile audacity I am already beginning to suffer fate's cruelest punishments. Dearest Doravra, possessor of the essence of angelic charm . . . (Ibid., 23)

> [Доравра, любезнейшая Доравра, что значат сии перемены? Ты мной огорчена! Ах я начинаю чувствовать следствия моей дерзости! Но ты всех приятностей собор, для чего неспокоишься? Ежели я позабыл о благопристойности, если сказал то, чего вежливость вам слушать воспрещает, когда я не умел отгадать достойнейшие почтения обыкновения

---

2. Iurii Tynianov and Boris Eikhenbaum, eds., *Russian Prose*, trans. and ed. Ray Parrott (Ann Arbor, Mich., 1985), 21–22.

вашей земли, вашему благородству и прекрасной вашей особе, то я за подлую мою дерзость уже жесточайшее от судьбины претерпевать начинаю наказания. Дражайшая Доравра, естество ангелов прелести в себе имеющее . . .]³

Nicholas Karamzin had attempted to reform Russian prose. His innovations were language oriented, involving a simplification of syntax patterned on French and English models. He favored calques, neologisms, euphony, prose rhythms, alliteration, and assonance and opposed the use of Church Slavonic and Old Russian morphological forms.⁴ Diminutives predominated, with birds becoming "little birds" and nests "dear little nests." His measured, rhythmic period based on parallelism, an equal number of accented syllables per cola, and a marked musical intonation together with an avoidance of conjunctions and the long period, created an immediate sensation in the reading public. Against the heaviness of the previous period, Karamzin's prose tales sounded like poetry in prose, as the following extracts show:

He is an orphan in the world but God loves orphans while Novgorod loves the magnanimous. [On sirota v mire no Bog liubit sirot, a Novgorod velikodushnykh.]

I often come to this place and almost always greet the spring here. I come here too in the gloomy days of fall to grieve together with nature. [Chasto prikhozhu ia na sie mesto i pochti vsegda vstrechaiu tam vesnu, tyda zhe prikhozhy i v mrachnye dni oseni / gorevat' vmeste s Prirodoiu.]

Reckless young man! Do you know your own heart? Can you always answer for your actions? Does logic always rule your feelings? [Bezrassudnoi, molodoi chelovek! Znaesh' li ty svoe serdtse? Vsegda li mozhesh' otvechat' za svoi dvizheniia? Vsegda li rassydok est' tsar' chuvstv tvoikh?]

3. Russian text cited in Iurii Tynianov and Boris Eikhenbaum, eds., *Russkaia proza* (The Hague, 1963), 16.

4. Viktor Vinogradov, "Stil' prozy Lermontova," in *Literaturnoe nasledstvo*, vols. 43–44 (Moscow and Leningrad, 1941), 519.

Never had the larks sung so beautifully, never had the sun shone so brightly, never had the flowers smelled so pleasant. [Nikogda zhavoronki tak khorosho ne pevali, nikogda solntse tak svetlo ne siialo, nikogda tsvety tak priiatno ne pakhli.]

Without your eyes, dark is the bright moon, without your voice, dull is the nightingale's song, without your breathing, the breeze is unpleasant to me. [Bez glaz tvoikh temen svetlyi mesiats, bez tvoego golosa skuchen solovei poiushchii, bez tvoego dykhaniia veterok mne ne priiaten.][5]

Karamzin's lexicon was rigid. Common speech was not allowed because of its coarseness and crudity; Church Slavonicisms were inadmissible because of their association with elevated genres such as the ode. Karamzin took the speech etiquette and manners of polite society as a linguistic norm: "The role of conversational language was limited by the . . . principle of 'pleasantness.' 'Coarseness' and 'tenderness' [were] the two stylistic poles which were keenly felt in Karamzin's epoch" (Tynianov and Eikhenbaum, *Russian Prose,* 30). As he narrowed the linguistic register to a variation of Lomonosov's middle style, Karamzin's prose came under attack from Admiral Shishkov, particularly for its gallicisms. By Bestuzhev's time, these innovations had become so codified that handbooks of sentimentalist style had been written. One of them, "On Circumspection in Style," ("Ob osmotritel'nosti v sloge," 1812), listed the pitfalls of a "noncircumspect" style as compared to the mellifluous symmetry of a "correct" period structure:

By a circumspection in style, writers avoid as much as possible the confluence of vowels (hiatus), of similar syllables (cacophony), and ambiguity in expression. They try to avoid presenting two or three words in the same case in sequence, and also avoid using two or three words of varying relations [in different cases] with one preposition; they are wary of incorrect repetitions within phrases. They subject their sentences to the laws of symmetry. They observe an equal number of adjectives (epithets) and nouns (elegance), and strive for a smoothness of phrase, a fullness of period, for precision in turns of speech, and pleasantness in the

---

5. Tynianov and Eikhenbaum, eds., *Russian Prose,* 25, 27–28; *Russkaia proza,* 18, 21.

sounds of words. They change the singular into plural, or plural into singular, a noun and verb into other parts of speech, etc., etc., in order to avoid hampering the reader in the slightest way, in order to provide him with every pleasure . . . for which, let us say in passing, he often does not know the reason. And there is no need for him to know. The artist loves his work, and indefatigably so. (Ibid., 32–33).

Although Bestuzhev had discussed and debated stylistic matters in his literary criticism, he chose to avoid what the critic in 1812 maintained was the most rigorous task for the writer—editing:

> Artists of the word know what a meticulous style is, and what difficulties must be overcome to achieve it. Only a talented author can be circumspect in style, can ponder [the effect of] a period, a phrase, a word, a turn of speech, and so on. Another [lesser writer] cannot. Finally, the closer style is to perfection, the further readers are from surmising its perfection. What comes without difficulty to readers seems to them to have come to the writer without difficulty. (Ibid., 33)

Instead, Bestuzhev produced spontaneous speech, following what appeared to him to be the style of automatic writing established in late-eighteenth-century England by Laurence Sterne (1713–68). In an article translated from the French that appeared in *The Northern Messenger* (1803) the point was made unequivocally that "one need only sit down and write whatever comes into his head, and he will have a book in the Sternian manner. Its arrangement is even more important than its content. Neither order, nor harmony, nor connection between ideas is necessary. One can leap from a cemetery to an ale house without the slightest break. Herein lies its poignancy" (49). In effect, Bestuzhev's natural writing style was sanctioned by this carefree canon.

Between 1820 and 1823 Bestuzhev's prose laboratory was the travel genre with its focus on anecdotes. Not only was he familiar with it from his reading, he was a traveler himself in the service of Duke Wurtemburg. The genre made perfect sense both as a literary form and a repository of personal experience. It joined literary text and life-text in a manner that particularly fit Bestuzhev's desire to encode himself in life and art. His models came from Europe and America in Sterne, Louis

Dupaty (1775–1851), and Washington Irving (1783–1859). Karamzin's *Letters of a Russian Traveler* (*Pis'ma russkogo puteshestvennika*, 1791–96) had introduced the Russian variant of the form. Bestuzhev's first publication in prose, "A Journey to Revel" ("Poezdka v Revel'," 1820) was cast in the loose form of a travelogue. It was quickly followed by a succession of popularly received anecdotes and travel tales presented as a cycle of military episodes narrated by the same officer.[6] He enjoyed great success with these texts and followed them up with two anecdotes of a similar stamp.[7] Anecdotes made comparatively fewer demands than longer forms, and from this genre it was a natural move to travelogues, which are still centered around an anecdotal structure but with a more definitive depiction of the narrator. He followed this track, which carried him to ever more complex narrative structures and culminated in his production of historical fiction, the genre that won him fame in the 1820s.

The Anecdote

Bestuzhev's earliest anecdotes reflect an ambivalence toward eighteenth-century prose in general and Karamzin in particular. On the one hand, he parodied sentimentalist stylistic conceits, and on the other, he replicated them in genre selection, thematic interest, and narrator image. "A History of Punctuation Marks" ("Istoriia znakov prepinaniia," 1821), published only posthumously, is strictly parodic. It is the story of a young princess and her love for the foreigner Punctuatio (*Prepinani*) who scorns her. In order to evade the ever watchful eye of the suspicious queen, the princess develops a system of communication based on punctuation marks. In her mind they suffice in expressing all her emotions.

---

6. "A Page from the Diary of a Guard Officer" ("Listok iz dnevnika gvardeiskogo ofitsera," 1821); "Another Page from the Diary of a Guard Officer" ("Eshche listok iz dnevnika gvardeiskogo ofitsera," 1821); "Night on Board Ship (From the Notes of a Guard Officer on the Return to Russia after the Campaign of 1814)" ("Noch' na korable [iz zapisok gvardeiskogo ofitsera na vozvratnom puti v Rossiiu posle kampanii 1814 goda]," and "The Castle Wenden (A Fragment from a Guard Officer's Diary)" ("Zamok Venden [Otryvok iz dnevnika gvardeiskogo ofitsera]),″ 1823).

7. "An Evening at a Bivouac" ("Vecher na bivuake," 1823) and "Another Evening on Bivouac" ("Vtoroi vecher na bivuake," 1823).

When she is jilted, she continues writing in her secret code until she dies of a broken heart.[8]

Bestuzhev's satire begins immediately with a polemical salvo: "They say that we are indebted to the love of a shepherdess for our ability to paint nature, but I have found out too that punctuation is indebted to the same sentiment for its existence."[9] Communication between author, narrator, and reader is founded on an *a priori* knowledge of the literary canon. By reducing it to a series of set moves, Bestuzhev rendered it inflexible, formulaic, and predictable. Thus, Bestuzhev's princess and lover communicate without needing to complete their thoughts. Since they are conditioned by literary models, everything is understood in advance. Their conversation represents a collective anacoluthia:

"Beautiful princess," Punctuatio once said to the shy beauty, "your glances . . ."

"Prince," she responded, "you always speak so intelligently that I must always listen to you with keenness! Because, well because . . ."

"I am in rapture," Punctuatio cried falling at her knees. "Allow me to kiss your little hand, and . . ."

"Stop!" the trembling voice of the princess broke in, "My heart has long belonged to you, but . . ."

At this point the prince acted the fool, like all lovers. And, of course, the princess grew angry like all women, and the rest you can read in any novel.

(Ibid., 183)

As speech predicated on literary cliché need not be completed, Sentimental tales could be reduced to anecdotal plots and sentimentalist writing to minimal gestures of the pen:

---

8. In a final irony that indicates the new literary world he would discover, the narrator reminds the reader that punctuation marks derive their name not from the princess, but from the jaded lover Punctuatio: "Thus Amerigo Vespucci gave his name to the land discovered by Columbus." A novel approach to art was to be won by the romantic hero, not his refined, sentimental victim.

9. Aleksandr Bestuzhev-Marlinskii, *Vtoroe polnoe sobranie sochinenii* (St. Petersburg, 1847), vol. 4, part 10, 181. Henceforth cited in the text as *Vpss* with reference to volume, part, and page.

The princess took up a pen, for lack of anything better to do, and wrote a few remarks. "What are you doing?" inquired Punctuatio with tenderness. "I am engaged in our love," the princess responded. "Look at this sign ?. It will signify: Dear prince, do you indeed love me?" "Do I love you? Oh, ye gods!!" Punctuatio cried. "This answer," she remarked, "shall be noted down in two ways. The first part, that is 'Do I love you?' is marked by , a comma; and the second, that is 'Oh, ye gods!' by !, an exclamation point. : a colon, one dot over the other, will be a signal that we have something to say to each other. In this manner we will be able to communicate with each other without danger of discovery." "How smart this is!" Punctuatio repeated four times. "Listen, dear prince," the princess continued, "let us develop this sign system in more detail. ; the semicolon, for example, will denote some sort of obstacle obstructing a meeting. - a dash or hyphen, signifies that our meeting will take place at a more felicitous time. And if it so transpires that we must scold one another (for a tender love always has such a moment in reserve), then we shall express our reproaches with `, an accent grave; and making up by a ´, an accent ague, and the lachrymose word 'farewell' by =, a short double stroke, and a private meeting with (), parentheses, which signify our separation from others. (Ibid., 185)

Sentimentalism was laid bare by the absurdity of the notion that meaningful communication between lovers can be codified so succinctly. Missing from the princess's conception of plot, however, is the permanent loss that comes from a love that is false. She is not equipped emotionally to lose Punctuatio. When she does, she comes to a full stop and dies.

By negative analogy Bestuzhev claimed that his own writing was up to the task of encompassing experience. To Karamzin's symmetry, isocolon, parallelism, alliteration, and assonance (in abundance to reinforce the parodic intent of the work), Bestuzhev added marlinist rhetorical devices. Paregmenon occurs at the tale's conclusion to mark two coincident terminations—the story's and the princess's: "Finally [nakonets] death placed a period at the end [konets] of her life's sentence and the princess was no more" (ibid., 183). Polyptoton and chiasmus depict the presence of a new narrator image: "She blushed at the very thought of love and already loved to blush at the very thought of it" [Ona krasnela ot odnoi mysli o liubvi i uzhe liubila krasnet' ot sei mysli] (181).[10] This anecdote belongs, in fact, to a boundary genre that combines fiction and criticism, the feuilleton. It is alternately sententious and ironic and abounds in Bestuzhev's stylistic techniques—puns, witticisms, and sundry rhetorical games. Bestuzhev attempted to surmount the limitations of the Karamzinian school, especially in terms of language. He accomplished this feat under the impress of Lord Byron. Lauren Leighton suggests that Bestuzhev superseded literary tradition in Russia by investing his early tales with Byronic elements, especially the intrusive narrator and bilious hero.[11]

Byron also supplied Bestuzhev with material for the justification and elaboration of the self-image he had already developed in his criticism (combative, witty, confident, competitive), giving it shape and *literariness*. It was the literariness that attracted Bestuzhev, for life was given a special piquancy when reality and literature conformed one to the other. Lotman argues that romanticism (in our case Byron in Bestuzhev's life) was a "movement which transformed artistic texts into programs for behavior in life."[12] Furthermore, in order that the literary text might affect actual behavior, people like Bestuzhev selected personae from literature to project in their writing and in public. Lotman states that "romanticism demanded a consistent mask which would as it were become part of the individual's personality and form a model for his behavior" (159). Byron's art, as Bestuzhev read and interpreted it, supplied him with a persona by which to fuse his literary self-projections with the mask he was wont to wear in society. This attitude toward art, particularly Byron's art, had a powerful impact on Bestuzhev's understanding of the meaningfulness of life. Life derives its meaning from literariness: theatrical life consists in a chain of events. Human beings are not passive participants in the impersonally flowing course of time; liberated from everyday life they exist as historical persons, choosing their behavior, making an active impact on the world around them, and either going under or winning.

10. Paregmenon denotes the use of the same root in different words within the same utterance (discrete/discretion); polyptoton the use of different cases of the same word in a single utterance (sister/sister's); and chaismus, in which the main elements of an utterance are reversed (When the going gets tough, the tough get going).

11. Lauren Leighton, *Alexander Bestuzhev-Marlinsky*, 85. Henceforth *ABM*, when cited parenthetically in text or notes.

12. "The Theater and Theatricality as Components of Early Nineteenth-Century Culture," in *The Semiotics of Russian Culture*, ed. Ann Shukman (Ann Arbor, Mich., 1984), 147.

Viewing real life as a performance fills individuals with the expectation that things are going to happen. As Lotman put it, "Eventfulness, that is, the possibility that unexpected phenomena would happen, became the norm" in society (160). The literariness of the Byronic pose, assumed by his narrators in art and by authors in daily life, brought life together and introduced the egocentric notion of the self as part of a historic drama. It is not coincidental that Bestuzhev joined the Secret Society just as he was growing more fascinated with Byron's literature as a model (and encouraging Pushkin to read him in the original).

But the Byronic narrator's strong presence, his self-aggrandizing remarks, and his self-conscious style are not always apparent in Bestuzhev's anecdotes. These features had their antecedents in sentimentalism.[13] Bestuzhev cannot be credited with being the first to introduce a willful narrator into Russian fiction, because he advanced rather than dismissed the tradition initiated by Karamzin, a lesser accomplishment than promised in the parodic "History of Punctuation Marks."

Bestuzhev's most popular anecdotes of the 1820s, "An Evening at a Bivouac" ("Vecher na bivuake," 1823) and "Another Evening at a Bivouac" ("Vtoroi vecher na bivuake," 1823), introduced the hussar, his milieu, his habits of speech, and his behavior. The military anecdotes had a decidedly masculine ring. Leighton praises these minor works saying that "the 'bivouac' or 'hussar' tales are heavily stamped with the influence of Byron, particularly in their narration and the characterization of the heroes. . . . they are anecdotal in structure, with a setting in military bivouacs during the War of 1812. If they are . . . affected by false heroics and hyperbole, their structure is sophisticated, and they are distinguished by a quick-paced witty dialogue. The tales are identical in theme and structure, as well as by characters" (*ABM*, 87). If anything, however, the structure and theme are as derivative as the protagonists, but the significance comes from the introduction of a unique context for the usual fare of lachrymose tales of the Punctuatio variety. Although

13. Karamzin had already introduced the Sternian voice into his historical fiction, for example in his "Natalya, the Boyar's Daughter" ("Natal'ia, boiarskaia doch'," 1803). It is something of a commonplace to assert that against Karamzin's "feminized" prose Bestuzhev introduced a more masculine style. Such a view is predicated on a selective reading of Karamzin's accomplishments rather than upon his whole corpus, which evolved rapidly and summarized the early stages of romanticism well in advance of Bestuzhev's career. See Lewis Bagby, "Notes on Sentimental and Romantic Prose (and Literary Evolution)," *Russian Literature* 14 (1983):103–48.

Bestuzhev's anecdotes were simultaneously derivative (in plot and character) and innovative (in context), they enjoyed such great success that he published sequels. This repetition of a successful formula characterized his career as a popular writer. His stories delivered up precisely what the audience sought and thus realized a handsome sum. As such Bestuzhev represents an example of a new commercialization of art in early-nineteenth-century Russia.

The two "Bivouac" pieces are frame stories after the style of Washington Irving rather than that of Byron.[14] They use the device common in travel literature of a reliable and unobtrusive narrator who describes a scene and is told or overhears an anecdote. The traditional freedom governing the anecdote and travel tale is handled with subtlety by Bestuzhev. It appears at first glance that the anecdotes are loosely strung together without thematic connection, but this is not the case.

The first anecdote is about an officer, Olsky, who is stationed at the front within earshot of the French. He is fiercely hungry and crosses from the starving Russian lines to the opulently supplied French side where he requests a meal. The commander and his officers are at table when the Russian introduces himself, and they invite him to dine. After agreeing with his hosts that in the next day's battle they will do their best to "split each others' skulls," Olsky returns to his side. An interlude follows in which a hussar, Lidin, recounts a brief tale. Then a second anecdote is narrated by a young officer, Mechin, who had been jilted years earlier. He was in love with Sofia and was seriously wounded in a duel fought over her. Confined to bed for over a month, he does not see his love, for he does not want her to see him in a weakened state. He recovers, finds her in his rival's nuptial embrace, and flees to the front in an effort to forget her and his disgrace. Later, by chance, he meets his unfaithful Sofia. She had married his rival, who quickly abandoned her. She is broken-hearted and dying of consumption. As Mechin's compassion overwhelms him, his anger disappears. He embraces her, whereupon she expires.

These anecdotes are connected by the theme of reconciliation, either momentary (between Russian and French soldiers) or eternal (between lovers). But reconciliation is balanced by opposing concepts, rivalry and death, which intertwine to form a unifying theme of mutability. In the

14. Carl Proffer, "Washington Irving in Russia: Pushkin, Gogol, Marlinsky," *Comparative Literature* 20 (1967):329–42.

first anecdote, enemies are briefly transformed into "friends," after which they fall back into their original hostile relationship. The reverse occurs in the second anecdote—the lovers become estranged only to find each others' hearts again. In both tales, the fluctuation of primary emotions works its charm from beginning to end. Love, death, reconciliation, and rivalry are linked in shifting relations that never find resolution. Death may sound the final note, but the final chord is left to the imagination of the narrator and his listeners (and, by extension, to the author and his readers). In the first anecdote in a series of paradoxical challenges, Olsky flees the threat of death by starvation to risk his life among his enemies, and then returns to face the chance of death in battle. In the second, Mechin moves from symbolic death to the threat of a real one. In both narratives the theme of thanatos is linked at a structural level to the theme of flight. Bestuzhev here selects (and represents) the heroic persona as a weapon against death.

In the tales, relationships are doubled, replicating the struggle between the conscious and the unconscious. Although Mechin is thwarted by his rival, they represent a similar ethos, each daring, vengeful, frivolous, and witty. Their competition for Sofia (wisdom) is a plot guise in which Bestuzhev, perhaps unwittingly, examined the contradictory impulses of a single identity. The young woman is more symbolic than real. The villain possesses her, then the hero embraces her again, acquiring his rival's power. In thematic terms, the final act can be read doubly as the victory of good over evil (comedic romance) or vice versa (tragedic romance). But at a deeper level, within the very structure of the tale, a competition between facets of *one* identity is enacted. Since the rivals represent mirror images of each other, integration remains out of reach as long as the two do not seek unity. Bestuzhev, therefore, introduced a mediating third party, Vladov. Similar to the rivals, but more guarded, Vladov is capable of giving sound advice, which Mechin follows to absorb the wisdom Sofia symbolizes. As Bestuzhev's hero searches for identity outside himself, as though for a lost limb, his identity development proves to be a triangular event in which the traits are shared by three individuals (two self-destructive rivals and a *raisonneur* representing self-preservation). Due to the mutability that destabilizes his position, the split in the romantic hero cannot be permanently mended. If circumstances change, the characters' roles change as well.

In the second "Bivouac," Mechin narrates an anecdote about his friend Vladov. Vladov predicts his own death in battle, and his prediction quickly comes true. When Mechin finds his friend dying on the battlefield (one of Bestuzhev's favorite motifs), Vladov cries out, "Don't pity me, because I regret only the friendships I have had [and now lose] on this earth. I have been incapable of living and that is why I am able now to die." Here is the sine qua non of Bestuzhev's hero, the justification of his entire life (and of Bestuzhev's fiction)—death with a heroic flourish, the right word, the correct pose. After Vladov dies, it is obvious that he is no different from Mechin and his rival. In the first "Bivouac," hero, villain/rival, and *raisonneur* are in fact interchangeable.

In many respects, the difficulties encountered in the life of the hero are a function of language. Words deceive as often as they represent the truth. The hero's misapprehension of the world affects his life profoundly. Mechin misreads his beloved's insincere avowal of love before she gives herself to his rival. Vladov misreads reality and as a consequence seeks death on the battlefield. Thus, a wisdom that adequately describes reality becomes the prized object. Ironically, since Sofia's words don't amount to much, such a quest seems pointless.

Since literature was presumed to represent a model for life, of what value are Bestuzhev's words in the "Bivouac" anecdotes? Bestuzhev expanded the limited lexicon of the sentimentalists in these early prose experiments, especially in the voice of his narrator. Military jargon, technical language, and camp slang were injected into the Russian literary language from its periphery (military memoirs of the War of 1812). The story begins, "Boundless flames, like stars, were burning about the field and the shouts of soldiers and foragers, the squeal of wheels and the neighing of the steeds animated the smoke-filled picture of the military camp" (*Vpss*, 3.8.113). Olsky rides into this scene and initiates a typical marlinist dialogue marked by colloquialisms, elliptical constructions, figurative speech, sundry rhetorical devices, word play, and witticisms:

"Greetings, friends!"

"Welcome, Prince! We've been wondering when you would show up. Where have you been all this time?"

"Need you ask? At my usual place at the front of my unit, chopping, flailing about, winning out—but for that matter even you hussars proved today you don't wear your mantles on your right shoulders. My thanks to you. But first, sergeant major, have my donets [steed] put up and fed—he has tasted naught today but dust and smoke."

"But listen, your excellency [poslushai-ka] . . ."
"My excellency doesn't hear or heed a thing until he's downed
a bit of glintwine, without which my excellency can neither excel
nor see. Bring here a cup and be quick" [Moe siiatel'stvo nichego
ne slyshit i ne slushaet, pokuda ne vyp'et glintveinu, bez kotorogo
emu ni svetlo, ni teplo; davaite skoree stakan].[15]

In 1823 such reference to the traditional drinking habits of the hussars,
their daring forays into the thick of battle, and the casual attitude about
themselves and their bloody work represented something of a novelty in
fiction. Bestuzhev's readers were taken by this verbal bravado as well as
by the animated dialogue, which in formal terms was based on paregmenon, polyptoton, and chiasmus. Although it sounds forced to our ear,
as in the play with the word "excellency" (related conceptually to
svetlost', "light") and listening/hearing (*poslushai-ka; slyshit, slushaet*),
this bombastic and assertive style delighted the reading public for its
freshness.

When Olsky is asked to relate a tale around the campfire, his jocular
narrative reflects the speech mannerisms of the introduction. It combines
colloquial speech, military jargon, common parlance, and laughably
mundane (rather than lachrymose, sentimentalist) figures of speech.
Olsky's opening lines are representative:

> Once, not too long ago, we hadn't had a crumb from our provi-
> sions for more than three days. All about, thanks to your kind-
> ness and that of the Cossacks, everything was as empty as my
> pocket. And to make things worse, they were not allowing the
> cavalry to forage. What could I do? My hunger grew even worse
> at the sound of cattle lowing from across the French lines. The
> sound echoed off the sorrowfully empty walls of my stomach.
> Thinking of man's vanity, I rode wrapped in my felt cloak and
> chewing a dry crust of bread so mouldy that you could have
> studied botanical fungi on it, and so hard and stale that you'd
> have to cram it down your throat with a ramrod. Suddenly a most
> happy thought flashed in my mind. Now I'm in the stirrup and
> it's forward march. (*Vpss*, 3.8.114)

15. "An Evening on Bivouac," trans. Lauren Leighton, in *The Ardis Anthology of Russian Romanticism*, ed. Christine Rydel (Ann Arbor, Mich., 1984), 206. My adaptations in the translation are based on the text in Bestuzhev-Marlinskii, *Vpss*, 3.8.113–23.

His lively narrative is challenged by one of the hussars, Nichtovich:[16] "Is this not taken from some story or other?" Olsky responds to Nichtovich's implied criticism, "Sure it is, but even if it is from a story, it's gotta be news to you." Undaunted for the moment, Nichtovich continues, "And after what military 'affair' did this take place?" To which Olsky replies, "After the battle where you were wounded in the boot."[17] Outmatched by Olsky's superior wit, Nichtovich falls silent. The narrator picks up the thread and continues in Olsky's manner: "Nichtovich popped the bitter pill and vainly stroked his mighty mustachios seeking a tit for tat. But this time his wit wilted" (*Vpss*, 3.8.116). Like Olsky, the narrator dramatically turns from matter-of-fact description to stylistic pyrotechnics, condensing sound through alliteration, assonance, paregmenon, and polyptoton: "[Nichtovich] za*pil pil*iuliu, i na*pras*no tere*bil* usy, ishcha *otveta* na *otvet:* na *etot raz ostro*umne ego *oseklos'*." With Bestuzhev drawing the narrator and Olsky together, in speech and behavior, and the readers' propensity to see narrators as their authors (Bestuzhev was a military officer with a life similar to his narrator's), the space normally separating characters, narrator, and author was eliminated.

Mechin's melancholy story is replete with clichés and marked by sententiousness and sentimental epithets and figures of speech, which set it apart stylistically from Olsky's anecdote. Mechin's hyperbole is the measure of his ecstatic love for Sofia: "About two years before the campaign, Princess Sofia attracted all the hearts and lorgnettes of Petersburg. Nevsky Boulevard boiled with sighs when she took her walk along it" (ibid.). Mechin's similes serve a similar function: "They say, however, and I believe it, that love soars down to take one in no other way than on the wings of hope" (117). "On the evening of the engagement announcement I was dancing with the princess at Count T's. I was as happy as a child, intoxicated with hope and with love" (118). This simile, often encountered in Bestuzhev's fiction and criticism, is used to suggest Mechin's innocence. It is acquired directly from the sentimental canon, as are the figures of grief at the tale's conclusion: "But I discovered how very much I loved her when, instead of a proud beauty, I saw before me the wretched victim of high society." "But life, like a flickering lamp

16. The name Nichtovich is based on the root for "nil."
17. In the hussar's world, this remark is an insult. By it Olsky is suggesting that Nichtovich was lying about on the job. It was more appropriate (i.e., heroic) to be hit in the chest, arm, or leg.

about to be extinguished by a faint breeze, flamed up suddenly for a few days [before her death] as of old" (122).

In appealing to sentimental formulas, Bestuzhev effectively avoided analyzing his protagonist's behavior. When Mechin is tempted to commit suicide, his friend Vladov persuades him to desist. Instead of presenting Vladov's eloquent plea, which holds power sufficient to forestall Mechin's thanatic urge, the narrator remarks aphoristically, "He who advises another to live is always eloquent" [Kto zhit' sovetuet, vsegda krasnorechiv] (ibid., 120). More often than not, sententious formulations of this type are elicited to avoid descriptions that might overtax the analytic skills of the speaker (the writer in this instance) to explore a character's interior life. This lapse can be ascribed to the sentimentalist endeavor to draw character, narrator, and reader into a close emotional relationship. In considering how Mechin overcame his grief, the narrator responds, "Time is the best counsellor" [Vremia luchshii sovetnik] (121). When seeing Sofia for the first time since her engagement, Mechin states simply, "There are inexpressible feelings and scenes [in life]" [Est' nevyrazimye chuvstva i stseny] (122).

By injecting marlinist discourse into the stock language of the Mechin anecdote, Bestuzhev signaled the beginning of a new era in prose. In the midst of Mechin's sorrowful tale, Bestuzhev introduced a note of humor as his hero recounts a dramatic moment when he demanded his rival apologize to Sofia for an insult made behind her back. Knowing that his gallantry had worked to his disadvantage, Mechin remarks, "This Mr. Captain [the rival] thought he might extract himself by making a joke. He said he didn't remember his words. But I, my dear sirs, have the misfortune of having a fortunate memory" [No ia, m(ilostivye) g(osudari), po neschastiiu, imeiu ochen' schastlivuiu pamiat'] (ibid., 118). Marlinist paregmenon reinforces the irony and shows that time brings perspective on the past.

Deflating the duel in which he was seriously wounded, Mechin states from a jocular distance, "We fired at five paces and his first shot, his by lot, almost killed me. Some Spanish poet or other (I can't remember his name or patronymic) said that it's the blow of the physician's bill that really rings your death knell" (ibid.). The shift in tone from sentimentalist cliché to romantic bravado brought with it a sense of novelty, but it could not illuminate the fashionable pose of the postsentimental protagonist. The language Bestuzhev introduced into the ossified sentimental tale in no way penetrated the reality for which he presumed it adequate. Mechin exclaims, "I wanted the princess to love me not for my cloak, my ability to dance, my witty words, but me myself without any superficial signs" [mne khotelos', chtoby kniazhna liubila vo mne ne mundir, ne mazurki, ne ostrye slova, no menia samogo bez vsiakikh vidov] (118). The desire to be known beyond the normative behavior patterns not only in fiction but also in life posed a serious linguistic problem for the Bestuzhev hero. The tension that existed between the projected persona and the potentially expressible self is precisely encapsulated in Mechin's discourse. If self-understanding is a function of language, then the elaboration of the protagonist along a linear axis suggests that Bestuzhev had no language equivalent to reality.

Bestuzhev did not explore the interior of his characters' lives; rather, he sought to entertain with glittering surface utterance. At the conclusion of Mechin's anecdote (when Sofia dies), the frame narrator resumes his account: "Touched deeply, the officers all fell silent, and a tear even rolled from beneath the captain's eyes, fell down over his mustache and vanished in his silver cup of glintwine. Suddenly a shot rang out, then another, and yet a third. Cossacks flew past the squadron. . . . 'Mount up,' shouted the lieutenant. 'Flankers, check your pistols. Sabres ready! Move out by threes! At a trot! Forward march!' " (ibid., 123). The narrator superficially describes the reactions of those listening to Mechin's tale. Conditioned readers of sentimental tales, the soldiers weep. As the discourse shifts from the lachrymose to the matter-of-fact, the circle closes on the anecdote, ending where it had begun in a mixture of language codes in an uneasy alliance. The experiment in language clearly required further work.

In the process of creating his tale, Bestuzhev made important claims about the hussar's identity. He is witty, vulnerable in love, impulsive, carefree, daring, proud, vengeful, but also sensitive, in great need of recognition and acceptance, and forever committed to a life of action, competition, and storytelling. These were all components of Bestuzhev's Marlinsky persona. His self-idea was a linear elaboration of narratives in which plot governed behavior and the marlinism was presumed to be sufficient to reality.

In aesthetic terms, none of the early anecdotes is of high aesthetic merit, but their literary and social value was significant. Bestuzhev's first prose was not as dull as his brother Nicholas's writing, was less vulgar than Faddei Bulgarin's, and less awkward than Vasily Narezhny's.[18] His early contribution lay in introducing a virile Russian language, assimilating and propagating English models, and developing a literature suited to the tastes of a growing popular readership. The anecdotes were significant in putting Bestuzhev's name forward as an innovator. They helped him develop a distinctive, if not completely unique, style, solve narrative problems pertaining to story motivation, and elaborate, in miniature, motifs, themes, and character types that he would explore in greater detail in his historical fiction. He set his work apart by its excesses—an affective style marked by varied levels of diction, an egocentric and dramatized narrator, an interest in unfamiliar places and people, emotionally charged dialogue, and the doubling of protagonists involved in love intrigues. He used the same bag of tricks that to this day informs formula literature.

The Travelogue

Extending the anecdote, Bestuzhev experimented with the travelogue, a hybrid form that permitted the author great liberties in creating the text. With the travelogue, he attempted to stake a claim on the unexplored territory of Russian prose fiction of the 1820s. He wrote several travel accounts, beginning with his first published work, "A Journey to Revel" (1820). It was followed by "A Page from the Diary of a Guard Officer" (1821), "Another Page from the Diary of a Guard Officer" (1821), "A Night Aboard Ship" (1822), related to the "Bivouac" anecdotes, and "The Castle Wenden" (1823), a gothic tale that reflected Bestuzhev's interest in British fiction.

Just as the novel of love evolved out of the adventure novel, the travelogue developed from the anecdote. Characteristic features of the travelogue were "extensive use of quotations and the interpolations of verse" (Tynianov and Eikhenbaum, *Russian Prose*, 55–56). They found their way into "A Journey to Revel," which was a quasi-fictional ac-

18. Vasily Narezhny (1780–1825) was one of the most popular eighteenth-century novelists. The archaic structure and style of his novels did little to influence nineteenth-century Russian prose, but his satiric approach to storytelling continued to enjoy some popularity until the time of his death.

count based on Bestuzhev's military assignments in the Baltic where he supervised road construction and maintenance. These trips left many impressions, for they were his introduction to the West. He made extensive studies of Estonia (Livonia) and its history. The fruits of this labor were gathered both in his travel notes and in the cycle of historical tales Bestuzhev penned from 1823 to 1825. The "Journey" holds an important position in Bestuzhev's development as a writer of historical fiction.

Bestuzhev's "Journey" conforms to dominant genre patterns of the time. Cast in the traditional form of an epistle to an unidentified addressee, the narrator freely mixes prose and poetry. Based upon Karamzin's *Letters of a Russian Traveler* (1791–96), it is constructed on two planes. The first focuses on the travel events themselves, presented chronologically and apparently based on an actual journey (or journeys). Descriptions are matter-of-fact and objective. The second plane focuses on the narrator, his impressions, responses, and thoughts. The dual structure allows the author a great degree of freedom to take the work in any direction. Bestuzhev's narrator, unlike the narrators in works from the sentimental school, breaks into verse whether or not his emotional state calls for it.

Bestuzhev's freedom, however, is a ruse, for the "Journey" is a sustained cliché. The opening lines of the text confess as much:

> You requested and I promised
> my exacting friends
> that I dedicate my stories
> and describe for you, like Dupaty,
> the leisure of my momentary rest
> and the events of my travels.

> [Желали вы—я обещал
> Мои взыскательные други!
> Чтоб я рассказам посвящал
> минутных отдыхов досуги
> И приключения пути
> Вам описал как Дюпати.]
> (*Vpss*, 2.6.3)

By 1820 the motifs of missing one's friends, longing for the homeland, comparisons of the foreign land with Russia, melancholic responses to the landscape, and apologies to the reader for deficiencies of style were entirely formulaic. Stylistically as well as structurally, Bestuzhev conformed to Karamzin's model, especially in terms of prose rhythms and sounds. "The frost was harsh, the sky clear, and my thoughts darkened" [Moroz byl zhestokii, nebo iasnelo, mrachilis' mysli moi] is governed by Karamzinian isocolon, rhythmic impulse, inversion, assonance, and alliteration. The narrator's self-conscious effusions were also copied from the Karamzin school: "My thoughts, having burst forth, disappear just as the momentary shadow of a hawk of the heavens disappears in the valley below" [Mysli, sverknuv, ischezaiut, kak ischezaet na doline mgnovennaia ten' sokola podnebesnogo] (66). The derivative nature of Bestuzhev's "Journey" can best be understood as a novice writer's obeisance to the canon.

In 1821 Bestuzhev published "A Page from the Diary of a Guard Officer." This work again reflected Karamzin's dual structure, but Bestuzhev developed a language in which sentimental cliché and a more assertive military argot were mixed. The tale sings a paean to Russia's greatness and praises the hero's aspiration to glorify the homeland through self-sacrifice. It is not as interesting a piece as its sequel, "Another Page from the Diary of a Guard Officer" (1821). Similarity between the two works ceases with their titles, for the second "Page," which was cast within the conventional frame of a travelogue, represents Bestuzhev's first experiment in the English gothic tradition.

Written in diary form, the narrator assumes a limited first-person role in order to build suspense. The tale begins with a journey to the Baltic far from the homeland. As a candle flickers its last, the narrator falls asleep. He is awakened by a friend who invites him to an evening hunt by the light of the full moon. Despite warnings from their guide that thieves and villains are about, they proceed into the deepest regions of the forest. There they discover a head half eaten by wolves, fall into a ravine, witness the capture of their guide by brigands, then attempt to save him. The narrator is captured by the villains, who instruct him to dig his own grave. He is set before a firing squad. When the shots ring out, the narrator announces glibly, "Dear ladies and gentlemen, it was all a dream!" (ibid., 4.10.150).

Pushkin parodied this convention in his tale "The Undertaker" (1830),[19] but in 1821 the climactic twist was entirely acceptable.

---

19. N. N. Petrunina, *Proza Pushkina* (Leningrad, 1987), 76–100.

Mikhail Dmitriyev (1796–1866), a contemporary of Karamzin, attested to the audience's willingness to be charmed by such jokes:

> The horrific and the sentimental, these two were the two genres most to the public taste. . . . I recall even the reading of novels in the provinces. All our family gathered together into a circle. Someone read as the others listened, particularly the ladies and girls. What horror the glorious Radcliffe disseminated then. What fate was suffered by the sensitive heroines of Genlis! . . . The fact of the matter is that upon such readings, during these moments, the entire family lived by its heart, by its imagination, and was conducted to another world entirely, which at this minute seemed real, and what is more important, was experienced as even more vivid than our own dull and ordinary lives.[20]

Bestuzhev became known for his fast-paced plots with twists and turns, rapid shifts in locale, and sudden denouements. He clearly benefited from practicing in the genre that represented these stylistic maneuvers in capital form.[21] Throughout the tale he ridiculed gothic literature and played with the ambiguous line that separates fiction from reality: "Our path would really be a perfect scene for a supernatural novel," the narrator says laughingly to his friend. "Yes, and the night is straight Radcliffe" [Da, i noch' samaia radklifskaia] (Vpss, 2.10.146), the latter responds. But this play becomes dangerously complex when the two characters are captured. Their inability to distinguish literary form from "reality" blinds them to such an extreme they end up endangering their lives: "Of course these aren't robbers! . . . I've seen them in vignettes and

---

20. Cited in I. I. Zamotin, *Romantizm dvadtsatykh godov XIX stoletiia v russkoi literature* (St. Petersburg, 1911), 2:83. John Mersereau Jr. comments that the gothic tale in its Russian variant was accepted only in comic terms. Flights into fantasy, beyond laws of common sense, logic and nature, were not appreciated other than as jokes: "In the twenties, French and Russian translations of E.T.A. Hoffmann and Washington Irving became available, and Russian authors, who were still working primarily with short forms, quickly began to imitate these imported works. From the mid-twenties on, the supernatural tale becomes one of the most popular types of fiction. Oddly, despite their obvious attraction to the supernatural, Russian authors always treated it satirically, ironically, or comically" (*Russian Romantic Fiction* [Ann Arbor, Mich., 1983], 75). Bestuzhev had Scott in mind as well.

21. Although he found it difficult to accept Zhukovsky's ventures into the supernatural, his experiments in the genre were beneficial to him in formal terms.

in the German theater more than once, and they always wear red capes and hats with feathers in them. But these don't have either Spanish caps or capes" (148). The readiness to read fiction into real life was a major problem of the time, which drove true believers toward death, suicide, exile, flight, or any number of lesser disasters.[22] While Bestuzhev made fun of the confusion of literature and life, he simultaneously revealed and masked the central dilemma in his own life, especially as it expressed itself in the imagery of dreams.

His final contribution to the travel genre written during this period was a gothic work with an overtly political theme, "The Castle Wenden" (1823). It is a diary entry of the same guard officer who narrates the earlier travelogues. Within the travel frame, the work contains a thirteenth-century tale of horror taken from Livonian chronicles. The evil knight Rohrback, the lord and founder of Wenden castle, is introduced as a cruel exploiter of the folk. His tyrannical authority is attacked by Serrat, champion of the people. Rohrback orders Serrat flogged for insubordination, whereupon the hero challenges the villain to a duel. When Rohrback refuses, the humiliated Serrat steals into Wenden castle to murder the despot. Serrat succeeds and is executed.

It is no accident that the publication of "The Castle Wenden" coincided with Bestuzhev's entry into the Secret Society. The antifeudal message, displaced to Livonia from Russia, sounds a populist note. Comic devices and literary reference disappear with the infusion of Decembrist thematics. The story attests to Bestuzhev's growth as a writer, as he more carefully honed the building blocks of fiction. His study of Baltic peoples and their history led him to recreate the exotic environs of Livonia and its people's knightly code of behavior as well as their customs, clothes, and manners. Character development remained shallow with the dramatis personae functioning merely to embody simplistic moral categories through which the plot is developed. Actual historical names and dates are used to create a degree of verisimilitude. The historical focus of

22. Lotman discusses this problem in "Poetika bytovogo povedeniia v russkoi kul'ture XVIII veka," *Uchenye zapiski Tartuskogo Gosudarstvennogo Universiteta: Trudy o znakovym sistemam VIII* 411 (1977):65–89, as well as in "The Theater and Theatricality as Components of Early Nineteenth Century Culture." Pushkin's secondary characters in his Belkin tales underscore the danger inherent in the unquestioned linkage of art and life. The stationmaster's confusion of the story of the Prodigal Son with the story of his daughter is the most striking example. But the pattern extends to the unnamed suiters in "The Snowstorm" and "Baryshnya-Krestyanka" and to the narrator of "The Shot."

"The Castle Wenden" represents a major reorientation of Bestuzhev's prose toward historical writing.

In Bestuzhev's fiction from 1820 to 1823, there is a concomitant development of literary technique, from simple anecdotal structures toward more sophisticated narrative forms. The early texts show Bestuzhev working out formal problems of narration. In them he discovered his voice. As the short pieces were received with excitement and acclaim by the public, Bestuzhev's confidence and skill continued to grow.

Noteworthy but by no means outstanding in Bestuzhev's early work were his expansion of the lexicon beyond the strict parameters established by the Karamzinists and his willingness to treat topics other than the lyric sentiments of young couples falling in and out of love. The military elements Bestuzhev introduced into his work had a striking effect. But as he expanded the lexical categories permissible in art, he simultaneously aligned himself with the story models established by Karamzin. In fact, there is nothing Bestuzhev accomplished in terms of themes, character types, plot structures, narrator personae, or emotional manipulation of the reader that Karamzin had not already introduced. Karamzin clearly foresaw the direction in which literature would evolve, but, curiously, he was not emulated by writers between his and Bestuzhev's time. Bestuzhev picked up where Karamzin had stopped two decades earlier. Although Bestuzhev complained that imitation ruled all too many writers and was dedicated to the idea of originality, European and Russian literary models influenced him directly. He had as his models Byron, Irving, E. T. A. Hoffman (1776–1822), Ann Radcliffe (1764–1823), and Walter Scott (1771–1832). They had a powerful impact on his subject matter, settings, the voice of the narrator, stylistic technique, and even political thematics. Lauren Leighton argues that Bestuzhev did not imitate but adapted these models to Russian situations and character types (*ABM*, 82–86). Since Karamzin had already accomplished this feat twenty years earlier, less can be claimed for Bestuzhev. Nevertheless, Bestuzhev popularized Karamzin's achievements before a readership not available to Karamzin in his time.

The travel frame, which supplied motivation for his earliest work, and the travelogue, which allowed him to experiment with prose techniques, were soon to be replaced by the historical tale, which he composed exclusively from 1823 to 1825. But Bestuzhev did not discard all the paraphernalia of his experimental genres; he kept plot and character typologies, a narrator with multiple guises, and marlinisms. His syntagmatic conception of utterance constituted the central issue in the development of an aesthetic language that could duplicate the world he wished to create. The anecdote and the travelogue did not permit a thorough test of the adequacy of Bestuzhev's language. The historical tale represented a logical extension of the experiment.

5

Historical Fiction and the Fictionalized Self

Prose style demands a knowledge not only of
the grammar of the language but of reason as
well, not only variation in cases but a
roundedness to the period, and it never
permits repetition.
—Bestuzhev-Marlinsky

Russian History

Bestuzhev established a place for himself in Russian literature by writing
historical tales. From 1821 through 1825 Bestuzhev penned six of them.
Three recount Russian history prior to the eighteenth century; three
recast Livonian history prior to the seventeenth. Except for the interest
in chivalry reflected in each tale, especially in the heroic persona of the
knight, the works have little in common.

In 1821 Bestuzhev completed "Gedeon," a tale of the Time of Trou-
bles (1598–1613), which was not published until after his death. "Gedeon" consists of two brief scenes reminiscent of the anecdotes and travelogues that occupied him at that time. Its setting is the same as that of the
"Journey to Revel." (The Bestuzhev family estate was located just to the

east of this region.) Its protagonist is one of Bestuzhev's forebears. In this work Bestuzhev imbues the past with personal significance.

The story recounts Gedeon Bestuzhev's refusal to pledge allegiance to the False Dmitry: "Whoever would not pledge to Ivan the Terrible will not [pledge] to the Pretender as well," he states in the tale's opening lines.[1] Thirty years earlier, and on behalf of the Russian state, Gedeon had plundered and pillaged Estonia. His violent past is the source of the work's complexity and of its dramatic conclusion. The Pretender Dmitry is dead, and the Poles are to be driven from Russia. To celebrate this great occasion, Gedeon holds a feast at which his daughter, Evpraksiya, is formally engaged to Vsevolod Gorsky. The evil warrior, Edgard Shreiterfeld, storms into the castle, holding everyone hostage while he sets the estate on fire and steals the bride. He promises that he will kill Gedeon as well, for Gedeon had killed Edgard's parents and siblings, sacked the Shreiterfeld estate, and taken Edgard prisoner.

The scene shifts from Gedeon's estate to the woods near the Narva Fall. Edgard has Evpraksiya in tow and promises she will witness her father's death at the very spot where his family had been murdered. But Edgard's plans are foiled by Gedeon and Vsevolod. In a fury, Edgard turns on Evpraksiya, stating that the suffering of the child is the same as the parent's and that by killing the daughter he will in effect murder the soul of his enemy. He pulls the wedding band from Evpraksiya's finger and loads it in his pistol. At the very moment Vsevolod and Gedeon arrive, he fires it into her heart. A battle ensues in which Vsevolod and Edgard fight to the death; both fall into the abyss. Gedeon returns to Russia to fight with Pozharsky against the Poles. The narrator concludes that violence breeds violence.

In "Gedeon" we find, in embryonic form, narrative elements lacking in the travelogues and anecdotes, such as a relatively early representation of romantic "confession." Through it the villain explains his behavior and justifies his base deeds in terms of the past and the curse (of revenge) visited upon him. Bestuzhev borrowed the confession from Scott and Friedrich Schiller (1759–1805). Bestuzhev complicated the moral dimension of the story by using the confession to explain Edgard's motivation and Gedeon's violent past.

Bestuzhev loved dramatic scenes in which central characters speak

1. Note that Bestuzhev dissociates his forebear from a tyrant. This family myth was soon to affect his own political behavior.

eloquently before acting heroically, especially when facing death. His criticism had focused on this moment, and he wrote it out again and again in his fiction. It is a moment whose sacrality is witnessed in accompanying symbols. Evpraksiya is executed on the very spot where Gedeon had slaughtered Edgard's family and Edgard had taken an oath to avenge them. Edgard fulfills his oath under the sign of Evpraksiya's wedding band, the circle that symbolizes the motion of the narrative. Violence and the sacred are joined in "Gedeon," introducing a mythological dimension to Bestuzhev's tragic narratives. As in European romanticism, myth occasionally merged with folklore, the secret and mysterious forces of life displaced to a supernatural level. Bestuzhev concluded his tale on this note: "It is timidly suggested that to this very day at the hour of midnight when lightning flashes in the dark waves of the Narva's rapids, a frightful specter arises over the waters and the shadows of the murderers wander over the adjacent fields. And there, where the murders were committed, where innocent blood flowed, the grass neither grows, nor does the swallow weave a nest of its own."[2] Against this folkloric background, Bestuzhev's characters replace each other in psychologically interesting ways. Evpraksiya's death replaces what should be Gedeon's, and Vsevolod substitutes for Gedeon's absent sons. "My sons are fighting far away; stand in the place of my son!" Gedeon declaims. After Vsevolod's death, Gedeon takes on his role: "I am too old to value my life, but young enough to bring death to the enemies of our homeland" (Vpss, 4.10.152). Heroic qualities are sacred and thus ageless. They defy the biological clock. At the end of the tale Gedeon goes off to war like a youth, endeavoring not only to drive the Poles back but to undo time. At this level, the mythological impulse of the tale is deepened profoundly. Not only death, but time itself is to be cheated.

Although remorse is not a feature of the hero's personality, Gedeon's challenge to time constitutes a symbolic representation of remorse. He cannot retrieve his daughter, his son-in-law, or the Shreiterfelds; but he can behave like a young hero, restore Russian independence, and reestablish his life as it had been in the past. But to do so is to accept the principle of inversion. The configuration of shifting signs is linked in a vital way to life and death. Even at the tale's conclusion, life conquers

2. Bestuzhev-Marlinskii, *Vtoroe polnoe sobranie sochinenii*, vol. 4, part 10, 161. Henceforth cited in the text as *Vpss* with references to volume, part, and page.

death. The titanic combatants live forever, wandering the moon-swept fields near the Narva Falls. Within this pattern, the most profound substitution is the offspring who dies instead of the father. From a psychological perspective, the principle of inversion operating here creates suggestive parallels in regard to Alexander Fedoseyevich's demise and its impact on his son.

In the "Journey to Revel," the narrator Alexander Bestuzhev travels from Russia to Estonia and back; and in "Gedeon," Gedeon Bestuzhev makes the same journey. The intimate connection between the two Bestuzhevs is enacted figuratively in the metaphoric sense of narrative, with the younger walking in the footsteps of his forebear. These two literary journeys were duplicated in life by Alexander Bestuzhev. His military travels took him over the same ground, suggesting a meeting of fiction and reality. Narrative and life were drawn together intimately, the present taking on personal meaning the more it conformed to a prior, heroic, and tragic past.[3]

If "Gedeon" represents the aesthetically humble but psychologically profound origins of Bestuzhev's historical fiction, "Roman and Olga" (1823) is the summit of his pre-Decembrist achievement. It is organized around two plots centering on Roman. The first is a love story. Roman and Olga are in love, but her father, the insensitive materialist Simeon, will not allow their marriage. The second intrigue is political. Moscow seeks to subjugate the independent and democratic peoples of Novgorod. The two tales interweave allegorically with Roman representing heroism and Novgorod, Olga personal freedom and political independence, Simeon Moscow and tyranny.

Roman is an impoverished nobleman who persuades Olga to elope with him during Twelfth Night celebrations.[4] At that time Novgorod learns it must either resume its allegiance to Moscow or become a vassal to Lithuania. Whichever choice Novgorod makes through its *veche* (its democratic, public, and legislative body), the offended party is sure to retaliate. As the *veche* meets, Olga, awaiting Roman's arrival, decides she will not go with him because she cannot betray her father. No matter—Roman never appears. At the behest of the *veche* he has left on

3. Iurii Lotman, "The Theater and Theatricality as Components of Early Nineteenth-Century Culture," 147.

4. N.B. the sacred orientation of time and the dependence of this plot on Karamzin's "Natalya, the Boyar's Daughter" (John Mersereau Jr., *Russian Romantic Fiction*, 53).

a secret mission to Moscow to discover what the Russian Prince Vasily will do in response to Novgorod's drive for independence. On the road to Moscow, Roman is taken by thieves. He is freed by his abductor, the "good" villain Berkut, when Berkut learns that Roman is a Novgorod patriot. Roman resumes his journey and arrives in Moscow as the *veche* reaches its decision. When the news is heard in Moscow, Roman is arrested and thrown into prison. Olga remains secluded in a tower for a year while Roman pines away for her in a dungeon. As Moscow prepares for war on Novgorod, Simeon leaves with his troops to confront the enemy beyond the city walls. Roman is freed from prison by Berkut's men, and they ride off together to fight in defense of their native city. On the way there they come upon a small platoon of Moscovites holding Simeon captive. After freeing him, they all continue to Novgorod. During the battle Berkut dies heroically. It seems that Novgorod will win the day but Roman, like Berkut, has fallen. In the final chapter, presented in part from Olga's perspective, Simeon returns to his domicile in triumph with an unidentified rider. He informs his horrified daughter that she must marry the stranger. To everyone's great joy—and to no reader's surprise—that man is none other than Roman, the hero of the battle and Simeon's deliverer. The tale ends happily as the couple weds.

Bestuzhev's fantasy works within the confines of traditional romance. The story involves a movement from peace and stability toward trauma and chaos. The conclusion is marked by a return to peace and stability. In Northrop Frye's terminology, "Roman and Olga" is marked by a descent into the night world with a subsequent return to the idyllic world symbolized by marriage. Thematically, too, "Roman and Olga" fulfills the many expectations of comic romance: triumph of the young over the old, freedom's victory over tyranny, and the constancy of purity over threatened despoilment.[5] In each character (including Novgorod and its *veche*) identities are reestablished, family and community triumph over isolation and subjugation, and life conquers death whether it be real or symbolic (except in Berkut's case).

There is, however, one significant feature of Bestuzhev's story that overarches traditional comic romantic structure, modifies expectations of the hero, and consequently challenges the nature of heroism in the

5. Northrop Frye, *The Secular Scripture: A Study of the Structure of Romance* (Cambridge, Mass., 1976), 84, 117, 129, 132, 147.

world. Bestuzhev's departure from the norm, unconscious though it may be, pertains to the specific form that Frye's "loss of identity" motif takes in Roman's depiction. In Frye's description the hero moves into an unfamiliar world where he loses touch with himself and undergoes a severe test of his authenticity *qua* hero. Frye labels this characterological event "amnesia" (emphasizing that this is a literary rather than pathological category) (ibid., 54, 104). In the very nature of Roman's near defeat but final victory over the adversary (his descent and ascent), Bestuzhev altered expectations concerning Roman's bout with amnesia. His loss of identity and the adventures that proceed from it do not take place at the story's outset, but at its midpoint. Viewed from the perspective of the tale's logic, this delay allows for a conventional development of the love intrigue; for the introduction of Novgorod and its *veche* as central sociopolitical themes pertaining to democratic self-government; for the inclusion of Scottian historical local color; and for the presentation of documentary evidence from the Novgorod chronicles to verify Bestuzhev's "history."[6] Most important, the suspension of the hero's quest allows for the representation of Roman in an epic heroic mold.

In Simeon's estimation, Roman Yasensky is handsome and comely. He has served Novgorod faithfully and has suffered much for sacred Rus'. He speaks effectively before the people's assembly, Simeon admits grudgingly, and has waged successful battle in tournaments. He is bright, as his surname suggests, learned, and friendly. Yury, Simeon's brother,[7] adds that Roman has given his blood and youth in sacrifice to his homeland and that he selflessly defended Novgorod by setting fire to his family estate so that its enemies could not use it to lay siege to the city. Roman came from a noble line of boyars and, unlike others his age, he has a generous heart.

From Olga's perspective, we apprehend in Roman a storyteller and bard. His tales and songs teach her that he has been a captive of the Mongols, that he was forcibly removed from his homeland to Astrakhan and the Caucasus where he was a prisoner of Tamerlane himself. His songs recount his escape from the Black Sea region and, after many dangerous and exotic adventures, his return home. His stories are

6. Details of setting in the Russian historical tale often displace plot and character (Mersereau, 53).

7. Yury represents the pairing of opponents at a secondary level.

bogatyrskie, or epic in proportion. Quite naturally, Roman represents Olga's ideal of the fearless, dashing warrior with a heart.

As bard, Roman accompanies himself on the *gusli,* an ancient stringed instrument similar to a small harp, and sings a romantic ballad that parallels point by point his own love story. It also presages the tale's happy end. In the song, however, the hero (Harold) is not depicted in the epic proportions that Bestuzhev uses to portray Roman. Instead, the song conforms to the structure of the Russian folktale with its hero modeled after the folk protagonist Ivan the Fool:

> Roman tuned his *gusli,* shyly glanced at the gathering, and began to sing of the love of Yaroslav's daughter, Elizaveta, for the brave Harold, knight of Scandinavia, driven from his homeland but kindly received at Novgorod's court. "Prince," the wise Yaroslav addressed him, "You are dear to my daughter, and that in itself is sufficient. Exchange hearts and rings forthwith. But you must know, too, that you shall not purchase Elizaveta's hand as long as honor and glory do not intercede for you." "Go and serve me!" uttered the stunned and half-alive princess. Harold flew to Greece, fought many years for the sacred cross in the Crusades, reigned victorious many times. But only because he loved. Having disdained the passions of the Empress Zoya he returned amidst countless dangers with his trusted band of Varangians to Novgorod and lay his glory, honor and very self at the foot of his ever-faithful Elizaveta.[8]

There are significant differences between the Russian epic hero and the Russian folk hero, and they inform Roman's portrait as he moves through a cycle of descent and ascent (perceptible in Harold's life as well). The epic hero, endowed with first name, patronymic, and surname, is self-sufficient and without peer. He is repeatedly opposed by an immense force in epic narratives, but he continually defeats his enemy without the aid of supernatural powers. He is immortal and timeless. The hero of the Russian epic tradition is patriotic even when ruled by a weak older king. This hero never marries the king's daughter. The well-known epic hero Dobrynya Nikitich has many of Roman's characteristics, especially at the story's outset. Dobrynya also enchants his public

8. *Sochineniia v dvukh tomakh,* 1:13.

with song, accompanying himself on the *gusli*. He, too, is a skillful warrior willing to sacrifice himself for the homeland.[9]

Although Roman conforms to these epic traits at the outset of the story and at its conclusion, his loss of identity in the middle portion is presented as a fall from epic stature. He becomes more like Harold, the folkloric hero about whom he sings. In contrast to the epic hero, the folk hero has no patronymic or surname. He is not self-sufficient but requires a Helper in order to succeed in his task. Because he fights supernatural powers with supernatural weapons, he cannot be considered representative of this world but belongs to some other order. And finally, at the tale's end he weds the king's daughter.

In Roman's song Harold participates in epic heroic qualities only at the beginning of the song; thereafter he resembles the folktale's Ivan (and follows the pattern of Roman's life). When Roman leaves Novgorod and Olga for Moscow, his surname is no longer used; his adversary is a nonhuman, impersonal entity (Moscow); and at the tale's close he is wed to the king's daughter. On his quest he requires the aid of a Helper (Berkut) and a power bestowed on him by that Helper (guile). Roman's self-sufficiency is undermined when he is captured by Berkut, which fulfills the folktale expectation of a chance meeting between the hero and his Helper. Roman's folk-hero identity is underscored when Berkut's men help him escape from prison and impending death; then Roman, in accordance with the folktale, has a second meeting with the Helper.[10] Like Ivan the Fool, Roman doubts his ability to perform his appointed task. Bestuzhev describes Roman's thoughts as he departs on his quest: "With disturbing thoughts imprinted upon his sullen brow he went on farther and farther. Conscience reproaches us all the more when decisiveness in performing a poorly conceived deed is in vain; for the vexation of a certain failure goads it—that is how it was with Roman" [S dumoiu na ugriumom chele pustilsia on dalee. Sovest' uprekaet nas sil'nee, kogda reshimost' na khudoe delo naprasna, ibo dosada neudachi ee podstrekaet—to zhe samoe bylo s Romanom] (*Sochineniia*, 1:21).

The intrusion of a false hero as well as a trial by temptation (both typical of the folktale) also appear in "Roman and Olga." In the first instance, Simeon threatens to force another suitor on Olga. In the sec-

9. Alex E. Alexander, *Bylina and Fairy Tale: The Origins of Russian Heroic Poetry* (The Hague, 1973), 4, 8–9.

10. Vladimir Propp, *The Morphology of the Folktale* (Austin, Tex., 1968), 35–36.

ond, Evstafy the Sated (Evstafii Syta), a former Moscow ambassador to Novgorod who is well acquainted with Roman's amorous plight and his poverty, entices the young man: "Listen, Roman! I know your worth and I know how little it is valued in Novgorod. It is not like that here. I give my word that the Prince [of Moscow] will shower you with gifts and honors. And I myself shall do more. Since I have loved you for so long, I shall give my daughter to you in marriage. She knows you well, and I believe Roman himself has more than once been attracted by her" (ibid., 30). In exchange for the promise, Roman would have to remain in Moscow forever. He refuses, accepting death on the executioner's block instead; here he represents the passive, solitary image of the hero.

As Frye points out, in romance a confrontation with death usually culminates in a new vision. In this story the knowledge gained by Roman is not psychological, philosophical, metaphysical, or spiritual. Reflective capacities and analytic tools are apparently not available to the hero. It is political knowledge that he gains. Roman does not come to any new understanding about the homeland, life, or love; but what he knew at the story's outset is confirmed at a deeper emotional level. Bestuzhev was grounded in the concrete rather than the abstract world, which differentiated him from the romantic writers imbued with the spirit of German idealism.

Only upon the second intervention of the Helper does Roman begin to recover from his amnesia and regain his epic-hero status. Together with Berkut, Simeon, and Novgorod, Roman is transformed into his former (prenarrative) condition. Of the four, only Berkut dies. Because of Berkut's role as Roman's folkloric Helper during the bout with amnesia, and because of their juxtaposition in the central portion of the narrative, their dual portraiture is of considerable importance in testing the adequacy of Bestuzhev's conception of the hero when faced by the death-dealing forces of real existence. In many respects Berkut's story intensifies the threat to Roman's life, for what has happened to Berkut might happen to Roman (if the two figures substitute for each other, as is characteristic of Bestuzhev's dramatis personae). Both Berkut and Roman have been unjustly treated by an authority figure. Both are patriotic native sons of Novgorod. Both are proud, honorable, educated men and experienced warriors. What distinguishes them, however, are not only the choices they have made in life but also the conditioning of their choices. Berkut is the son of a deceased nobleman. He squandered his entire estate, borrowed beyond his means, was publicly shamed for his debts and thrown into an adventurous life of violence to compensate for his loss of social standing. He was betrayed by a rival who falsely accused him of treason. Berkut was found guilty, and his estate burned to the ground. To avenge the lie, Berkut killed his rival and fled to live the life of an outlaw. Roman, on the other hand, is of a poor but noble family. In contrast to Berkut, he burned his own home to protect Novgorod. In his life he has not known the ambiguous pleasures of profligacy, debauchery, and material well-being. In many respects, Berkut recalls the villains in Bestuzhev's anecdotal fiction who represent a catalogue of the human vices that governed Bestuzhev's generation. Roman is the antidote, the cure to the poisons that drive well-intentioned souls from society.[11]

The differences between Berkut and Roman reflect the story's mundane conflict of values presented in the first chapter, in which the brothers Simeon and Yury discuss Olga's love for Roman. In fact, the first chapter introduces all the tensions that are resolved at the conclusion of the story: false pride / authentic pride, right / wrong, age / youth, surface / substance, materialism / idealism, selfishness / selflessness, dearth / plenty, and wealth / poverty. As we have seen, these conflicts were current in Bestuzhev's time, separating Decembrist ethics from the hedonistic impulses of the nobility. But Roman's and Berkut's differences reflect an even deeper inquiry into the nature of the hero in a complex world. Together they represent Bestuzhev's image of the romantic hero and supply the constant presence of the heroic throughout the story. When Roman slips from his epic status during his amnesia, Berkut is there to take his place. And when Berkut dies, Roman resumes the role.

When Roman is reduced to folkloric hero, the features that identify his personality stand in direct opposition to those characteristics which identify Berkut. It is possible to juxtapose folk hero traits taken from Vladimir Propp's study with those of the epic hero, not as an arbitrary venture in the limitless production of binary oppositions, but to distinguish the intrinsically identified features of heroic types inherent in "Roman and Olga." It should be noted that the folk hero's features are fallible and human, whereas those of the epic hero are precisely that—epic and heroic:

11. Eugene Onegin flees a morally bankrupt society the same year "Roman and Olga" is published.

Folktale Identity	Epic Tale Identity
(Roman in mid-story)	(Berkut)
ambivalent	self-assured
uncertain	confident
inexperienced	experienced
dependent	independent
tyrannized by circumstances	in control
misplaced heroic identity	continuous heroic identity

Bestuzhev's narrator also exemplifies the qualities of an epic hero. The narrator authoritatively comments on the story's characters and events: "In those days people were not ashamed of their tears, and did not conceal their hearts behind a friendly smile. They were themselves before friends and enemies alike," he states in the aphoristic style reminiscent of Karamzin (*Sochineniia*, 1:9).[12] The narrator claims allegiance with these "good people" of bygone days and consequently vaults himself beyond the tyranny of his current social circumstances to join them in their ideal behavior. He controls his material within the confines of the fictional world he creates. And in the narrator's unabashed use of striking metaphors, outlandish similes, sententious commentary, and veiled allusions to the story's outcome, we perceive a character who is assertive, assured, experienced and self-sufficient—at least in his literary task. This "epic" image of the narrator is typical of Bestuzhev's historical fiction of Russia. Because of this consistency, Bestuzhev's narrator represents an aperture through which Bestuzhev's readers are allowed to see what they consider to be the author's authentic self.

There are indications in "Roman and Olga" that generic patterns and psychological issues meet, unifying life and art in a manner typical of Bestuzhev. In Roman's song and its interpretation within the story, metatextual signals appear that aid us in seeing Bestuzhev as a writer grounded at the center of his fiction. In the person of the "implied" author, generic features of the epic and the folktale fuse to release a complex, quite human personality from self-imposed restraints.

After Olga has been enraptured by Roman's romantic song, she asks her nanny, "Can it be that what is sung in songs is true?" Her nurse responds that "a fairy tale is make-believe, but a song is true" [V skazke-

12. The remark is as critical of contemporary mores as it is descriptive of an idealized code of behavior.

basnia, a v pesne—byl'] (ibid). This remark suggests that the nurse adheres to a pagan belief, held by Slavs even into the twentieth century, that the song of the Russian minstrel (*skomorokh*) has magical powers. Roman's song, therefore, is to be considered historically accurate. Since that song encapsulates Bestuzhev's tale itself, the story "Roman and Olga" represents proof of the nurse's belief: both the song and the Bestuzhev tale are adequate to the reality they describe. This metatextual reference, of course, to Bestuzhev's own fiction takes place in the narrative he has himself created, but it distinguishes an important feature of Bestuzhev's vision of art and its relation to reality.

Northrop Frye examines romantic narrative in its identification of fictions that are, on the one hand, oriented toward the real world and those which are, on the other hand, oriented toward fantasy. They represent an interesting analogue to the nanny's definition of fairy tale and song. Frye's scheme may be summarized as follows:

Reality	*Fantasy*
World	Idyll
Fact	Make-believe
True life processes	Idealized life processes
mortality	immortality
tragedy	comedy
violence	guile
Praxis	Wish fulfillment

According to Frye, no matter how it begins, at its conclusion a fictional narrative will be found to belong on only one side of this divide. Plot is impelled by the interaction between the two opposing orientations. Tragedy is grounded in harsh fact, comedy in make-believe. With the nurse's voice Bestuzhev equates reality to Roman's song, and by analogy Russian history to his own fictional account. Roman's narrative, therefore, corresponds to Frye's Reality configuration, his songs and stories telling of actual horrors in life (tyranny and death) and of military subjugation by autonomous national entities such as Tamerlane, the Mongols, and the Tatars. In the face of Moscow's belligerence, Roman's narratives beget an understanding of civil and personal responsibility, of the need for a people to act forcefully, even violently when necessary, if it is to fulfill its mandate. Surely Roman gives direct voice to Bestuzhev's ideological sentiments here. But "Roman and Olga" shifts (as Roman's song) from an initial grounding in Reality to a final allegiance to Fantasy. When Roman, Novgorod, Simeon, Yury, and Olga face life's real dangers (misery, violence, and death) they are moved to heroic action in pursuit of the ideals of the idyllic world (happiness, peace, and immortality).

Bestuzhev discovered the ultimate substitution during these years: Fantasy for Reality. Since Roman's song is factual, "Roman and Olga" is similarly true, not because it represents mundane reality, but because its critical consciousness is based on reality. Acknowledging from the outset that the Real represents the foundation for the initiation of his narrative, Bestuzhev then asserts that the Real may be superseded. His narrative transcends the limits imposed by reality and ultimately finds peace in an idyllic order. From Bestuzhev's perspective, when imagination creates romantic historical fiction (initiated in Reality and culminating in Fantasy), it serves higher truth. Furthermore, imagination in the service of a superior depiction of reality is more potent and all-encompassing than the commonalities of banal existence (and its mundane fictions). In a personal discovery of a romantic verity, the Ideal superseded the Real in his fiction. The consequences of this discovery were profound for Bestuzhev.

Since Bestuzhev believed imagination allowed contact with an incomparable knowledge, he recognized two tangible goals for his fiction. He would have his narratives entertain by transporting the reader to an elevated view of life. He would also enlighten his public by leading it toward a radical vision of its civic duties. He delighted his readers with fast-paced narrative and witty dialogue, all delivered with elaborate metaphoric flourishes by strong narrators. He then instructed them to attend to the social myths and prejudices that governed their lives (the divinity of the tsar, political passivity, crass materialism, debauchery). Bestuzhev diminished worldly anxieties with the fabulous and simultaneously harkened his public back to the real world from his heroic perspective with its superior understanding of dream and reality.

This dynamic relationship constituted a vital linkage of author and audience. Bestuzhev's readers accepted both his view of the world and the persona he projected through his heroes and narrators. His social self was seen as proof of the ideal in the world. As his heroism became his readers' model, he was no longer his own man; he chose to play out his and his audience's desires in his Marlinsky persona.

A dramatic sign of the two conscious functions inherent in Bestuzhev's stories is the recurring theme of disinterest in the idyllic and demonic worlds. He was principally interested in this world, the one he would change through heroic activity. The game of chess Simeon and Yury play at the conclusion of the story symbolizes the kind of action Bestuzhev felt would be required of him (and others) in time. The game represents the idea that life is for warriors who conceive of a better world, which may be attained through violence and guile. Chess suggests Bestuzhev's idea of the hero's essential skills and talents. For him the pursuit of social and political goals demanded heroism out of the epic mold, transferred from the chessboard and fiction into real life. Heroics required the steadfastness and strength of character shaped through adversity, which Bestuzhev portrayed not only in his fiction, but also in his own life as romanticism's original swashbuckler. The hero, like Tolstoy's Prince Andrei and Dolokhov in *War and Peace,* was undaunted by the specter of imminent demise. The fear of death had no place in Bestuzhev's conception of the heroic persona, so it was consigned to an area outside the hero's description.

Bestuzhev was unwilling or unable to appreciate fully the power of reality over imagination. Confronting the harshness of life over and against his ideals, he was not only moved to take action against injustice, but to prepare himself emotionally and mentally for requisite action in life. To gird himself he replaced his understanding of the Real with the language of the Ideal. His transformation of the language of the mundane necessitated structural alterations in "Roman and Olga." Changes were made that inevitably made Bestuzhev vulnerable to disillusionment à la Berkut after the failure of the Decembrist Revolt.

In the final analysis, Bestuzhev failed to understand that despite his prodigious romantic will, Roman's song, like the fairy tale, is make-believe. "Roman and Olga" is not real but wish fulfillment. In Bestuzhev's hands, historical narrative was more than the product of creative urges. It was a psychological precursor to a deeply held belief that life like art can be shaped by one's own hands. For him the historical genre constituted a necessary component in the creation of a revolutionary and heroic persona. In Bestuzhev, genre and psyche met unconsciously to give birth both to an innovative narrative form in the early nineteenth century and to a new Russian character as well—the Marlinsky persona.

In spite of the number of layers on and below the surface of "Roman and Olga," the historical tale suffered at Bestuzhev's hands. Because of the extra-aesthetic burdens that he attached to his fiction, Bestuzhev scaled down his composition, reduced its imaginative scope, failed to submit it to critical analysis, and rigidified a diachronic process (genre development) at the historical moment in which he engaged it. Bestuzhev's political motives for writing contributed to the ossification of the genre as he practiced it, for his approach diminished aesthetic considerations while advancing ideological programs. From a psychological perspective, the historical genre bore such incredible emotional weight in its insistence on the viability of the heroic persona in the real world that Bestuzhev could hardly question its aesthetic form. As Bestuzhev claimed in Roman's case, doubt undermines conviction.

Although in the 1830s the historical genre would be viewed by the likes of Alexander Pushkin as a medium for discovering prose techniques (and simultaneously a more authentic conception of Russian historical narrative, of national character and identity),[13] in the 1820s Bestuzhev saw it as a container into which he could pour his preformed ideas about the heroic persona and the hero's ideological quest. In contributing to the sudden growth and equally sudden fossilization of the genre, Bestuzhev did not seek historical facts to enliven the representation of Russia's past. He sought situations in which the hero could step forward to be counted in times of social unrest and upheaval. This focus on the hero prefigured Bestuzhev's own heroic involvement in the Decembrist Revolt two years after the publication of "Roman and Olga." This parallel between his fiction and life was an invariant feature of Bestuzhev's aesthetic program in which his readers assumed that his hero protagonists (and his Marlinsky persona) reflected his personality. In this era, society not only sanctioned, but came to demand that art and life be closely linked through the personae of its artists, and like genres, writers came to live in the expectations of the audience.

The personal encoding of "Roman and Olga" was isomorphic to its social context—it marked the advent of a genre and a character type (Marlinsky). Because Bestuzhev desired recognition, revolution, success, and fame, and because his public desired fulfillment of its expectations in word and in deed, Bestuzhev overloaded his historical tales with cultural information. Author and audience worked together to shape a peculiar type of historical narrative and ultimately to consign it to oblivion. "Roman and Olga" had the dubious honor of depicting a dynamic

13. N.N. Petrunina, *Proza Pushkina,* 162–98, 241–88.

moment in the development of Russian prose and of Bestuzhev's prose in static terms.[14]

Livonian History

There is little difference between Bestuzhev's Russian and Livonian historical tales. To explore the chivalric code Russian culture lacked, Bestuzhev moved his settings west and back in time to the pre-seventeenth century and altered the sound of proper nouns. Although it is aesthetically faulty, "The Castle Neuhausen" ("Zamok Neigauzen," 1824), subtitled "A Knight's Tale" ("Rytsarskaia povest'"), is *quantitatively* one of the more sophisticated works of this period. Bestuzhev's control of diverse plot threads, the large number of dramatis personae, the variety of ways in which they are depicted, and the presentation of character from various points of view, all indicate his growing maturity as a writer.

"The Castle Neuhausen" is a love story that brings with it the inevitable battle between the forces of good and evil. Emma stands at the center of the various plot lines. She is married to Evald von Nordek, is coveted by the evil Romuald Mei, and is sister to Vseslav, a Russian captive of the Nordek family. That Emma is Vseslav's sister is not revealed until the end of the story. Through the machinations of his henchman, Konrad, Romuald almost succeeds in having Evald killed so he can take Emma for his own. Vseslav and his brother Andrei ensure the resolution of the conflict and the restoration of the prenarrative condition (peace), sig-

---

14. The monotony of Bestuzhev's prose is discussed by Abram Lezhnev in *Pushkin's Prose,* trans. Roberta Reeder (Ann Arbor, Mich., 1983), 134–37. The duality that constitutes Bestuzhev's creative and thanatic urge is manifested in the second and final Russian historical piece, "The Traitor" (published in the last issue of *The Polar Star* before the revolt). In "The Traitor" Bestuzhev elaborates an antiplot. He does not reconsider the fictional universe that operates in "Roman and Olga," but simply reverses all its elements: the hero becomes an antihero, the rival a real hero, the romantic marriage at the tale's conclusion is replaced by a tragic death. This suggests that Bestuzhev's sense of plot development was isomorphic to the rhetorical stock in trade of his fiction. The elaboration of plot and utterance operate on the same principle: linear directionality. If "Roman and Olga" moves forward along an axis, then "The Traitor" moves backward *along the same axis.* Like the rhetorical devices polyptoton, paregmenon, anaphora, assonance, alliteration, parallelism, and isocolon, all of which in sound and grammatical structure refer to each other back and forward along a uniform axis of speech, Bestuzhev's plots conform to the same horizontal design. He composes plots that resemble sentences.

naled in this instance not by marriage, but by a recognition scene between siblings and a reunification with their parents.

The narrator is presented in the third person. Although he is for the
most part unobtrusive, he does appear directly on two occasions, first, to
draw the firm moral categories that govern the tale, and second, to
apostrophize the characters and the reader. These two functions are
common in Bestuzhev's narratives, as are the sentimentalist stylistic features and the marlinisms that occur throughout the work. In the introduction to the third chapter Bestuzhev writes, "Bright and gay the morning mounted above the castle, but within all was gloomy and sad"
[Svetlo i radostno vstalo utro nad zamkom, no v zamke vse bylo
ugriumo i pechal'no] (*Vpss*, 1.3.112). In the original there are eight
instances of an unaccented *o* surrounded by the consonant clusters *sv, vs,*
and *vs,* all of which poeticize the prose. Alliteration abounds as well. In
the utterance "Their flame wafted at the will of the wind which penetrated the uneven lead transom of the gothic window" [Plamia ikh veialo
po vole vetra, pronikaiushchego v nerovnyi svintsovyi pereplet gotiches-
kikh okon] (107) there are five alliterations based on the consonant *v*
and four based on the consonant *p,* which create an overall effect of
compactness and symmetry when joined with the sound repetitions *la /
al / ol, ra / ro / ro,* and *vn / vn / vin.* These features direct attention to the
narrator who uses sound to establish intimacy with his reader.

"The Castle Neuhausen" contains language of several specific types:
martial, maritime, Old Russian, bureaucratic, biblical, folkloric, common, gothic, elevated, and exotic (chivalric terminology). These distinct
levels assist in the delineation of character. Konrad's common speech
discloses his low social station; his folkloric turns show his wit; and his
coarseness reveals moral bankruptcy. Through the mixture of stylistic
registers Bestuzhev established multiple narrative tones, moods, and
sensations previously unmet in his work. Now serious, now comic, at
one moment frightening, at another happy, and finally triumphant and
resolute, the moods re-create the atmosphere of the broad world.
Bestuzhev's emotional coloring brings the voice of the narrator to the
reader's consciousness.

But the story ends on an ambiguous note. The traditional Bestuzhev
plot ends happily enough with the family restored to its prenarrative
integrity, but the mutability of life and the inevitability of death enter the
text from the narrator's temporal frame. He describes the ruined castle
as it appears to him in the nineteenth century—harmless and peaceful,

rather than the locus of a life-and-death struggle. The past cannot be recaptured from the debris even through the agency of fiction and its fantasies. Bestuzhev's literature enacts desire but not fulfillment, hope but not reward.

For all its structural similarities to "Roman and Olga," "The Castle Neuhausen" is not as successful as its predecessor. This is the result of several factors. Despite the number of devices utilized to delineate character, the potential for multiple perspectives is not realized; and what remains are stock two-dimensional dramatis personae out of Bestuzhev's youthful puppet shows. Perhaps there are too many characters for Bestuzhev to control successfully. Although of great interest in its potential for delivering a complex image of the world, the expanded narrative time and space are obstructions rather than dynamic plot devices. Furthermore, Bestuzhev introduced familiar romantic motifs (incest, recognition) but without real conviction. In the final analysis, Bestuzhev's characters lack some fundamental wit. Vseslav and Evald believe Romuald's patent lies. Although their gullibility is necessary for the complication, the reader's intellectual identification with the hero is undermined. Plot supersedes character only to be supplanted by the image of the narrator.

"The Tournament at Revel" ("Revel'skii turnir," 1825) is a comedy, unlike Bestuzhev's other attempts at historical fiction. The protagonist, Edvin, is a wealthy young merchant who loves Minna, the daughter of a knight, von Burtnek. The father, disqualifying Edvin as a suitor for obvious reasons, announces that Minna will preside as queen of the annual tournament and be given as bride to the victor. Von Burtnek trains a protégé, the bully and drunkard Donnerbats, so that his rival, Ungern, might not win his daughter's hand.[15] At the tournament Donnerbats is felled by drink. Ungern vanquishes all challengers until a stranger defeats him. This is none other than Edvin. After a great scandal scene in which Edvin's right to Minna's hand is argued vehemently by the middle and upper classes, von Burtnek gives Minna to her beloved Edvin, the merchant of proven knightly qualities.

The motifs of "The Tournament at Revel" organized around the theme of love are similar to those of "Roman and Olga": resistant father versus worthy suitor, threat of marriage to a third party, heroic deeds

---

15. Other than the class distinctions, the plot complication is the same as in "Roman and Olga." Here, the father prefers an uncouth and undisciplined knight to a rich, sensitive, and well-educated merchant.

performed to prove one's worth, and a Helper (Doctor Loncius) who attempts to intercede for the young couple. Unlike "Roman and Olga," however, this story does not proceed in chronological order. The narrator exercises a willful control over the story through a proliferation of conversations, usually unrelated to the intrigue, and through digressive intrusion. The first chapter, for example, represents approximately one-fifth of the narrative. But it does no more in terms of plot development than introduce von Burtnek and his enemy Ungern. The expansion of narrative space beyond basic plot requirements is accomplished by the inclusion of a free, unmotivated dialogue (that is, dialogue not related to plot) between von Burtnek and Doctor Loncius concerning affairs of state, matters of health, philosophy, society, as well as the doctor's satiric description of the practice of chivalric competition. Their conversation is laced with verbal play and Bestuzhev's standard rhetorical pyrotechnics:

> Loncius . . . continued to persuade the blustering Burtnek, who swore to the entire world that he would not give his daughter to Edvin, even though he had been the victor.
> "But your word, Baron, your knight's word!"
> "But my ancestors, sir doctor, my ancestors! It is better to go back on one's word when necessary to uphold one's name. Putting it bluntly, Edvin assumed too much. Never, ever, will I give Minna to a man without a name."
> "But with a good reputation?"
> "To a man whose genealogy is an account book, who has no coat-of-arms?"
> "He has thousands of them, Baron, and all on a field of gold."
> "Let him be made of ducats, I will not agree to split my shield with a signboard."
> "Remember, Baron, that with his blood Edvin returned to you that which Ungern had taken away. Certainly you wouldn't repay generosity with ingratitude?"
> "Virtue is not a title."
>
> (*Vpss*, 1.3.114–15)

Chapter 6, representing another fifth of the narrative, engages in extended dialogue for its own sake. The greater part of the fifth chapter is devoted to a description of the knights, their regalia at the tournament, the tournament scene itself, and Loncius's satiric description of the same while in conversation with Edvin. The entire sixth chapter is dedicated to a social history of Livonia and brings the already halting forward progress of the story to a standstill. In this chapter, however, Decembrist themes are introduced (such as the castigation of the class system). The political portion of this penultimate chapter of the story deserves more extensive citation, particularly since it was penned during Bestuzhev's participation in the Secret Society's *duma* (the governing board):

> The events which I am presenting here took place in 1538, that is, fifteen years after the introduction of the Lutheran faith. The order of Livonian Knights of the Cross had recently lost control of the Prussian Order, which had become attached to Sigismund, and already it had become feeble in its terrible isolation. The long peace with Russia had rusted the sword with which Plettenberg had once threatened her. Having become used to luxury, the knights knew only how to hunt and feast, and their military spirit was maintained only by infrequent skirmishes with Novgorod horsemen or Swedish Varangians. If they did not inherit the manliness of their ancestors, still their pride grew greater and greater with every year. The spirit of the age divided even metals into noble and base categories, so is it any wonder that while convincing others the knights themselves became convinced, quite ingenuously, that they had been fashioned at the very least from noble porcelain? One must remember that the gentry, which was made up at that time of landowners, supported this idea. It sought to fuse with the knighthood, and consequently excited in the latter a desire to keep exclusively for itself those benefits which, God knows why, we call rights, and to degrade spiritually any new rivals. Meanwhile, the merchants, in general the most active, honorable, and useful of all the inhabitants of Livonia, with flattering ease became members of the gentry by purchasing real estate, or desirous of intimidating the gentry with splendor, abandoned themselves to luxury. The gentry, in order not to be outdone and to be on a par with the knights, had recently exhausted the estates they had acquired. The knights, in conflict with both groups, closed their castles, disarmed their vassals for good . . . and the fatal results of such unnatural class arrogance were imminent and unavoidable. Discord reigned everywhere. The weak undermined the strong, and the rich envied them. The military-trade society of

Black Heads (Schwarzen-Haupter), as the city militia of Revel, enjoyed almost knightly privilege and consequently was hated by the knights. The hour of destruction approached: Livonia resembled a desert, but its towns and castles glittered with the bright colors of abundance, like an autumn leaf before falling. Banquets resounded everywhere, tournaments called the young men and all the beautiful girls together, and the Order noisily lived out its fame, wealth and its very existence. (110–11)

Bestuzhev's political diatribe was directed at nineteenth-century Russia. The profligate aristocracy and its illusory notion of power are juxtaposed with the rising force of the merchant class. Bestuzhev created a fictionalized synthesis of these forces in Edvin and Minna, who represent a new order that might fill the ideological vacuum in a society in crisis. Bestuzhev carried his political message forward in the transition from the sixth to the seventh chapter. Mersereau notes that

Bestuzhev ends [the sixth chapter] abruptly with a rhetorical question which underscores the digressive character of this chapter: "Now just where had we stopped?" This is followed immediately by the epigraph to Chapter VII: "What will be, will be, and what will be is what God wills." Significantly, the quotation belongs to Bogdan Chmielnitski, the liberator of the Ukraine, and it represents the entire text of his response to the Sultan's threat to destroy the Ukraine and all its inhabitants if Chmielnitski refused allegiance [to him]. Taken in context with the preceding chapter, it suggests the inevitability of an apocalyptic conclusion to the class conflict prevailing in nineteenth-century Russia. (Mersereau, 60)

The message was a dangerous one, so Bestuzhev displaced the action from nineteenth-century Russia to fifteenth-century Livonia. In addition, the comic tone dominating the narrative, the sheer delight in language, and the willful play in the persona of the narrator shifted attention from the (political) object to the subject.

Unmotivated dialogue worked as a deflection as well. Bestuzhev's reliance on verbal tricks for emotional intensification, on wit and clever repartee, and his use of diverse language levels (mixed both for dramatic and comic effect) comprise the dialogues' most salient features. When von Burtnek tells Loncius that he will have "a great deal of work" during the tournament, the doctor responds:

"Work, Baron? What do you think I am, a smithy?" the doctor replied, marking each word with a gulp of beer. "What do you need surgeons for when you don't break ribs but armor?! Since the time when these damned coats of mail were invented, our brother now has to think about trials in battle as though he were in some silly folkloric tale about the seven Simons. Oh, it is really brave to pour yourself into some iron skin and stand in battle like an anvil! In truth of fact, the horses suffer more from the armor and weapons than do your opponents. (*Vpss*, 2.4.76)

Bestuzhev did not hesitate to use burlesque techniques either. Loncius mentions a bridge on von Burtnek's property that is in disrepair and cannot be used for commerce or passage to his rival's land. Von Burtnek responds:

"Let him rebuild the damned bridge himself. I quite frankly don't give a damn. I'll never go there on a visit anyway."

"So, you won't go, and why should you. But I pity the poor travelers who have to. They're not cranes, you know. They can't fly over the bog."

"That's their business, not mine."

"But the highway is everyone's business. And since it travels right through your property . . ."

"For that reason I have the right to do with it as I please, which is to do nothing."

"That means that were people to do what they want, everyone else would have to suffer what they don't want."

"I won't second that, doctor."

"Then how about a third?" Loncius announced pouring out yet another flagon.

"I'm talking about business!" von Burtnek shouted with vexation.

"And I thought you meant another business," Loncius replied.[16]

16. *Vpss*, 2.4.92. This silly banter would seem far removed from the political import of the tale. But, curiously, there is a reminder (albeit in inverted form) of Karamzin's letters to the tsar

Bestuzhev's dialogues of 1825 overcame the limitations of the sentimentalist style of his early fiction. He almost completely abandoned Karamzinian baggage. He packed satiric and political content in such a way that plot and character development were stifled. Attention, therefore, shifted to the narrator who functions (with Loncius) as a comic entity: "I can guess my reader's curiosity, not of course about the apples of the knowledge of good and evil, but about the apple which bears Minna's dear name. So I hasten to satisfy the reader, first because I want to be liked by you and second . . . I shan't hide it! I love to talk about young beauties, although I have trouble speaking with them" (Vpss, 2.4.81). Since readers were apt to apprehend the literary facts through the filter of biographical information, the pretense is ironic. The literariness and conventionality of the tie between author and reader is quite clear in another digressive aside: "Edvin spoke his greeting in a quivering voice, but he was satisfied that he uttered it, of course even more than the reader whom I ask, even if just for me, to forgive my hero, first because he had read not even one French dictionary of compliments, and second because he stood before a beautiful girl toward whom he was hardly indifferent. Ah!" (83).[17] The figure of the narrator-jester mediates the tale's two plots, forming the glue that holds the loosely conceived work together. At the conclusion, readers are not presented the ideal world Bestuzhev sought to describe in this bold political story, nor do they reach its antithesis. The narrator's persona and the subjective confines of his wit represent the main content of the fictive enterprise.

The final story of the pre-Decembrist period, "The Castle Eisen" ("Zamok Eizen," 1824), was scheduled to be published in a smaller publication of The Polar Star as a supplementary and final edition of the almanac. Bestuzhev and Ryleyev, who edited the journal, "had become increasingly occupied with revolutionary activities, and, moreover, they had been losing contributors to Northern Flowers (Severnye tsvety, Delvig's rival publication). Therefore, they had decided to reduce the size of their almanac for the 1826 issue, and to withdraw from the field" (Mersereau, 60). By the time of the revolt, some of this final edition, entitled The Little Star (Zvezdochka), had already been printed.

---

on the condition of Russia's highways, something Bestuzhev himself knew about in his work for the duke. Perhaps the facetious, apparently digressive dialogues of the story are not as remote from the political theme as might appear.

17. Additional examples are to be found on pages 78 and 88.

Immediately after the Decembrists had been crushed, the government seized all the printed portions of the almanac and baled
them up. Orest Somov, as editorial assistant to Ryleev and
Bestuzhev, had received proofs of the printed portions, which
included his own story, "The Rebel" ["Gaidamak"]. Somov kept
these proofs, and in 1826 sent Aladin, editor of *The Neva Almanac*, the printed pages of his own story, inadvertently including
"Blood for Blood," unsigned [by Bestuzhev] and with a new title
"The Castle Eisen." Since convicted revolutionaries were not sup-
posed to publish or be published, both Somov and Aladin had
some questions to answer. Somov insisted he had sent Marlinsky's work to Aladin through an oversight. (60)

The political intrigue surrounding the publication of this work is a fit
testimony to its revolutionary theme. It also reveals the moral and psychological quandary into which Bestuzhev was thrust as a member of the
Secret Society's northern branch.

Set in sixteenth-century Livonia, "The Castle Eisen" is a tale of double
revenge. It is ostensibly a continuation of the travel notes of Bestuzhev's
Guard Officer and is, therefore, directly linked to "The Castle Wenden"
and "Another Page from the Diary of a Guard Officer," especially the
latter's Radcliffe orientation. The facetious tone of the narrative undermines at every step the horror of the story's plot. Bestuzhev introduces
the story in a brief foreword that establishes the ironic tone in which it is
to be read. His narrator recounts a tale told him by a fellow officer, "a
well-known amateur teller of historical tales and of ancient legends."
Bestuzhev's self-reference reflects the narrator's complete dominance of
the story line. In "The Castle Eisen," there is a clearly thematized self in
the image of the narrator. He thrusts himself into the foreground at
every turn in order to dominate reader perception of the text. The shift
from object to subject underscores a dramatic turn in Bestuzhev's writing during the period of his most intense political activity. The reorientation is not only Sternian, but Byronic.

"The Castle Eisen" is constituted of yet another Bestuzhev trio: a
tyrant, Bruno von Eisen, his nephew, Reginald, and the latter's be-
trothed, Luiza. The evil Bruno is "coal black spiritually and physically,
along with his armor and his horse" (ibid., 61). His mistreatment of his
serfs and of people in general is demonstrated at length—half the narrative is dedicated to his rank dealings with others. When Bruno decides to

marry, he throws Reginald in prison and marries Luiza. This standard Bestuzhevan romantic fare (separation, prison, tower) is set within folkloric parameters. One day the superstitious Bruno visits a witch who warns him, in the ambiguous language understandable to the reader but not the character, that he will die soon at the hand of someone close to him. Guess who. Reginald escapes, somehow, and soon thereafter Bruno finds his wife (there is an indication that the marriage has not been consummated) in the arms of his nephew. Reginald and Bruno go at each other. Reginald subdues Bruno, ties him to a tree, delivers an obligatory tirade on the latter's baseness and prepares to dispatch him. Bruno pleads for his life, begging Luiza to dissuade Reginald from committing such a heinous crime—the murder of a relative. Since she would rather be Bruno's widow than his wife, she doesn't try very hard. Six months later Reginald and Luiza prepare to marry. At their wedding Bruno's ghost arrives, smites Reginald, and buries Luiza alive.[18] When Bruno's twin brother arrives soon thereafter to continue his sibling's tyrannical ways, it is apparent that no ghost avenged the murder. Typically, the story's fantastic element is explained away.

There is a rather transparent fascination with treason and regicide / parricide in this tale. Its importance, however, is to be measured not simply by the confluence of fiction and imminent Decembrist fact but by the stark depiction of the crime's consequence—death. Yet the story is not just a horror tale; it is also a real laugh. As Mersereau argues, "The fate of the protagonists is unimportant, since all are culpable, and, moreover, we learn so little about them that empathy is out of the question. . . . Rather it is the narrator's idiom which is intriguing. The same lightly humorous conversational tone is maintained throughout, regardless of the subject matter. This homogeneity of tone . . . obviates emotional reactions on the reader's part, since dire deeds are related with the same insouciance as mundane matters" (Mersereau, 61). As an example, Mersereau cites the following passage:

> Yet a long time ago a castle stood here called Eisen, that is, *iron*. And by rights it was so strong that no tale could tell it and no pen describe it. Everyone said it got its name by its fur. The walls were so high that when you looked up at them your hat would fall off,

18. Robert K. Massie reports that this was the usual punishment for such a crime among the Slavic peoples (*Peter the Great* [New York, 1981], 33).

and even the best archers couldn't shoot an arrow to the sphere on top of the tower. The gully on one side served in place of a moat, and on the other side thousands of poor Estonians spent entire seasons after harvest digging, and they dug down to active springs, and that's how they made the castle so there was no approach from any side. I won't even talk about the gates: oak planks set with nails like the studded sole of a Russian [foot-soldier]. Thirty bolts with locks fastened it, and so many bushy-mustached men guarded it that there's nothing more to say. On each merlon was an iron stake, and even in the gutters there were gratings, so that not even a mouse would think to crawl here or there without asking. So why make such fortresses if you were living in peace with your neighbors? To tell the truth, peace in those days was worse than war is today. They'd shake hands with one hand and slap you in the face with the other, and then the fun started. And he who won out was right. And the knights were not fools. Just as they build their castles with their people's hands, so they spoke; this is for defense against foreigners, and when they had built their castles and settled in them, like in an eagle's nest, then it turned out they were for pillaging their own land. (Ibid.)

Уж очень давно стоял здесь замок, по имени Эйзен, то есть железный. И по всей правде он был так крепок, что ни в сказке сказать, ни пером написать: все говорили, что ему по шерсти дано имя. Стены так высоки, что поглядеть, так шапка валится, и не один из лучших стрелков не мог дометнуть стрелой до яблока башни. С одной стороны этот провал служил ему вместо рва, а с другой тысячи бедных Эстонцев целые вспожинки рыли копань кругом, и дорылись они до живых ключей, и так поставили замок, что к нему ни с какой стороны приступу не было. Я уж не говорю о воротах: дубовые половинки усажены были гвоздами, словно подошва русского пешехода; тридевять задвижек с замками запирали их, а уж сколько усачей сторожило там—толковать нечего. На всяком зубце по железной тычинке, и даже в желобах—решетки были вделаны так, что мышь без спросу не подумай пролезть ни туда, ни оттудова. Кажись бы, за чем строить такие крепости, коли жить с соседями в мире? Правду сказать, тогдашний мир хуже нынешней войны бывал. Одной рукой—в руку, а другой в щеку, да и пошла потеха. А там и прав тот, кому удалось. Однако и рыцари были не промахи. Как строили чужими руками замки, так говорили: это для оборны от чужих; а как выстроили, да засели в них, словно в орлиные гнезда, так и вышло, что для грабежа своей земли.

(Vpss, 1.1.79–80)

The special conversational lexicon, idiomatic expressions, substandard utterances, and syntactic constructions (ellipsis, folkloric figures of speech, and sayings) establish the unique tone of the work. It is entirely conversational and jocular with many borrowings from actual folktales. Bruno's visit to the witch who divines his fate is based largely on the legendary Baba Yaga: "Finally he found himself in front of the hut which, as is told, stands on chicken legs" [Nakonets ochutilsia on pered izbushkoi, kak govoritsia, na kur'ikh nozhkakh] (ibid., 91). The facetious tone continues even at the most terrible moments, as when Bruno lops the head off one of his Estonian serfs:

> He would catch sight of an Estonian and gallop up to him with upraised sword.
> "Recite 'I beleive in One God,' you good-for-nothing." And that peasant would faint to his knees, not knowing a word of German.
> "Ey moistr." [I don't understand.]
> "Recite, I say!"
> "Ah ha! So you're stubborn in your paganism, you animal! Then I'll christen you!" Bam, and the head of the poor fellow would fly to the earth like a bowling ball, and with a laugh the Baron would gallop on, saying "Absolvo te!" which is "Thou art absolved," because as spiritual knight they could at the same time kill the body and save the soul.

(83)

It is striking that Bestuzhev depicted such frightening and serious subjects in a playful manner. The ambivalence of his position is dramatically captured in this text. The political import overtly and didactically worked toward the goals of the Secret Society; but the tone of the narrative subverted them at the same time. As in "The Tournament at

Revel," the narrator's comic voice functions as a mask to hide the tale's radical ideology, but the story's suppression by the government bears witness to the inefficiency of Bestuzhev's technique.[19] Although the juxtaposition of a comic voice and horrific content fragments the text at one level, it unifies the reading at another. The tension created between voice and subject matter renders an aesthetically deformed object, torn between two unintegrated impulses—hiding versus revealing the truth. On the eve of the Decembrist Revolt, this hardly seems surprising.

Bestuzhev's dualistic presentation of death also displays his ambivalence. On the one hand, death is terrible—burial alive. On the other hand, his representation of it is comic. In "The Castle Eisen" thanatos comes closest to the surface. The story thus speaks of more than aesthetic fragmentation. If Bestuzhev's fiction discloses his desires, it simultaneously betrays an anxiety that can be resolved only in reality. This tale placed Bestuzhev precisely on the border between the script and life, between his Marlinsky persona and his authentic Bestuzhev identity. But historical fiction could not solve the ultimate dilemma for the literary hero in his confrontation with daily life. The authentic challenge was to come beyond the texts which prepared him for December 14, a day that could "kill the body and save the soul."

19. All the material for *Zvezdochka,* the supplement to Ryleyev and Bestuzhev's *Polar Star,* was confiscated, even the most innocuous items. "The Castle Eisen," therefore, was not alone in this one respect; but the possibility for interpretation along social, psychological, political, and aesthetic lines increases because of the tale's content, its suppression, and its fragmentation. The other material planned for this supplementary final edition of the almanac cannot be treated in this manner.

6
Ritualized Identity

I am more a Democritus in image than at
heart.

         —Bestuzhev-Marlinsky

Decembrism

Bestuzhev's liberal sympathies were nurtured in his youth, but his active participation in political reform can be traced to 1820 when he joined a group of poets in the Free Society of Lovers of Russian Literature (Vol'noe obshchestvo liubitelei rossiskoi slovesnosti). In this organization, where discussions were devoted to Enlightenment ideals, he met future Decembrists such as Kondraty Ryleyev, Nicholas Turgenev, and Wilhelm Küchelbecker. The first Russian political radical Alexander Radishchev was highly revered by this society.[1] Ideas of armed revolution fomented by disillusionment with Tsar Alexander I were further encour-

---

1. William Edward Brown, *A History of Russian Literature of the Romantic Period,* 1:164.

aged by the ill-fated uprising of the distinguished Semenovsky guard regiment, which had protested Minister of War and unofficial prime minister Count Aleksei Andreyevich Arakcheyev's despised military settlements and harsh corporal punishment for small breeches of military conduct. Bestuzhev visited his friends incarcerated in the Kronstadt Fortress immediately after the mutiny and signaled his allegiance to their cause. He joined the revolutionary Secret Society in 1823.

The Secret Society had emerged in 1821 as an outgrowth of the Union of Welfare. As political events in Europe became heated, with rebellions in Spain, Italy, Portugal, Piedmont, and Greece,[2] a group of military officers in the Union became more radical. They secretly formed the first revolutionary organization in Russia, the Northern Society in St. Petersburg and the Southern Society in Tulchin. Their manifestos supported civil liberties and the abolition of autocracy.

Although the society represented a wide range of intellectual perspectives, from Enlightened to romantic, the group was cohesive during the planning stages of the revolt. Like other conspiratorial groups, the Secret Society bestowed upon its members a way to satisfy their need to glorify the self.[3] By conforming to a coded language and shared behavior, the members differentiated themselves from the larger social group (96), which contradicted the prevailing belief in heroic individualism. But as Eric Hoffer observes, "The adherents of a rising movement have a strong sense of liberation even though they live and breathe in an atmosphere of strict adherence to tenets and commands" (36).

The poet radical Kondraty Ryleyev was inducted into the Northern Society in 1823 and recruited his friend Bestuzhev. The two formed close bonds. Ryleyev had been raised by a cruel father who administered beatings regularly. He was a loner who usually elicited enmity from those he met, but he found in Bestuzhev his first friend. His famous mythological re-creation of the lonely exile of the revolutionary Mazepa's son, Voinarovsky, who suffered exile in Yakutsk in the terrible cold of northeastern Siberia, contained the categories on which

2. Andrzej Walicki, *A History of Russian Thought from the Enlightenment to Marxism* (Stanford, Calif., 1979), 57.

3. Eric Hoffer argues that "faith in a holy cause is to a considerable extent a substitute for the lost faith in ourselves. The burning conviction that we have a holy duty toward others is often a way of attaching our drowning selves to a passing raft. What looks like giving a hand is often a holding on for dear life. Take away our holy duties and you leave our lives puny and meaningless" (*The True Believer* [New York, 1966], 22).

Bestuzhev and Ryleyev modeled their behavior. Ryleyev wrote a dedication to Bestuzhev that is interesting for its fusion of literary cliché and reality (itself fictionalized):

As a sorrowful and lonely wanderer
amidst the empty steppes of Arabia,
From land to land in deep melancholy
I wandered in this world an orphan.
A hateful cold toward other people
pervaded surely all my soul,
and in madness I dared not believe
in friendship that was selfless.
Then suddenly you appeared before me:
The blinders from my eyes fell low
and I learned to believe all over again,
and anew stars of hope shined
in the heaven's heights.
Accept the fruit of my labor,
the fruit of careless leisure;
I know, friend, you will accept it
with all the care of a true friend.
As Apollo's stern son
you will not see in them art.
But you will find vivid feelings.
I am no Poet, but a Citizen.

[Как странник грустный, одинокой,
В степях Аравии пустой,
Из края в край с тоской глубокой
Бродил я в мире сиротой.
Уж к людям холод ненавистный
Приметно в душу проникал,
И я в безумии дерзал
Не верить дружбе бескорыстной.
Незапно ты явился мне:
Повязка с глаз моих упала;
Я разуверился вполне,
И вновь в небесной вышине
Звезда надежды засияла.

Прими ж плоды трудов моих,
Плоды беспечного досуга;
Я знаю, друг, ты примешь их
Со всей заботливостью друга.
Как Аполлонов строгий сын,
Ты не увидишь в них искусства:
Зато найдешь живые чувства,—
Я не Поэт, а Гражданин.][4]

Ryleyev's poem established a literary archetype of Yakutsk exile for Bestuzhev, and later, when Voinarovsky's and Bestuzhev's fates were merged, life conformed to the literary text. Nicholas I effected the linkage, but Bestuzhev played his part well, insisting during his exile that it was foretold in "Voinarovsky."[5]

Bestuzhev wrote an introduction to the work in which he inaccurately described Ryleyev's ambivalent hero as unshakable:

Such was the life of Voinarovsky and his moral stature is visible in his actions. He was brave, for Mazepa would hardly have trusted him in leading a band of independent detachments had he not manifested those personal qualities which can bring another person under its will. He was eloquent . . . decisive and unshakable . . . and was clever and inventive. In a word, Voinarovsky belonged to that small group of people whom Peter the Great considered dangerous. Without doubt, Voinarovsky, gifted with a strong character which the times allowed to develop fully, belongs to that number of most curious personages of the last century who are appropriate for history and poetry alike, for the whimsi-

---

4. K.F. Ryleyev's dedication to Bestuzhev is contained in "Voinarovskii, poema," in *Russkaia romanticheskaia poema pervoi poloviny XIX v.: Antologiia* (Moscow, 1985), 102–3.

5. Lauren Leighton discusses Bestuzhev's reading of his own fate in Ryleyev's poem, an interpretation, moreover, his audience entertained willingly. Georg Adolph Erman's account of his meeting with Bestuzhev in Yakutsk lends credence to the mythological presentation of Ryleyev's and Bestuzhev's personae: "[In 'Voinarovsky' Ryleyev] beholds in spirit the dreams of the conspirators at an end, their plans wholly frustrated, their views stigmatized, his friend Bestujev expelled from society; he discerns beforehand every fine line and touch in the suffering of years, and finally, sees himself in the hands of the executioner" (*Alexander Bestuzhev-Marlinsky*, 28). Rather than submit to this persistent view of Bestuzhev's relation to the poem, it is salutary to observe the cultural and psychological point of departure for interpreting literature and life in the early nineteenth century.

cal nature of his fate gives credence to the inventions of romance. (Afanas'ev, 108–9)

Bestuzhev often distorted the historical record (Voinarovsky did not possess the qualities Bestuzhev imputed to him) in order to project and simultaneously protect the romantic ego's colossal will.

The year Bestuzhev joined the Secret Society, he traveled to Moscow to propagate conspiratorial ideas and to meet with other Decembrists and their sympathizers, such as Prince Peter Vyazemsky,[6] Naryshkin, Raich, Mukhanov, and Nechayev. Under the cloak of official military business, Bestuzhev attended to recruitment and policy. His brief diary of 1824 mentioned contact with the future Decembrists Orzhitsky, Mukhanov, Akulov, Pushchin, Torson, Baten'kov, Pleshcheyev, and others.[7] In the winter of 1824–25, Bestuzhev lived with his former literary opponent Wilhelm Küchelbecker in Prince Alexander Odoyevsky's apartment, which was a center of Decembrist activity. During that time he brought many members into the society: his brothers Nicholas and Mikhail, Odoyevsky and his brother, Torson, Orzhitsky, and Baten'kov. He also introduced Alexander Yakubovich and Peter Kakhovskoy to the group.

Bestuzhev and his brothers worked collectively to reassert the Bestuzhev family name in Russian culture. It was not only their liberal upbringing that brought Alexander, Nicholas, and Mikhail to the Decembrist cause, it was also the urge to restore their family's power. They hoped to find themselves within the select few, in the *Duma* (the small central body of the group's inner circle) of a new government. They forbade their younger brother Peter from active participation in the revolution, but he stood on the bridge adjacent to Senate Square and harangued passersby. The youngest, Pavel, was arrested after the revolt because of his family's involvement and stated unequivocally, "I must be punished because I am the brother of my brothers!"[8]

Bestuzhev believed wholeheartedly in the cause he served. He was familiar with constitutional forms of government in the West, and he

6. Vyazemsky's Decembrist relations and leanings are discussed by Iurii Lotman in "P. A. Viazemskii i dvizhenie dekabristov," *Uchenye zapiski Tartuskogo Gosudarstvennogo Universiteta: Trudy po russkoi i slavianskoi filologii III* 98 (1960): 24–142.

7. S. A. Ovsiannikova, "A. A. Bestuzhev-Marlinskii i ego rol' v dvizhenii dekabristov," in *Ocherki iz istorii dvizheniia dekabristov* (Moscow, 1954), 430.

8. M. K. Azadovskii, *Vospominaniia Bestuzhevykh*, 58.

was versed in the manifestos developed by the Secret Society, which guaranteed the freedoms for which all enlightened Russians longed. These were the same ideals that his father had espoused.

After Bestuzhev's entry into the inner circle of the Secret Society in April 1825, he recruited more members in preparation for an uprising against Alexander I, planned in conjunction with the Southern Society for the following year. Although he was privy to all information pertinent to the workings, tactics, dissension, and compromise within the group, he did not distinguish himself as a thinker in this inner circle. His brother Nicholas recalled that Ryleyev trusted his (Nicholas's) objectivity over Alexander's "rashness."[9] But they counted on Bestuzhev to inspire others to follow the decisions of the ruling group.

The Secret Society had two distinct voices. Nikita Muraviev's was conservative and rational; Ryleyev's was liberal and intuitive. Anatole Mazour characterizes the two:

> Muraviev came to his political creed through a cold logic, Ryleyev through ecstatic feeling; if the former came into the Society attracted by a certain goal, Ryleyev was drawn into it like a moth drawn by the flickering flame in the night. This he seemed to have sensed prophetically when he wrote in his well-known poem, *Nalivaiko:*
>> My coming doom I feel and know
>> And bless the stroke which lays me low,
>> And, father, now with joy I meet
>> My death; to me such end is sweet.
> Ryleyev was too emotional to elaborate political doctrines, conceiving them rather as a poet conceives ideas of some beautiful form. If Muraviev was the brains of the Society, Ryleyev was its soul.[10]

Bestuzhev's brothers belonged to Muraviev's camp, but he was clearly aligned with Ryleyev by temperament and intellectual predisposition. They were well matched and represented what Ya. Gordin calls its improvisational wing. Like Ryleyev's, his style was declamatory and rhetorical,

9. Nikolai Bestuzhev, "Vospominanie o Ryleeve," in ibid.
10. Anatole G. Mazour, *The First Russian Revolution, 1825* (Stanford, Calif., 1961), 127.

not rational and analytic. Neither Bestuzhev nor Ryleyev were prepared to deal with the revolt in practical terms. Together they had composed several underground songs, which they circulated among the soldiery and common folk:

> As a writer of high merit, Ryleyev awakened many people. His inspiring poetry praising liberty and passionately condemning the rule of Arakcheev, his "verses not smooth but delightful because of their bitterness and audacity," as Grech said, were read by many people in Russia and circulated in handwritten form, since they often failed to pass the censor. Written in collaboration with A. Bestuzhev, his popular verses, "Oh, how nauseating even in my own land," or "Where are those islands?" were set to music and sung in virtually all circles, in conservative circles as in the home of Bulgarin as well as in those whose participants openly advocated the necessity of "d'en finir avec ce gouvernement." The government used every means to eradicate the songs and destroyed them whenever found. But, written in the form of folksongs in which the sad conditions of the masses were well reflected, they passed from mouth to mouth and no power could have stamped them out. (130)

These agitational songs were sung over a bottle, in taverns, and in private gatherings of friends. Unfortunately, their translation cannot capture the pithiness, abruptness, and humor of the originals. "Tell Me Now, Speak Up True" ("Ty skazhi, govori") is representative:

> Tell me now, speak up true,
> How the tsars try to rule in Russia?
> Tell me now, near and far,
> How the Russian tsars are crushed?
> How the corporals lead
> Peter [III] from his palace quietly,
> While his wife [Catherine] before the gates
> Pranced her stallion at her mate boldly?
> How the snub nosed Evil One [Pavel I]
> became the tsar after her. Grief.
> But The Lord, Russia's own,
> Helped the poor folk all alone. Relief.

[Ты скажи, говори,
Как в России цари
    Правят.
Ты скажи поскорей,
Как в России царей
    Давят.
Как капралы Петра
Провожали с двора
    Тихо.
А жена пред дворцом
Разъезжала верхом
    Лихо.
Как курносый злодей
Воцарился по ней.
    Горе!
Но господь, русский бог,
Бедным людям помог
    Вскоре.]¹¹

The reference to the problem of succession in eighteenth-century Russia amounted to a history lesson. Through such songs Bestuzhev and Ryleyev hoped to arouse popular distrust in the crown. The words indicate the authors' ability to assimilate the audience's perspective and deliver what the people wanted to hear, including the harshness of autocratic rule, God versus the Devil, and deliverance from suffering. The Decembrists attempted to substitute themselves for the God of the song in their plan to deliver the Russian people from bondage.

There are other songs that elicited hostility while instilling hope for governmental change. The following verse is based upon the widely despised penchant for parades, military precision, proper uniforms, and other "empty" forms characteristic of Alexander I's reign. It associates these traits with Alexander I's Germanic obsession with order, precision, and cold logic:

Our tsar is a Russian German,
Wears a dress coat made in Prussia.
    Ai da tsar, ai da tsar,
    Orthodox and Sovereign star.

11. Bestuzhev-Marlinskii, *Sochineniia v dvukh tomakh*, 2:511–12.

So he governs! Where's his rule?
Every day at the riding school!
  (refrain)

. . . .

He governs land, sea, air and rocks
Then stoops to straighten out his socks.
  (refrain)
An enemy to Enlightenment
but still on study [military maneuvers] he is bent.
  (refrain)
All our schools are barracks armed.
And all our judges are gendarmes.
  (refrain)

[Царь наш—немец русский,
Носит мундир узкий.
    Ай да царь, ай да царь,
    Православный государь!
Царствует он где же?
Всякий день в манеже.
  (припев)

. . . .

Царством управляет,
Носки выправляет.
  (припев)
Враг хоть просвещенья,
Любит он ученья.
  (припев)
Школы все—казармы,
Судьи все—жандармы.
  (припев)]

(Ibid., 512)

It continues with satires aimed at specific government officials, such as
the hated Arakcheyev.[12] The last barbs aimed at Alexander I delighted
the soldiery:

12. See Michael Jenkins, *Arakcheev, Grand Vizier of the Russian Empire* (New York,
1969).

He is afraid of Russian laws
and the Masons one and all.
(refrain)
Distinction's won but for parades,
The tsar's rewards are mere charades.
(refrain)
And for a little compliment
Our tsar a pretty ribbon sent.
(refrain)
And for the truth, our mother truth
He sends us all out to Kamchatka.
(refrain)

[Трусит он законов,
Трусит он масонов.
(припев)
Только за парады
Раздает награды.
(припев)
А за комплименты—
Голубые ленты.
(припев)
А за правду-матку
Прямо шлет в Камчатку.
(припев)]
                    (*Sochineniia*, 2:513)

This song would be used by the next generation of radicals to attack Nicholas I.[13]

Other songs called for revolt directly. Appealing to desires for power in the empire's hierarchical order, Bestuzhev and Ryleyev hoped to attract potential members to the conspiratorial group:

Along the Fontanka River
Regiments are quartered.
Glory!

13. Iu. G. Oksman, "The Politically Inflammatory Song 'Our Tsar is a German Russian,' " in Egolin, 59:69–84.

Regiments are quartered
All of them Guard regiments.
  Glory!
They teach them, torture them
Both night and day.
  Glory!
Both night and day
For the tsar.
  Glory!
Don't they have arms by which
To free themselves from torture?
  Glory!
Don't they have bayonets
For the little snot-nosed princes?
  Glory!
Don't they have rifles
To aim at the tyrant scoundrel?
  Glory!
Well the Semenovsky Regiment
Will show us how it's done!
  Glory!
Whosoever seeks shall find,
Whosoever finds will win
  Glory!

[Вдоль Фонтанки-реки
Квартируют полки.
  Слава!
Квартируют полки
Все гвардейские.
  Слава!
Их и учат, их и мучат,
Ни свет, ни заря,
  Слава!
Что ни свет, ни заря,
Для потехи царя,
  Слава!
Разве нет у них рук,
Чтоб избавиться от мук?
  Слава!

Разве нет у них штыков
На князьков-сопляков?
Слава!
Разве нет у них свинца
На тирана-подлеца?
Слава!
Да Семеновский полк
Покажет им толк!
Слава!
Кому вынется, тому сбудется,
А кому сбудется, не минуется.
Слава!]
(*Sochineniia*, 2:513–14)

Bestuzhev was swept up by the message as much as his audience. A victorious revolt on behalf of justice might win him the fame he sought.

In the fall of 1825, Bestuzhev lived on the Moika Canal in the same building as Ryleyev. Together the two radicals attempted to win the support of the Kronstadt officers and troops considered crucial for the success of the revolt. "Throughout all of November and the first two weeks of December 1825, and particularly in the days immediately preceding the revolt, Ryleyev and Bestuzhev's apartment house was literally the center of preparations for the revolt."[14] By September Bestuzhev was a member of the *Duma*, the ruling central group selected from within the inner circle. (Ovsiannikova, 421).

On November 27, 1825, news of Alexander I's death in southern Russia reached St. Petersburg. The *Duma* and the inner circle were thrown into a frenzy of activity as they attempted to decipher what was happening in the Winter Palace concerning succession and what the disposition of the military was (both in the rank and file and among the officers). Since many of the conspirators were attached to the most trusted military generals of the tsar and acquainted with members of the Senate and Synod (where the battle of succession would be fought), information flowed into Ryleyev's apartment. The confusion that pervaded the Secret Society early in the day disappeared by late that night when the members decided to exploit the infighting of palace factions during the interregnum.

Regicide certainly weighed on the minds of Alexander I's successors,

14. M. V. Nechkina, *Vosstanie 14 dekabria 1825* (Moscow, 1951), 64.

Constantine and Nicholas. Their father Paul I had been assassinated in 1801 at their brother Alexander's behest. Their grandfather, Peter III, had been murdered in a palace coup in 1762. Constantine had renounced his right of succession several years earlier in a secret letter. Although Nicholas knew about the renunciation, he was reluctant to assume the throne. Because he was seen as a petty tyrant, he was not popular (Nechkina, 68). Constantine was favored because of his quasi-constitutional rule of Poland. It was believed that Constantine would renew the dreams of Alexander I's early reign, but that Nicholas would continue the nightmare of Arakcheyev's harsh punishments and military settlements. Constantine represented something of an ideal in comparison to his brother,[15] although this appears to have been an illusion perpetrated upon a naive public.[16] If Nicholas had any support at all, it was to be found at Court. Its members felt that Constantine's liberal tendencies would reduce their privileges, but that Nicholas would sustain their special place.[17]

Nicholas was afraid of the Guards, who had assassinated his father, and was hesitant to appear to be wresting the crown from Constantine. Count Mikhail Miloradovich, governor of St. Petersburg and a member of the Senate, frightened Nicholas by telling him that he was in great danger. Under pressure, Nicholas swore allegiance to Constantine, while one of his father's assassins, Pavel Golenishchev-Kutuzov, stood next to him (Gordin, 36). In his panic Nicholas had the Guards swear an oath to Constantine even before the Senate and the nobility had done so. One member of the Court wrote, "The Grand Prince was quite in haste. He ordered all about to swear allegiance to Constantine with no regard for proper order, which led to the rank and file pledging before the ruling class" (24).

When the Senate met to consider succession, they were confused about what to do. They asked Nicholas to visit their chambers in order to help them make a decision, but he refused, saying he was not a member of the Senate. Miloradovich was sent to persuade Nicholas to come but used the opportunity to manipulate him to his own ends. When Nicholas entered the Senate pale and agitated, he pleaded, "Gen-

15. Ia. Gordin, *Sobytie i luidi 14 dekabria* (Moscow, 1985), 37–42.
16. Nicholas Riasanovsky, *Nicholas I and Official Nationality in Russia, 1825–1855* (Berkeley, Calif., 1969), 37; W. Bruce Lincoln, *Nicholas I: Emperor and Autocrat of All the Russias* (Bloomington, Ind., 1978), 26–27.
17. A. E. Presniakov, *14 dekabria 1825* (Moscow, 1926), 62.

tlemen, I beg you, I implore you for the peace of the kingdom, that you immediately follow the example set by me and the military to swear your allegiance to Tsar Emperor Constantine Pavlovich. I will accept no other measures nor will I hear of any others from you" (ibid., 35–36). The Senate proceeded to take the oath, and after them the Court, government officials, and the military as well.

Nicholas's insecurities went back to his infancy, and his "behavior in regard to the imperial succession had . . . deeper psychological roots" than usually ascribed to it by historians (Riasanovsky, 32). He was virtually abandoned by his mother upon his birth. His grandmother Catherine the Great was interested in him, but she died when Nicholas was only five months old. It was his father Paul I who cared for him and took time to play with him. The assassination of Paul I was traumatic for the young prince. He became obsessed by routine and order, suspicious, defensive, cold, rigid, and austere. One of his contemporaries studied his visage and social behavior and drew a picture of him in which the persona is distinctly felt and with it a terrible separation from any consciousness of the self:

> The usual expression of his face has something severe and misanthropic in it, something that does not put one at all at one's ease. His smile is a smile of civility which is not at all a result of gaiety or of spontaneity. The habit of repressing these feelings has become so inseparable from his very being that you see in him no awkwardness, no embarrassment, nothing studied; and yet all his words, as all his movements, follow a cadence as if he had a sheet of music in front of him. . . . There is nothing in the tone of his voice or in the construction of his sentences that indicates pride or dissimulation; and yet you feel that his heart is closed, that the barrier is impassable, and that one would be mad to hope to penetrate the privacy of his thought. (Cited in Riasanovsky, 9–10)

The Decembrists had no quarrel with Constantine, but they were afraid that if Constantine sat on the throne, he would thwart their plans for total political reform by instilling hope for a liberal future. In order to move the public to revolt, on the evening of November 27 Bestuzhev and his fellows went about spreading lies to create discord (Ovsiannikova, 425). They stopped soldiers and spoke to Guards, telling them that Alexander I's will, which promised freedom for the peasants and reduction of military service from twenty-five years to only five, had been suppressed. Bestuzhev subsequently wrote about this ruse: "You cannot imagine the eagerness with which the soldiers listened to our news, or the rapidity with which our word spread about the army. By the next day we were convinced of our success" (425). With the news on December 6 that Constantine would not take the throne, Nicholas quickly consolidated his power. During the week before Nicholas's coronation, the conspirators used more lies to mobilize soldiers against the tsar.

The meetings at Ryleyev's were not without conflicts concerning tactics and the delicate matter of regicide. It had been contemplated for most of the year, since Alexander Yakubovich had come to St. Petersburg with inflammatory speeches and plans to assassinate Alexander I because of the tsar's "unjust" treatment of him (Nechkina, 58). Yakubovich told stories about his feats in the war against the Caucasian mountain tribesmen and played the archetypal romantic hero before a captivated audience (Gordin, 29).

Ryleyev and Bestuzhev were attracted to Yakubovich but taken aback by his independence within the group. Although Radishchev was their model from the past, Yakubovich was their first direct encounter with a military hero who appeared to have walked off the pages of their beloved epic poems and tales. They were willing to use him as an assassin in the event the organization decided on regicide, but they were worried he might precipitate events before the activities of the Northern and Southern Societies could be coordinated. Bestuzhev described his first meeting with Yakubovich in Moscow in 1823: "He is a remarkable person in many ways and we became friends. . . . We spoke together on liberal ideas [liberal'nichali], but we really didn't quite open up to each other then" (ibid., 27). Ryleyev's account gives more detail about this same meeting:

> His words, voice, movements and wound [to the head suffered in the Caucasus] made a strong impression on me, which I, however, attempted to hide from him. I proposed that [regicide] might actually do him a dishonor, and that with his gifts and having already made a name for himself in the army, he might be more useful to the homeland by satisfying other passions. To this Yakubovich responded that he knew only two passions, both of which move the entire world. These are gratitude and revenge, and all other passions are but nothing. He also said that he didn't

send his word [of regicide] into the wind for naught and that he would complete the deed immediately. He had already selected two possible dates: upcoming military maneuvers or the imminent holiday festivities at Peterhoff. I left with A. Bestuzhev and on the way told him that we must try at all costs to stop this Yakubovich. Bestuzhev agreed. (29–30)

Although Bestuzhev and Ryleyev were intimidated by Yakubovich's rash stance, on the day of the insurrection Yakubovich proved to be all pose—he defected to the loyalist side. If Yakubovich's example was important for Bestuzhev in the days preceding the revolt, his actions on December 14 must have been unsettling. Indeed, Yakubovich's comportment prefigured Bestuzhev's own defection during the investigation that began on December 15.

There is evidence that Bestuzhev and Yakubovich spent a great deal of time together during the days preceding the revolt. They solicited the support of the Marine Guard at Kronstadt; after speaking with several company commanders, they prepared to leave. "With hat in hand Yakubovich stood before the young sailors wishing to encourage them. Not letting any opportunity to wax eloquent escape him, Yakubovich said, 'Gentlemen, although I have no doubt that you are brave, I also know that you have never been under fire before. I set myself as an example to you.' Here he and Bestuzhev reassured the warrant officers that the Guards were sympathetic to the cause and that they had no doubt as to their success" (ibid., 158).

Bestuzhev gradually moved to a peripheral position in the activities of the Secret Society, even though he was a member of the *Duma*. He was not of advanced military standing, so when surrounded by experienced officers of the Napoleonic Wars or by noblemen of superior social status, he held himself in respectful reserve. At Ryleyev's meetings Prince Sergei Trubetskoy, Prince Evgeny Obolensky, Nikita Muraviev, and others were equipped to deal rationally with the serious business of organizing a revolt and an interim government, to develop maneuvers to emasculate the Senate and Synod, and to formulate a constitution. These men and their ideas are extensively documented in the literature on Decembrism (see Mazour, 117–37).

Although Bestuzhev was not a theoretician, he was eager to fight. Trubetskoy, the revolutionaries' elected leader (who deserted the cause and absented himself on December 14), remarked "on his hotheadedness and fiery imagination."[18] Baten'kov thought him a fanatic and steered clear of him: "A. Bestuzhev was known to me as a man whose eyes expressed a readiness for every extreme, and I consequently avoided conversation and open discussion with him whenever I could."[19] The historian S. A. Ovsiannikova said that "Alexander Bestuzhev, feeling the imminence of [a revolt], was in a particularly excited and combative frame of mind. Three days before the revolt he met in the palace a member of the Northern Society, Rostovtsev, and told him, 'it looks like it will soon come to broadswords' " (Ovsiannikova, 427).

Like Yakubovich, Bestuzhev wanted to cut a heroic figure, but his actions vacillated between extremes. He recruited Yakubovich and Kakhovskoy, who were intent on regicide, but dissuaded them from carrying out their plans. He convinced Kakhovskoy not to shoot the tsar but loaned him a pistol anyway. He supported Ryleyev's assassination plans in *Duma* meetings but consistently sabotaged them in other venues. He recruited his brothers to carry out their portion of the revolt at Kronstadt but subsequently tried to persuade them to withdraw.

The careful military planners were inclined to call off the revolt if their forces could not effect entry into the Winter Palace and arrest Nicholas and his family according to plan; the improvisors were willing to forge ahead even in disaster, inventing spontaneously what needed to be done next. On December 13 Trubetskoy and Mikhail Bestuzhev argued that a well-planned and precisely timed military operation would increase their likelihood of success. Historians agree that the Decembrists had an excellent chance of succeeding. Ryleyev and Bestuzhev felt that the revolt must go forward: "For Ryleyev the mere fact of revolt was valuable regardless of the consequences" (Gordin, 151). Trubetskoy recounted that "Ryleyev shouted, 'No, it is too late to quit this business. We have gone too far. Perhaps we have already been betrayed [to the tsar].' [Trubetskoy] responded: 'So, you are willing to sacrifice others for your own neck?' Alexander Bestuzhev replied, 'Yes, for the sake of history,' and added, 'pages will be written [about us].' [Trubetskoy] answered, 'So, that is what you are after' " (151). Bestuzhev longed for renown, and he sought it through heroic action at all costs, even at others' expense.

The revolt constituted the supreme test of Bestuzhev's self-idea. Ef-

---

18. Cited in Neil B. Landsman, "Decembrist Romanticism: A. A. Bestuzhev-Marlinsky," 68.

19. M. V. Dovnar-Zapolskii, *Memuary dekabristov* (Kiev, 1906), 175.

fecting the persona of a self-sacrificing hero in reality called for a theatrical organization of scene to guarantee an audience to bear witness to the authenticity of the heroic self. On the stage of Senate Square in St. Petersburg, he was "ready to sacrifice his true, transitory self for the imaginary eternal self he [had built] up, by his heroic deeds, in the opinion and imagination of others" (Hoffer, 65). Regardless of political victory or defeat, the revolt represented his chance to write Marlinsky the romantic literary hero into his life-text. But with characteristic ambivalence, Bestuzhev alternated between enthusiastic support for the revolt and gestures of flight. Bestuzhev and Marlinsky appeared as his own interchangeable fictional characters—decisive hero, duplicitous villain, rational thinker, and jester-fool. Through adherence to a romantic heroic persona, he and his fellows felt that "they were not their real selves but actors playing a role, and their doings a 'performance' rather than the real thing. Dying, too, they [saw] as a gesture, an act of make-believe" (69). This moment represented the apotheosis of the hero.

Bestuzhev was drawn toward the dying warrior as toward an authentic self. His hero orientation amounted to a profoundly held belief that resisted the realities of life and sometimes common sense. It was predicated on an unwillingness or inability to reflect or analyze. As Hoffer proposed, "The readiness for self-sacrifice is contingent on an imperviousness to the realities of life. He who is free to draw conclusions from his individual experience and observation is not usually hospitable to the idea of martyrdom" (ibid., 75). In December 1825, Bestuzhev set out to prove his romantic point of view to himself and to others.

Carnival in St. Petersburg

Succession is frequently accompanied by carnival traditions to mark the cyclical nature of natural and cultural phenomena. Carnival is the celebration of the mysterious intertwining of life and death and can be found in many unrelated traditions. It represents a syncretic pageant that sweeps up all members of the community. It usually occurs in a central square and spills over onto adjoining streets, wherein the participants perform ritual acts that celebrate the cycles of the death and rebirth of the collective entity. All the festivals of the season's turning throughout the ages animate its spirit. These occasions are sometimes accompanied by political unrest and occasionally turn into political revolt.[20] The outpouring of primal vitality within the community occurs on the border of chaos. Sometimes the rites are consciously acted out, such as in Mardi Gras or Saturnalia, but often the carnival rises out of an unconscious impulse. During carnival celebrations at the winter solstice the community witnesses the death and rebirth of the sun, the giver of life.

The carnival spirit was the secret source of the revolt. As Rene Girard points out in his study of violence accompanying rites of passage for kings, the transfer of rule is often attended by blood sacrifice.[21] In effect, the process by which a group, or society, reestablishes order is through a ritual of violence that entertains chaos in order to dispense with it. Several features of the Decembrist Revolt liken this event in Russian cultural history to other societies during tense moments of transition that threaten to tear apart the fabric of the existing order.

In Northrop Frye's terminology the ritual marks a descent from an ideal state into chaos wherein death is confronted. Victory in the lower depths signals a reemergence to the ideal condition that predates the narrative. Carnival celebrations duplicate this narrative order, attesting to simultaneous rebellious and conservative tendencies. The rebelliousness is obvious; and as LeRoy Ladurie observes, once carnival is spent, there is a return to the hierarchical order that governs the daily life of the community (Ladurie, 301–2).

The day of the revolt was replete with real and symbolic life-and-death struggles suffused with laughter and propelled by ritual instincts that dramatize the duality of existence. The interregnum had produced an atmosphere of loosened behavioral norms, and consequently the quest for order could be set aside in the enjoyment of the libidinous moment. Since the high might now be rendered low, it was a time for the powerless to celebrate power. The Decembrist Revolt supplied the right mood and called forth the theme of regicide so deeply embedded in the carnival tradition.

Ritual and carnival elements infused the interregnum and the revolt on December 14 and infected the behavior of all the participants. The Decembrist insurgents took Senate Square early in the morning. Bestuzhev successfully brought out a battalion of the Moscow Regiment,

20. LeRoy Ladurie, *Carnival in Romans*, trans. Mary Feeney (New York, 1980), 305–24.
21. Rene Girard, *Violence and the Sacred* (Baltimore, Md., 1977), 105.

which was the very first to appear on Senate Square. He immediately set his men in formation and awaited the arrival of support troops. Not many would appear. The influential Semenovsky Regiment and the Finland Regiment refused to participate, upsetting the plans of the revolutionaries who expected them to challenge Nicholas I. Mikhail and Nicholas Bestuzhev were the only others successful in bringing troops forward. Throughout the morning and until mid afternoon the insurgents held their position surrounded by regiments loyal to Nicholas I. Negotiations were conducted with the rebels until three o'clock when Tsar Nicholas ordered his troops to disperse them with cannon and grapeshot. The conspirators were rounded up and interrogated.

Carnival includes the dissolution of hierarchical order ruling everyday life. Reversal and inversion occur at many levels. According to Mikhail Bakhtin, "Carnival brings together, unifies, weds, and combines the sacred with the profane, the lofty with the low, the great with the insignificant, the wise with the stupid."[22] A fool, who is selected from among the people and crowned king of the festivities, is deposed at the end of the ritual, and in ancient times was sacrificed to the new cycle of the sun. In the streeets rude speech, crude gestures, gross noises, sexual license, inebriety, and gluttony work in concert to worship the lower body. Clothes are worn inside out; men and women use each others' dress. Mock battles take place with the transformation of kitchen utensils and foodstuff into weapons. A mixture of derision, joy, madness, sarcasm, and play permeates the carnival with cosmic laughter reigning over all. The "joyful relativity" (124) of life's structure and order is worshiped under the raucous laughter of life's mysterious jester-creator. "Ridicule is fused with rejoicing" (126–27).

The celebration goes to the depths of the unconscious, drawing forth from each individual the mysterious apprehension of a life that cannot be understood fully. The specter of death is omnipresent, for the events of an upside-down world are meant to magically influence the uncontrollable forces of nature to benefit the community. Bakhtin summarizes the carnival participation:

22. Mikhail Bakhtin, *Problems of Dostoevsky's Poetics*, ed. and trans. Caryl Emerson (Minneapolis, 1984), 123. Bakhtin puts entirely too happy a face on the carnivalesque, carnival rituals, and rites of passage. There is always the day after the celebration when hierarchical relationships, turned upside-down for a moment, are reestablished. Ladurie's and Girard's accounts are more in keeping with the whole cycle of events surrounding carnival (both its festive and darker implications).

Carnival is a pageant without footlights and without a division into performers and spectators. In carnival everyone is an active participant, everyone communes in the carnival act. Carnival is not contemplated and, strictly speaking, not even performed; its participants *live* in it, they live by its laws as long as those laws are in effect; that is, they live a *carnivalized life*. Because carnivalistic life is drawn out of its *usual* rut, it is to some extent "life turned inside out," "the reverse side of the world" ("*monde à l'envers*"). (122)

In St. Petersburg on December 14, 1825, according to the Russian calendar, the sun rose at 9:04 and set at 2:58. This was the winter solstice. Mummers would soon be about, profaning the sacred in a carnivalesque mixture of Christian and pagan symbolism. The crowd was in a festive mood, but it was ambivalent about the succession and agitated by the problems of the interregnum. A place would be needed if the rite were to be enacted. The Decembrists fixed the location. When Bestuzhev marched the regiment out onto Senate Square the morning of December 14, an unplanned, unconscious carnival ensued that occupied the ambiguous ground between play and reality, between life and death.

Girard cites examples of transition ritual particularly appropriate for the Decembrist Revolt and Bestuzhev's place in it. The revolt may be read from a ritualistic perspective. "In some societies the whole enthronement ceremony takes place in an atmosphere of blood-stained confusion" (Girard, 105). Carnival requires a sacrificial victim, a fool king who falls as suddenly as he rose, and that role was played by a variety of actors. Count Mikhail Miloradovich was the first of a series of sacrifices, randomly selected out of the chaotic movement of undefined events. Vaulted suddenly to power at the time of Alexander I's death, he was felled by a shot while confronting the Decembrists in an attempt to persuade them to return to their barracks. Gordin briefly discusses Miloradovich's double role as he moved ineluctably from a position of (relative) power to the position of ritual sacrifice. "In Miloradovich we meet the first signals of metamorphosis. He turned from a political gamesman into a tragic figure" (193). The duality of his position, shown in his dealings with the Decembrist conspirators, identified him with the tragic forces of the carnival's movement from joyous crowning to tragic sacrifice. The fool king was also played by the coward Trubetskoy, the commander of the revolt who turned tail and hid throughout the day at his cousin's house, and by the traitor Yakubovich, whose courageous words before the revolt proved empty. They appeared quixotic and paradoxical to their fellows (and later generations) because of their ambivalent behavior.

Yakubovich, who represented the heroic persona in absolute terms for Bestuzhev, went through a sudden and dramatic change the day of the revolt: " 'The daring Caucasian,' who had formerly amazed everyone by his audacity and whom the Society had often feared to 'unleash,' lost his revolutionary ardor. Evidently, as M[ikhail] Bestuzhev [later reported], the audacity of a soldier and that of a conspirator are far from the same thing" (Mazour, 170). He played the fool in mixing mutually exclusive roles (hero-traitor). Mazour gives a memorable account of Yakubovich on December 14:

> On the day when the issue was at stake, that same posing Marat marched to the Square carrying his hat on the tip of his uplifted sword, shouting "Hurrah for Constantine!" Here he stood for only a moment, then, under the pretense of a frightful headache, left the place just as the order was given to load the rifles. "Noticing the criminal intentions of the rebels," he went to Nicholas and declared that his presence on the Square "was a result of exclusive zeal and sincere attachment to the young Emperor." Praised by Nicholas for his loyalty, Yakubovich returned to the rebels and advised them to hold on firmly, for Nicholas was afraid of them. After that he turned around, went home, loaded his pistol, ordered that no one be allowed to see him, and sat down contemplating, as [Nicholas] Bestuzhev says, "how to betray more heroically." He remained at home until he was arrested there by a government official. Yakubovich's later fate was as tragic as that of the other rebels. (170–71)

It appears that the romantic persona was prone to the principle of inversion, and that the internal conflicts created in the disparity between persona and personality bore a tragic weight.

Girard points out that the carnival king does not represent a sum of human virtues as much as a sum of human vices. Alexander I fulfilled this expectation in both political and personal terms, but the transition to Nicholas was the trading of one set of human faults for another. When the king is sacrificed at the closing act of the carnival, the historically prevailing hierarchical order is restored in a renewed and sanctioned form. "It is because of this impurity that the king, in the course of the enthronement and renewal ceremonies, is subjected to the ritualistic insults and abuse of his people. A hostile crowd denounces the misconduct of this miscreant, who is as yet nothing more than a criminal and a social outcast. In some instances the royal army stages a mock attack on the king's personal bodyguard and even on the king himself" (105).

The anxious Nicholas took up the cloak of the fool king. He falsified the record in his memoirs when he wrote that he had not been informed about Constantine's abdication. Furthermore, he played up his role in dramatic terms, creating a picture of himself as humble victim willing to sacrifice for the good of the country (Gordin, 61).[23] His ambivalence during the interregnum gave license to the festive occasion and allowed it to develop into a full pageant.

The substitution of one party for another is a common feature of the ritual of enthronement and renewal. While Nicholas was convincing everyone to pledge allegiance to Constantine in Moscow, Constantine had all of his attendants in Poland swear an oath to Nicholas. The European press made great sport of the empty throne with two reluctant brothers deferring to each other. Constantine and Nicholas played into the hands of the carnival by pairing off against each other. As Girard notes, "At the core of this royal magic contest . . . appears the old theme of *enemy brothers*. Factions congregate around the various claimants, and the surviving brother is accorded the throne" (Girard, 109). That Nicholas and Constantine did not compete for the throne, but rather competed to put the other on it, rendered the enthronement ritual comic and carnivalesque, for each brother was playing the role of the "unworthy king" traditional in carnival. "But once the carnival is over the anti-king is expelled from the community or put to death, and his disappearance puts an end to all the disorder that his person served to symbolize for the community and also to purge it" (109). They fulfilled the ancient and subliminal function of the competing brothers, but in reverse to produce a burlesque effect on a crowd of common people recently intoxicated by that spirit in pre-Advent and solstice celebrations.

---

23. It is possible that Nicholas I was dissimulating, establishing himself as reluctant candidate only to manipulate his family and others into demanding that he become tsar. This conjecture in no wise alters Nicholas I's *self-depiction* in a series of guises suited to carnival tradition.

Not only was the folly of the interregnum something tragicomic, but "Russia faced the impossible situation of having an Emperor who refused to recognize himself as such, and who would not even formally abdicate the throne which he did not want to occupy" (Lincoln, 31). Within twenty-four hours of the revolt, Nicholas sought the advice of his minister of war, General A. I. Tatishchev, on the matter of conspiracy of which he had been forewarned. "Tatishchev proposed that any known conspirators who could be found in the capital should be put into prison immediately. But [Nicholas] refused to see his reign begin with a flurry of arrests and therefore rejected the general's advice. . . . Tatishchev pointed out that, if the arrests were not made, then the chances for a revolt would be greater. 'Then let it be so,' responded the Grand Duke [Nicholas]" (34). By postponing arrests Nicholas guaranteed that the events would take place in a specific time frame that, by Russian folk beliefs, was considered unlucky (40).

Traditional carnival relations were established with the collision of opposing forces on the day of the revolt when Nicholas discovered who the conspirators were. He ordered their immediate arrest. As commandant of the city and chief of the city police, Miloradovich did not arrest the conspirators but merely conducted surveillance of them. Decembrists met with Miloradovich; officials conducted government business in the presence of conspirators. One of the Decembrists, Yakov Rostovtsev, even alluded to the revolt in Nicholas I's presence, although it is not clear whether his veiled words constituted a betrayal of the Decembrist cause or a tactical maneuver to lead Nicholas to believe a revolt was imminent elsewhere in the kingdom (Gordin, 105–12). Gordin states: "The paradoxicality of the situation was such that the relations of Miloradovich and Yakubovich, cohort of Ryleyev and friend of Alexander Bestuzhev, were closer in fact than relations between Miloradovich, the governor-general of the city, and Benckendorf, the chief of police and Nicholas I's friend" (66).

If carnival is a celebration of the loss of distinctions in society, then regicide constituted a grand signal for the populace to engage in this celebratory act.[24] The Decembrists considered killing Nicholas and the

24. "The act of regicide is the exact equivalent, vis-à-vis the polis, of the act of patricide vis-à-vis the family. In both cases the criminal strikes at the most fundamental, essential, and inviolable distinction within the group. He becomes, literally, a slayer of distinctions" (Girard, 74).

royal family, although there was no complete agreement on this matter even up to the final moment. After the revolt it was Bestuzhev who first informed the investigating commission that regicide was part of the plan.

Important in carnival celebrations is the participation of the masses. On a coronation day the populace expects a spectacle. With the rumors spreading that a revolt was in progress, the citizens flocked to the heart of the city. Although they were explicitly excluded from the Decembrist's plans for revolt, a large crowd of common people gathered throughout the day around the perimeter of the square where the insurgent troops had assembled. Bonfires were lit, drinking and eating persisted throughout the day, and shouts in support of the rebels continued from the beginning of the uprising to its bitter end. Cries against the tsar and his supporters are noted in many accounts of the revolt. Nicholas I heard curses shouted at him from side streets leading out onto the square. "As the French journalist J. H. Schnitzler recalled, Nicholas was displeased at the presence of so many idle spectators. He advanced . . . and several times requested the crowd to retire. 'Do me the favor,' he said, 'to return home. You have nothing to do here.' They retired a few steps, and then, impelled by curiosity, returned. I did the same, and near me some old women remained, in equally flagrant disobedience, repeating, 'He comes to ask us himself! and how politely too!' " (Lincoln, 44).

The tsar, who was according to Russo-Byzantine tradition the most sacred figure in society,[25] was treated no more like an emperor than any member of the rabble. In a striking image of the profanation of the sacred, Nicholas described workers throwing lumber down on him and his retinue from St. Isaac's cathedral (which was under construction at the time).[26] When the metropolitan, Serafim, arrived on the square, he beseeched the rebels to return to their barracks, to honor the rightful tsar, the homeland, and the Church and to lay down their arms. He was told, "What kind of a metropolitan are you when in just two weeks you have sworn an oath to two tsars? You are a traitor, a deserter . . . get thee hence. This matter does not concern you!" (Gordin, 262). An armed crowd gathered around him and his deacons and they were forced to flee through a rent in the fence surrounding St. Isaac's. From there they were carried in a humble rig to the Winter Palace. When questioned about

25. V. M. Zhivov and B. A. Uspenskii, "Tsar' i bog: Semioticheskie aspekty sakralizatsii monarkha v Rossii," in *Iazyki kul'tury i problemy perevodimosti* (Moscow, 1987), 47–153.
26. Iu. G. Oksman, ed., *Dekabristy: Otryvki iz istochnikov* (Moscow, 1926), 329.

what had happened, Serafim responded that he had been roundly cursed and sent packing (Nechkina, 120). When Grand Duke Mikhail Pavlovich attempted to persuade the insurgents to reconsider, he too was met by a barrage of carnival curses and had to retire in order to save his life. Bestuzhev attests that Küchelbecker attempted to shoot the grand duke, but his pistol misfired. The Decembrists represented the carnival impulse transformed into outright rebellion.

Carnival laughter is deeply ambivalent, for it expresses the joyous experience of the living while reaching into the darkest recesses of personal anxiety over mortality. Bakhtin argues that the laughter which brings these opposing forces to the surface is most often linked to crises in those spheres of existence where the individual has little power to influence events. "Ritual laughter was always directed toward something higher: the sun (the highest god), other gods, the highest earthly authority were put to shame and ridiculed to force them to *renew themselves*. All forms of ritual laughter were linked with death and rebirth, with the reproductive act, with symbols of the reproductive force. Ritual laughter was a reaction to *crises* in the life of the sun (solstices), crises in the life of a deity, in the life of the world and of man (funeral laughter). In it, ridicule was fused with rejoicing" (126–27).

In an anecdote that has long been considered apocryphal, the crowd shouted for Constantine and "for his wife Constitution," a fine joke in the spirit of carnival fun and the joyful expression of a topsy-turvy world. M. V. Nechkina considers the anecdote the result of Shchepin-Rostovsky's attempt to diminish his role in the revolt in the Secret Society. He drew the pun before the Investigating Commission (Nechkina, 153–54), which subsequently circulated it at Court as a form of ridicule of the insurgents and their political ignorance. But in his memoirs Butenev witnessed that "the crowd shouted 'Hooray, Constantine! Constitution!' and someone in the crowd, *as a joke,* added: 'His wife!' " (153). Although Nechkina considers this the least likely explanation, she is nevertheless willing to admit that the crowd would have understood the irony of the remark. And, of course, they would have, for they appreciated intuitively the carnival spirit that infused the events of the mass spectacle on December 14.

When the tsar was cursed and the metropolitan scolded, the crowd laughed. Violence was also accompanied by laughter. On the morning of the revolt, when Bestuzhev attempted to incite the Moscow Regiment, the occasion was marked by the day's first bloodshed and laughter:

On December 14, 1825, early in the morning, Mikhail and Alexander Bestuzhev succeeded in inciting a battalion of the Moskovsky regiment to rebel. After informing them of the request to take the oath to Nicholas they added: "All this is a lie; we are compelled to take the oath by force; Emperor Constantine Pavlovich has not abdicated the throne, but is in chains," and they therefore advised the soldiers not to take the oath until Constantine in person requested them to do so. Alexander Bestuzhev told the soldiers that Constantine intended to lower the term of military service and raise their pay. The soldiers unanimously shouted, "We want no Nicholas—Hurrah! Constantine!" and agreed to join the rebellion. (Mazour, 169)

Mazour misses an important feature of the morning's activities when he states that "some of the officers who showed resistance were beaten and several of them seriously wounded," for the fact of violence, significant in its own right, is met by what, without the perspective of carnival, would otherwise be inexplicable—laughter.

Nechkina presents a clearer picture of what transpired once the battalion had decided to follow Bestuzhev. As he led the troops from their barracks, Generals Shenshin and Frederiks tried to turn them back:

"Stand aside, general!" Alexander Bestuzhev shouted, aiming a pistol at Frederiks. [The pistol misfired.] Several soldiers cried from behind him, "Stand aside or we'll kill you!" At this moment Prince Shchepin-Rostovsky, a captain in the regiment, drew his saber and with one blow knocked Frederiks off his feet. . . . Brigadier Commander Shenshin, taking his turn in attempting to keep the troops from leaving the barracks, was knocked to the ground by a blow from Shchepin-Rostovsky, who then proceeded to deliver him several saber wounds. Then he wounded with three saber thrusts Lieutenant Khvoshchinsky, who also attempted to interfere with the soldiers' exit. Leaning upon Shchepin-Rostovsky with upraised hands [in submission], Lieutenant Khvoshchinsky elicited the laughter of the soldiers. (Nechkina, 74)[27]

27. Nechkina's account exaggerates Bestuzhev's violence, thereby participating in the mythologization of Bestuzhev's role in the revolt.

Frightening scenes of violence and laughter within the rebel and loyalist groups were matched by burlesque stage comedies in the vicinity of
Senate Square. An example of low comedy appeared when the traitor
Yakubovich told Nicholas I that the insurgents refused to acknowledge
him as tsar:

> Nicholas I commanded Yakubovich to inform the insurgents that
> Constantine had forsaken the throne "freely several years ear-
> lier." Yakubovich . . . refused to take the message to the rebels,
> fearing for his life, then reconsidered, only to have Nicholas direct
> Durnovo to perform the service. Durnovo quite picturesquely
> describes how he "fulfilled" his mission: "Having crossed myself,
> I set out toward the rebels. I opened my mouth to speak when one
> of their commanders shouted to me that I should get out of there
> or else he would order that I be shot. And then he in fact com-
> manded two soldiers to hoist me on their bayonets. But I was
> faster than these rogues and with all my might I managed to run
> back to our side. I really overcame a great personal danger, for
> the two soldiers ran after me quite a ways. But they couldn't catch
> me." (Nechkina, 90)

In another comic scene, Nicholas I had his family escorted in the nick
of time from the Winter Palace to Tsarskoe Selo. The Grenadier Guards
had been sent to the palace to capture the family and had arrived minutes too late at the unguarded (!) gate. Seeing their plans foiled, they
rushed to join the rebels on Senate Square. Without recognizing him,
they ran toward Nicholas I, a frightful moment for the new tsar to be
sure. He cried, "Halt!" to which they responded, "We are for Constantine!" "Because they did not recognize their new emperor, the rebel
Grenadier Guards, who a few moments before had been foiled in their
efforts to seize the Imperial Family, marched directly past the young ruler
whom they were hoping to overthrow. Had but one soldier recognized
him, Nicholas would have fallen into the hands of the insurgents" (Lincoln, 43).

Enthronement rituals can be viewed within a society as renewal rites
in which the sins of mankind, once vested in the former king and now
transferred to the new king, are cleansed. Girard finds that such rituals
"are accompanied by mock combats between two factions . . . sometimes enlisting the participation of the whole community" (109). The

Decembrists hoped for success, but Ryleyev announced on the eve of the revolt, "I foresee that there will be no success, but an upheaval is necessary, for it will awaken Russia, and we with our failure will teach others" (Mazour, 154). In many respects, the combat on Senate Square may be seen as a mock combat, for the rebels stood throughout the day in an aggressive military formation, but they did not attack. It was a *show* of confrontation. The violence of regicide was reduced to an idea and enacted as a miniature tableau of conflict. Like Ryleyev's pronouncement, the Grenadier Guards running past the tsar is symbolic of the ritual nature of the event.

The tsar's forces were not well prepared for the day's events, suggesting, too, the ritual nature of the pageant:

> Nicholas . . . resolved that decisive measures must be taken. He ordered first a cavalry attack against the insurgents. The Horse Guards, resplendent in their red-collared white uniforms, their brass helmets glinting dully under the darkening winter sky, attacked in squadrons against the massed rebel force, but because their horses were not properly shod for attacks over icy pavements, they were unable to gain the momentum necessary for a charge, and slid rather than galloped toward their objective. . . . As Nicholas later recalled, "they could accomplish nothing because of the confined space, the icy pavement and, in particular, because they did not have sharpened sabers." Indeed, because they were more prepared for parades than for combat, all the cavalry that day answered the Emperor's summons with unsharpened parade-ground sabers. (Lincoln, 44–45)

The rank and file maintained the carnival dissolution of distinctions as well. Many of the loyalist troops maintained an ambivalent position vis-à-vis the rebellion, and consequently ignored differences separating them from their rebel brothers. One of the Decembrists recounts the following illustrative scene:

> On December 13 . . . [Alexander] Bestuzhev and Ryleyev informed me about their planned revolt and ordered me to observe the movements of the Grenadier Guards Regiment. . . . As a consequence on the following day I visited the Cavalry Artillery in the morning where Lukin told me that his officers had agreed to hand in their

sabers so that they could not be forced to move against the insurgents, whom they considered defenders of the former oath [to
Constantine]. Then, passing yet another regiment I met Muraviev
(Alexander Muraviev, younger brother to Nikita Muraviev, a member of the Society), who told me that his regiment would swear an
oath [to Nicholas], but that they would not fire at the insurgents.
(Gordin, 185)

The rebel soldiers refused to fire at their brother loyalists, choosing
instead to fire throughout the day into the air or at the highest representatives of the government sent to negotiate with them. Fluid relations
defied class distinctions, brought opposing groups together, and fed the
mass confusion.

It would be impossible to argue that any of these carnivalistic events
happened at a conscious level. Rather, ancient traditions were visited
upon the populace and the major figures of the revolt on December 14 as
an unfolding of historical destiny. On the fusion of the historical and the
ritualistic, Girard writes that in modern representations of ancient rituals, "in a conflict whose course is no longer strictly regulated by a
predetermined model, the ritualistic elements disintegrate into actual
events and it becomes impossible to distinguish history from ritual"
(109–10). In the aftermath of the insurrection the role of antisovereign
was played out by a number of pretenders among the Decembrists. The
intensity of the competition superseded the clashes of literary polemics
and confrontations on the field of honor. Ultimate power over society
constituted the final grounds for testing one's strength, one's fate, and
one's identity.

Ryleyev seems to have participated in the revolt in some degree of
consciousness of the roles appropriate for the carnival occasion. When
Nicholas Bestuzhev came to Ryleyev early on the morning of the revolt,
he found him preparing to dress in a costume. Ryleyev's carnival gesture
fused historical and ritual forces:

Ryleev was planning to dress in peasant's costume with a knapsack on his back and a rifle in his hand, to symbolize the union
between the soldier and the peasant "in the first act of their
mutual liberty." [Nicholas] Bestuzhev objected to this masquerade; he considered it dangerous because the Russian soldier did
not understand "these delicacies of patriotism," and besides, he

felt that the time for the National Guard had not yet arrived in Russia. Ryleev agreed that it was too "romantic" and determined to proceed with his plans without putting on any kind of "make-up." (Mazour, 169)[28]

The dualism within the Secret Society is once again apparent in this episode. Ryleyev saw his action in literary terms, staging and costuming it to symbolize political categories, and Nicholas Bestuzhev viewed it in concrete terms in which the event represents itself without any mediation. The rationalist rejected the carnival spirit, the romantic embraced it, but both perforce lived it on December 14.

Ryleyev could not free himself from the literary aspect of his conception. Reality prepared for him dramatic scenes in which he was entirely willing to perform:

As [Ryleyev] started to leave, [his] wife seized Bestuzhev by the arm and commenced imploring him with tears in her eyes to leave her husband alone for she felt he was going to his doom. Both men endeavored to persuade her that there was no danger involved in the undertaking, but she refused to listen. The tragic moment was heightened by the appearance of Ryleyev's six-year-old daughter, Nastenka. In despair Madame Ryleyev shouted to her daughter at the top of her voice: "Nastenka, beg your father for yourself and my own sake." The little girl embraced her father's knees, pleading with him not to go, and the mother completely collapsed. Ryleyev placed her on the divan, tore himself away from his daughter, and ran out toward the Square. Here Nicholas Bestuzhev soon appeared leading the Marine Guard, and Ryleyev joined the rebels. He greeted his colleagues and in a dramatic tone proclaimed the beginning of freedom for which he was willing to give his life. (Mazour, 170)

This account is given by Nicholas Bestuzhev and has subsequently entered into the lore concerning Ryleyev's sacrifice to the cause. This fusion of literature and life must have impressed the romantic Alexander Bestuzhev. He also participated in the revolt as a literary phenomenon,

28. Küchelbecker wore a dashing costume in keeping with his own idea of the revolt and his part in it.

with his "saber in one hand, and pipe in another." He also wore his parade coat and highly polished hussar boots (inappropriate for the occasion or the uniform) and, making a display of himself, continually inspected the troops he had set in line before the gathering crowd of onlookers (Gordin, 179). Bestuzhev hoped to conquer his fear of death in this drama by facing it directly.

Not only Yakubovich and Trubetskoy, but many other military/ literary figures disappeared that day. Colonel Bulatov, a right-hand man to Trubetskoy, turned back from Senate Square when he saw it was only half-occupied by the rebels. Then he took the oath of allegiance to Nicholas and surrendered himself to the authorities with a confession of his part in the conspiracy. "On January 18, 1826, after being arrested and questioned a few times, he committed suicide by smashing his head on the cold walls of the fortress" (Mazour, 171). December 14 and its aftermath might appear a mockery of the heroic cause the Secret Society served, but only if we refuse to accept the carnival impulse at root in the affair and the dramatic ritual at the core of the succession.

Senate Square remained a static site for most of the day as rebel and loyal armies confronted each other. Without leadership, the Decembrists did not know what to do, although their mere presence fulfilled the rules of the ritual they were enacting. Command of the insurgents was offered to several capable men, including Nicholas Bestuzhev, who refused for lack of expertise and experience. Prince Obolensky assumed the role, but in the confusion he served only passively. The tsar's loyalists and a growing crowd of spectators gathered about the rebels. In the bitter cold, opposing forces faced each other hour upon hour.

Those imbued most with the spirit of literary heroism were on Senate Square and acted in accordance with the model they felt obliged to enact. On this day their behavior was consistent. Bestuzhev had his first opportunity to prove himself in the face of death. It was paramount for him to realize his heroic persona, for his whole idea of self, imagined in his writing, rested on it. What Bestuzhev could not anticipate was his participation in a carnival pageant with its foregone conclusion— legitimate succession to the throne. Because Bestuzhev was implicated in a drama where his success at the conscious level (in confronting death) would be matched by failure at an unconscious level (the insufficiency of heroism to control reality), he could not foresee that the most profound test of his heroic persona remained ahead of him in the aftermath of the revolt. Again and again Bestuzhev would have to test his actions against a new, emergent set of words extracted from him in the stressful circumstances of incarceration, isolation, interrogation, and the threat of torture. Although steadfast on December 14, Bestuzhev would find these conditions extremely difficult to handle. The notion that he might gauge himself against his persona on December 14 was soon shattered. He could perform heroic acts, defy power, stand up to a hailstorm of bullets with his chest forward against the enemy guns, but the following six months forced him to recognize that he could not sustain the effort. He reversed his heroic stance, declaring himself a criminal to Nicholas I and promising to make amends by giving frank testimony and full cooperation.

The ritual of renewal required a final act. The carnival, which celebrates the mysterious forces of life and death, must close dramatically. Out of the ritual there is delivered up to the populace a once impure, but now wholly cleansed ruler absolute in his power. This is precisely that kind of ruler Nicholas turned out to be, as though his intense fears and deep insecurities during the interregnum were released through the ritual application of violence so that a superhuman force might be rendered out of a mere man, a tsar out of an unprepared and ill-educated pretender to the throne. In Girard's terms, "The ceremony unleashes an increasing exaltation, a dynamism that draws its energy from the very forces it puts into play; forces that initially seem to claim the king as their victim but from which he eventually emerges as the absolute ruler. . . . He brings down the curtain of blood which finishes the event" (111).

With the news that some of the loyal troops surrounding the rebels on the square might defect to their side at nightfall, Nicholas I attempted a cavalry charge. The mob became more daring as the sun inclined toward the horizon.

> Nicholas who himself was on Senate Square [as required by the rules of enthronement ritual] saw that the increasing hostility [of the crowd] was likely to become serious. The growing mass was openly against him, and many people asked the officers to hold on for an hour or so and everything would go well. Some even dared to throw firewood which the mob had found piled nearby. Bullets were showered, though none hurt the Emperor. Later, in recalling to Prince Eugene, of Wurtemberg [Bestuzhev's own Wurtemberg], the sad experience of that day, [Nicholas I] said:

"What seems to be most inconceivable in this story is the fact that both of us were not shot down." (Mazour, 178)

As night fell (about mid afternoon that day), Nicholas forced the engagement toward the final act Girard describes. Under the advice of his generals, and to "save the Empire," he gave the command to open cannon fire on the rebels and crowd.

In primitive rituals of enthronement, this climactic moment is usually very stylized, with the king emerging from his enclosure to hurl projectiles at the enemy forces, after which they disband entirely defeated (Girard, 111). Nicholas's cannon shot disbanded the insurgents, killing many of them as well as several observers. But in the aftermath of the revolt, cannon fire was exchanged for accusations and verbal abuse hurled at the rebels (from the Winter Palace) in order to strike down the guilty for inflicting this rite of passage on Nicholas I. Prince Wurtemberg wrote in retrospect that Nicholas was a veritable Caesar by the conclusion of the revolt.[29] The carnival had worked its magic.

"In the spirit of purification which pervades all the important stages of the ceremony" (Girard, 111), Nicholas I ordered all evidence of the day's violence removed from Senate Square and its environs by morning. The stones of the streets adjacent to the square, the square itself, and the surrounding building facades marked by shot were cleansed of blood and repaired. Bodies were slipped through holes cut in the ice of the Neva, some alive as well as dead, it was rumored. The man who perpetrated this gruesome act, Alexander Shulgin, St. Petersburg's chief of police, was later discharged for not understanding the delicacy of Nicholas's constitution, but he knew how to deal with the cleansing ritual in symbolic as well as practical terms. In primitive societies the effects of ritual enthronement can be set aside as the new year blossoms into spring, but in Russia the effects of the revolt could not be so quickly erased. Bodies bobbed to the surface at the spring thaw, and the investigation of the rebels continued well into the summer, when five more bodies were produced from the scaffold.

With the failure of the insurrection, all power was firmly held in the hands of Tsar Nicholas I, a clever and cruel man. He was a man "seething with passions, especially with rage and with fear, but also [visible in

29. B. E. Syrochkovskii, *Mezhdutsarstvie 1825 goda i vosstanie dekabristov v perepiske i memuarakh chlenov tsarskoi sem'i* (Moscow, 1926), 119.

the] kind of exultation . . . he felt [when] he was striking telling blows against [his] enemy" (Riasanovsky, 7). "Relentless harshness became the outstanding characteristic of his reign" (13). Nicholas's subsequent role during the investigation of the rebels arose out of a confluence of ritual and historical forces. In Girard's assessment, "At first almost sacrificed himself, the king then presides at rites which show him to be the sacrificer *par excellence*" (111). During the first day after the revolt, Nicholas played a dominant role in interviewing and interrogating the prisoners. Seeing that he was too personally involved (something unbecoming a ruler), he appointed an Investigating Commission to pursue the matter and to determine the extent of the conspiracy in Russia and the degree of guilt of each participant in the revolt.

Despite his attempt to extract himself from the proceedings, Nicholas's hand can be seen in all the interrogations, including the physical and psychological tortures, which delivered up to the Commission a remarkably complete picture of the conspiracy. From this information, punishments (ranging from drawing and quartering to five years exile in the Caucasus) were fixed. Nicholas I knew the Decembrists professionally as well as socially. He decided each man's fate in accordance with the individual's personality.[30] As Nicholas Riasanovsky asserts in his study of Nicholas I, the tsar's aesthetics inclined toward symmetry and precision, and fitting the punishment to the crime was ultimate in "the regularity of design." Nicholas sent five men to the gallows, including Kondraty Ryleyev (21). Although Ryleyev seems to have been proud to claim the honor of political martyr,[31] it was Bestuzhev's testimony that sealed his comrade's fate. Bestuzhev's behavior after December 14 besmirched his name, if not immediately before conspirators and loyalists alike, then to posterity and to himself. Ten days after the revolt Alexan-

---

30. Nicholas I showed a brilliant understanding of the men he confronted after the revolt. He knew whom to frighten (e.g., Bestuzhev), whom to tearfully swear undying love and devotion, and whom to flatter. He understood Bestuzhev perfectly as a conflicted persona and personality. He observed Bestuzhev's dandy dress and his acting the role of smiling penitent with complete understanding, consigned him to the category of frivolous gentleman and then dealt with him summarily as someone who would confess all to save his own neck.

31. The others were Pavel Pestel, Mikhail Bestuzhev-Riumin (a relative of the Bestuzhev family), Peter Kakhovsky, and Sergei Murav'ev-Apostol. Ryleyev announced to the Investigation Committee in April 1825: "If an execution is needed for the good of Russia, I am the only one who deserves it. I have long prayed that it will all stop at me and that others will be returned by God's mercy to their families, their fatherland, and their noble tsar." Cited in Patrick O'Meara, *K. F. Ryleev* (Princeton, N.J., 1984), 276.

der Izmailov, minor fabulist and president of the Free Society of Lovers of Literature, Sciences, and the Arts (Vol'noe obshchestvo liubitelei slovesnosti, nauk i khudozhestv), wrote to a friend about events surrounding the revolt: "And on the next day [after the insurgency], imagine my surprise, I hear that the ringleader of the rebels was . . . guess who . . . that loudmouth Aleksasha Bestuzhev. Calling himself an adjutant to the Great Prince [Würtemberg], he deceived two battalions of the Moscow Regiment and brought them out to Senate Square with a saber in one hand and a pipe in the other!" (Oksman, *Dekabristy*, 239–40).

Deceit and treason were more than enough for Bestuzhev to bear, but burdensome too was the low opinion others would have of him for his failure to realize the image of self he had actively created. Under the weight of a potential public shame, it became crucial for him to develop a means of atoning for his sin and renewing himself before his audience. There could be no atonement, however, without an appropriate punishment, which Tsar Nicholas I readily supplied.

On the morning following the revolt, Bestuzhev dressed up like a dandy and presented himself at the Winter Palace for arrest. He was initially sentenced, after six months interrogation, to beheading. Because of his willingness to cooperate with the Investigating Commission this punishment was mercifully commuted to a loss of noble rank, hard labor for twenty years in Siberia, and permanent exile. Later, the twenty-year sentence was reduced to fifteen (Ovsiannikova, 434). Nicholas I fused literature and life in his own way for Bestuzhev, forming an aesthetics of punishment with a personal touch, an art he perfected during his reign.[32] The specific nature of Bestuzhev's exile could hardly be considered coincidental: Nicholas fashioned it from Ryleyev's "Voinarovsky."

Crucial to Bestuzhev's resurrection in society as a heroic persona was his experience of death and rebirth through the agency of interrogation, confession, punishment, and the assumption of his pen name Marlinsky. For over half a year of imprisonment in the dreaded Peter and Paul Fortress and months of sporadic interrogation, Bestuzhev alternately donned the carnivalistic masks of hero and traitor. But when his scenery fell and his puppets refused to operate effectively, Bestuzhev swung the jester out from the wings to save the moment through comic improvisation.

---

32. In 1849 Nicholas I staged the mock execution of members of the Petrashevsky circle, including Dostoyevsky.

7

Incarceration

Not by daring and rash dreams, which are
always destructive, but gradually, and from
above, laws will be issued, defects remedied,
and abuses corrected.
　　　—Nicholas I, Coronation Manifesto

Nicholas and Alexander

When Bestuzhev turned himself in at the Winter Palace the morning after
the revolt, he was dressed for a ball. His interrogation began on December 26, 1825, and continued for approximately six months. There were
periods during this time when he was under intense scrutiny and was
required to meet with the Commission to write long responses to its
questions. On other days he sat and waited in isolation while death
stared at him from the walls of his cold and silent cell. The romantic and
heroic rebel, imprisoned in the winter of 1825, would leave the Peter and
Paul Fortress in the spring of 1826 a traitor, not only to his tsar and
country, but also to his cause. "The Prisoner of Chillon" proffered no
model for Bestuzhev here.

The members of the Commission had to collect and collate complex and contradictory evidence from the Decembrists to discover the extent of the conspiracy, the principal parties involved in the rebellion, and the degree of guilt of each participant. They probed conflicting testimony, examined inconsistencies between individual accounts, and forced prisoners to confront each other when their recollections did not coincide. Bestuzhev suffered through confrontations with the turncoat Yakubovich, the impetuous Kakhovsky who had killed Miloradovich, and his close friend Ryleyev. It was a grueling experience for all the Decembrists, especially as they realized that in the course of their interrogations they were implicating one another in ever more serious crimes. Painfully, they saw how differently each of them viewed the events of December 14 and the preceding days. Bestuzhev, like his fellows, became demoralized as he observed the gradual disintegration of their individual and collective resolution, of their romantically conceived heroic will. After months in prison, a thorough diminution in their health, and doubt about each individual's future, fear and temptation contributed to the phenomenon known as Decembrist confession. The conspirators responded in different ways to the interrogation, but almost everyone eventually confessed the whole plan, implicating themselves and one another in so doing.

Bestuzhev was the first to reveal the entire scope of the conspiracy, including regicide. He wrote a confession, cast in a literary design to be sure, to Nicholas I so that he might explain his behavior. It is clear from evidence within the letter (his response to charges about inflammatory speech) that it was written during the first two months of the investigation. Bestuzhev began with typical ambivalence, on the one hand assenting to the authority of the tsar, but on the other claiming his own authority in explicating "the historical development of free thinking in Russia":

> Your Imperial Highness!
> Convinced that You, Sovereign, love the truth, I dare to lay before You the historical development of free thinking in Russia and in general of many ideas which constitute the moral and political basis of the events of December 14. I speak in full frankness, without concealing evil, without even softening expressions, for the duty of a loyal subject is to tell the Monarch the truth without any embellishment. I commence.[1]

1. Thomas Riha, ed., *Readings in Russian Civilization*, 2:298–99.

Bestuzhev did not present an original exegesis but a document of clichés borrowed from comrades during both casual and formal gatherings of the past two years. Through (or perhaps even despite) the occasional use of marlinisms, he wanted to create a coherent argument by drawing a picture from which the tsar might view his behavior:

> Thinking is like gunpowder, only dangerous when pressed. Many cherished the hope that the Emperor would grant a constitution, as he himself had stated at the opening of the Legislative Assembly in Warsaw, and the attempt of some generals to free their serfs encouraged that sentiment. But after 1817 everything changed. Those who saw evil or who wished improvement, thanks to the mass of spies, were forced to whisper about it, and this was the beginning of the secret societies. . . . Since the grumbling of the people, caused by exhaustion and the abuses of national and civil administrations, threatened bloody revolution, the Societies intended to prevent a greater evil by a lesser one and began their activities at the first opportunity. (Ibid., 299)

Bestuzhev moves on from this dramatic moment in his narrative to a description of the various classes in Russia and how they had become disaffected during the final years of Alexander I's reign. Historical facts confirm in large measure what Bestuzhev had to say. He catalogued abuse of the lower classes by the nobility and landed gentry and discussed graft, privilege, and deceit in the ruling class, citing specific examples from his and his brothers' own experiences. He summarized the many problems of military life:

> The soldiery grumbled wearily over their studies, the many inspections and doubled guard duty; officers complained about the scarcity of assignments and the insufferable harshness [of their daily routine]. Sailors were dissatisfied with their heavy physical labor, which had doubled due to abuses [by government officials]. (For example, in the Petersburg and Krondstadt admiralties ninety horses were assigned to the task of carting logs. . . . Not one horse works in this fashion; all are used to cart various officials off to visit their friends. In their place the poor sailors are harnessed to the task. My brother Nicholas and K. L. Torson can give more detailed information about the great many abuses that

occur in the navy.) Talented people complained that their attempts to make improvements in the civil service were blocked at
every step; instead they were required to display a quiet subservi-
ence. Academicians complained that they were not allowed to
study and learn, and youth that they were not allowed to study. In
a word, from all corners peered dissatisfied faces. Shoulders were
shrugged on all the streets, and everywhere people whispered.
Everyone wondered where it would all lead. All the elements
[working dissatisfaction] were abroad. Only the government care-
lessly drowsed upon this volcano, only the court officials increased their fortunes, for only for them was Russia a promised
land.[2]

He uses metaphors, elliptical constructions, and parallelisms in order to
shape the literary form of this confession. When describing why the
Decembrists took up arms on December 14, Bestuzhev lied:

> You, Emperor, already know how, inflamed by this sorrowful
> state of Russia and seeing all elements prepared for a change, we
> came to the decision to revolt. Now let me dare to elaborate
> before Your Highness that we, in doing this, thought our actions
> founded on the laws of the people. . . . In addition, Batenkov and
> I said that we had at this time (that is, close to December 14), a
> political right [to revolt] based on the fact of the interregnum. For
> Your Highness had refused the crown, and we knew that the
> Grand Duke's abdication was already here. (Our error consisted
> in the fact that we did not know that Your Highness had been
> named the Heir to the throne [in Alexander I's will].) (40)

Justifying his actions on the basis of the historical record, Bestuzhev
recounted those occasions in the eighteenth century when there was a
conflict between the government and the rights of the people. He added,
"We were bound already to our first oath, so a second we could not
take. Your Highness may readily comprehend the incorrectness of this
position [we took], but at that time I was convinced of its propriety and
acted on this presupposition" (ibid., 43).

Bestuzhev then listed twelve goals of the Secret Society pertinent to the

2. A. K. Borozdin, ed., *Iz pisem i pokazanii dekabristov* (St. Petersburg, 1906), 39–40.

composition of the Senate, the creation of a people's house, education and financial reform, land distribution, and the reformation of the courts. Confessing to be a novice in these matters, he referred Nicholas I to Nikita Muraviev's constitution, "which was nothing more than an experiment," in the writing of this genre. He continued to diminish his role: "As pertains to me, other than being an ultra-liberal *in word only to win the trust of my comrades,* I privately inclined toward the Monarchy and the moderate ideas of the aristocracy" (ibid.). He confessed that he had been deceived, falling for the temptations Baten'kov set before him: "Enticing me, Baten'kov said that as a member of the nobility and as a man participating in the overturn of government, I could hope to become a member of the governing aristocracy of the country" (43). He admitted that had the Izmailovsky Regiment joined the insurgents on December 14, he would have taken command and, having a plan already in mind, would have ordered an attack on the loyalist forces.

In an astounding penultimate paragraph, Bestuzhev turned from incriminating himself to analyzing Nicholas I. He marshaled his literary talents in order to bring the tsar into his confidence:

> Your Emperial Highness, let the following confession of how we viewed Your personal character before [December 14] serve as proof of the respect which I have for Your magnanimity. We were quite familiar with the gifts which nature bestowed upon You; we knew that you, Emperor, were engaged in the study of governance and that you read a great deal. . . . The anecdotes which bespeak the harshness of Your Highness frightened many of us. But I must confess that never once did I ever say that the Emperor Nicholas with his mind and strictness would ever become a despot all the more dangerous because his perspicacity threatens all intelligent and well-intentioned people with exile; or that He, being enlightened Himself, would deliver death blows to enlightenment [in Russia]; or that our fate would be decided from the moment He would take the throne, or that consequently we may as well die today as tomorrow. (Ibid., 43–44)

In refuting an accusation leveled at him by another conspirator during the investigation (that he maligned the new tsar), and in a symbolic verbal gesture, Bestuzhev prostrated himself before the tsar who had only recently been sacralized through ritual violence:

Experience has revealed to me my errors, repentance has washed clean my soul, and I am pleased now to be disposed to whatever Providence delivers. . . . From the few signs that have penetrated my dark cell, I doubt not that Your Royal Highness will heal the ills of Russia, will quiet and correct for the better the wandering of misguided minds and thus exalt the Fatherland. I am convinced that the Heavens themselves have bestowed on us through You another Peter the Great, even greater than he, for in our time and with Your gifts, Emperor, to be such as Peter is but a small task. This thought for the time being lessens my sufferings for myself and for my brothers. Prayers dedicated to the happiness of a Fatherland which is not separated from Your Highness's true glory now fly [from my cell] to the throne of You, the Most High.

> Most devoted servant of
> Your Imperial Highness
> Alexander Bestuzhev (44)

In his letter and in his testimony, Bestuzhev revealed a conflict between his personality and his persona, between Bestuzhev and Marlinsky. His bravado paled as he confronted the consequences of his actions. He quieted his liberal goals, confessed his errors, and condemned his intemperate behavior.

Interrogation

The record shows that complete confession was typical. The causes were many. First, neither European literature nor Russian society had created a revolutionary prepared to deal with failure. Bestuzhev wrote, "I sought death during the battle. A bullet pierced my hat one hair from my head. But God preserved me . . . for repentance."[3] Bestuzhev (and other conspirators) held a fatalistic idea about their revolt. Victory would prove them right; defeat would prove them wrong. Second, they carried forthright speech, the code of behavior within the salon and literary circles, into prison. Third, they were disoriented during the inquiry, not only

---

3. A. A. Pokrovskii, ed., *Materialy po istorii vosstaniia dekabristov* (Moscow, 1925), 1:452.

because of their failure and the carnage they had precipitated, but because of their familiarity with the members of the Court who interrogated them. The Decembrists even knew Nicholas I from his days among them as Grand Duke. In this artificial creation of a military club,

> It amused Nicholas I to punish the prisoners by putting them on a diet of bread and water or ordering them to be shackled. He had a vast and instinctive knowledge of how to extract confessions, and he seems to have invented the psychological trick of bringing the prisoners blindfolded into a room filled with junior officers jingling their spurs, joking, and telling stories, behaving exactly as they behaved in their military clubs. At such moments the blindfolded prisoners would feel that they had been suddenly transported into the carefree and innocent past. Then they would be led into a narrow anteroom, the handkerchief would be whipped away from their eyes, and they would find themselves standing at the end of a table covered with a red blaze cloth, facing their accusers. . . . If he refused to confess, he was hurried back to his cell, heavy arm and leg fetters were attached to him, and the prison doctor was ordered to determine how much more torture he could endure. Priests in the pay of the government came to their cells and promised them the comforts of religion if they confessed in secret, and some time later these secret confessions would be read out to them by one of the members of the Secret Committee.[4]

Over twenty Decembrists gave testimony about Bestuzhev's part in the revolt. Nicholas, Mikhail, and Peter Bestuzhev have the least to say about their brother, confessing merely that he was a member of the Secret Society. Ryleyev was equally circumspect about Bestuzhev's activities. Yakubovich, on the other hand, testified extensively to Bestuzhev's involvement in the plot to assassinate the tsar. This charge was the focus of many questions put to Bestuzhev. Attempting to juggle both the demands of his hero persona and his survival instinct, Bestuzhev admitted that he participated in discussions of regicide but never took those discussions seriously.

Like Bestuzhev, most of the improvisational Decembrists submitted to

4. Robert Payne, *The Fortress* (London, 1967), 48–50.

the unconscious forces of the carnival ritual and returned to the hierarchical position suited to their station. These men had the greatest difficulty dealing with the circumstances of incarceration. In his confession to the tsar written twelve days after the revolt, Yakubovich concluded: "You will be the benefactor and savior of the Fatherland from many calamities, and the love of Your grateful fifty-two million subjects will only be the beginning of Your immortal glory."[5] Ryleyev was an exception. He sacrificed himself to the heroic ideal.

A few Decembrists held their ideological ground to the very end, but not many. The rationalist, who was inclined to make both constitutional and tactical plans for the revolt and its aftermath, continued to hold to his political ideas in exile. In prison, for example, Muraviev put the finishing touches on his constitution. It seems the more integrated the psyche of the individual, the more consistent his behavior. Nicholas and Mikhail Bestuzhev had cultivated the qualities that would carry them through such adversity. Vladimir Shteingel also held firm: "No matter how many members there may be found of the Secret Society or those who had only known of it; no matter how many be deprived of freedom on account of it, there still remain a great many people who share those ideas and sentiments. . . . In order to eradicate free thinking, there is no other means than to destroy an entire generation, born and educated in the last reign. But if this is impossible, there remains one thing—to win hearts by kindness and attract minds by decisive and evident means toward the future prosperity of the state" (ibid., 279–80).

Bestuzhev's confession was ambivalent, motivated by both cowardly and selfless impulses. His testimony was frequently inconsistent and fundamentally self-conflicted. At a deep level Bestuzhev was ruled by a fear of death. He spoke openly and freely to preserve his own skin but also to shield his family. Throughout the proceedings he protected his brothers and friends from accusations that might have ensured their deaths, but he condemned his rivals within the Northern Society at every opportunity. He even incriminated his friend Ryleyev. Bestuzhev could not have possibly conformed to his heroic persona less.

Ryleyev accepted primary responsibility for the actions of the conspiratorial group; he was prepared to die for the holy cause. On the eve of the revolt he had pronounced: "I am certain that we shall perish, but the example will remain. Let us sacrifice ourselves for the future freedom of

---

5. Anatole G. Mazour, *The First Russian Revolution, 1825*, 280.

our country!"[6] Although his testimony made no attempt to hide his role in the Society, it is significant that Bestuzhev protected his friend less than his brothers did. In fact Bestuzhev seemed angry with Ryleyev in the aftermath of the revolt for having enticed him and his brothers into the Society (437, 440, 446). He was unhappy with himself for having allowed his younger brother Peter into the fray: "[Peter] was so young that he did not know what he was doing. For him and my brother Mikhail I am answerable to God and the Emperor. I am guilty for their behavior. [Peter] never was at a council meeting, knew little and knew even fewer members" (447). In fact, young Peter only became aware of the revolt on its eve, when he observed his brothers loading their pistols.

Bestuzhev's January 27, 1826, account implicated Ryleyev in every stage of the conspiracy. Patrick O'Meara, Ryleyev's biographer, does not fault Bestuzhev for this, concentrating instead on the vicious and damning testimony given by Kakhovskoy. But Bestuzhev wrote about Ryleyev:

> [He was] one of the most zealous members of the Society, a man who lives completely by imagination. But other than his liberalism, which constituted, so to speak, the center of his madness, he was of the purest moral character. He believed that if a man, convinced of the rightness of his deed, acts not for himself but for the common good, then Providence will guide him. This opinion was shared by many of us. Although he was [!] my best friend, for the sake of the truth I cannot hide that he was the mainspring of the undertaking [the revolt]. He inflamed everyone with his poetic imagination and shored us up with his persistence. . . . He often chided me for my laziness and indifference to the Society. I responded that I was conserving my energies for action. (Ibid., 444)

Bestuzhev played up his innocence against Ryleyev's guilt. Here Bestuzhev's conviction that the imagination can create the image and stuff of real life fell under critical scrutiny, but only in relation to Ryleyev, to whom he imputes the belief. Still no reflection, just self projection.

In his testimony to the Investigating Commission on December 26, Bestuzhev gave a brief account of his participation in the Secret Society. When the Commission asked him what propelled him to join, he re-

6. Cited in Patrick O'Meara, *K. F. Ryleev*, 233.

sponded, "Upon entering the Society by dint of youthful delusion and wild imagination, I thought that it would be possible to perform a service to the homeland through [the Society] at some future time, if not by deed, then by broadcasting liberal ideas. The enticements of something new and secretive also played more than a small part [in my decision to join] and little by little criminal thoughts enticed me" (Pokrovskii, 1:431).

On December 27 Bestuzhev gave an extensive account of the Society and the revolt. His testimony, volunteered while he still had his wits about him,[7] reveals the desire to ingratiate himself. Bestuzhev lied feebly, claiming the revolt "was a chance occurrence . . . and was produced by circumstances and not by prior planning" (433). In his testimony there are many such attempts to obfuscate the truth to seduce the Commission into believing his claims of loyalty. This confession is literary—yet another Bestuzhevan frame narrative in which he shaped the apprehension of his Marlinsky image:

> From age nineteen I began to read liberal books, and this turned my head. At the age of twenty-two when I was promoted to adjutant to General Betancourt, I had no constructive idea [about what to do with my liberal ideas], and like all young men [of my age] I cried into the wind without any purpose. Then I met Ryleyev, and since he and I sometimes returned together from meetings of the Society "The Advocate of Enlightenment and General Welfare" [Sorevnovatel' Prosveshcheniia i Blagotvoreniia] we dreamed together. With his ardent imagination he enticed me more and more. (433)[8]

The Commission questioned Bestuzhev's election into the *Duma*, especially in the face of his claim that he was not deeply committed to the aims of the Society. Bestuzhev lied:

7. After five months of incarceration, Bestuzhev admitted being unable to remember exact times, dates, people and plans (Pokrovskii, 1:458). The causes of his memory loss were not purely physical. An anxiety which lay at the foundation of his identity was brought to the surface—the fear of death. He was hard pressed to discover which of his multiple roles he should play in these (for him) extraliterary circumstances. Only his pen permitted him the literariness that shaped his responses.

8. Bestuzhev cites the name of the Society's publication; the society was called Vol'noe obshchestvo liubitelei literatury (The Free Society of Lovers of Literature).

Then in April, I think, Ryleyev told me that I was elected to the *Duma*. I received this news rather indifferently, and up until September I never met with its other members in session, except in one instance when I was called to Obolensky's to hear part of Nikita Muraviev's constitution about land reform. This was the one time I was in fact in the so-called *Duma,* and there I became thoroughly convinced of the Society's vacuousness. I decided to continue my acquaintance with them as a kind of game. Furthermore, since I had long wished to travel to Moscow for the winter . . . I thought this a good excuse to distance myself from the Society and from there I could engage in travels for a year or two. (Ibid., 433–34)

Bestuzhev's journey to Moscow at this time was to participate in conspiratorial matters, not to fly from them.

In the same account, Bestuzhev disclosed Decembrist plans of regicide. Describing the social round in Moscow (balls, theater, aimlessness) and his meetings with Yakubovich, Bestuzhev suddenly informed the Commission that for personal revenge Yakubovich wanted to assassinate the tsar. Bestuzhev also confessed that the Secret Society concurred. This tactical mistake had severe consequences, particularly for Ryleyev, but Bestuzhev's information was later rewarded by the tsar. "We three [Bestuzhev, Ryleyev, and Odoyevsky] began to get to know Yakubovich better. He confessed to us that he had come to Petersburg with the unalterable intention of killing the emperor out of the need to avenge himself. 'I do not want to belong to any Society,' he said, because he did not want to dance to anyone else's tune. 'I will do what I must, and you can use it however you want. And if you can rouse the soldiery after the deed, then I will unfurl the banner of freedom and sacrifice myself. I have grown weary of life.' This sudden pronouncement shocked us" (ibid., 434). Bestuzhev quoted Yakubovich in direct speech. This literary device allowed Bestuzhev to distance himself from it, but it also enabled him to engage in the rhetorical bombastics of the warrior-poet. Building the drama of his account in this fashion, Bestuzhev could play up his and Ryleyev's heroic role—dissuading Yakubovich: "As his best and oldest friend, I managed to convince him to set his plan aside" (434).[9] In the Commission's summary of Bestuzhev's first month of testimony, they concluded that he had been responsible for thwarting the plans of regicide.

9. Bestuzhev would repeat this technique again in reference to Kakhovskoy.

Throughout the ordeal, Bestuzhev obscured his part in the discussions of regicide: "Then the question was considered [in the *Duma*] about what to do if the emperor [Alexander I] refused to agree to a constitution. Since Spain had already proven that the emperor's opinion on the matter is not necessary, Ryleyev told me that the Southern Society rejected the monarchy. The [Spanish] option was adopted by us as well, and with this decision came the plan to eliminate the emperor if the opportunity were to arise. I should mention that [by this time] I had become more experienced and had begun to cool toward the society" (Pokrovskii, 433). There is little evidence to support Bestuzhev's argument. In fact, as the time approached for action, he was all the more involved in the decision-making processes of the *Duma*. Anticipating a question about his remaining in an organization in whose aims he was no longer interested, Bestuzhev went on to say, "I observed at first hand the impossibility of accomplishing this task and my distrust in the conspirators [grew during our meetings], which then convinced me of the madness of the plan. Nevertheless I remained among them as before, for I did not want to bear their scorn, which at that time appeared more dangerous to me than the far off deed [regicide] itself" (433). As he hid the nature of his involvement in the assassination plots, he revealed a powerful motive operating in his life—the desire to be accepted, the need to have his persona confirmed by the group.

There was a price to pay for Bestuzhev's depiction of himself as patriot among conspirators. While partially revealing the truth about the conspiracy (to diminish his role in it), he was forced to present an image of himself which was not in keeping with his heroic persona. He depicted himself as something of a buffoon, a jester who engages in empty speech:

> Obolensky and Ryleyev said . . . that it was necessary to eliminate the whole [royal] family. I don't know what their reason was, but it seemed [they reasoned that the destruction of the tsar's family] would eliminate the possibility of a royalist counterinsurgency. I adhered to this plan for I knew that you might find one assassin, but not enough [to murder the entire royal family]. . . . I was convinced that it would be impossible to find such people. Yakubovich and I insisted that no less than ten [assassins] would be required [for the job], and thus by this colossal figure the blow to the Sacred Head was avoided. In a word, I made a loud noise [*ia byl krikun*], but I was not a villain. (Ibid., 435)

Bestuzhev's representation of himself as an activist in word but not in deed severed the linkage he proclaimed in his pre-Decembrist fiction and criticism. The incantational effect of language to influence reality proved to be illusory and thus redoubled Bestuzhev's crisis of identity, forcing him to confront the vacuousness of a word-generated persona.

After the revolt, Bestuzhev was forced to reassess the relationship between rhetoric and action, between literary persona and actual identity. If he now claimed "[Plans of regicide] were simply empty bravado, and when the issue came to action, our plans changed entirely" (ibid., 457), what was the connection between word and deed? Bestuzhev was forced to examine that relationship when the committee requested an explanation of his cry for the elimination of the monarchy: "I repeat that it was surely some sort of bravado which brought such evil thoughts to my mind. For example, before many other comrades I once entered Ryleyev's study and while stepping through the door I announced with a laugh, 'I am crossing the Rubicon, for Rubicon means *rubi kon,* that is, anything that might happen.' But in no way did I have in mind regicide in so speaking" (451). Bestuzhev's attempt to obfuscate the remark (which made specific reference to revolutionary figures of ancient Rome) is entirely unconvincing. He tried here to reinterpret a typical Marlinskian romantic gesture, played to the crowd for its immediate approval, and consequently negated himself: "On the question of parricide [!] and the removal of the reigning family, [Ryleyev] always was of the notion to leave Constantine in peace so that the new government would not be divided into factions threatened from abroad. It is evident from this what childish calculations we made" (444). "The Society had great plans and no means [to effect them]. It consisted for the most part of young people with a fiery imagination and no maturity of mind" (442). In short, Bestuzhev approaches self-knowledge momentarily, then veers away by referring to the behavior of the group.

With the diminution of the heroic persona and the severing of word and deed, word play, puns, and figures of speech were altered and moved from strict literary parameters toward a whole new configuration. In effect, during the investigation Bestuzhev was held accountable for frivolous speech, cleverness, and the propensity to play the wit and jester in serious circumstances. Bestuzhev was required, then, not only to question the nature of his heroic self-image, but to examine the consequences of his discourse. As Bestuzhev utilized the marlinism both to repress personal guilt and to obscure his part in the conspiracy, the literary techniques became a repository of the unconscious, expressing in a symbolic language the content he wished to hide. Bestuzhev directly expressed his deficiencies with a rhetorical flourish: "Long live [Tsar Alexander I's] memory. I saw little [in the Secret Society] of substance, and only dreamed how to remain true to my word while turning away from complicity in the Society's criminal intent. Enticed by my imagination, by my rhetoric, which worked on my impressionable mind, I was separated from my heart" (ibid., 435). In a reflective mood perhaps for the first time in his life, Bestuzhev delivered an image of himself as a weak and impressionable person, very different from the persona he had projected throughout his youth and early adulthood. Bestuzhev himself may not have fully appreciated the division of mind and heart (persona versus self) he confessed to the Commission.

Bestuzhev used rhetorical tricks to deflect his readers (on the Investigating Commission) from the matter at hand. When asked to describe how one of the officers of the Moscow Regiment was injured, Bestuzhev was hard pressed to absolve himself of guilt. Consequently, he used "marlinist" figures of speech and sound play to reduce the impact of the content: "In response to Captain Shchepin-Rostovsky to the effect that I cut Lieutenant Khvoshchinsky [with my sword], I refer to private Kolokolnikov who carried my Cherkes sword (sabre), which I only strapped on when the Cavalry Guard fell upon us [on Senate Square late in the day] and not earlier. Up until that time only a dress blade did I carry, and such a delicate one, like a gesture [kak zhest], and by which it would neither have been possible to cut or gut a man [i kotoroiu ne tol'ko rubit' no dazhe i ushibit' nevozmozhno] (ibid., 450). Assuaging his guilt on another occasion, Bestuzhev concluded his report with a grand verbal outpouring: "My heart overflows with blood when I consider that fate ordained I play the role of enticer to my friends and brothers whom I love more than myself. But God is my witness that faintheartedness does not control my quill. Having mistaken errant ways for truth, I have brought many to their deaths. What shall I not do now to serve truth?" (448).

Under the duress of the investigation, the archetypal figures of Bestuzhev's earliest drama and fiction gradually emerged. Hero and warrior were replaced by braggart, jester, and traitor:

My complete disenchantment with the means of the Society when I saw the workings of its supreme *Duma* was the cause of my inactivity in regard to details [pertinent to the conspiracy] and my incompetence on many matters put in my hands. Everything seemed to me to be undeserving of my attention, so much so in fact that Ryleyev and Obolensky more than once argued with me that I joked too much and made puns all the time while they were discussing serious matters. They called me a braggart and said that I would exchange the constitution [they planned to invoke] for a promotion in the service. I responded that they were dreamers and that I was a soldier born to act, not to think. (Ibid., 435)

The roles compounded themselves, twisting on one another in a manner that defied the simplistic conscious definitions Bestuzhev had given them in his fiction. The investigation brought to the surface the content of the unconscious Bestuzhev had not been willing to acknowledge. Bestuzhev's confession is remarkable for its directness in depicting himself in less than flattering terms. The heroic persona is rendered a villain and traitor. The jester mediates the two images, using figures of speech, puns, and word play to lend the confession of crimes a jocular air.

The young and successful author readily sensed what his interlocutor wanted to hear from him and appealed to categories that might prove ingratiating. His repentance was dramatic and timed to come only at the final moment, when he felt sure that he had created an image of an utterly loyal and contrite servant who was no longer led astray by imagination, romantic dreaming, the enticements of fame and power, or the beguiling voice of people like Ryleyev. He appealed to patriotism: loyalty to the homeland, the tsar, and the Romanov family; devotion to the Church, to God, and to the people. He asserted that he was a misled patriot who had attempted to serve his homeland through a revolutionary zeal that proved callow (ibid., 433–34, 437). Not infrequently Bestuzhev linked the tsar to God, the government to the Church, fusing distinct phenomena commonly united in the popular mind. Bestuzhev subordinated himself to each:

When I was going to the Moscow Regiment [the morning of December 14] I prayed to God with fervent tears "if our task is just, then aid us, and if not, then Thy will be done." I now know his will—and both God's accusing finger and the tsar's anger are directed at me. . . . I now feel that I have used my gifts to an evil end, but I could bring honor to my fatherland by sword or by pen—[I could, if allowed,] live usefully and die honorably for the emperor! But the tsar is God's law on this earth. God forgives the repentant. . . . If by chance this paper falls into his Highness' hands, then let him see on it the tears of one who deserves his punishment, the tears of true repentance. (437)

Soldiery and writing ("sword and pen") were indeed the two forms his punishment took, thanks to the tsar.

Within days after this testimony, the Commission went back to Bestuzhev with additional questions concerning his incitement of the Moscow Regiment, the violence inflicted on the officers who had resisted his insurgent plans, the identity of the one who shot Miloradovich, and Küchelbecker's complicity in the crime. Bestuzhev's response was in keeping with the secret carnival heart of the revolt. He confessed that he indeed had held the pistol in question and that while addressing the Moscow Regiment, he had threatened General Mayor Frederiks and Captain Muller with it: "But in order that the pistol would not fire by accident, I had uncocked it and had done so in such a manner that it could not be fired, I think, later on" (ibid., 438). At the barracks of the Moscow Regiment, Bestuzhev claimed that he "fired at no one . . . and gave the pistol back to Prince Shchepin, who then, it seems, passed it on to a soldier to carry unloaded" (438). Then Bestuzhev transformed the discussion into another form of discourse, describing Küchelbecker's role from a comic perspective, deflating the horrific import of violence through the injection of sarcastic laughter: "The Collegiate Assessor Küchelbecker did not belong to our Society, at least not until the eve of the revolt. I think this was because we always thought him crazy" (438). Bestuzhev slipped into the easy banter of society and the comfortable chatter of the salon where literary enemies were the constant target of one's wit. Confession became club chat filled with cleverness and condescension toward the civil servant.

While aiming his barbs at Küchelbecker, Bestuzhev unwittingly implicated himself in the comedy: "He walked about [Senate Square] with a pistol and I recall that when I ordered 'Shoulder arms!' he repeated the same command after me. So I told him not to interfere, that no one would obey him [a civilian]. Then, because he is so nearsighted and hard-of-hearing, he asked me if I knew where Grand Prince Mikhail Pavlovich was located. Whatever became of [Küchelbecker], I don't know" (ibid., 438). Küchelbecker parodied Bestuzhev's serious, official demeanor, repeating his commands like a parrot. When Bestuzhev found it necessary to explain his role to Küchelbecker, he enacted a burlesque. The parting jab about nearsightedness and Küchelbecker's hearing defect served no point in the official proceedings. It reveals Bestuzhev's attempt to move the occasion into a behavioral setting familiar in society. The dormant content of his self-understanding escaped his control and removed his heroic mask.

In January Bestuzhev could state clearly what personality characteristics were sought in potential recruits of the Secret Society, but by May his behavior indicated that he had lost those characteristics: "A member must not be marked by a single base deed; he must be recognized as selfless, of strong character, as brave as possible (either in war or in duels) and of a sound constitution so that he might serve the Society without being cowardly, remaining faithful to it even in the event of its failure" (ibid., 441). Many others failed this test as well.

Describing the technique by which he sought potential members of the Secret Society, Bestuzhev wrote the Commission that "in order to discover [someone's] bent of mind you must begin to contradict [everything he says]. And when he flares up, you observe his true character" (ibid.). Before the Investigating Commission, Bestuzhev revealed the breadth of his whole personality. On December 14 Bestuzhev's heroic persona remained intact. Once removed, however, from the dramatic and literary circumstances that delimited the experiment on Senate Square (and from which he did not expect to return alive in the event of a failure),[10] the persona could not hold up to another assault, an unexpected confrontation with mortal dread in the aftermath of the revolt. If Bestuzhev were to restore any semblance of his self-idea, he would need to create a heroic image able to rationalize his fear and cowardice.

The Commission demanded that Bestuzhev examine his behavior and the motivation behind it. The inquiry thus supplied Bestuzhev with an opportunity to develop faculties that had been lacking in his development previously. If Bestuzhev could marshal reflective and analytic powers, he might be able to heal the split between his self-image and his self. Bestuzhev, however, chose avoidance, recasting his persona in the darker hues of a romantic hero whose past is shrouded in mystery—crime and personal tragedy. This was a moment when the dark Byronic model could be acquired with a vengeance.

10. "We were so absolutely convinced that we would either succeed or die that we did not make even the least plan in the event of failure" (Pokrovskii, 1:452).

In Bestuzhev's work of the 1820s prior to the Decembrist Revolt, the confessions of literary villains and traitors come at dramatically timed moments. The villain presents a rationale for his behavior, laying blame at the door of an evil society that has treated him unjustly. No matter whether the criminal is sympathetic (Berkut in "Roman and Olga") or overwhelmingly evil (Sitsky in "The Traitor"), fault lay first with society, then perhaps with the Evil One, but only rarely with the individual. Rousseau's idea of cruel fate was consistently utilized to manipulate the reader's judgment of the villain and to attack simultaneously the egregious crimes perpetrated in feudal (medieval European or contemporary Russian) society. Bestuzhev ascribed human faults to a philosophy that diminished the importance of personal choice or characterological weakness. He could no longer cling to this opinion.

The Commission understood Bestuzhev falsified a great deal of his record and saw that he had been involved in each stage of the planning of the revolt and regicide (Pokrovskii, 1:466–69). Nevertheless, in its findings against Bestuzhev, the Commission took a lenient position. Their report summarized:

> [In the *Duma* meetings Bestuzhev] became convinced of the Society's insignificance. He says that he had been drawn into it by his imagination and his tongue, but not by his heart, and that he continually considered quitting the Society so as not to compromise his word of honor. In confirmation of his testimony that he was cold toward the group, he cites evidence that he had grown weary of Ryleyev's and Prince Obolensky's reproaches, that he recruited but two people, Prince Odoyevsky and his brother Peter Bestuzhev, and that Ryleyev and Obolensky often told him that he would give up the Society for a pair of epaulets and aglets of an adjutant. (470)

The Commission apparently believed Bestuzhev when he stated that he called out for the assassination of the tsar frivolously:

> Ryleyev told Bestuzhev that the southern branch of the Secret Society renounced the Monarchy and that their position had been confirmed [in the northern branch], and that the southern branch would remove the tsar given the least chance to do so. Obolensky and Ryleyev also said that in the event of a southern branch

insurgency it would be necessary to remove the entire Imperial family so as not to give the counterinsurgents any advantage. Bestuzhev confesses that he agreed with this opinion, suggesting that it would be possible to identify one assassin, but not as many as would be required. Furthermore, Bestuzhev asserted that he should be used for the [assassination], but he assures us that he pronounced these words as a braggart [*krikun*] and not as a villain. (470–71)

The investigators apparently were willing to submit to Bestuzhev's description of himself as an actor rather than a revolutionary, as a mask rather than a person of substance. It claimed that Bestuzhev was swayed by the moment and an ill-placed patriotism, but when the reality of regicide was before him, he actively worked against the plan's fulfillment:

[On the eve of the revolt, Bestuzhev], having entered Ryleyev's study, found Kakhovskoy, Pushchin, and Obolensky there at the very moment when the latter two bid Kakhovskoy farewell and kissed him. After Bestuzhev too had done the same, Ryleyev told Bestuzhev that "Kakhovskoy will await the Tsar on Palace Square in order to deliver the [fatal] blow." Bestuzhev fell silent and when the others were departing he invited Kakhovskoy to come see him in the morning [of the fourteenth]. At that time Bestuzhev managed to convince Kakhovskoy that he should not perform the deed assigned him.

The Commission described a repentant Bestuzhev who turned himself in, "begging forgiveness and regretting his crime completely" (472).

During the course of the investigation, Bestuzhev had presented ample evidence of his willingness to play a double role, speaking out in favor of the revolt before his comrades, but working diligently to avert disaster for the Crown. The Commission was well aware of Bestuzhev's underlying "patriotism" in the conspiracy:

In proof of his consistent position against regicide and violence, Bestuzhev mentions the following: first, his extreme efforts to dissuade Yakubovich from murdering the deceased emperor [Alexander I] and Kakhovskoy from assassinating the ruling emperor on December 14 . . . ; second, he removed General Neidgart [from danger], saved a captain of the Pavlovsk Guards from the mob, and restrained the rank and file insurgents from firing their weapons; [third], he delivered General Adjutant Levashev from a wound (or worse). [This occurred in the following manner.] When General Levashev attacked [the insurgents] fearlessly, Bestuzhev noticed that but five paces from him someone was taking aim at [Levashev]. The gun was cocked, the flint in place, and aim taken, prepared for firing, but Bestuzhev grabbed the pistol, saying "What are you doing, sir? Who commanded you to do this thing?" by which he succeeded in forestalling the shot. Bestuzhev himself did not mention this episode because, he asserts, he could bring no witness forward to attest to its veracity. (Ibid., 473)

The investigating board concluded its report with Bestuzhev's words of repentance where he identified the sword and pen as the tools of his penance.

In the guise of a faithful citizen and dutiful soldier willing to serve the government by being the first to confess, Bestuzhev was the only Decembrist allowed to resume a literary career, although under the pseudonym Marlinsky. His sentence was not as severe as his brothers', who were less active in the Secret Society. But in the role of the rebel prepared to destroy the dynasty, Bestuzhev was viewed with enmity by the emperor. Nicholas I was to monitor his every move. The tsar insisted that Bestuzhev use a pen name, selected Yakutsk as his place of exile, transferred him to the military in the Caucasus, and ordered that he never be promoted. Nicholas I continued to display a more than passing interest in his prisoner. He seemed to understand Bestuzhev's psyche very well.

Bestuzhev's language was an extension of desire and thus entirely subjective. In his fiction, criticism, and letters, and in his confession, his language only seems to be describing its object. Bestuzhev's texts were subject-oriented, and that fact suddenly came to haunt him. In a state of internal chaos Bestuzhev enacted the shifting roles of his many dramatis personae—traitor to the tsar, but hero in his group; traitor to the group, but honest patriot before the Commission; hero in his own eyes on December 14, but comic jester with Küchelbecker; abject hero-captive, but powerless pawn of the state.

Lotman states that during this historical period individuals conceived of their lives in terms of plot, and with it came a need for a "fifth act" that would render the life remarkable.[11] The months of investigation were pivotal for the development of Bestuzhev's persona. From the period of the investigation until the end of his life, Bestuzhev would live within the contours of a new literary visage, creating a Life-text that bore the stamp of a more mature romantic literature. He was forced to examine the inconsistencies of his behavior and to integrate the sundry visages at the heart of the split between his persona and personality.

Restoring the Fictionalized Self

Bestuzhev began to reinvigorate his persona prior to his arrival in Siberia. After sentencing there were many prisoners to be escorted to the East, which necessitated temporary incarceration in regional facilities. Bestuzhev was sent to Fort Slava in Finland. After six months in the Peter and Paul Fortress, the trip to Finland was quite refreshing, even a happy time for the prisoners. Ivan Yakushkin was sent with Bestuzhev and recalled how they were met at station houses by relatives. It is not known whether Bestuzhev's mother and sisters attempted a meeting.

The commander of Fort Slava was inconsistent in his treatment of the prisoners, allowing, then revoking without explanation, certain liberties. He would have tea with them, inquire about their personal lives and their recent experiences, and then suddenly send them to solitary confinement without the privilege of taking fresh air. He fed them rotten corned beef, which made them ill. When he ordered their stoves to be heated to high temperatures in their ill-ventilated quarters, Bestuzhev almost died from the inhalation of charcoal fumes.[12] They were not allowed to have books.

During his confinement in Fort Slava from August 1826 until the end of October 1826, Bestuzhev worked on an epic poem titled "Andrei, Prince of Pereyaslavl" ("Andrei, kniaz' Pereiaslavskii," published in 1829 under the pseudonym Marlinsky). In a letter several years later, he defended the factual errors in the text, saying it had been written without a library and reference materials. He went on to describe how he jotted

---

11. Iurii Lotman, "The Theater and Theatricality as Components of Early Nineteenth Century Culture," 125–42.
12. N. Kotliarevskii, *Dekabristy Kn. V. F. Odoevskii i A. A. Bestuzhev-Marlinskii,* 149.

at night on tobacco wrappers, using metal scraps from which, with his teeth, he fashioned writing tools (ibid., 149). This ironic bit of exaggeration shows he was still capable of making a jest. The poem consists of two of the five cantos Bestuzhev had planned to write plus a few odd stanzas. It reflects Bestuzhev's greater comprehension of how verse can condense and aestheticize cultural information, specifically, the era's dilemmas over the natural succession of power, the relationship of national and personal identity, epistemology, and the contents of the unconscious. But Bestuzhev's idea for the poem was so large in scope that it never got off the ground even after its first two cantos (which are devoted to the depiction of its many characters). His plot, recorded from memory, involves a competition for succession by Andrei and Vsevolod, prince of Kiev, heirs of Vladimir Monomakh.[13] He used their conflict as the work's constructive principle. The dialogues and monologues that make up the text refer to the political questions that interested Bestuzhev and the Decembrists.

Like his callow verse of the early 1820s, "Andrei, Prince of Pereyaslavl" indicates that the author is not a poet. Although the verse dispenses with insipid couplets and exact grammatical rhyme, it still suffers grammatically, rhythmically, and lexically. Thus, when in the poem's fictional introduction "Marlinsky" claims that he was born a poet, irony is compounded by the knowledge that Bestuzhev was aware of the contrary:

By Greek chronologic calculation, in the summer dated 7335 from the beginning of the creation of the world, I, whose signature is affixed below, lay in my bed leafing through Doctor Hall's phrenology study . . . , vexed that nature had not set numbers upon my cranial organs [to match with those in the text] for ease in finding the specific parts to which it refers. However, feeling here and there, then rubbing yet again all the mounds on the surface of my genius, I was entirely amazed when my first finger found a hump of imagination and a pyramid of comparison, two indubitable companions of poetizing. "Devil take me!" I exclaimed (sinner that I am, that is my favorite ejaculation). "How

---

13. This was a political theme which engaged many Decembrists before and after the revolt, including Ryleyev, Rayevsky, and Alexander Odoyevsky (V. Bazanov, *Ocheriki dekabristskoi literatury: publisistika, proza, kritika* [Moscow, 1957], 360). Vladimir Monomakh's rule (1113–25) saw continual battle with Livonia, Finland, the Volga Bulgars, the Poles, and the Hungarians. He was a fine administrator, writer, and city builder.

stupid that for so long I have been itching to try my hand at versifying [and have done nothing about it]. Nature ordained that I be a poet after all!"

[В лето, от сотворения мира, по Греческим хронографам 7335, я нижеподписавшийся лежал на кровати своей, перелистывая черепословную систему доктора Галля . . . , и очень досадуя на природу, что она не выставила нумеров на мозговых моих органах, для легчайшего прииска. Щупая и перещупывая, однакож, все выпуклости на кивоте моего гения, весьма был я изумлен, когда указательный мой перст встретил на нем шишку воображения и потом пирамиду сравнения, двух несомненных спутников поэзии. Чорт меня возьми! вскричал я тогда (грешный человек, это мое любимое восклицание); мудрено-ль, что у меня издавна чесались руки на стихотворство, когда сама природа предназначила меня быть поэтом!][14]

Bestuzhev's comic tone contrasts neatly with the apocalyptic reference to 7335. The temporal setting emphasizes the importance of this moment in his life in fanciful and ironic terms, and prepares the reader for "Andrei, Prince of Pereyaslavl" as a structure of some as yet undetermined significance for its author (whoever this Marlinsky might be).

It is not Andrei who grabs our interest, but Roman, a secondary character, who represents a figure in transition (from one set of beliefs to another). Bestuzhev indicated Roman's importance in two ways. First, he used the same name as he had in his well-known tale "Roman and Olga." This was an allusion to the poem's connection with his pre-Decembrist works and thus to his identity. Second, he included Roman in the majority of the poem's patchwork scenes, wherein we observe the gradual abandonment of his tyrannical political beliefs.

Roman's quest is similar to the author's. Bestuzhev emphasized the pertinence of a double reading of his text by asserting in the introduction that he was in the process of evaluating his beliefs: "There is no need to doubt it, by taste and the spirit of the times, I was a romantic to the ends of my nails" [Nechego i somnevat'sia, chto, po dukhu vremeni i vkusu,

---

14. *Vtoroe polnoe sobranie sochinenii*, vol. 4, part 11, 3–4. Henceforth cited as *Vpss* with reference to volume, part, and page.

ia byl romantik do kontsa nogtei] (15).[15] The questions before Bestuzhev were whether the romantic hero's identity was authentic, whether the persona could decipher reality and deal with it, how the hero's integrity would hold up under fire, and whether he could be successful in effecting morally sound ideals in reality:

> It goes without saying that I wanted my first endeavor [in poetry] to be poured into a historical mold. I simply lacked a hero, and heroes in our time . . . have become so rare that Byron himself could not find one even after reading about one hundred and two of 'em. I had to scratch through the dust of ancient Russia, but unfortunately at that time I was living in a foreign land without Russian books and even without Russian acquaintances. Digging through the sack of my memory (which I can hardly praise as a fortress of strength), I happened upon Andrei, Prince of Pereyaslavl, called "The Good" in later times. So I took him up as my hero, you might say. He, ya know, had to take upon himself all the errors of my memory. One, two, and there you are—a story comes along bearing his name, crawling out of my head halfway, like Minerva from Jupiter's.

> [Нечего и сказывать, что я хотел первую попытку свою вылить в историческую форму. Не доставало мне только героя, а герои, в наш героический век, от стечения их на базар славы, стали так редки, что сам Байрон перечел сотни две имен, не зацепясь ни за одно. Надобно было просевать пепел русской старины, а на беду я жил тогда в чужой земле, без русских книг, даже без русских знакомцев. Перерывая в сумке памяти (которой крепостию не могу похвалиться), попал я на Андрея, князя Переяславского, проименованого *добрым:* его-то избрал я моим героем; он-то должен был взять на себя все ошибки воспоминания. Раз, два—и повесть, носящая на себе это имя, вылезла из головы моей до половины, как Минерва из головы Юпитера.] (*Vpss*, 4.11.5)

---

15. "By taste and the spirit of the times" ["Po dukhu vremeni i vkusu"] is a hidden quotation of Griboyedov's response to his arrest after the Decembrist Revolt (A. S. Griboyedov, *Sochineniia v dvukh tomakh* [Moscow, 1971], 2:18).

Bestuzhev played with the reader through the ironic voice of a comic narrator. At the same time he alluded to the conditions of his exile by revealing that he wrote in isolation far from his homeland. Thus, the contours of a new, tragicomic romantic persona began to emerge upon the publication of his first work from exile. The mask was that of a writer whose fate was to suffer separation from his audience in utter equanimity, as though he were superior to his circumstances.

At the time of the poem's publication, readers must have wondered who Marlinsky was. He was no novice, as he spoke and wrote with authority and projected a confident image of himself. He represented a mystery, an unknown name detached from any discernible reference. Deciphering the identity of the author was beyond the power of most readers except his Decembrist friends, publishers, and family. The multiple encoding of "Andrei, Prince of Pereyaslavl" with its facetious introduction constituted Bestuzhev's first attempt to divulge his identity through the thematics and structure of his text. He penned barely masked allusions to the Decembrist political program, its tragic misunderstanding of reality, and its collapse. On the one hand, this material represents a means by which Bestuzhev analyzed himself and attempted to uncover deficiencies in the political program. And on the other, the poem was presented in a manner that permitted him to encode a new identity with specific reference to the historic personage Alexander Bestuzhev.

V. Bazanov notes that "Andrei, Prince of Pereyaslavl" is striking for its courage, cheerfulness, and for the absence of any reflection or despondency (Bazanov, 361). Despondency is missing from the poem, but Bazanov misses an important event in Bestuzhev's life when he finds no introspection in it. Although it is not made a theme, reflection engages each character at some point in the narrative. From the perspective of a failed political program, Bestuzhev began to take intellectual account of himself.

The disaster of the Decembrist Revolt, the exhausting and demeaning experience of interrogation, the initial sentence of death, and the reality of exile forced Bestuzhev to confront what went wrong. The second canto of "Andrei, Prince of Pereyaslavl" expresses the Decembrist crisis directly through Andrei and Roman. Soviet criticism has focused on this material for its ideological content, specifically, the representation of two types of political rule: either by force or through the consent of the ruled. Vsevolod, prince of Kiev, represents the former; Andrei the latter.

Roman figures into the narrative as a mediating third party—first convinced by Vsevolod that violence brings order, then assured by Andrei that one rules best when respectful of the people and their rights.

Against the background of these two beliefs, questions pertinent to political behavior are raised. An unidentified character from Vsevolod's camp states in the first canto, "Words without deeds are like a bow without arrows" [Slova bez del, chto luk bez strel!] (*Vpss*, 4.11.31). This marlinism encapsulates an assumption made by the Decembrists prior to the revolt. Prince Andrei, however, refutes any causal linkage between the two terms, explaining to Roman that "brilliant words" are sometimes accompanied by "darkest deeds" [blestiashchikh slov i chernykh del] (46).

In the second canto there are four related issues which are explored as replacements to the linkage of words and deeds. Two have to do with positing true versus false values. For example, one of the many secondary characters in the text, Lyubomir (a name that connotes ironically one who loves peace and the world), claims that the acquisition of glory, fame, and wealth are the driving forces that govern youth (ibid., 66–67). By proffering these treasures to the young and impressionable, one easily takes control of their minds.

Andrei's ideology is Lyubomir's antithesis. He claims that rule must be approached humbly and with a deep and abiding respect for one's fellows. Nature supplies the model for life, government, and love. The figures of the ideal are metaphorically assimilated in the shapely body, sonorous voice, or finely tied braid of a beautiful young woman's hair (ibid., 55) or in the radiant horizon against which the moon rises upon a "choir of stars" (48). Beauty in nature demonstrates the manner in which one must relate to his or her brothers and sisters in society. Andrei exemplifies this ideal.

Another secondary character, Svetovid (whose name means "he who perceives the world / light"), equates the experience of nature with personal depth. Like Bestuzhev, Svetovid feels most connected when isolated from society. In his loneliness Svetovid finds a poetic center to his being, which heightens his awareness of the world about him and the music awakened in his soul. In some of Bestuzhev's finest verse, Svetovid recollects his childhood and youth:[16]

---

16. Like the allusion in the work's introduction, this passage recalls how Bestuzhev would read on the couch in his father's library.

Dear friend, from childhood I was taken
by upland sounds of shepherd's reed!
Enticed was I, a lad, by miracles awakened—
Tales and songs were sung to me
Of ancient days gone by,
And of our mighty warriors' deeds.
And in the dark, my future told,
I loved to glimpse the faint outline
Of our beloved knights, so bold,
To hear astounding legends fine,
To dream unheard of things.
Sweet and bright my reveries
All in the breath of spring beguiling.
They bore me to that land of dreams
Where apples ripen gold the while
And Paradise's firebirds weave
Their nests of twigs and flying leaves.

. . . .

Seeing this and hearing all
I raved within the thrill of songs.
Then as I grew, my dreams
Grew with me unseen.

[Так, милый друг, от колыбели
Нагорный звук пленял меня
Пастушьей утренней свирели!
И чудом отрока маня,
Мне повести и песни пели:
О былинах минувших дней,
О подвигах богатырей.
И я любил во тьме гаданья
Старинных доблестей черты,
Невероятные преданья,
Неисполнимые мечты!
И сладостны и светлы были
Мои, в дыхании весны,
Очаровательные сны!
Они в тот край меня носили,
Где сияет яблок золотой;

Где вьются райские жар-птицы,

. . . .

Все это видя и внемля,
В восторге песней бредил я!
Я возрастал; мои мечтанья,
Росли невидимо со мной.]

(*Vpss*, 4.11.52)[17]

These tales present an illusion of reality in that the hero confronts an underworld that duplicates horrors confronted in life. The happy endings underscore the hope that heroic deeds will reign victorious over evil. Fiction, consequently, leads to the political arena, the testing ground of romantic ideology. Out of his love for legends and his despair over the discontinuity between his ideals and the real world, Svetovid, like Bestuzhev, becomes a rebel:

> Then suddenly within my breast
> A fire glowed without arrest
> From which I sang most daring tunes.
> And suddenly my gift unfolded,
> Wedding winged word to thought,
> Surrendering fancy to great passion,
> With song joining secret voice
> Known only to impassioned hearts,
> Who quietly, at times by chance,
> From nature's lap, and even death,
> Blew deep in me a living breath.
> My heart in rapture fluttered, beat,
> Much as a leaf from wind blown tree;
> So songs in floods of flaming heat
> Poured forth all harmonized from me.
> Then echoes harkened, drank
> My rapturous and heartfelt angst,
> Whereon they cited me by heart—
> My song resounds from mountain tops.
> These tunes of my youth

17. "I raved" ("Bredil ia") implies the "madness" to which the poet succumbs during composition.

And my pensive reed's cry
Are not seen by men's eyes,
Nor man's ear do they soothe;
Like a vision of swans
Or the leap of a hart,
So they live in me down
In the depths of my heart.

[Тогда-то к смелым песнопеньям
В груди моей затлелся жар,
Тогда-то развился мой дар:
Мысль окрылят воображеньем,
Давать живой язык страстям,
Сливая в думы голос тайной,
Знакомый пламенным сердцам,
Который тихо и случайно
Из лона жизни, из могил
Певцу понятно говорил.
Восторгом сердце трепетало,
Как ветром сорванный листок,
И думы пламенной поток
Ладами, стройно изливало!
И эхо резвое внимало
Мою восторженную грусть,
И, повторяя наизусть,
Скалам от скал передавало.
Но песни юности моей,
Моей задумчивой свирели.
Незнаемы умам людей,
Как стаи вольных лебедей,
Звуча, в поднебесье летели,
Иль досель кипят они
В моей сердечной глубине!]

(*Vpss,* 4.11.53–54)

Svetovid is arrested by a reflection linked to memory. It takes a political crisis to initiate his reflection; he senses the depths of his being only when his ideals have been shattered. Significantly, this is also the first time one of Bestuzhev's characters has attempted to ascertain how he has become himself, a self whose psychological function is embedded in his name—perceiving (*vid*) the world / light (*svet*) in adequate terms.

If Vsevolod / Lyubomir and Andrei / Svetovid represent opposite poles, Roman mediates between them. Convinced earlier that might makes right, Roman accepts Svetovid's and Andrei's arguments that rule must be won through the love and respect of the governed. There are many parallels between Roman's autobiographical discourse and Bestuzhev's past. Inspired by Svetovid's example, with its union of nature and man through an introspective life of exile and isolation, Roman recounts how he was drawn into radical politics.

Of signal importance was the death of his father after the "dawn" of his youth:

> The very will of the heavens
> could not assuage the tears of old;
> it would not waft an anguished sorrow
> from off my face with kindest bliss!
> The dawn of my years
> found me at my father's grave!

> [Так воля самая небес
> Не усладит минувших слез
> И злой кручины покрывала
> Не светят негою с лица!
> Денница лет меня застала
> На гробе милого отца!]
>
> (Ibid., 56–57)

Roman attempted to restore himself in the face of his loss and to assuage his anguished soul:

> Not out of love, but out of sorrow
> my breast beat first
> when covered by tempered steel.

> [И не любовью, но печалью
> Облечена военной сталью
> Впервые билась грудь моя.]
>
> (57)

To compensate for the trauma, Roman recovered some of the value of existence by turning to the life of a warrior. His armor suggests its psychological function. Weighed against the conditioning event (the father's death and, by extension, his own death), his breastplate, shield, and helmet represent both physical and symbolic protective coverings. Roman arms himself against a hostile world ("the very will of the heavens") that might at any moment take *him* away. The armor he dons is more than a physical object, a necessary tool of the military trade, and a sign of his calling. It is also a symbol of his fear of death and his willingness to confront it in combat. Like Bestuzhev, Roman throws himself into a test to see if he will be protected. In battle he wins glory, fame, and honor and secures an *idea* of safety based on his talisman, the armor.

During this phase of his life Roman meets Vsevolod, prince of Kiev. Roman finds in him a surrogate father, completing in psychological terms a circular quest that had begun in his childhood:

> And then, at last, amidst the hue and cry of the hunt
> On the fields of our native Chernigov
> Vsevolod opened up his soul to me.

> [И наконец под шумом лова
> В полях Чернигова роднова
> Мне душу Всеволод открыл.]

(Ibid., 57)

Vsevolod speaks to Roman of ancient times and the glory of his heroic forebears, Vladimir and Svyatoslav (who safeguarded the homeland). He argues for a patriotic cause by which all Slavs might be unified under his rule. Roman is convinced; he does not question the morality of Vsevolod's claim that the ends justify the means and assents to the violence Vsevolod identifies as necessary.

Roman represents in symbolic form Bestuzhev's reflection on the Decembrist Revolt. His story delivers up Bestuzhev's understanding of his own past, from the trauma of his father's death to the violence induced by a surrogate authority figure. Bestuzhev's reconstruction of the Decembrist fiasco in the figure of Roman reveals that the wellsprings of Bestuzhev's behavior were deeper than his quest for fame and glory.

Together with the issue of false models, Bestuzhev raised a related problem—the profoundly moral nature of identity formation when faced by one's mortality. The military life temporarily bestowed on the hero both a real and figurative armor:

> The daring soul balks at nothing
> the agile mind sees what it must do.
> I gave my oath to Vsevolod bravely
> to word and deed combined.
> I swore my sharp sword and youth would serve the
>   homeland true.

> [И—смелый дух на все решится
> И все решит способный ум
> Тогда на слово и на дело
> Я дал обет Всевладу смело
> И острый меч, и юный век
> На службу родины обрек.]

(Ibid., 58)

But the solution produced problems of its own. Over time Roman discovered that he had been led astray: "And then, at last, freely wed to wander / I overcame my self" [No nakonets, stradalets vol'nyi / Ia sam sebia preodolel] (59). Uncertainty entered his consciousness and with it came a reconsideration of the presuppositions underlying the violent life he was leading:

> But I must confess that doubt
> suddenly spoke to me in Andrei's voice
> for the first time in my life:
> Is there really salvation to be found in titanism?
> Can one remove ill by doing ill?
> Can one establish rule through untruth?
> And why had Vsevolod described to me
> an Andrei in such dark colors
> when from Andrei there had only come
> thanks and praise for Vsevolod?

> [Но признаюсь, о том сомненье
> Лишь только здесь, Андрея глас

Во мне посеял в первый раз
Уже ль в огромности спасенье?
Беду ль—бедами излечать?
Права ль неправдой водворят?
И для чего мне князь великий
Вчерне Андрея описал
Когда ему несутся клики
Благодарений и похвал?]

(59)

Svetovid responded, "You have become doubtful—this is / the bitter fruit of an unjust service" [Ty somnevaesh'sia! i vot / Nepravoi sluzhby gor'kii plod!] (59). Roman turns abruptly from Vsevolod and his ideology of might.

Svetovid helps Roman see that there is no causal connection between word and deed, that the pursuit of a laudable goal is negated completely by ill intent, and that a finely wrought word is nullified when put in the service of an evil plan. Andrei, too, attempts to convince Roman that glory and fame are mere egoism and emptiness:

What is glory? A brittle piece of nothing,
The ruddy glow of a leaf's decaying!
It is the booty, not a reward,
Of the goal you win by daring deeds!
Great rulers pass, fall away,
And in their gilt-edged graves
The glow of their northern fame
Can hardly warm their frigid dust,
Nor bring the soul a peaceful rest.
The centuries trample the scribe's fine words
With a heavy heel that shows disdain;
The plow will heave up pieces of their tomb,
And ungrateful scion forget their glorious names!
Tell me, who were the leaders
Of the fearless Slavs who from darkened lands
Fell upon the Roman walls?
What do we see? Near, far,
And all around, great peoples,
Great in their victories, flow by

And, like mountain waters in the spring,
Disappear without a trace
From the face of the earth!
What are their names? Where is their rusty might?
Where is the glory of their embattled life?
Only the steppe winds waft upon
Their unanswering burial mounds!
And what of the bards, you ask?
They do not sing about everyone,
Elevated sons of reverie though they may be.
Their momentary creation's drawn down, too,
In the depths of life's rapids.

[Что слава? ломкая скудель,
Румянец тленья листопада!
Она добыча, не награда
И душ и дел, пробивших цель!
Падут владельцы величавы,
И в позолоченных гробах
Сиянье северное славы
Не согревает хладный прах,
Не придает душе покою:
Века тяжелою пятою
Сотрут златые письмена;
Изроет плуг гробниц обломки
И нерадивые потомки
Забудут славных имена!
Скажи мне: кто такие были
Вожди безтрепетных Славян,
Когда они с полночных стран
Пределы римские громили?
Не то ль мы зрим! вблизи, вдали,
Окрест великие народы,
Шумя победами, текли
И, как весной нагорны воды,
Изчезли вдруг с лица земли!
Где имя их? где силы рьяны?
Где слава жизни боевой?
Лишь развевает вихрь степной

Их безответные курганы!
И не про всех поют баяны,
Мечты возвышенной сыны,
И тонут в бездне быстрины
Их мимолетные творенья!]

(Ibid., 62–63)

Through Andrei's voice Bestuzhev effectively fashioned a new form for his warrior-hero-poet archetype. He did not dispense with the prototype altogether but added another element that offered the hero a new perspective on himself and his place in the world. If the hero were now to pursue fame and glory, he would do it in recognition of his limitations, the greatest of which is his mortality. Thanatos has become conscious.

Another question haunting Bestuzhev was the adequacy of the models acquired in life. It begged more than passing treatment in "Andrei, Prince of Pereyaslavl," for it is connected fundamentally with epistemology. For the first time in his life, Bestuzhev asked how the hero might perceive reality accurately. Roman's quest is instructive. Roman fell under Vsevolod's grip because he remained unconscious of the forces that brought him to the warrior's ethos and ultimately delivered him up to a surrogate father whose model proved false. In examining how this had happened to him, Roman became introspective. But reflection is not sufficient in itself to define its own perceptual adequacy. To treat this fundamental epistemological issue (how we know what we know and whether or not we are in possession of a complete knowledge), Bestuzhev resorted to the tool he had utilized throughout his life—image-making. Roman's model, therefore, did not reach Bestuzhev's own experience, for the discourse of *fiction* separated the question from the rigorous answer it deserved in *reality*.

The fictionalization of Bestuzhev's response is a departure from the direct treatment of other significant themes addressed in the poem. This is signaled formally in the text—Bestuzhev set the passage apart from the preceeding stanzas by inserting a hiatus in his text (the first encountered in the poem). As a second cue he initiated the discussion (in Andrei's voice) with a paradox: "In matters of truth I believe / enemies are our best friends!" [Tak, v dele pravdy veriu ia / Vragi nam luchshie druz'ia!] (ibid., 50). This inversion of common sense is predicated on a union of opposites, a reversal of expectations, and an examination of self from the position of a distant other. We cannot know what a true friend is without the experience of a real enemy. Erase grief from the world and we lose our appreciation of happiness. Andrei asserts a commonplace romantic thought—we cannot attain to a full understanding of good if we have not experienced its opposite. Enemies help us establish the truth by showing us what it is not.[18] There are limitations, however, to the understanding acquired in an intuitive, nonrational fusion of antitheses. Yet other techniques are required in the quest for adequate knowledge.

In Svetovid's story, deficiencies in knowledge caused by a literary and fanciful conception of reality are compensated for by anamnesis. Svetovid tells Roman that frustrations in life are diminished by the certain knowledge that comes from memory. Although he could not realize his ideal of love in life, "Fate ordained that I retain the recollection" of that ideal (*Vpss*, 4.11.56). Andrei repeats this notion when he later states that possessing an ideal must be seen as its own reward, for dreaming an ideal does not make it real (64). The individual must remain in touch, therefore, with the absolute, with the image of perfection, through memory and contemplation. Yet memory itself is imperfect since it maintains the disparity between the real and the ideal that produced romantic longing in the first place.

Neither the fusion of opposites nor memory permit access to the certain knowledge sought within the text. Consequently, Bestuzhev turns in an entirely different direction. From the analytic discourse that issues from the mouths of the sundry characters, Bestuzhev has his narrator speak. Omniscient storytelling takes over narrative responsibilities originally invested in the dramatis personae. The burden of narrative is shifted from direct speech to metaphor, from dialogue, confession, and analysis to the symbolics of plot and character. Bestuzhev based the next phase of his epistemological inquiry on associative cues symbolized in visual acuity. Svetovid's name indicates the value of sight in the text. Andrei's hunting is yet another symbolic representation of the same. Bestuzhev used the hunt in "Andrei, Prince of Pereyaslavl" to depict a ritual enactment of the age-old conflict between chaos and order. But "seeing" is the pivotal concern

---

18. From another perspective, Bestuzhev's friends brought him to the greatest crisis of his life (barring his father's death), drew in his brothers against his own expressed wishes, martyred five, and traumatized an entire nation. What kind of friends were these? What kind of friend had Bestuzhev been to those he inducted into the Secret Society and whose lives had been tragically altered through the trust they placed in him? Friendship, raised to a cult in the early nineteenth century, was placed in doubt. At a deeper level, however, where Andrei's speech takes effect, had it not been for his friends, Bestuzhev might not have been forced to face the epistemological, psychological, and political issues addressed in the poem.

in it. To catch his prey, the hero must be capable of encompassing in his sight more than the object of his attention. He must also envisage the field of his action, his position in it, and his effect on it. Bestuzhev concentrated much of his description of the hunting scenes on the power of individual vision. In effect, he reduces epistemological issues to questions of adequate sight. This act crystallizes imagistically Bestuzhev's inquiry into the relationship between word and deed, ideals and reality, fathers and sons (whether biological or surrogate), authentic and fictionalized identity, and true and false understanding.

Andrei participates in two hunting episodes, the first of which emphasizes the theme of sight in the figure of a hawk (representative of the Prince):[19]

Shocked by the light of the new day's sun,
Shaking itself and opening wide its clear pupils,
The predator bird does not quit
His master's hand too soon.
Andrei's first hawk sights his prey from afar,
And like an arrow alights beneath the clouds
With whistling wings soaring,
Higher and higher it flies until
It strikes the heron as though with lead.

[Поражены лучем денницы,
Расширив ясные зрачки,
И отрясаясь, хищны птицы
Не вдруг кидаются с руки,
И первый сокол князь Андрея,
Добычь узрев издалека,
Стрелой взвился под облака,
Свистящими крылами рея,
Все вверх и вверх, и наконец
Ударил в цаплю, как свинец.]
(Vpss, 4.11.50–51)

19. In War and Peace, Tolstoy's hunter (Nicholas Rostov) and his dog (or bird) are interrelated, dissolving the separation felt between the natural order and man. Nicholas is his hound, just as much as the other hunters are identified with their dogs. The hunter mediates between chaos and order. Lermontov's "Mtsyri" uses similarly the struggle between man and nature to suggest an affinity between them.

The image of sight is encountered again between the two hunting scenes, specifically in an interlude that introduces a love theme into the text. Roman beholds Svetovid's infatuation with a young maiden:

> Why do you blush?! I have observed
> That at her first glance at you
> In her eyes there shone the light of love,
> Suddenly in yours it blended,
> Enraptured by some sweet bliss.
>
> [Зачем краснеть!—Заметил я,
> При первом взоре на тебя,
> В ее глазах любви зарницы,
> И вдруг в твоих слиялся он,
> Какой-то негой упоен!]
>
> (54–55)

Each of the first four lines indicates that vision possesses an essential communicative function. Through it reality and truth are illuminated. Both the girl and Svetovid fall in love with each other "at first sight." Roman's eye beholds their love. He comments,

> You bowed your head toward her just so
> that you might not take your eye
> from her shy beauty even for a moment! . . .
> Or has my vision deceived me, your friend?
> Or did you wish to seduce [her]?
>
> [Но ей в поклон едва, едва
> Твоя склонилась голова
> Чтоб глаз не свесть ни на мгновенье
> С ее стыдливой красоты! . . .
> Иль друга обмануло зренье
> Иль обольстить желаешь ты?]
>
> (55)

Roman's queries allude to his competence as an observer, which he himself doubts, not because he does not know what he has seen, but because he is aware that one's point of view can be contaminated by its own subjectivity. Svetovid, however, confirms Roman's perception. Like the hawk sighting its prey from a great distance only to capture it in one swift move, Roman perceives the object of his sight quite clearly, captures what he has observed, then renders it in a language that encompasses reality.

Since Roman is a reincarnation of an earlier, more naive hero of Bestuzhev's fiction, the theme of discernment takes on added significance. Roman overcomes his conceptual blindness and has his vision restored: "A fog has fallen from my eyes" [Upal s ochei moikh tuman] (ibid., 62), he announces to Andrei, who then repeats for Roman a lesson about ideals in a world that assaults them at every turn. He recounts his dream of a unified nation and a world united by brotherly love and self-sacrifice. Roman perceives Andrei's ecstasy as prophetic:

[Andrei] fell silent. His brow shone,
His vision alighted on the heavens
As if he saw through a veil
The face of the future.

[(Андрей) Умолк. Чело его сияло
На небо светлый взор летел
Как будто он сквозь покрывало
Лице грядущего узрел.]

(64)

This, too, is a vision of love.

Bestuzhev expressed the movement of a newly acquired contemplative mind in the hero's quest for adequate knowledge predicated on morally informed insight. In raising the many issues that burst forth chaotically from the text at random moments, Bestuzhev allowed his intuitive side to explore perspectives that had not formerly entered his texts. By treating directly the trauma of the revolt and its aftermath, and by examining what had gone wrong, Bestuzhev opened himself to the philosophical wellsprings of romanticism, the most profound perspective of which had to do with epistemology. Yet if vision is important to it, it remains undefineable, nonanalytic, and, consequently, suspect as an intellectual category.

Dreams, beloved by the romantic, were put to use as Bestuzhev's epistemological inquiry began to lose impetus. He applied all three Russian terms to indicate dreams and sleep: *son,* which signifies both a sleeping state and a dream itself; *mechta,* which is a state more akin to reverie, longing, or even idealistic hope; and *snovidenie,* which refers directly to the series of images, emotions, or thoughts encountered during sleep. The emphasis of this last term is on two roots—*son* (sleep /dream) and *videnie* (which is related to seeing or vision). It is also connected to the question of perception and links dreaming to the epistemological question. Each of these nouns occurs in the song that closes the first canto:

> Rest thyself, young traveler.
> Thou art tired and troubled.
> My golden strings will enfold thee
> Into a deep sleep [*son*].
>
> Bending down upon thy pillow
> The beauty of dreams [*snovidenie*]
> Will surround thee with love,
> A lightwinged reverie [*mechta*].
>
> [Успокойся, путник юный,
> Ты разбит и утомлен;
> На тебя златые струны
> Назвенят глубокий сон.
>
> И приникнув к изголовью,
> Сновидений красота
> Обоймет тебя с любовью
> Тихокрылая мечта.]
>
> (Ibid., 38)

The song brings sleep (*son*), which in turn delivers the weary visions (*snovidenie*), which constitute one's personal desires and longings (*mechta*). Bestuzhev in effect asserted through his bard that the unconscious is equivalent to one's conscious wishes. This is an important claim illuminated by the dreams of various characters in the narrative.

Significantly, sleep and death are immediately associated—Roman's first dream is introduced through a visit to a graveyard. He contemplates his forebears, heroic defenders of the homeland, as he begins his quest for a thorough understanding of life. Having prayed that he might complete his quest and be fulfilled in life, he partakes of the morning's catch, lies down on the grassy steppe, and falls asleep. Unbeknownst to Ro-

man, two enemy Polovetsians, Konchak and Topaz, plan to murder him
while he sleeps. Roman foils the Polovetsians' plan. He has a dream in
which he finds himself on a hunt. The wild bull he tracks turns to engage
him in battle. The bull overturns Roman's horse and lifts Roman on his
horns, throwing him ever higher until he reaches the heavens (ibid., 24).
The dream of death and transcendence is immediately followed by another in which Roman meets his troops at their campsite. They appear as
strangers to him, but he sits with them nevertheless and shares a cup.
When it is passed to him in a toast "to friendship, inalterable love, and to
Vsevolod," Roman notices that it is not wine they drink, but blood.
Thunder breaks through the fog, and then a battle cry. Roman awakens
to find he is indeed under assault—by the Polovetsians. He throws himself into the fray against Konchak. Topaz readies an arrow, but Roman
turns at the last moment, and Konchak's back meets the dart. Konchak
(as his name indicates) dies, Topaz flees, and Roman thanks fate that he
has been saved by a dream that awakened him to an equivalent reality.

   Through the dream, Bestuzhev presented a fictionalized answer to the
problem of how one attains knowledge to handle life's challenges. As
Roman dreams, he is educated to meet reality. The warrior's intuitive
powers prove superior to analytic skill. In effect, Bestuzhev dispensed
with analysis and introspection when he realized that they cannot totally
encompass reality. His investigation reestablished the value of intuition
and spontaneity as appropriate tools for dealing with the world. Despite
its extensive probing, this poem contains no new program of behavior
for Bestuzhev's fiction or his life. Rather, "Andrei, Prince of Pereyaslavl"
reaffirms the romantic ethos. Out of the trauma of interrogation in
which Bestuzhev encoded for posterity the deformation of the romantic
persona, he sketched in prison the contours of that persona's next stage
of development. Not analytic by nature, Bestuzhev initiated a new phase
in his writing, as he attempted to ascertain impressionistically the limits
and powers of intuition and of reason. Although finally dismissing syllogistic reasoning, epistemological rigor, and the value of logical inquiry,
Bestuzhev nevertheless benefited from their assistance, for they allowed
him to assimilate the mortal imperfections of the hero.

8

Siberian Exile

Do not forget a man who has ceased to be a
fable.

—Bestuzhev-Marlinsky

Yakutsk

Bestuzhev's journey into exile began on October 27, 1827. His brothers
Mikhail and Nicholas had left for the East two or three days before.
Andrei Rozen (1800–1884), who was sent to the East several months
later, noted that Bestuzhev left Fort Slava in an unusually jocular and
even excellent frame of mind.[1] Bestuzhev was taken by boat to the
Schlesselburg Fortress where he awaited Matvei Muraviev-Apostol
(1796–1828), who would travel with him. The two were placed in irons
and escorted to St. Petersburg, where Count Ivan Ivanovich Dibich

---

1. Cited in N. Kotliarevskii, *Dekabristy Kn. V. F. Odoevskii i A. A. Bestuzhev-Marlinskii,*
151.

$(1785-1831)^2$ informed Bestuzhev that he would be spared hard labor, and that he would be allowed to pursue his writing career on the condition that he "not write anything stupid" (Kotliarevskii, 151). They then traveled to the Tikhvin Station where a Mason met them and gave Muraviev-Apostol a gift of six hundred rubles. Although embarrassed by the generosity, he accepted it since "neither Bestuzhev nor I had any money."[3] The Decembrists journeyed on to Yaroslavl, Vyatka, Perm, and then to Ekaterinburg where they were astonished to receive a heroic welcome by provincial officials:

> Here we were met by the postmaster who received us with particular delight. After a short rest in an adjacent room, the doors were opened to us into the dining room where a table was laid out in exceeding luxury. The postmaster's entire family gathered together [for the meal]. Bestuzhev and I, after a two-year incarceration that was both difficult and sorrowful for us, and which had made us grow unaccustomed to all amenities in life, not to mention the travails of the road, found ourselves quite by surprise amid hospitable hosts who showered upon us every kindness and served us with unfeigned delight. Goblets were drained to our health. Although our position did not promise any happiness in the future, we nevertheless forgot for an hour our grief and with all our hearts expressed our gratitude for the generosity of their welcome, so surprising was it to us. ("Vospominaniia," 525–26)

Much to the travelers' delight, they were shown similar respect and hospitality in Tobolsk and Krasnoyarsk.

When Bestuzhev discovered that his brothers were not far ahead of them, he grew impatient to push on and became vexed with Muraviev-Apostol for wanting to prolong the pleasures of the road. The latter proved sensitive to Bestuzhev's desires:

2. Count Ivan Ivanovich Dibich was close to Alexander I and continued to serve the new tsar, Nicholas I, upon the former's demise. Dibich informed Nicholas I of the December revolt well in advance of the fourteenth. He was placed in charge of arrests in its aftermath. Thus, Bestuzhev's subsequent address to the count was well calculated in terms of influencing the tsar on matters pertaining to the revolutionaries.

3. "Vospominaniia Matveia Ivanovicha Murav'eva-Apostola, zapisannye Aleksandrom Petrovichem Beliaevym v 1883," *Russkaia starina* (1886): 525.

Along the road from Tobolsk the unreachable wish to overtake our comrades traveling ahead of us continued to torment us, especially Bestuzhev whose brothers Mikhail and Nicholas were among them. Marlinsky's impatience to meet them redounded on me. The official accompanying us, taking into consideration the Tobolsk governor's kind disposal toward me, asked politely at each station if I would like to rest or have the horses harnessed immediately. Because of this Bestuzhev came to the conclusion that everything depended on me to convince the guard that we must take the opportunity of meeting his brothers. But I learned from him that our timetable and route was strictly laid out and that it was not allowed to arrive in advance at any given station. Taking pity on the guard, I decided not to lead him into temptation [and bribe him to hasten on]. Our difference in opinion on this matter led to heated debate between us, which nevertheless did not detract from our friendly relations. Given his impressionable and passionate nature, Alexander Bestuzhev was nonetheless gifted with a kind heart and an uncommonly easy disposition. (Ibid., 526–27)

Bestuzhev arrived in Irkutsk on November 22, 1827, two months after leaving Fort Slava. He and Muraviev-Apostol were placed in a prison cell where, on the following day, Bestuzhev finally was reunited with his two brothers. No one has left a description of this meeting. Ironically, since Bestuzhev and Muraviev-Apostol were sentenced not to incarceration but to surveillance in distant communities, the governor of Irkutsk apologized for having placed them behind bars. They protested that they would rather be with their comrades than elsewhere, but they were removed to quarters consistent with their punishment.[4]

Ivan Yakushkin recounted his meeting with Bestuzhev in Irkutsk as a literary event: "[I found] Matvei Muraviev and Alexander Bestuzhev in

4. Muraviev-Apostol wrote, "This untimely reduction of our punishment was bitter for us" (ibid., 528). The ties among the Decembrists were very strong at this time and remained so for many years, each following the fate of his comrades with keen interest and deep compassion. Many fell ill, others went mad, and several died unexpectedly, including some of the Decembrist wives. For details, see I. D. Yakushkin's account in Glyn Barratt, *Voices in Exile: The Decembrist Memoirs* (Montreal, 1974), 293–99. For the Decembrist wives, see Christine Sutherland, *The Princess of Siberia: The Story of Maria Volkonsky and the Decembrist Exiles* (New York, 1984).

Fig. 3.   Mikhail A. Bestuzhev (1800–1871), watercolor by Nicholas Bestuzhev, 1837–39

Irkutsk; they were both free and awaited their departure up the Lena River to Yakutsk. Bestuzhev sent me [a copy of] 'The Gypsies' ["Tsygany," 1824]. I read this new Pushkin work with the greatest delight." Yakushkin went on to describe events that presage in miniature the bathhouse scene in Fyodor Dostoyevsky's *Notes from the House of the Dead* (1861–63):

> That same evening we were taken to the bathhouse where we were served very politely and adeptly by people in chains. These were the most grievous sinners with brands upon their foreheads, some with nostrils removed. Together with them we made up the prisoners of the camp. Such close contact with them was not without benefits for me personally. Instead of repulsion toward them, whom society, with all its prejudices and institutions [of law], attempts to isolate from itself, I could not help but experience some kind of compassion for these poor people. Suddenly, to my great amazement, Alexander Bestuzhev walked into the bathhouse all covered in soap. I jumped up from my bench and embraced him. It goes without saying that we could not meet here long and indeed we only had a few moments to speak to each other about Pushkin's gypsies. [I might mention in passing that] Bestuzhev even found some way to get into the prison camp to meet his brothers just before their departure for Chita.[5]

After three weeks Muraviev-Apostol and Bestuzhev continued their journey northward. Accompanied by a Cossack sergeant, they went downriver (north) and saw fellow Decembrists exiled to various villages along the distant reaches of the Lena. Muraviev-Apostol recalled that they arrived in Yakutsk on Christmas Eve, 1827; but in his letters, Bestuzhev claimed that it was New Year's Eve. Both dates are important festivals, each related to new beginnings. The symbolism of this timing was not lost on Bestuzhev, who marked this date in his initial correspondence of the Yakutsk period.[6] On January 6, Epiphany, another symbolically laden date, Muraviev-Apostol dutifully noted in his memoirs that he left

5. "Iz zapisok dekabrista Iakushkina," *Russkii arkhiv* 8–9 (1871): 1584–85.

6. For Bestuzhev's correspondence, see "Aleksandr Bestuzhev v Iakutske: Neizdannye pis'ma ego k rodnym, 1827–1829," *Russkii vestnik* 5 (1870): 213–65; and "A. A. Bestuzhev-Marlinskii v Iakutske," in M. K. Azadovskii, *Pamiati dekabristov* 2:189–226. Three additional letters may be found in "Pis'ma A. A. Bestuzheva iz ssylki," *Byloe* 5 (1925): 114–20.

Bestuzhev to travel another 450 miles north to Vilyuisk. Bestuzhev, knowing that Muraviev-Apostol was more isolated than he, kept up an active correspondence with him and made purchases on his behalf.[7]

Objective data on remote Yakutsk in 1827 is not as scant as might be imagined. Although the governor of the territory did not visit the small community until 1836, Yakutsk was contained in the territory census. It held approximately 2500 inhabitants, consisting of Buriat and Tungus natives, Great Russians in government service, and Siberians (*sibiriaki*) of Russian extraction. The Russians who composed society there could hardly be called polite; many were illiterate. One family subscribed to a Russian journal, but read it rarely. Set in the midst of a vast emptiness, the village was made up of nothing more than indigenous yurts, a few huts, and several log cabins.

The Lena lay a mile away and did not enhance the immediate territory with its immensity, islands, and geologically varied basin. Vegetation in Yakutsk was sparse and lacked variety. Due to the short summer and arid climate, Bestuzhev had difficulty growing flowers and vegetables. Winter at 62° north is long and severe, and Bestuzhev's mica windows were covered in frost for many months at a stretch. The only light was the dull glow afforded by candles. The temperature was often forty degrees below zero. It was impossible for Bestuzhev to leave his cabin, let alone take a walk. The post came to Yakutsk twice a month, sometimes only once. Bestuzhev was forced to spend his time during the long winter in his two rooms reading books supplied by his mother, his former English teacher, friends, and the publisher Nicholas Grech. He smoked fine tobacco, wrote letters, entertained fantasies, and indulged memories.[8]

Mikhail Semevsky (1837–92), editor of *Russkaia starina* (1870–92) and the Bestuzhev family chronicler, remarked that this was the gloomiest period in Bestuzhev's short life ("Aleksandr Bestuzhev v Iakutske," 214).[9] G. Prokhorov contends, on the contrary, that this was a time of renewal for Bestuzhev (Azadovskii, 2:189). The truth of the matter probably lies somewhere between the two. Bestuzhev's letters are full of enthusiasm for discovering the glories of a land that had boded ill for exiles. He used his year and a half to read Homer and Dante in the

---

7. Those letters have not survived.
8. All accounts verify these facts with regularity and conform to Bestuzhev's own record in detail. See Azadovskii, *Pamiati dekabristov*, 2:195, 199, 203, 209, and 211. See also "Aleksandr Bestuzhev v Iakutske," 231, 239, 250–51.
9. Semevsky collected provincial and family archives for publication in his journal.

original, to study German in order to read Schiller and Goethe, and to continue his favorite reading—Shakespeare and Byron, as well as Thomas More. He made careful observations of the local inhabitants, particularly the Buriats and Tungus,[10] and in conjunction with these scientific research projects, he assisted the German natural scientist, Georg Adolph Erman (1806–77),[11] in gathering astronomical data. Despite protests to the contrary, Bestuzhev kept himself very busy.[12] In exile, he became something of an ethnographer, a folklorist, a linguist, and even a natural scientist.

While Bestuzhev lived in isolation, his letters expressed a deep longing to be with his mother and sisters on their estate, to share Nicholas and Mikhail's fate in Chita if only to be with them, or to fly to his younger brothers Peter and Pavel in the Caucasus to fight the "infidel." He was troubled, sometimes depressed, but he managed to dispel his anguished moments by staying busy, a technique most Decembrists found helpful (263). He complained of boredom and his habitual laziness: "For the time being I lie about for days on end with my feet propped up against the wall just staring at the ceiling."[13] He referred to his rooms as a tomb or a grave and longed for an awakening (238).

Bestuzhev, however, did not remain alone very long. In June 1828, Zakhar Chernyshev, another Decembrist, was transferred from Chita to Yakutsk. They lived together in the same cabin for eight months, after which Chernyshev was sent to another location. During that time Bestuzhev enjoyed the company of this quiet and unassuming man.[14] Chernyshev brought news directly from Bestuzhev's brothers and described in detail their life in Chita. On Chernyshev's arrival Bestuzhev wrote Nicholas and Mikhail a letter that did not pass through the censor, but went directly to them (carried in all likelihood by the official who

10. See, in particular, "Otryvki iz rasskazov o Sibiri" ("Fragments of Stories about Siberia," 1830–32) and "Sibirskie nravy: Isykh" ("Siberia Mores: Isykh," 1831). These works most likely were written between 1827 and 1829.

11. Erman reached Yakutsk in 1829 and was assisted in his research to some extent by Bestuzhev, *Sochineniia v dvukh tomakh,* 1:614.

12. For a list of many of the books Bestuzhev had with him in Yakutsk, see the letter to his mother dated June 3, 1829 (Azadovskii, 2:226). In it he lists many dictionaries, histories, natural science studies, seventeen volumes of Schiller's work, sixteen volumes of the Latin classics, Byron, and others.

13. This letter is dated Spring 1826. See "Aleksandr Bestuzhev v Iakutske," 229.

14. E. Tarasov, "Iakutskaia ssylka Bestuzheva-Marlinskogo," *Dekabristy na katorge i v ssylke* (Moscow, 1925), 8–9:254.

accompanied Chernyshev): "Zakhar has broken my forced isolation. I am now entirely satisfied [with my lot] both as a man and king" ("Aleksandr Bestuzhev v Iakutske," 234). Later in the month he wrote that Chernyshev "arrived emaciated and jaundiced, but he is already gradually improving in health. We live together; unhappiness draws people close together and joins them as brothers. It looks like we won't be quarreling with each other. I am happy, so happy that I now have someone with whom I can share hours of sorrow and minutes of joy" (234–35). Bestuzhev continued the same letter with an announcement of the arrival of many books from his mother. He mentioned that Chernyshev had brought a substantial library with him. "I don't know where to begin [with my reading]. At dinner and over tea we talk about you, ourselves, about our ancient entertainments [a reference to life in St. Petersburg and to Decembrist activities], and about what is going on in the world, news I should add that is hardly fresh off the press. The weather is fine, the fields are green, and the river water plays about; I am coming alive, though just for a moment" (234–35).

In this expansive mood, Bestuzhev noted in a postscript that Chernyshev showed him a portrait painted by his brother Nicholas. He made a request that his portrait be done as well ("If it is possible, do my portrait—mustache down and without sideburns"),[15] thus showing his inclination to create an image of himself had not disappeared. He was as careful in how he presented himself in public in Yakutsk as he had been in St. Petersburg. His first letter to his mother, dated January 9, 1828, is an elaborate request for supplies—money, clothes, amenities, books, dictionaries. He wanted a fur coat, neckerchief, several pairs of colored gloves, a half-dozen socks for summer wear, a single-breasted evening jacket in black, and material from which he might fashion other articles of clothing (Azadovskii, *Pamiati dekabristov*, 2:193). In his private letters to his brother he dramatically displayed the care he took with his attire: "L'argent ne me manquait pas d'autant plus que je suis frugal de nature; la seule manie qui ne me quitte pas, c'est celle de m'habiller elegamment; je suis la vignette de mode a Jakoutsk [I haven't been in need of money, especially since by nature I am frugal;

15. "Aleksandr Bestuzhev v Iakutske," 234. Nicholas Bestuzhev's paintings and portraits of the Decembrists, of their life in exile, of Chita, and of Petrovsky Zavod are famous and are frequently included in studies and publications by and about the Decembrists. The portrait Bestuzhev requested of his brother appears, among other editions, in Iu. S. Postnov, *Sibir' v poezii dekabristov* (Novosibirsk, 1976), 52.

the only mania I can't escape to this day is dressing elegantly; I set the fashion in Yakutsk]" ("Aleksandr Bestuzhev v Iakutske," 233). Apparent in his boasting is his need to authenticate his Marlinsky persona. His intentions in so dressing are clear in his next remark: "Je ne fréquente point les assemblés et ne suis connu qu'avec deux maisons. On vient parfois me voir et m'ennuyer; même j'ai vu des jolies dames chez moi . . . [I do not attend social gatherings and I am received in only two houses. People sometimes come to see me and bother me. I've even seen good-looking women at my place]." The ellipsis is Bestuzhev's and clearly signals to his brother that his womanizing had not ceased in the remoteness of northern Siberia.

Despite the deficiencies of local society, Bestuzhev was an attraction and may have had liaisons with one or two women. Bestuzhev, living as he did for a year and a half in Yakutsk, managed to make solid contacts in society. The regional governor, Miagkov, a good man and well disposed toward the Decembrists, gave balls and on high festivals organized dinner parties to which he invited the Decembrists, who were, to be sure, the center of attention. "Miagkov even invited them on other occasions to visit him, and himself visited their quarters from time to time" (Tarasov, 261–62). An eyewitness account delivered by N. S. Shchukin states, "It was quite well known that Alexander Alexandrovich was his own man even in Miagkov's home; that he was received in A. P. Zlobin's home as well (the latter was the director of the salt works in Yakutsk), and that he tutored Zlobin's children; and that he frequented the home of A. I. M-aya on her nameday, subsequently dedicating a poem to her . . . which includes the lines:

> In this land of winter and winter friendship
> Believe me—you and only you alone,
> Your kind and generous conversation,
> recalled to me and to my friends
> unforgettable days of old."
>
> (262)

Tarasov, Bestuzhev's biographer of the Yakutsk years, writes, "Even in cold Yakutsk Bestuzhev remains true to himself, aspiring there to taste 'sweet tears and an eternal first kiss.' [Bestuzhev] admits that even in Yakutsk he 'drank the perfidious mead of love, taking not my lips from its cup' " (ibid.).

Bestuzhev also passed his time by documenting life in this obscure part of the realm:

Such lifelessness occurs for lack of unanimity amongst the population, and perhaps even from a lack of animus. I have believed little up to this time in treatises by the mister physiologists on the impact of climate on temperament, but in my Northern Palmira I have met but rarely all those passions associated with Italy. Thus, my disbelief has turned [north], like a compass arrow, so that at each [gloomy], philosophical gaze [I encounter], I am more and more convinced of the theory's truth. Here the people's mind and sensitivities are in some kind of hibernation: their movements are awkward and heavy, their speech monotonous and drawn out. Sitting is their greatest pleasure, and silence is not even difficult for women to acquire. Only bilious passions are animated here: self-interest, envy, and vanity. That's what flows in the blood congealed and lifeless.

They marry for economic reasons and continue to live together merely because it is virtually impossible to separate. As a consequence their children are weak and consumptive and rarely live to adolescence. Moreover, the custom of giving a child to a wet nurse, or, as they put it here, "to a Yakut," ruins the children more than diseases. You can judge for yourself their customs when at the age of three or four the children are brought home to a mother whom they do not recognize and who has entirely forgotten them. Negligence and spoiling conclude their rearing, so that at eighteen years of age a lad encompasses in himself all the prejudices and deficiencies of both peoples, possessing not a single direct idea nor a single language, for he has not sufficiently acquired the Yakut language, and no one is capable of teaching him Russian. . . .

Nowhere else is there as little interest in holidays as there is here. Women sit about with each other for hours on end without anything to occupy them; but, then again, there is nothing to do at home, and when there is, it pertains only to necessity and never to pleasure of any sort. Fine and beautiful hand work is virtually unknown except to maybe two or three ladies. Showing themselves off merely in expensive fur coats, they do not attend to their dress in the least, and not infrequently you will find a wealthy merchant's wife in a soiled dress, black stockings and holding a particolored kerchief in her hand. Men's attire is even more outrageous. They haven't the slightest inkling of the pleasures associated with good, clean linen. At meals they do not even change plates between courses, and two cups serve a dozen mouths. This is all the more incredible in that for important meals where guests are invited you can see a table covered in European style with European cuisine. Clearly, they know what is good and what is bad. But, it seems, they consider cleanliness a silly adornment which is worn only for show. I shall not even begin to speak about the laziness and uncleanliness of the Yakuts. ("Aleksandr Bestuzhev v Iakutske," 250–51)

Bestuzhev's despair in the isolation and provinciality of Yakutsk, especially after Chernyshev was transferred,[16] is hardly surprising. It was a time of stasis. A healing alternative was to further his reading.

An Isolated Reader

While in exile, thanks to the generosity of his family and friends, Bestuzhev was well supplied with books.[17] Of the forty-four letters available from the Yakutsk period, all but four comment on the books he has received, the nature of his reading, and his interpretation of what he has read. Literature is the overarching theme of his correspondence, which attests not only to his love of verbal art but also to art's seminal role in the restoration of a fallen soul. Bestuzhev wrote his brother Peter:

> I live with my books and with my dreams [mechtania]. I observe the frozen asters on the mica windowsills and rarely bathe in the winter fogs, that is, I sit and sit like [the epic tale hero] Il'ia

16. Bestuzhev's despairing remarks were penned upon Chernyshev's departure.

17. Kotliarevskii, 157–58; Postnov, 55; and Tarasov, 8–9:256. Interestingly, Bazanov does not attend to this topic at all, and the eyewitness, P. S. Shchukin, categorically states that he saw no books about Bestuzhev's quarters when he visited him there (Shchukin, "A. Bestuzhev-Marlinskii v Iakutske," 142). There is a striking resemblance between Shchukin's words and the fictional editor's in the introduction to Dostoyevsky's *Notes from the House of the Dead* (1860).

Muromets. You must, my dear brother, justify the blessings of Providence which saved you [by exiling Peter to the Caucasus where he might fulfill the calling of the warrior] so you can prove yourself worthy of life. The book of the world lies before you and in it you shall discover that there is no other wisdom in this world other than truth and justice. God protect you in battle and in peace for the sake of our unfortunate mother. ("Pis'ma iz ssylki," 120)

The figure of the world as a book was not new in Bestuzhev's time. It underscored the notion of life-texts and implied that the tools required to read the world are the same ones used to decipher literature. Bestuzhev questioned these assumptions when he asked Peter, who had recently been wounded in battle, to write his responses to the Caucasus: "Do me the favor of writing what kind of impression mountain nature, your first battle, and first assault had on you. I am attempting to study man in all conditions in life and I depend upon your truthfulness more than on the stories of scribblers: I want to compare their opinions with the real thing" (119). Although Bestuzhev expressed a sceptical view of literary description, he thought that his brother could produce a true picture of reality. He was unaware that writers select, shape, and thus distort, even when attempting to be objective. He ignored his own caveat about scribblers and suggested what Peter might narrate about his life:

And so now you are resting on your laurels, even in a literal sense. I imagine you see over you a sapphire sky, beneath and about you monuments to your heroic deeds, and in the distance (or perhaps even close at hand) dark-eyed beauties of the East who surely transport a man and inspire in him pure rapture!! Of course the physical conditions and coarse prose of the soldier's life must fold in the wings of imagination for a time. But still, the minutes of joy must be passionate and vivid. As Mickiewicz says, "One moment in May is more dear than a week in autumn." (203)[18]

Bestuzhev juxtaposed his flowery style with the humdrum routine of the common soldier's life. As he penned a figurative phrase ("fold in the

18. Adam Mickiewicz (1798–1855) was Poland's leading romantic poet. Like Bestuzhev, he was a revolutionary; like Pushkin, he was a great poet.

wings of imagination"), he sustained the poetic vision by which he was inspired, which found its deepest attraction in fantasies of sensuality:

> I have grown old by experience, but I am still young at heart and life still flows in my veins thanks to my imagination. Now allow me to ask in a whisper, has not some obliging zephyr blown your way a veil attached to a concubine? And have you not rendered some manner of service, as one might expect, in the name of kind gratitude. And is there not a serenade sung (*a propos*, do you not strum on the guitar?); and a jealous Moslem at hand; and even . . . so on and so forth? This is all very well for turning one into a poet, not to mention for chasing my garrison and platonic boredom away. ("Pis'ma iz ssylki," 119–20)

In his letter Bestuzhev was alluding to Pushkin's "Prisoner of the Caucasus" (1822) and "The Fountain of Bakhchisarai" (1824)—love between a Russian officer and a native beauty, a jealous Moslem suitor, and all the accoutrements of this triangle (veils, dark eyes, gentle breezes, the mountain air, a sapphire sky, and the night of consummation). Here he reveals a great deal about his understanding of writing and reading. He requests a "realistic" description of Peter's life but hopes that it will replicate his literary preconceptions. The inconsistency underscores Bestuzhev's belief that literary structures constitute reality, that literature can encompass the real world.

Bestuzhev's presuppositions about art infected his reading practice. Several years earlier, on March 9, 1825, Bestuzhev had written to Pushkin in response to the first canto of *Eugene Onegin* (1823–28). He criticized the choice of poetic topics, and, in response to a letter from Pushkin, wrote, "You deftly parry my objections about the object; but I am not convinced that it would be a great service to fertilize the impoverished soil of your object, although I agree that it requires much art and great labor to do so. It is a miracle to graft apples to a pine; certainly this can happen, and it causes one to be amazed, but the apples will smell of pitch no matter what you do."[19] Bestuzhev argued that poetry, indeed all art, seeks not any object, but lofty ones. Pushkin's genius brought with it the obligation that he address something grand (not the good-for-

---

19. "Pis'mo A. A. Bestuzheva (Marlinskogo) k A. S. Pushkinu," *Russkii arkhiv* 1 (1881): 425.

nothing fop Onegin): "In order to bring down an eagle from its heights, one requires art and a good weapon. The weapon is your talent, the bird the subject you treat. Then why in heaven's name do you fire a cannon at a butterfly?" (425).

Advancing his idea of an appropriate object for poetry, Bestuzhev asked, "What could be more poetic than Peter [the Great]?" (ibid.). Here he displayed his bias toward historical subjects, for in them the grandeur of man unfurled against life's adversities. The ideal could be embodied only in greatness. Onegin did not fit the bill, as Bestuzhev noted in a letter to his mother and sisters: "[I notice] no taste for romanticism among us Russians, for Pushkin, the god of current fashion, has very little of the *ideal* (that is, the Romantic) in him" (Azadovskii, *Pamiati dekabristov,* 2:206). Bestuzhev challenged Pushkin:

> That you can describe grand society in a poetic manner cannot be denied. But have you given Onegin poetic form other than the fact that you have written about him in verse? Have you placed him in contrast with society so that you might show him in sharper contours against the cutting malice [of society]? What I see is a fop who in body and soul is given only to fashion. I see the type of man [in Onegin] whom I meet by the thousands each day. For them all coldness, misanthropy and the desire to be strange are kept on the shelf with one's toilet articles these days. Of course many of the pictures you have drawn are charming, but they are not complete. You have captured Petersburg society, but you have not penetrated it. Read Byron. Even without knowing our Petersburg, he described its likeness, and this is the case especially because he understands people as they really are. Even his affected empty-headed speech hides within itself keen philosophical observation, and when it comes to satire, what can one say! ("Pis'mo k Pushkinu," 426)

Byron supplied the literary archetypes that rendered the world comprehensible to Bestuzhev. Most significant was Byron's persona. The contact between reader and writer was also important to Bestuzhev:[20] "I do not know a person who better than [Byron], more vividly than he, has

---

20. Wolfgang Iser, *The Act of Reading: A Theory of Aesthetic Response* (Baltimore, Md., 1978), 152–54.

described character and captured in them new passions and vices which at this historical moment are only emerging. And he is so cruel, so fresh in his satire! Don't think, however, that I do not like your *Onegin*. On the contrary, all the parts of reverie [the digressions] are charming, but here I do not see Onegin at all, only you" ("Pis'mo k Pushkinu," 426). In a letter written much later (June 1828), Bestuzhev states his views more directly than he could have in his pre-Decembrist correspondence:

> I must confess that I would greatly like to have all Pushkin's verse. Write to him directly. This would not be a gift to me in the least, for I purchased a fragment of Onegin from him for three hundred rubles so that I might publish it in the *Star*. I was not able to put it in print. He, of course, is not at fault for my not using his verse, but, consequently, sending me an edition will cost him nothing but only make up for my losses. I already have the first two cantos here, and I have memorized them already, even though I do not envy the hero of the novel. He is some kind of unnatural decoction of the eighteenth century with a little silly Byronic spice added to it. (Azadovskii, *Pamiati dekabristov*, 2:205)[21]

Claiming that he did not need Onegin because he saw thousands of them each day, Bestuzhev equated literature and life in absolute terms. He resisted the cues Pushkin encoded to guide his readers toward the text's fecundity. Onegin's propensity to play the fop, to dress for public display, to use bons mots, to engage in affairs, and to stand above the crowd, all conform to the gentleman officer's behavioral code to which Bestuzhev adhered. There may in fact be little difference between Onegin's "silly Byronism" (*baironovshchina*), which Bestuzhev emphasized in his letter to his sister Elena, and his own dedication to Byronism and English literature as mentioned in a letter to Pushkin: "I will say this about myself. I am in the process of swallowing with passion English literature, and I am grateful with all my soul to the English language. It has taught me how to think and has turned my attention to nature, this inexhaustible spring! I am even prepared to say: il n'y a point de salut

---

21. Pushkin had returned the three hundred rubles as early as 1827 to the families of Ryleyev and Bestuzhev. Bestuzhev apparently did not know about this gesture on Pushkin's part toward the destitute Madame Ryleyev and the hard-pressed Bestuzhev women.

hors la littérature anglaise [There is no salvation outside of English literature]. If you can, study it. You will be repaid for the effort a hundredfold" ("Pis'mo k Pushkinu," 427). If he were to meet Pushkin fully in his reading, he would have had to become conscious of his own *baironovshchina*.

Bestuzhev may have committed the several hundred lines of *Onegin* to memory as a means of experiencing the exquisite verse aesthetically, in which case he could have remained aloof from Onegin. But his repulsion and attraction to Pushkin's seminal text suggests its psychological value. His reproof may have been matched by a secret understanding of Pushkin's antihero, an understanding that motivated him to take the text within himself as a facet of his own identity and investigate its unfolding significance. As the text resides within the psyche of the reader, the subject-object division essential to cognition and perception disappears (Iser, 154). Pushkin's text thoroughly involved Bestuzhev in the process of struggle. Engagement in reading to this extent holds the potential of "becoming conscious" (157–59).[22] Bestuzhev, however, rejected the path toward critical consciousness, and his opinion of *Eugene Onegin* persisted to the end. On Christmas 1828, he wrote a bilious commentary to his brothers Mikhail and Nicholas: "By the way, the further Pushkin takes his *Onegin* the worse it becomes. In the last three cantos you won't find a half dozen poetic strophes. The verse is playful, but burdened by trifles as well as slovenly carelessness. Eugene's character is simply vile. He is an unfeeling beast with all the sins of petty passion" ("Aleksandr Bestuzhev v Iakutske," 249).

Commenting on reader response to *Tom Jones*, Wolfgang Iser describes a similar style of reading: "By setting the hallowed norm against an unfamiliar background, the text illuminates those aspects of the norm that had hitherto remained hidden, thereby arousing an explosive reaction from the faithful followers of that norm" (202). Bestuzhev's vehemence about Onegin *qua* hero fits precisely Iser's condition of interplay between the familiar and the unfamiliar. We know from Bestuzhev's

---

22. The conflict Bestuzhev experiences in reading *Onegin*, suggested by the fact that he memorizes it and simultaneously rejects its hero, establishes the conditions, Iser argues, that enable a text to affect a reader. In an attempt to resolve such a conflict, a reader will utilize the text as a means toward entering into his or her own psyche: "The significance of the work, then, does not lie in the meaning sealed within the text, but in the fact that meaning brings out what had previously been sealed within us" (157). This is particularly important in regard to the Onegin prototype in Bestuzhev and to Bestuzhev's attempt to comprehend himself in exile.

remarks that the social background of the novel was contemporary society. But Onegin's callous disregard of others' emotions and his propulsion toward morally reprehensible behavior based on indifference did not portray the ideal qualities Bestuzhev would endow in a Byronic hero. The deficiencies, which covertly governed the Byronic type in Russian culture and which were laid bare by Pushkin, created a dilemma for Bestuzhev (because he was wont to read texts as programs for daily life). He was challenged by Pushkin to see the reality of *baironovshchina* behind the public mask of heroic *baironizm*.

The themes of perception and reflection in Bestuzhev's first work in exile, "Andrei, Prince of Pereyaslavl," have no equivalents in Bestuzhev's response to *Onegin*. Bestuzhev could thematize the value of reflection, but he could not engage it. Pushkin offered him the possibility of viewing from without the norms by which he lived, wrote, and, one day, died; but he chose to cling to the very romantic preconceptions Pushkin assaulted. He was reluctant to take a sufficiently critical attitude toward the codes, causes, beliefs, and ideas that had led him into isolation and exile.

Stasis

On February 10, 1829, Bestuzhev wrote to Count Dibich, the official who had offered compassion on his journey to Yakutsk, to seek his favor. The count's recent commission as commander of the Second Army stationed in the Caucasus occasioned Bestuzhev's letter:

> Your Honor, and Kind Sir,
> Your highness's generous mercy, which I have had the pleasure of experiencing before, emboldens me to make a request of you which is both humble and impassioned: I ask that Your highness intercede for me before the most generous Monarch that I might be assigned the post of common soldier to serve you in pursuit of victory. A great soul reared in battle can well understand the suffering of a soldier who has been sentenced to wither away in frivolity while the glory of Russian weapons thunders above the cradle of the ancient world, above the grave of Mohammed. But in beseeching your mercy, I seek neither reward nor distinction. I seek only the opportunity to spill my blood for the glory of the

Emperor, that I might honorably end my life, a life given by him, so that over my dust the name of a criminal shall not hang. Forgiven by the most highly generous of Monarchs, I feel all the more the magnitude of my crime, and am more completely consumed by repentance. But together with these feelings my consciousness opens before me the limitlessness of His mercy, and therefore I beseech you to inform His Imperial Highness of my humble request. If he, who decides the fate of battles and of empires, might have a free moment to take from civic and military duties, please turn his attention to his unfortunate servant.

Only in the Emperor's mercy lie my hopes, only in your intercession can I find anyone to take my part. Other than Your highness I have no other protector, no other means by which to serve in word and in deed the Most High Emperor, whose throne you, by unalterable right, may approach.

Awaiting with great trepidation a word on my fate, and suffused with great respect for you and a zealous devotion to you, I have the honor of abiding, Your highness and most kind sir, as your most devoted servant Alexander Bestuzhev.[23]

The letter made a circuitous route from Yakutsk to Irkutsk, and from there was carried by intermediaries, the last of whom was General Adjutant Potapov, who recommended the letter to Count Dibich with the personal words, "I feel that Bestuzhev's letter is worthy of Your highness's reading" (887). Dibich forwarded the request to Nicholas I, who responded succinctly: "Alexander Bestuzhev shall be transferred as a common soldier to the active regiments of the Caucasus Corps with the proviso that in the event of distinction in battle he will not be promoted, but that word of his accomplishments will be reported to us" (887). A month after receiving the tragic news that his friend and fellow writer, Alexander Griboyedov (1795–1829), ambassador to Persia, had been murdered in a mob assault on the Russian embassy in Iran, Bestuzhev was sent from Yakutsk into active duty.

Life in high society, in the barracks, and at the club in St. Petersburg had afforded Bestuzhev the opportunity to display his persona and release his romantic energies. When he tired of the endless round of dance, drink, and debauch, or of Decembrist asceticism, literature served as an

23. "Pis'mo Aleksandra Bestuzheva—grafu Dibichu," *Russkaia starina* 11 (1881): 886–87.

Fig. 4.   Alexander A. Bestuzhev (1797–1837), engraving from a self-portrait sent from the Caucasus to his sister, Elena, 1833

alternative outlet. In remote Yakutsk, despite some diversions, the creative expression of the persona was difficult for Bestuzhev to sustain. Yakutsk represented a symbolic death.

On Christmas 1828, Bestuzhev wrote his brothers, "in my heart feelings are born, in my mind thoughts flash and glitter, but to no avail. There is no purpose [in pursuing] either one or the other. I am not taken by poetry enough to create something for worms and mice, and I cannot prepare dry prose for hanging on a wall" ("Aleksandr Bestuzhev v Iakutske," 249). The reference to stasis in creativity refers to a discovery Bestuzhev made while in Yakutsk concerning one of his forebears. In a letter to his sister Elena, Bestuzhev remarked that he had been wandering about the Yakutsk environs in search of Voinarovsky's grave and the stone of his "unfortunate relative, [Anna] Bestuzheva, who died here." He continued:

> There are still old ladies here who remember her. They say that she was unusually beautiful, but always walked about in a veil. You know, I think, that her tongue had been cut out and that she spoke indistinctly and hardly audibly. She lived entirely alone by the Church of the Holy Mother and went to services each day. She gave alms to the poor and in general left fond memories of her as well as compassion for her situation. They called her Countess hereabouts (although this was incorrect) and did not know the reason for her exile. You should not be unfamiliar with her. In my papers you will find the order by Empress Elizaveta on the matter. From them it should be clear that she was in an alliance (of the heart, it seems, and not a political one) with doctor Lestok who was accused of insulting the Emperor. Thus one day my dust, thrown by a great storm into the cold tundra of Siberia, will too be sought out! (Azadovskii, *Pamiati dekabristov*, 2:204)

In 1723 Anna Bestuzheva (née Golovkina) had married a highly placed official and soon thereafter became Ekaterina I's lady-in-waiting. Her husband died thirteen years later, and in 1743 she married Bestuzhev-Riumin whose brother held a high government post. Her position at court became precarious, for her brother's exile to Siberia brought suspicion upon her. She fell into court intrigue and was sent to Yakutsk, where she died in 1749. Alexander Bestuzhev sought her papers, which were rumored to be located somewhere in the village:

I have been seeking hereabout the grave of Anna Gavrilovna Bestuzheva . . . who ended her life of exile here. She was banished out of the empress's jealousy, was flogged and had her tongue cut out. An old lady remembered her and told me that she was pretty, went about in a veil, and spoke inaudibly. She did much good as well. I almost found a trace of her papers and those of her brother, but found them (Oh Vandals!) papering a cabin wall and covered with paint. Thus indeed perish all traces of the past in these parts. ("Aleksandr Bestuzhev v Iakutske," 240)

The misuse of "Andrei, Prince of Pereyaslavl" by less than honorable publishers earlier that year and the discovery of the ruined Bestuzheva papers dampened his spirits and deterred him from engaging in his craft. Overcome by lethargy and purposelessness, in Yakutsk he was indifferent toward his own work. He wrote a few Siberian poems and used the paper on which they were written for cigarettes. He told his brothers in Chita: "I write absolutely nothing in prose; I haven't sufficient sources or adequate resources for treating serious subjects. And as for writing sentimental pieces, I have become altogether too serious a person. I live alone, leaf through my books, and cover the ceiling with smoke from my pipe. I smile only when I recollect the fond past; and I *laugh* as rarely as my cat. Oh, why am I not with you, my friends! Together again with you I would wipe from my face this uncharacteristic sadness" (ibid., 241). Only in his letters could Bestuzhev express himself in a romantic guise (isolated, bored, yet hopeful, strong, and prepared to suffer whatever fate might bring): "A person who has little to narrate but much to tell needs find himself in great difficulty when he must in very few words say something to the point. I am not in such a circumstance. Feelings are a waterfall, but words are a sieve! One look, one touch of the hand would communicate to you more than [my words can], and would make us happier than the carefulness [with which we usually write our] frozen lines. They are like worms in the snow" (238).

It was not uncommon for Bestuzhev to refer to his mortality in his epistles to his family. In describing the Lena River, for example, he noted that it was surrounded in places by "minarets or crowded churchyards where thousands of gravestones stand one behind the other" (Azadovskii, *Pamiati dekabristov*, 2:195). He depicted his brothers' place of exile as a "silent domicile, like a grave" ("Aleksandr Bestuzhev v Iakutske," 231). In a letter dated June 10, 1828, Bestuzhev stated directly: "Death would not improve my fate, nor can it give hope to my dreams, for everything else may change for the better. Who in life can dare say: 'This shall be', or 'this shall never be!' " (Azadovskii, *Pamiati dekabristov*, 2:203). It is not fortuitous that Bestuzhev saw death as an escape, even if only to reject the idea, for during the initial decades of the nineteenth century in Russia Wertherian suicide was considered an honorable exit for those grown weary of life.

A theatrical demise possessed unique charms, for it dramatized an otherwise boring existence. On July 25, 1828, Bestuzhev wrote his mother and sisters a decidedly literary description of his plight and his future:

> I am writing to you, mother dearest, just at the end of our local summer. It is still warm, but the heat has passed, and amidst the beautiful days we occasionally find that it isn't superfluous to fire the stove. The Yakutsk climate doesn't want us to forget it even in fine weather. However, the thunderstorms have occurred only twice this whole time, and I have taken pleasure in the night watching the lightning run along the clouds to disclose the sky. At these times I have been carried into the past; I have always loved a storm! Many, many recollections ignited together with the heaven's fires, like lighthouses from different periods of my life— a life which, viewed superficially, appears entirely uniform, but in fact is the most romantic of lives. Now, it seems, I am in the final chapter of my novel—and certainly the Yakutsk snow will be its and my cover. The sooner the better. (Ibid., 2:203)

If this was literary posturing, then it projects a persona which Bestuzhev felt was endowed with substance. In typical fashion, he viewed the unfolding of his existence in narrative terms, as the development and elaboration of a plot. He continued his letter with reference to the texts he used as models:

> The proximity of the [north] pole has instilled in me a greater indifference to life [than before] because, as the saying goes [and here Bestuzhev cites the passage in English], "I am not thirsty of mere being, but of well-being," that is [in Russian], I do not thirst for bare existence, but for well-being. Do not think, however, dear mother, that I am bored with life, or that I have fallen to that

fashionable illness which covers all printed pages—that spleen [in English] from Byron's shop; on the contrary, I would consider it a sin to even think about grumbling, for I feel strongly that the beneficence of God and of the Tsar have protected me from a thousand great and well-deserved misfortunes. (203)

In distancing himself from fashion, Bestuzhev asserted that social norms are empty, mere posing, purchasable for next to nothing in the shops. Spleen of this cheap variety was a counterfeit copied poorly from the true coin (Byron); its value resided in the bard's historical authenticity. Bestuzhev claimed that he conformed not to the social norm but to the literary phenomenon, and thus represented Byronic authenticity.

Bestuzhev made another distinction concerning the interpretation and inculcation of texts. If the authentic text modeled behavior and language, it was only a conditional modeling, for it could potentially be superseded by a greater code (if not ontologically, then at the level of discourse). Bestuzhev's references to the beneficence of God and tsar are not to be taken lightly, even though they were penned to appease the censor and the government apparatus, which made regular reports to Nicholas I about Bestuzhev's exile. Religious considerations represented a necessary part of Bestuzhev's confrontation with his mortality. His letter continues: "I bravely endure my fate, but I must confess that an existence without a purpose and without a goal diminishes its value daily. Thus wise Providence, little by little depriving [us] of life's pleasures, teaches us first not to fear, and then to even desire death. I have not reached this point yet and undoubtedly will not reach it before the time affixed by age or illness, but I nonetheless think about life coldly" (ibid.).

Bestuzhev's remarks about God and life's purpose are immediately followed by mortal thoughts. This is logical, of course, considering Bestuzhev's isolation in Yakutsk: "God gave us fruits, but also gave us hands so that we might obtain and improve them. God gave us reason, but ordained that man not darken, but enlighten it, otherwise why would he have sent us experience, otherwise why would he have allowed us a long life, if not in order to supply us with the means of correcting the past and preparing for what will come?" (ibid., 210–11). Pressed by anxieties about the future, Bestuzhev mixed his message to his mother. On the one hand, he announced that although he must one day "desire" death, he had not yet reached that point in his life. He stated his perspective in categorical terms—fate is governed by Providence and is unalterable. This could hardly have reassured his mother. On the other hand, Bestuzhev replaced his fatalistic model of life with a teleological notion—man is a product of God's manufacture, endowed with faculties that justify his existence. The two perspectives are not antithetical. Bestuzhev argued fatalism but delayed the "necessity" of seeking death willingly in order to develop his God-given gifts: "I am far from being an egotist, but just as far from self-abasement. I know my worth in the world of Russian letters, even though I have attained my value by chance, through the lack of prose writers in contemporary literature. Thus, I feel that I have services to perform for our native language" (220). He presented his argument within traditional spiritual categories. It was not *he* who determined his future, purpose or fate, but God. In rhetorical terms, Bestuzhev shifted authority from his own voice to that of the Supreme Deity. He replaced the literary with a religious code, not as an affirmation of faith, but as a gesture that might simultaneously satisfy his mother (who was deeply religious) and manipulate the censor. Thus, a nexus of categories come together at the surface of his discourse—thanatos, Providence / God, fate, confession, atonement, and literary activity. If there was a religious note sung in these letters, it was secularized, individualistic, and even solipsistic. It is not God who is served in Bestuzhev's affirmations.

It would not be entirely fair to claim that Bestuzhev's spirituality was totally lacking in substance. His letters begin and end with a prayer or a blessing ("God protect you," etc.). Certainly his remarks might be formulaic speech habits appropriate for his loved ones. He meant to comfort his mother by appealing to religion, but his relationship to his brothers Nicholas and Mikhail was intellectual, and they were not religious. The following March, in a letter to his brothers, Bestuzhev scarcely mentioned the God about whom he had written his mother in January. He replaced the spiritual lexicon with marlinisms: "It seems that I have already informed you about the departure of my compagnon de larmes, non d'armes [comrade in grief but not in arms]. If I haven't written to you about this, I am nevertheless alone now. He left so quickly that I hardly had time to say adieu. The last word Dieu in truth belongs more to the traveler than to me. Let Him guard him and send him success. I am more taken by the mysterious particle *a*. Fate shall show me where I am located, on a silent street or at a crossroads" ("Aleksandr Bestuzhev v Iakutske," 252). There is no reference to God as designer of texts, but rather to fate, a secular term the Enlightenment set in opposition to God.

He tailored his remarks for a different reader, understanding his brothers' beliefs and refraining from assuming a voice of authority. To his mother, Bestuzhev had maintained that grief is ordained to instruct man, but to his brothers he says he does not know its purpose. To the romantic Bestuzhev, God, Providence, fate, and fortune were synonymous. These references to higher authority indicate a revaluation of his place in a cosmic plan of an as yet undetermined shape.[24]

As he experienced his powerlessness, Bestuzhev yielded to mythological terms as fecund descriptive signs. They allowed him to comprehend anew the dimensions of his self-idea. Where once he considered himself central to any description of the world, he was now compelled to acknowledge forces beyond his control. This shift was represented by and conditioned through Bestuzhev's language, which introduced a religious and philosophical lexicon and was carried forward by stylistic structures that emphasized that lexicon's personal significance: "Formerly, it is true, I did not value [life], but this was because I valued too highly the illusion of glory and fame. Then I was daring intuitively; but now I lack fear by dint of reason. Formerly I put everything out on the table hoping that this might help me obtain what I then valued most; but now I wouldn't even wager a single stake, for there is nothing for me to gain" (ibid., 257).

These utterances are constructed on the opposition "then/now." The temporal construction suggests that Bestuzhev countenanced personal growth as an essential component of selfhood. This moment marked a significant alteration in Bestuzhev's idea of himself and must be viewed as part of a series of changes in his self-definition during exile. As the emergent persona entertained a larger and more inclusive world, however, he interpreted his condition from a fatalistic perspective. If these combined features rendered Bestuzhev more introspective and willing to examine deficiencies inhering in the early Marlinsky persona, they simultaneously suggest the parameters within which his future development took place. He did not dismiss the persona altogether, but modified the warrior-hero archetype to include his tragic and mortal dimensions.

This internal conflict sprang from Bestuzhev's determination of the

---

24. Bestuzhev's letters of April 10, 1829, to his mother, on the one hand, and to his brothers on the other, attest to the importance of the addressee in determining the lexicon and themes of his epistles. In the former Bestuzhev discussed almost exclusively his preparations for the Easter festivities and his hopes for his mother during the high holiday. In the latter Bestuzhev presented his thoughts on meteorology ("Aleksandr Bestuzhev v Iakutske," 255–57).

meaning of his life at a time when it was entirely static. Because he entertained little hope of change, he experienced dread and despair and struggled to overcome gloomy thoughts of death. He appealed to both religious and secular categories to try to assuage his anxieties (and those of his interlocutor). He used two distinct languages in his letters while in exile, one closed, fixed, and eternal (to his mother), the other open, ambiguous, and mutable (to his brothers). But these two codes can be ascribed to one central event—in Yakutsk he faced mortality directly and openly and was pressed to consider his fifth act. He read voraciously in search of solutions to life's problems. He pursued traditional religious ideas for an adequate perspective on his isolation. He adopted a descriptive terminology that issued from the Enlightenment and continued to exercise the marlinist language of the hero as a means toward comprehending the past. These sundry points of view interweave in his letters to his family and constitute an emerging self-idea that expanded, rather than abandoned, the narrow confines of the Marlinsky persona, which had governed his earlier life. If the voices he used in his letters individually and collectively describe the same problem, the persona of the warrior-hero delivered a potential solution—escape through heroic endeavor.

9

The Caucasus

The book is the man and creation is the
reflection of the Creator. This is what I
think, what I believe.
                              —Bestuzhev-Marlinsky

The Initial Test

The exotic Caucasus was associated with two great contemporary
authors—Byron and Pushkin. In addition to this literary interest, the
region was politically significant because it was the object of the government's expansionist policies. The fight being waged against Ottoman
hegemony was officially promoted as a war of liberation, although the
local tribes seemed as opposed to Russian liberation as they had ever
been to Turkish oppression. Reports from the front made popular reading in the journals and almanacs; travelogues were published regularly.
Bestuzhev entered a literary topography he knew well as a reader. He
arrived in the Caucasus ready to fight with both pen and sword. During

this period, Bestuzhev most effectively embodied the primary code of his existence—the fusion of literature and life.

Bestuzhev was a foreigner who initially did not command the language(s) of the resident communities. His life was situated on the boundary between two distinct cultures. This condition had an immediate impact on the conflict between reality and fantasy within him. It forced him to question the idea he brought with him to the Caucasus and to verify literary models in reality. Previously fiction had influenced his acquisition of the Marlinsky persona in society, the military, and the literary salon. Now, however, the relationship, if not reversed, was reapportioned. Daily life, which seemed exotic to the newcomer, played a significant role in the writing of his fiction. As life began to exercise a more profound effect on his art, Bestuzhev shaped more naturally the literary boundaries of his daily existence. A dialogical relationship emerged in which fantasy and reality commingled in dynamic tension, which was never fully resolved, but is dramatically enacted both in his texts and in his life-text. The first indication of this tension appeared in a work Bestuzhev wrote in Siberia and saw published soon after his arrival in the Caucasus. It laid out the parameters of Bestuzhev's new thinking about the power texts have to make individuals act.

After a long visit with his brothers Pavel and Peter and other Decembrists, and immediate engagement in military maneuvers against the Turks, Bestuzhev was suddenly moved from Tiflis to Derbent on the Caspian Sea. He spent the next four years in the garrison there, his existence alternating between boredom and military activity, humiliation at the hands of punitive superiors and support in the homes of sympathetic friends, by periods of poetic inspiration and bouts of writer's block, and by fierce engagements against the mountain foe and by sustained periods of parade ground exercise or night guard duty, which he considered beneath his dignity (though not his station).

Bestuzhev began publishing under his pen name Marlinsky almost immediately upon his arrival in the Caucasus. This was due to the persistence and acumen of Elena in dealing with publishers and the censors in Petersburg and Moscow. Within three years "Marlinsky" became the financial mainstay of the Bestuzhev family—his mother and sisters at the family estate, his brothers Peter and Pavel in the Caucasus, and Mikhail and Nicholas in Siberia. By 1835 Bestuzhev counted 50,000 rubles in deposits and interest for his stories, travelogues, and criticism,[1] the result of such popularity that publishers were willing to sign contracts in four figures (an unheard-of sum at the time) for a hundred pages of his work. In 1834 the renowned publisher Alexander Smirdin (1795–1857) paid Bestuzhev ten thousand rubles for three volumes of his collected works.[2]

There is dramatic representation of the commercial world and middle-class desires in Bestuzhev's first major publication of the Caucasus period, "The Test" ("Ispytanie"), which appeared in four successive numbers of *The Son of the Fatherland* in 1830. The story has been variously treated as a Decembrist tract and as a polemical response to Pushkin's *Eugene Onegin*.[3] It has been examined from the perspective of the further development of Bestuzhev's politically oriented, propagandist literature, and from the point of view of Bestuzhev's formal presentation of fictional personalities.[4] Mersereau dismisses these perspectives out of hand, summarizing the story line disparagingly:

> The entire plot of *The Test* is downright silly. A certain Gremin persuades his fellow officer, Strelinsky, to attempt to win the affection of Alina, a wealthy young widow with whom Gremin had previously been in love. The tester succeeds too well, which seems rather *de trop* to Gremin, who issues a challenge. Meanwhile Gremin has fallen under the spell of Strelinsky's sister, Olga, fresh from the Smolny Institute. Through Olga's intercession, a pointless duel is avoided and everyone lives happily ever after.[5]

Although accurate, this synopsis hardly does justice to the deeper purposes of the tale. In Bestuzhev's work, silliness does not preclude themes of import. "The Tournament at Revel" showed Bestuzhev's pro-

1. "Aleksandr Bestuzhev na Kavkaze, 1829–1837: Neizdannye pis'ma ego k materi, sestram i brat'iam," *Russkii vestnik* 7 (1870): 62.
2. "Pis'ma Aleksandra Aleksandrovicha Bestuzheva k N. A. i K. A. Polevym, pisannye v 1831–1837 godakh," 466.
3. Lauren Leighton, "Marlinskij's 'Ispytanie': A Romantic Rejoinder to *Evgenij Onegin*," *Slavic and East European Journal* 13, no. 2 (1969): 200–216.
4. V. Bazanov, *Ocherki dekabristskoi literatury: Publitsistika, proza, kritika*, 406–18; Lauren Leighton, *Aleksander Bestuzhev-Marlinsky*, 80–92; F. Z. Kanunova, *Estetika russkoi romanticheskoi povesti (A. A. Bestuzhev-Marlinskii i romantiki-belletristy 20–30-kh godov XIX v)* (Tomsk, 1973), 134–36.
5. John Mersereau Jr., *Russian Romantic Fiction*, 121.

pensity to mix the high and the low as early as 1825. "The Test" in fact addresses Decembrist themes from the perspective of failure. It asks what possibilities there are for political, social, and economic reform in the aftermath of unsuccessful rebellion. Bestuzhev's tale answers forthrightly that the courses of action available to characters like Strelinsky and Alina are personal rather than social—flight from vacuous urban existence to transform, à la Tolstoy several decades later, the conditions in which the serfs labor.[6]

Related to the theme of land and labor reform, Bestuzhev addressed romantic heroic behavior patterns, questioned their value, only to reassert them in their feminine representation (that is, in Alina and Olga, who are willing to step outside social convention in order to resolve the conflict between Gremin and Strelinsky). At story's end, Gremin's rash, egocentric, dramatic, and impassioned performances of the heroic code have endangered his and Strelinsky's lives and threatened Olga with high society's censure for taking charge in a man's world (the duel). Bestuzhev expressed some ambivalence about the heroic code. On the one hand, it leads to near disaster (Gremin and Strelinsky's duel); but on the other, it conditions the tale's resolution (Alina and Olga's intervention). In this story Bestuzhev challenged the gentleman's code of behavior, which had been accepted without any question, by bringing into focus the thanatic potential inherent in its "heroics."[7]

Interestingly enough, "The Test" contains a dimension lying completely outside the potentially deadly chivalrous code Bestuzhev examined. Chapter 2 digresses from the Gremin / Strelinsky plot to a description of the Hay Market in Petersburg made so famous by Dostoyevsky in *Crime and Punishment*. The epigraph, taken from Byron, motivates the chapter's tangential approach to the plot: "If I have any fault, it is digression." Having supplied this rationale, Bestuzhev occupies the reader for several pages with a description of the Yuletide bustle of the

6. This theme has been adequately treated in Soviet scholarship and hardly requires elaboration here. See, for example, Bazanov, 406–18.

7. Lermontov's and Pushkin's examples indicate the difficulties authors had in imagining a way out of the enchanted circle that encompassed behavioral choices. Onegin, Silvio, Hermann, Pechorin, and Grushnitsky and a host of other characters reflect the inevitability of death delivered through the code. These authors were hard pressed to find an answer to the question of identity. Underscoring the mutual inclusiveness of literature and life, Pushkin and Lermontov themselves died according to the romantic code—they were killed dueling. It appears, then, that release from the thanatic foundation of romantic behavior had to come from another quarter, beyond the genres, character types, plots, and themes governing literature at the time.

marketplace. Challenging the reader to make sense of the digression, Bestuzhev concludes with an imagined dialogue between reader and author:

"But please, Mr. Author!" I hear many of my readers exclaim. "You have written a whole chapter on the market which elicits more a feeling of hunger than of interest in your story."

"Yet, in each instance you have lost nothing, kind sirs!"

"But, at least tell us which of the two hussars, Gremin or Strelinsky, has arrived in the capital first."

"You cannot know this by any other means than reading two or three chapters more, dear sir!"

"I must say, this is a strange way to force us to read your story."

"Each person has his own fantasies, and each author his own way of telling a story. However, if you are that curious, send someone to the commandant's headquarters to check the list of recent arrivals to town."[8]

The irony inherent in Bestuzhev's conception of the reader formed part of the critical canon of the period. While exploiting the ambiguous ground of fiction and reality he had helped create in the early 1820s, Bestuzhev suddenly challenged his readers to reconsider their assumptions. It is difficult to imagine a reader who indeed would send someone out to discover who had stepped into Petersburg out of Marlinsky's fiction.[9]

The drama of fiction stepping into reality represented one of Bestuzhev's deeper concerns in taking up the pen again. He was painfully conscious that he was lost to Russian literature. The Marlinsky pseudonym masked who he really was. Fiction reaching into reality, therefore, takes on psychological importance. It suggests one of the dilemmas of Bestuzhev's art during the 1830s. While cautioning his readers about the romantic code and its inherent dangers, he sought through his art to reveal his identity. In the first instance, he asked the readers to question

8. Aleksandr Bestuzhev-Marlinskii, *Sochineniia v dvukh tomakh*, 1:183; Carl Proffer, ed., *Russian Romantic Prose: An Anthology* (Ann Arbor, Mich., 1979), 155.

9. Mersereau claims that it was an open secret that Marlinsky was really Bestuzhev (*Russian Romantic Fiction*, 120), a fact which appears to have gone unnoticed by Bestuzhev himself (as his letters attest).

the relationship of art to life, and in the second, to seek the coincidence of the two.

Escape from the confines of a literary identity was not as easy to fashion as a story or even a romantic life, but "The Test" presented an alternative in its digressive second chapter. Thematic ambiguities, Decembrist concerns, and literary polemics with Pushkin notwithstanding, this story contains a perspective on life almost entirely lacking in Bestuzhev's earlier prose. It is the stuff of mundane, lower- and middle-class existence—the Hay Market of Petersburg. It enters the story for a moment, retards the progress of the plot, calls attention to the whimsy of the narrator (and the implied author), and challenges the reader to attend to the connection between literature and life. The Hay Market chapter points in the direction prose of the next two decades was to take in the work of Nikolai Gogol, the naturalist school of writers, and many a realist.

The events Bestuzhev recorded in the second chapter of "The Test" are centered around festive holiday activities in preparation for the Christmas celebrations: "Yule-Tide more than any other holiday has the aura of the olden days, even in our Finnish Palmira, Petersburg" (Proffer, 151). If Easter in the Orthodox tradition represents the spiritual celebration par excellence, the lesser holiday which is Christmas, says the narrator, involves a more secular form of celebration and revelry reminiscent of earlier historical periods when pagan and Christian alike celebrated the winter solstice. These celebrations are reminiscent of the hedonistic lifestyle of the aristocracy to which the central characters of the story belong. As Strelinsky takes in "all the variety of forms and scenes that rear up before his eyes" (151), he is reminded of the code that belonged to Bestuzhev and his generation as well: "The material images awoke in his soul long-forgotten events, long-forgotten acquaintances and a multitude of wild escapades of his youth in society" (151).[10] Reference to the "olden days" and "wild escapades," which traditionally accompany the festival rebirth of the sun, indicates a carnival mood.

This chapter is replete with traditional carnivalesque features: masses of people gathered in an open, central meeting place; marketplace language; shouting matches; laughter; images of sacrificial slaughter; refer-

---

10. Just how long-forgotten those events and acquaintances are is a matter of conjecture, but it would seem to indicate the Decembrist Revolt. It is one of the many self-allusions Bestuzhev includes in the text.

ences to the lower parts of the human body (the stomach in this instance, and, by inference, any other parts of the body involved in "wild escapades" of youth).[11] These features appear in the chapter's introductory paragraph: "One of our heroes had entered there through the Moscow gate on Christmas Eve, and when the particolored and lively panorama of the capital city activity met his eye, all the joyful and pleasant recollections of childhood flooded his mind anew. While his dusty troika passed slowly amid the thousands of carts and pedestrians . . . a dashing young cabby, with his cap askew, stood and shouted, 'Watch out, out of the way!' in all directions with a smile" (Proffer, 152).

The succeeding passages of the text present detailed descriptions of each of the carnivalesque elements associated with the literary representation of the festive event: "Air, land and water here deliver their innumerable sacrifices for man's festival carnivorousness," the narrator writes, noting in mythological fashion all imaginable media which act as conduits to the gourmand's gut. In rabelaisian fashion the narrator catalogues these secular "sacrifices"—huge frozen sterlets, white sturgeon, and regular sturgeon "yawn out of boredom in these foreign environs," plucked geese "gaze longingly out of their carts awaiting a customer so to warm themselves over his spit." Hazel grouse and black grouse "have flown in by the thousands to taste the delights of capital city hospitality." Herds of curly-tailed swine prepare for the sacrifice by announcing, in a double inversion of carnival language (high flown, rather than base speech, to elevate the station of beast to that of man): "I am a striking example of the perfection of nature: I have long been a lesson to all on slovenliness and now I will become an example of good taste and tidiness. I deserve my laurels by virtue of my fine hams, hide, and hair which preserve your health, the clothes of your dandies, and the teeth of your beautiful ladies" (ibid.).

In drawing man and beast together in this fashion, the carnivalesque serves the critical purposes of language inherent in the celebration of life and death. The narrator's language is transformed into a marketplace tirade aimed directly at that vacuous society which had created men like Gremin who are vain, egocentric fops, and had produced an equally insipid literature: "Egotist calves, recollecting nothing but the saying, 'Keep your hide on,' do not hush their mugs for everyone else's sake and moo away the imminent loss of their motley clothes, which will surely

---

11. Mikhail Bakhtin, *Problems of Dostoevsky's Poetics*, 122–37.

attain a higher state of being, e.g., a soldier's knapsack or, even worse, a cover for some inane book" [Egoisty teliata, pomnia tol'ko poslovitsu, chto svoia kozha k telu blizhe, ne vnemliut golosu obshchei pol'zy i mychat, oplakivaia skoruiu razluku s pestroiu svoeiu odezhdoiu, kotoraia dostanetsia ili na soldatskie rantsy, ili chto eshche gorshe, na pereplety glupykh knig].[12]

Lest a naive reader miss the point of the narrator's barbs, the market-place and contemporary literature are immediately connected: "And how easy it would be for an apologist to pick up his quill here!" the narrator remarks. He turns his attention to the people who come to the market of necessity: servants indifferent to their masters' wishes, profligate butlers bent on cheating their barons, hausfrauen in oriental garb, red-nosed cooks, fat merchants, and the sorrowful, simple peasant. In this proletarian mass, all is cacophony, movement, and chaos bent on the processes of creation, sustenance, and destruction: "The market is alive. . . . Carriages and carts race each other, crash, get entangled, break up and fall apart" (Proffer, 153).

There is here a reverse movement toward that archetypal time of creation out of destruction, toward prehistory and the celebration of primal life forces, toward fecundity and death. The narrator likens this motion back in time to the individual's recollection of childhood, when hierarchical orders were leveled in the merriment of the festive season, and back to the collective past, and to pagan roots: "People are destined forever to chase after the toys [of their childhood]; childhood alone represents happiness to them, a happiness without [the need of] repentance" [Vechno liudi osuzhdeny goniat'sia za igrushkami, odno detstvo schastlivo imi bez raskaianiia] (Sochineniia, 1:182). The reference to guilt is significant from a psychological perspective, for carnival celebrations represent ritual purgations for individual as well as for collective bodies.

The carnivalized literature in which Bestuzhev engaged manifested a personal as well as sociocultural component relating both to the condition of the writing as well as to the content of the prose. Chapter 2 is Bestuzhev's excursus into heretofore closed areas of his psyche. Beyond any rationalization of behavior, outside the bounds of the persona's self conception, lay a bad conscience, which demanded release if only in ritualized form. Bestuzhev sought this release in the simultaneous critical and constructive power of creative writing.

Beginning with "The Test" there was movement in Bestuzhev's fic-

12. Proffer, 152; Bestuzhev-Marlinskii, Sochineniia, 1:179.

tion from folkloric fantasy toward a mythologically based fiction (in the sense that it attempts to create a coherent picture of the world and of self which could purge the experience of sin or inadequacy). The Hay Market represents the condition of mutual creation and destruction that allows for a transformation of a prior state of being. It is a primal impulse that stands outside the literary inheritance Bestuzhev had acquired and developed in his previous fictions. As such it is related to pagan traditions: "On the second day the real Yuletide celebrations get underway—that is, Christmas caroling, divinations, the traditional pouring of wax and tin into water in which the young women imagine they will see either a wedding wreath or the grave, either a sleigh or flowers with silver leaves—and finally traditional Christmas dinner songs, a race out behind the gates and all the pagan rites of old" (Proffer, 154). At the conclusion of the chapter, the equation of the pagan past with purgation/celebration can be seen as parallel to the ironic linkage of literature and life under the imprint of laughter. Rather than using the occasion to dismiss the connection between fiction and fact, and by extension between the author's persona and his real personality, Bestuzhev organized the fiction to serve both the destruction of the connection and its revaluation under new conditions. We are not meant to send our servant to the Moscow Gate, as the narrator facetiously suggests we should, because it is clear that there is no connection between the fiction we are reading and the world of romance we imagine as we follow the clichéd story that belongs to the dramatis personae. That story is a fable, as is its happy ending. If there is a connection between literature and life, however, it appears in the new elements of Bestuzhev's prose—the world of mundane reality, of commoners, beasts, and the unwashed masses.

This is not to suggest that Bestuzhev became a naturalist, an anthropologist, or socialist. On the contrary, the world represented in chapter 2 was decidedly *not* realistic (over and against the play of the aristocracy). What constitutes the message here is the reformulation of fiction's boundaries to include perspectives formerly inaccessible to Bestuzhev— the deromanticized, prosaic, and mundane world of the merchant and peasant classes.

Bestuzhev's years in Yakutsk had opened this stratum of society to him directly, reminding him in some measure of his inheritance through his mother.[13] Bestuzhev utilized this world not to destroy the illusions of

---

13. Bestuzhev's mother was of the merchant class, for which he felt a reverse snobbery.

romantic behavior to which he had subscribed earlier in life, but to reevaluate them. He wanted the behavior to serve more than youthful dreams of a better world and of a grander self. The materials of romanticism were marshaled in a new fashion to serve the emergence of a larger conception of the world and of one's place in it. The consequent movement was toward mythologization. "The Test" manifests this movement from folklore to myth in the dualistic forces of the carnivalesque. This story represents both an end and a new beginning, the death of one way of thinking and the emergence of another, not wholly divorced from the past, but transformed to absorb larger elements of life in a comprehensive and meaningful fashion.

In terms of the story's discourse, chapter 2 stands out, not as an anomaly, but as the narrative's interpretive center. The spirit of barter, trade, profanation, deformation, and celebration under the double imprint of death-dealing and life-affirming forces suffuses the entire story—its plot, characters, themes, and covert messages. From the first chapter, when Gremin and Strelinsky pillory the profligate and hedonistic ways of their comrades, to the summary comment of the doctor (the raisonneur) on "the felicitous foolishness of man" (ibid., 194), Bestuzhev's first tale of exile engaged the resources of the comic and absurd to impress a new order on his reader. From Gremin and Strelinsky's headlong rush toward mutual destruction to Olga's rejection of her expected role, a carnival spirit informs the story. From the cutting and satiric wit displayed by Strelinsky and Alina during the aristocracy's quintessential indulgence of genteel carnival (the masked ball) to the comic but dreadfully mindless discussion of appropriate behavior prior to the duel, the all-consuming destructiveness of time suffuses each chapter of the tale. And from the surgical analysis of "Decembrist" behavior to the apology of Decembrist revolutionary ideology, "The Test" constitutes a world of inversion and reversal unified throughout by a celebratory mood.

Several important questions concerning "The Test" remain unanswered. If Bestuzhev's tale was an effort to reverse Pushkin's gloomy vision of heroic identity and behavior, then how are we to evaluate Gremin and Strelinsky? Were it not for underlying wish-fulfilling prophecies on Bestuzhev's part (expressed through Olga's behavior), these two central characters might have met the same end as Lensky in *Eugene Onegin*. Given the inherent criticism of Gremin's rashness, impulsiveness, and competitiveness (all suggested in his name, *gremet'*, "to thunder"), and Strelinsky's stubborn adherence to ideological and behavioral principles (suggested, too, in his name, *strela*, "arrow"), "The Test" seems anything but optimistic. This early publication from the Caucasus represented an inquiry and an apology, neither of which was wholly satisfactory, but which indicated an altered purpose to Bestuzhev's fiction. It represents a means of describing life's problems, not their solution. The related questions of behavior and identity remained open. Bestuzhev would seek answers to them in his daily life.

Derbent

During the initial years of exile in the south, Bestuzhev created more than fiction under the pen name Marlinsky; he also invented and enacted a self-idea that grew out of the thinking evident in "The Test." It was the fusion of two images—one projected in fiction through his narrators, dramatis personae, and their implied author, the other displayed in daily behavior, encoded in personal letters, and recounted by memoirists and biographers—that has given rise to confusion about the man himself, the person secreted behind the ingenious persona Marlinsky. Of the more than one hundred and fifty letters that have appeared in print from Bestuzhev's exile archives, there are very few indeed that do not advertise the persona in stock literary terms—a poet-warrior given to bouts of ennui and laziness alternating with the whirl of social life (affairs, soirees, flirtations) and creativity. Like so many fictional characters who followed him, from Lermontov's Pechorin and Grushnitsky to Tolstoy's Olenin, Bestuzhev fashioned himself a Caucasian native, dressing the part to tear across the steppes or over the high mountains on a wild Circassian steed. In May 1831, he wrote the Polevoys that he had "taken up the Tatar language."[14] Ksenofont Polevoy noted that a Tatar friend of Bestuzhev's visiting Moscow testified: "Indeed [Bestuzhev] speaks like a real Tatar; we take him for anyone but a Russian" (150). Bestuzhev did everything in his power to project himself in the guise of a native, for he wished to engender in his audience a view of him from a romantic perspective. That audience apparently included Russians and natives alike: "All the natives of the mountains are crazy about me" (315). Bestuzhev's original archivist, Mikhail Semevsky, noted, "how quickly

14. "A. A. Bestuzhev (Marlinskii): 1798–1837," *Otechestvennye zapiski* 5 (1860): 150.

Bestuzhev managed to get on with the wild Asiatics and to be liked by them" (155). Bestuzhev explained his success in a letter to his brother Pavel in which he claims he "played the hero at [the battle of] Chirkhei." Semevsky adds that "in all military engagements Bestuzhev indeed showed himself to be a hero" (155).

Bestuzhev's rhetorical effectiveness cannot be overestimated. He wrote and acted on the boundary between fiction and life. Even transformations in the persona were conditioned by literature. By 1835, when he had left Derbent and participated in intensive and constant military operations, the image he projected was not merely of a warrior, but one who has grown weary of the fight: "Zass and I made two raids with the cavalry. We removed about eight thousand rams and took an inaccessible *aul* [village]. It was a very interesting journey, but it included a veritable pile of difficulties and deprivations. We fought not too foolishly, cut off a few heads, and, having spent fifteen days [in maneuvers] beyond the Kuban', we returned. Up until now I have been learning how to engage in battle [*voevat'*], but now I have learned how to plunder [*razboinichat'*]. Zass is a master at his trade" (ibid., 346). Bestuzhev would not have his readers view him merely in heroic form, but in the guise of the disillusioned warrior-poet. The image of a despairing hero deepened in a letter written to Mikhail and Nicholas just weeks before his death. In it he expressed personal doubts about the virtue of the war, his flagging interest in it, and the degree to which he had become servant to the habits of the fight:

In order to nourish you with Caucasian snowflakes, I am writing these lines with a state courier. I have the pleasure of yawning nowadays on the heights of the mountains which have submitted to us, that is, submitted as much as one can say here—without depriving [the natives] of the right to fire away at us victors at every opportunity. . . . I dreadfully feel like getting into the fray, for this political war of words with ragamuffins is growing tiresome as never before. It is strange that you make exclamation and question marks at the mention of my war madness. Glad would be my trigger to be placed on the table for good; [and happy would I be] to play the gay blade [khokhol volokut]. But once into the field [of battle], like a drunkard at a feast, I can hardly restrain from going the distance [ne sterpliu, chtoby ne poguliat']. Just one shot and my blood begins to boil, and whether or not I have to be under the hail of bullets [sled ili ne sled mne byt' pod puliami], I throw myself into the crossfire. (76–77)

It would be an error to claim that Bestuzhev manufactured the image of growing despair as a deliberate effort to delude his interlocutors and to win their sympathy by ruse. On the contrary, Bestuzhev expressed truthfully what he saw and how he felt. His lived experience and his persona happened to coincide completely.

The generation of a persona, which appeared to have absorbed all concrete historical and biographical reality, represented the power of romantic categories to subsume all experience. In a letter written just two months before his death, Bestuzhev urged his mother not to worry about his health:

I so completely rely on the Providence which has so far saved me from ill, that without the least anxiety, not to mention fear, I approach all dangers [with equanimity]. Fear is a feeling unknown to me. Whatever will be, will be; whatever will not, will not. This is my faith.

[Я так надеюсь на Провидение, спасавшее меня доселе, что без малейшего опасения, не только страха, иду на все опасности. Страх есть чувство, мне неизвестное. Что будет—будет; чему не быть—не бывать. Это моя вера.] (Ibid., 74)

What is remarkable about these remarks is that they are addressed to his mother, to whom he was prone to confess his thoughts and feelings. There is no dissembling here. This is the presentation of an inner consciousness that is complemented by a literary plot.[15]

Bestuzhev also perceived himself as a Byronic outcast, a loner, an isolated and doomed man. "My God, my God," he wrote to Pavel in November 1836,

---

15. It is as though we are reading Pechorin's fictional journal, and not Bestuzhev's personal letters, especially when we encounter the ideas of a personal destiny and the power of fate to determine the outcome of the protagonist's life plot.

when shall I end this paltry nomadism on foreign soil, far from every means toward gainful occupation?! I pray but for one thing—that I be given a tiny corner where I might lay down my staff and, serving the Emperor in some civil service, I might also serve Russian letters with the pen. They probably do not want this. Let it be so.

[Боже мой, Боже мой! когда я кончу это нищенское кочеванье по чужбине, вдали от всех средств к занятиям?! Об одном молю я, чтоб мне дали уголок, где бы я мог поставить свой посох и, служа в статской службе Государю, служил бы русской словесности пером. Видно, не хотят этого. Да будет!] ("A. A. Bestuzhev [Marlinskii]," 66)

The image projected here of the prophet in the wilderness, forsaken by his own people, reveals the grandiose dimensions of Bestuzhev's self idea: "I know of nothing more deadly than Caucasus society. True, there are some engaging fools, but here even with a lantern you might find none other than the vicious and boring" [Ia nichego ne znaiu ubiistvennee kavkazskogo obshchestva. Ved' est' zhe zanimatel'nye duraki—a zdes' tak, krome zlykh i skuchnykh, s fonarem ne vyishchesh'] (153). The persona has become a contemporary Diogenes who does not only seek the truth, but a homeland as well:

Not by gift of talent, but by fate I am like Byron. What calumny was not cast his way? What did they not suspect him of doing? So it is with me as well. My greatest misfortunes appear to others to be crimes. My heart [conscience] is clean, but my head is bespattered by disgrace and slander. So let it be! "Whosoever forbears to the end will be saved," saith our Savior.

[Не даром, но долей похож я на Байрона. Чего не клеветали на него? в чем его не подозревали? То и со мной. Самые несчастия мои для иных кажутся преступлениями. Чисто мое сердце, но голова моя очернена опалой и клеветою! Да будет! 'Претерпевый до конца, тот спасен будет,' сказал Спаситель.] ("Pis'ma k Polevym," 434–35)

The hero becomes martyr: "The gift of the word has not been given to me for long. I am not an inhabitant of the earth; but what can be done when, it seems, everything has conspired to hinder the outpouring of my unspoken truths!" (Ne nadolgo dan mne dar slova . . . ia ne zhilets na zemle; no chto zh delat', kogda, kazhetsia, vse soglasilos', chtoby me-shat' izliianiiu nevyskazannykh istin moikh!] (435).

The martyred self seeks refuge in quiet to the end of his days. A pastoral dream occurs in many letters, but with particular force in an epistle addressed to Nicholas from March 9, 1833:

> You and brother [Mikhail] are for me the constellation Castor and Pollux. Whenever I think of you my heart takes its ease; and upon this thought, each time the desire to live with you peacefully tucked away in a remote corner [of Russia] arises in my breast . . . there I would become a man of letters—two hours a day with you, the rest by myself, with books and with nature about. I confess, such a life is merely one of my fantasies, and as much a bright one, alas, as it is an impossible dream. . . . It is not only the towers of the Kremlin which I love so much that I shall never see, but the snows of the homeland I miss; snows for which I would give all the vineyards of the Caucasus and all the roses of Azerbaidjan, for the latter have only thorns for the outcast. (435)

Bestuzhev was wont to poeticize his conditions, using language to purge his emotions and recreate the persona in a new, tragic guise. In the formulaic style of travel literature, Bestuzhev wrote, "So I again move further away from the borders of my homeland, from you, and from all that is dear to me, one thousand versts, and hundreds of mountain tops shall stand between me and the winds which waft from my native north" [Itak ia opiat' udalius' ot granitsy moei rodiny, ot vas, ot vsego chto mne milo, na tseluiu tysiachu verst, i sotni khrebtov vstanut mezhdu mnoi i vetrom veiushchim s rodnogo severa] ("Alek-sandr Bestuzhev na Kavkaze," 70). Then debunking the sentimentalist turns of speech, Bestuzhev continued,

> This, if you will, is mere childishness. Is it not all the same if one is separated either by a stone wall or by mountain ranges, by six rather than seven thousand versts? But such are the eccentric beasts

called so by the poets: a mere trifle delights, but a half a trifle vexes us. And if you say, "the smoke of the fatherland is sweet and pleasant," it nevertheless does not waft to the Caucasus; here, even a man's scent sharpened by ill fortune cannot detect it.

[Это, если вы хотите, ребячество: не все ль равно быть разлучену каменною стеной или грядами гор, шестью или семью тысячами пространства? Но таковы эксцентрические животные называемые поэтами: безделка счастливит, полубезделка огорчает нас. А что ни говори: 'дым отечества нам сладок и приятен', а за Кавказ не долетает этот дым, его не чует даже обоняние изощренное несчастием.] (70)

Shifting tones to reflect yet another mood, Bestuzhev described the conflicting realities of his experience: "The Russians here are half Asians, and the Asians half beasts. Only nature, rich, grand nature, with whom I have become most intimate due to the absence of someone else [who can be considered] close to me, shall act as my comforter, my constant friend, though inconstant [in form] she be" [Russkie tam polu-Aziiattsy, Aziiattsy—poluzveri. Odna priroda, bogataia, velichavaia priroda, s kotoroiu srodnilsia ia za nedostatkom drygogò rodstva vblizi, budet tam moeiu uteshitel'nitseiu, podrugoiu neizmennoiu, khotia izmenchivoiu] (70). Bestuzhev concludes his multivoiced discourse with a combined romantic and sentimental foray: "Providence I thank even for this. In the mountains separation is sweet sorrow, but in the steppe it is melancholy. Thus nowhere and at no time does one feel his isolation as when admiring the richness of nature. Whom can I tell, 'Look how beautiful this is!' From whom might I receive an answer in a kiss?" (Blagodariu Providenie i za eto. V gorakh razluka—grust', v stepi—toska; za to nigde i nikogda tak sil'no ne chuvstvuesh' svoego odinochestva kak liubuias' roskosh'iu prirody. Komu skazat': posmotri, kak eto prekasno! Ot kogo poluchit' otvet potseluem?] (70–71). Bestuzhev's outpouring was sincere, authentic, even spontaneous, but the utterances represent a continuous citation from the literary canon. The reader is reminded of Pushkin's "Queen of Spades" where Hermann uses speeches from German novels to impress Elizaveta. Bestuzhev's myriad remarks of romantic angst were taken from novels and became the stuff of Russian novels: "My heart seeks love . . . the last years in which I might expect to find it as a mutual feeling are fading fast. Why, why, do the thorns outlive the flower, why does the flame not die when it cannot shine for others?" [Serdtse moe prosit liubvi . . . poslednie gody, v kotorye ia mog by ozhidat' ee vzaimno, vianut! Zachem, zachem shipy perezhivaiut tsvetok, zachem ne gasnet ogon', kogda on ne mozhet svetit' drugim!] ("Pis'ma k Polevym," 297–98).

Bestuzhev conceived his masculinity in terms of virility, both in war and in love: "After the rapture of love I know no higher rapture for carnal man than victory, for it mixes both the experience of glory with one's feeling of strength and power" [Posle vostorga liubvi ia ne znaiu vysshego vostorga dlia telesnogo cheloveka kak pobeda, potomu chto k chuvstvu sily primeshano tut chuvstvo slavy] (ibid., 466). The juxtaposition of sexual relations and military prowess was characteristic of the time. The idea of dominance brought feelings of well-being through status, power, and fame. In a letter dated February 24, 1832, Bestuzhev attempted to impress his brother, Pavel, with the image of a dashing, gay blade: "Since the New Year I have gotten into charming the ladies and quite successfully—I possess the finest lady in the entire town [of Derbent]. Elle fait des folies pour moi [She outdoes herself for me] and it is as if I am living out years of great kindness. . . . But I think you remember [what I looked like when we met] in Arzerum? I am still quite fresh for a thirty-three-year-old, and driving women crazy is nothing new for me. So—vogue la galère! [Sail on!] And consequently my work [writing] goes poorly, but then I am living for myself—and that is hardly a trifle!" ("A. A. Bestuzhev [Marlinskii]," 150).

The affairs in which Bestuzhev engaged possessed a narrative quality, containing a beginning with its complication, a middle that determines the form of the denouement, and a conclusion. Two months prior to his death, Bestuzhev reported an affair to brother Pavel. It reads like an anecdote from the romantic canon:

I was living in Kerch at an old acquaintance's and comrade in unhappiness [i.e., a Decembrist's], B. He has a wife—a woman the likes of which I have yet to meet again—in soul and shape charming; a monastic one to the ends of her nails, and a woman to the strands of her heart. She married from passion, but seeing her husband's coldness, at first from out of revenge, and then from passion, threw herself on me. What it cost me to possess her completely, however, the devil himself only knows. She put me through the whole gamut of madness, but finally fell. I can't tell

you how difficult it was for me to part from her, to join my
detachment, all the more so since her husband began to suspect
things and there had been some terrible scenes with him. On the
second of December I again traveled to Kerch. Not finding a
launch, I set off in a rotten old boat. I was one and a half days in
fear of my life, knocking atop the sea, for there was only one oar.
And can you imagine my happiness [when I arrived]—her husband was on leave and I occupied his place for a whole month. I
was entirely happy: c'était une femme divine; j'ai manqué
d'ailleurs d'avoir deux duels pour elle—avec son mari d'abord et
un officier depuis [this was a divine woman; I almost had two
duels over her—first with her husband and then with a certain
officer]. But I was prepared to do this for her. I wanted to take her
away with me, to carry her off, but two children hindered this.
She remained with her husband, but I love her to this very day.[16]

Bestuzhev's life encapsulated romantic fiction, and his fiction produced models for the persona's further elaboration. Bestuzhev thus
became an authentic hero of his own prose. Witness, for example,
Yakov Kostenetsky's (1811–55) recollection of two meetings with
Bestuzhev in Derbent.[17] Kostenetsky's prose reflects, too, the propensity of Bestuzhev's popular audience to read and re-create him as "Marlinsky." His account reads like fiction; it begins with an introduction to
warm the reader to the topic, and then enters into a narrative of intrigue. In fact, Kostenetsky's manner of writing is of more interest here
than the content of his description (Bestuzhev's love life), for it conforms completely to Bestuzhev's marlinist style:

Bestuzhev was at that time . . . a man of strong and healthy constitution, with a passionate heart. Could he therefore remain indifferent to the fair sex? And since such a handsome and captivating
man was liked by almost every woman, he was never lacking for
objects of his passion. Once, in response to my question concern-

16. Bestuzhev goes on to describe other affairs in Stavropol and Tiflis, and concludes with
an aside that he had recently written a letter of proposal to a family in Moscow (subsequently
refused). But more interesting than any catalogue of Bestuzhev's feats is the propensity to
encompass self in narrative form ("Aleksandr Bestuzhev na Kavkaze," 72–73).
17. His memoir of these meetings was published only in 1900, attesting to an interest in
Bestuzhev even at the close of the nineteenth and beginning of the twentieth centuries.

ing the affinity between Bestuzhev and lace, he responded, "Both one and the other are beloved by women." And in truth there were many women charmed now by his courageousness, now by his fascinating mind, one by his fame, and another by his bravery and decisiveness. I am convinced that on another scene of action, in different circumstances, Bestuzhev would have made a real Don Juan. Indeed, even in the Caucasus he had not just a few admirers; even the wives of stern asiatic, jealous, and blood-thirsty husbands, knowing that for the slightest indiscretion an inescapable death awaited them, were enticed by this dear Iskander-bek, as the asiatic often called Bestuzhev. More than once, with dagger in hand, in the darkest of night, in secret he would make his way along the Derbent wall and across the flat roofs of the houses to the embraces of some young Persian girl impatiently waiting for him.[18]

We cannot corroborate Kostenetsky's account, but the fictionali-zation of life through literary discourse finds engaging confirmation in his narrative:

It goes without saying that these were passing fancies. Finally there appeared a woman who reciprocated Bestuzhev more fully in terms of his passionate temperament and his mind—He fell in love with her with all his heart and soul. This was Alexandra Ivanovna N., the wife of a certain lieutenant. Her husband was some meager little man, coarse, uneducated, forever drunk and forever involved in card games, and consequently prone to leave his wife entirely alone and bored. Alexandra Ivanovna was a young woman, no older than twenty-two or twenty-three, very beautiful, with black eyes, abundant hair of the same hue, of average height, peaches and cream complexion, a real Russian beauty. In addition she was quite well educated, by standards then, and in possession of a most kind and pleasant disposition. And so it was this lucky lady who was the object of the most tender and ardent passion of our writer, our unlucky hero upon whom fate had not seen fit to bestow the pleasures of a legal domestic happiness. This woman gave herself to him completely,

18. V. Vatsuro, "A. A. Bestuzhev," 2:166–67.

without holding anything back. Neither the fear of punishment at her husband's hand for her infidelity, nor fear of obstacles and dangers, no nothing could keep her from meeting her beloved. When her husband would play cards long into the night and next morning, she would dress herself, as it would happen, in his clothes, and amidst the impenetrable darkness, along the circuitous and narrow streets, like a cat, she would make her way to that familiar apartment.

This string of clichés taken almost verbatim from the fiction of the early nineteenth century informs Kostenetsky's text throughout. Not, of course, that the writer falsified what may truly have been a torrid affair. Kostenetsky fashioned it to fit the image of Bestuzhev he carried within him, and in accordance with the dictates of Bestuzhev's own fiction:

The night excursions of the young and beautiful lady, to be sure, could not always remain free of danger, but in order to meet [Bestuzhev], despite his great daring, there was no other means that was any less dangerous than this in Derbent. As a comely woman Alexandra Ivanovna was adored by all the young officers of the battalion. In particular one of them, sub-lieutenant A., a Georgian, was enchanted terribly by her and followed her everywhere with confessions of his passions, needless to say, without success, which agitated him greatly. Once upon a time this officer was making the rounds along the Derbent streets in the wee hours of the morning, with lantern in hand and with a small escort of soldiers. Suddenly some officer or other attempted to pass him by without saying a word to him. "Who goes?" he shouted as he pushed the officer against the wall. Not receiving an answer he brought the lantern to the officer's face . . . and to his great amazement instead of an officer who should he see but Alexandra Ivanovna in officer's dress! A., who was torn frighteningly by this woman's coldness toward him in the past, and seeing that he had in his arms a defenseless woman who had herself been carousing, pressed her with his base demands. He threatened her that if she did not comply he would take her to the command post to be arrested, in which case her husband as well as everyone else would learn of her nocturnal visits in an officer's coat. . . . The unfortunate girl cried, begged him, implored him to let her go, but the drunken Georgian was inexorable and in no manner wished to let this fortunate occasion slip through his fingers. In despair the poor woman puts to use her last defense—distaff cunning. She makes a face as if she agrees with his demands. At the officer's command, the soldiers accompanying him set off, at which time the passionate A. attempts to take her into his arms. She hit him so hard in the face that he fell over backward onto the ground. Like a frightened cat she runs in the opposite direction from the soldiers and in this manner managed to escape from the insolent and drunken lout. It goes without saying that Aleksandra Ivanovna recounted all these events to Bestuzhev, who was so angered by it that he swore to punish the cad forthwith in the Caucasian native manner. When A., who on the next day himself repented his base deed, found out about Bestuzhev's grave threat to his life, he became so frightened that he immediately set off for Tiflis where he procured a transfer to our Kurinsky Regiment. There I became acquainted with him. He himself recounted to me this entire history.[19]

Bestuzhev's life and his audience's reception of it through his literature supplied models par excellence for his mythologization.

The Nestertsova Affair

To set Olga Nestertsova's death in Bestuzhev's room in perspective, mention must be made about the conditions of Bestuzhev's life in Derbent. Upon his arrival in the Caucasus, he made a significant impact on the Russian community. In Tiflis young officers for whom Bestuzhev's name worked a special kind of magic gathered about him, seeing in him the embodiment of all to which they aspired in life. His every gesture, word, and deed breathed the guard officer's ideal of extreme self-sacrifice mixed with hedonism. Civilians, too, were attracted to Bestuzhev. Newly attired in the latest Petersburg fashions, he cut a striking figure. Frightened by

19. Although this is a story about Aleksandra Ivanovna and her officer more than it is of Bestuzhev, we are nevertheless asked to observe indirectly Bestuzhev's effect on both principals (ibid., 167–68).

Bestuzhev's ability to influence impressionable youths, the government decided to send him to a less desirable location, Derbent.

To a certain extent Derbent life suited Bestuzhev. He kept intelligent company among the civilian population, had access to the books he required to foster his writing career, and enjoyed a military life of relative ease. Although Bestuzhev occasionally complained that he had to perform duties he considered asinine for a man of his standing and military training, his impression of his life in Derbent was rather more favorable than not. True, the commander of Bestuzhev's battalion, a certain Vasil'ev, demanded that Bestuzhev appear for drill and parade marches, which he would normally not have had to endure had he not been reduced in the ranks. By all accounts, Vasil'ev was a dolt, as were many of the young officers stationed at the Derbent garrison. By way of contrast, however, the commandant of the city, a certain Shnitnikov, was a refined gentleman at whose home Bestuzhev enjoyed a semblance of the old Petersburg style. In addition, Bestuzhev was well liked by a provincial Russian population still attracted to the theatrical behavioral code typical of the 1820s.

Bestuzhev was admired for the care he gave the native population. Bestuzhev frequently performed minor medical services for them, talked to them as equals in their native tongue (which he acquired quickly), and was free with his money when it came to humanitarian programs and cases of individual want. To complete the dual code of the officer and gentleman, Bestuzhev's Caucasus biographer, V. Vasil'ev, claims that Bestuzhev fell in with "an uncultured group of officers who spent their time getting drunk, playing cards, and filling time through involvement in petty intrigues and arguments."[20]

While stationed in Derbent, the military hero in Bestuzhev was given an opportunity to perform. In the fall of 1830 Kaza Mulla, the masterful strategist and learned spiritual leader of the natives of the region, lay seige to Derbent. Bestuzhev distinguished himself frequently in defense of the city at its walls, at the barricades, and in quick skirmishes outside the city. On each of these occasions, and even in the hottest moments of battle, Bestuzhev smoked a pipe. This was a deliberate and calculated gesture intended to attract attention from all sides. He quickly became the talk of the town, which recognized in him the hero they expected.

---

20. V. Vasil'ev, *Bestuzhev-Marlinskii na Kavkaze* (Krasnodar, 1939), 12. There is no connection between the biographer and Bestuzhev's commander in Derbent.

Smoking a pipe performed several symbolic functions. It made him seem distinctive, unusual, blasé in the midst of the fray, even casually heroic, as if he were engaging in an activity consistent with his everyday life. The pipe also guaranteed that no matter where he might be fighting he would be noticed by his commanders. This ensured as much as possible that his heroics could be mentioned in official reports. Bestuzhev achieved this end—his name is immortalized in Russia's military archives. Bestuzhev's pipe also singled him out in the enemy camp. He became a legendary figure among the natives. He was in his element, for life confirmed his belief in romantic fiction.

In the fall of 1832 Bestuzhev attempted to procure the Cross of St. George for his part in the defense of Derbent. "I have earned this cross with my breast, and have not sought it out deviously," he attested quite truthfully, if immodestly, to his brother. "When the matter reaches the tsar," he informed Pavel, "then the corps commander must make the presentation or else nothing will ever come of it" ("A. A. Bestuzhev [Marlinskii]," 159). Bestuzhev, however, was refused the distinction. Bestuzhev was not aware that the matter had reached the tsar, and that it was the tsar who had denied him this honor.

While enjoying recognition in his military career, if only unofficially, and wide popularity in Russia for his stories, if only as Marlinsky, Bestuzhev experienced two tragic events which affected him deeply. In 1832 his brother Peter dissolved into madness. A terrible sensitivity and a high-strung emotional nature increased the sufferings Peter endured at the hands of a petty commander. He began to lose touch with reality. Peter became paranoid, stopped eating his food for fear of poisoning, ceased trusting even his best friends, and eventually, after moving to Bestuzhev's so that he might receive adequate care, came to distrust his own brother. Bestuzhev had won the right to care for Peter in Derbent after months of entreaty. No sooner did Peter arrive than he began to drive Bestuzhev crazy; he remained in bed all day long, kept silent when addressed, refused to move or eat, but argued lucidly and with wit in the service of his disease: "Brother Peter is here [with me] and has already managed to cease loving me. Only those who are thousands of versts away are yet dear to him . . . and that is simply because they do not contradict him. His blood has become bilious. Do not blame him, however; it is his disease. You just cannot help but feel sorry that you cannot cure him by any means, that you cannot dissuade him that some magic potion exists on this earth that will cure him" (ibid.). Realizing that he could not help him, Bestuzhev obtained orders for Peter's retirement from the service and permission for his return home to their mother and sisters.

It is difficult to ascertain the effect Peter's illness had on Bestuzhev. The circumstances that gave rise to it, however, might have given Bestuzhev pause. Peter was serving a Caucasian exile similar to Bestuzhev's and was subject to the petty, even cruel, tortures of superiors whose role in life, it seems, was simply to make the Decembrists suffer. Distinction in battle had not brought Peter a promotion, and his lot became worse with each passing year. Bestuzhev's circumstances did not differ from his brother's, and his future in the Caucasus held for him similar challenges. Yet Bestuzhev was not of his brother's bilious temperament. He most likely felt confident that he could hold up under unfair treatment at the hands of myopic superiors. He was tested in this regard in the next year over the Nestertsova affair.

During the winter of 1833 the foreign section of the city of Derbent was continually on guard. Famine sent criminals and hungry residents into Russian apartments and homes under the cover of night in search of money, foodstuffs, and possessions. Russians were being robbed and murdered with some regularity. Bestuzhev kept a dagger and sometimes a loaded pistol between his two pillows in the event of an entry into his apartment. His neighbor had recently been cut up, two women had been stabbed, and a soldier in his neighborhood had been wounded. Because of his reputed wealth Bestuzhev thought himself a likely target. He wrote to his brother Pavel, "I am gaily, even eagerly ready to die on the battle-field, but I don't want to perish without a fight in my bed at the hands of some thief!" (ibid., 161).

Bestuzhev's preparedness had dire consequences. One evening Olga Nestertsova, the widow landlady's daughter who took in Bestuzhev's laundry and did his mending, came to his room when he was out. She was conducted to his quarters by the doorman, and she commenced sewing. Bestuzhev returned to find her there. They conversed and joked together, and their laughter resounded throughout the residence. Olga began to cavort about and suddenly threw herself on the bed. Bestuzhev's pistol fired when she hit the pillow where it was hidden. She was fatally wounded. Within fifty hours her lungs filled with blood and, in terrible pain, she drowned. Fortunately for Bestuzhev, Olga confessed her responsibility in the matter to her mother, the local priest, several officers summoned to the scene, and the doctor who attended her. She absolved Bestuzhev of any misdeed, and at the subsequent hearing on the case Bestuzhev was judged innocent of any wrongdoing.

Given the sensationalism of the event, its prurient interest, its melodramatic basis, and its literariness, the case did not end with Bestuzhev's official exoneration. For most of the next year Bestuzhev was subjected to social humiliation at the hands of officers, of people Bestuzhev had alienated in the normal rivalry that accompanied garrison life, and of those who were inclined to fill their lives with intrigue of this sort. The tragic affair offered Bestuzhev's enemies and detractors the opportunity to get their hands on a haughty Decembrist who clearly deserved a lesson in humility. Although a military trial had cleared Bestuzhev, these officers spread "the rumor that he had murdered his mistress in a jealous rage" (Leighton, *Alexander Bestuzhev-Marlinsky,* 32). Only after several months of additional hearings, examinations, and cross-examinations, was Bestuzhev's case finally laid to rest by the authorities. It was a difficult year for Bestuzhev, as his letters to Pavel and his editors, the Polevoys, attest.

This aspect of his life fit neatly the archetypal image of the loner, outsider, and misfit calumniated, like Byron, by base society.[21] Bestuzhev's tragic implication in Olga Nestertsova's death inclined toward narrative form, but not in the sense of building a fantasy in which imagination takes the dominant role in structuring discourse. From this perspective we observe how Bestuzhev's life became fictionalized, that is, renderable in the narrative shape in which he had educated his readers.

In being hounded and calumniated in society, Bestuzhev found himself in the equivalent position of so many of his beloved heroes—on the outside, alone, misunderstood, but firm and determined. Through all his traumatic ordeals his life and his art united to sustain him, and he and his sympathetic audience saw his heroic persona confirmed through the vicissitudes of his lived experience. As the worldview of Bestuzhev's hero proved capable of interpreting his personal life both in adversity and triumph, Bestuzhev's persona acquired mythic proportions.

21. It may have been a troublesome time, too, because Bestuzhev attempted to keep his relations with Olga a secret throughout the ordeal. There is circumstantial evidence that Bestuzhev kept an affair with Olga out of the public's eye and even from the inquiries from his family. In response to Pavel's queries concerning the nature of his relationship with Olga, Bestuzhev never actually denied that he was having an affair with her. He skirted the issue, choosing instead to praise her (and her mother) for the many happy and carefree hours they had spent together chatting and joking. Curious, too, is the fact that Olga's mother, after the tragedy, returned to Petersburg to find a large sum of money left her by Bestuzhev. Months later she again received several hundred rubles from Bestuzhev through his publishers, the Polevoys. Bestuzhev's letter to them is vague, even secretive.

262 Alexander Bestuzhev-Marlinsky

Inconsistencies

Bestuzhev relegated discrete functions of his persona to different audiences. When writing to the Polevoys, he was wont to propagate a literary image of himself that betrayed few secrets. In letters to his family, however, matters were discussed of a more revealing nature. Even within his family Bestuzhev differentiated the type of information he was willing to pass on. Erving Goffman defines the differentiation of audiences in terms of "frontstage" and "backstage" patterns, the first indicating the behavior the individual permits himself to maintain a public image, and the second the more inclusive behavior in which the individual engages daily in private.[22] A comparison of frontstage and backstage utterance reveals cracks in the Marlinsky facade. Bestuzhev, for example, clothed himself fashionably while in the Caucasus. Whether in the Shnitnikov's home in the latest dress of high society, or in military finery in the garrison, Bestuzhev projected a fashionable image. Procuring such finery, however, remained a backstage occupation. Were he to show the trouble it took to dress himself in this manner, the effect of his performance would have been diminished, for the heroic persona did not incorporate into itself the idea of mundane tasks or financial dealings.

Bestuzhev made use of his own and the Polevoy families to obtain his wardrobe and other items. Consequently, they were privy to backstage information, which required a shift in self-presentation that would do Bestuzhev's image the least harm. This was a delicate task, and Bestuzhev handled it with consummate skill. He made requests of the Polevoys that did not concern his toilet and dress. They purchased clothing to be given to friends and acquaintances (usually women). His backstage behavior thereby projected a frontstage image of the generous roué.

When Bestuzhev required goods for his own person, he sought exclusively the aid of his brother Pavel. From the women of the family he requested only books, information, and moral support. From Nicholas and Mikhail he asked opinions, criticisms of his stories, and their assessment of current literature. There was one exception—Elena. She possessed a fine business acumen, and he depended on her to see to the publication of his work. She operated with power of attorney (or its equivalent), handled his contracts and finances, and saw publication

22. Erving Goffman, *The Presentation of Self in Everyday Life* (Woodstock, N.Y., 1973), 106–40.

proceedings through from beginning to end. Since their relationship was both family and business oriented, neither seemed to have felt a discrepancy between the Marlinsky persona and the backstage activity of publishing in which Bestuzhev engaged. Consequently, in his letters to Elena, there was no attempt on Bestuzhev's part to convert backstage information into a different form. Since his publishing activity constituted a major source of support for the family, it goes without saying that the persona of the heroic son and brother was adequately maintained even through business dealings.

Bestuzhev consigned his many business activities to a narrow audience. He engaged in the legal and financial activities related to publishing, wrote directly to the Polevoys and to his sister about the price he should be paid per sheet, how the censor should be approached, and what binder to use for his collected works. He made it clear to these few people that he was in the business of selling his literature for income: "I am not one of those people caught up in little details and who fuss over each line like a child with a new toy. But I do have one request. Let me know about my works that appear in print, for they might escape me like lost goods. I live in such a fashion that after God, money is the first thing, but where in life is this otherwise?" ("Pis'ma k Polevym," 305–6). Bestuzhev often discussed monetary concerns, especially since he felt he was the only one who could support the family (327). He wrote about his debts and how to handle them, about the dangers of doing business with friends, and (to Elena) how to barter with the publishers. He commented on how he was misused financially by Grech and Bulgarin, and what his relations were with the publisher Smirdin.[23] Bestuzhev's financial affairs were complex, if only because he had to handle them entirely through the post. When he claimed, therefore, that personality (*lichnost'*) and business do not mix, he clearly had his persona in mind. If with the Polevoys and his family Bestuzhev allowed them of necessity into differentiated backstage domains, with all others he manipulated audience reception consciously, performing on the frontstage in conformity with his image.

A stark example of the discrepancy in his dual roles can be found in his discussions of his health. He mentions it frequently in his letters.

23. "Aleksandr Bestuzhev na Kavkaze," 56, 57, 58. Alexander Smirdin (1795–1857) was a bookseller, publisher, and bookstore owner. He held a virtual monopoly on publishing in the 1830s but fell into bankruptcy in the 1840s.

During the Derbent years he remained in excellent condition, but after 1834 he was exposed to tropical diseases and gradually succumbed to a variety of disorders that began to ruin his health and affect his emotional state. He was not loath to confess these details to his family and the Polevoys. Bestuzhev felt there was no incongruity between these backstage remarks and his frontstage image, for his failing health reinforced his romantic (martyred) visage. But Bestuzhev drew a strict line to discriminate between audience and information.

In 1833, while Pavel was yet stationed in the Caucasus (in Tiflis), Bestuzhev frequently requested articles for his toilet—combs, brushes, cloaks, and so forth. In November of that year, Bestuzhev wrote to his brother Pavel, "By the way, and without joking, I am sick with a disease that will not allow me to sit on a saddle" ("A. A. Bestuzhev [Marlinskii]," 330). Bestuzhev's delicacy in referring to his trouble suggests a reluctance to allow Pavel entirely into the backstage. But he depended on Pavel's help to procure the necessary medicine for him in Tiflis. A month later Bestuzhev complained that he was still suffering from the same disease: "I cannot depart from [Derbent for a new assignment in Akhaltsy] very soon. Hemorrhoids have fixed me to my place. And since the doctor says that not only riding but particularly the winter cold may turn my illness fatal, then I must wait for warm weather before I can improve" (332). January passed without his receiving the medicine, and Bestuzhev was faced with having to remain in the garrison: "[They say that] there is no good without ill. But in my 'no good without ill' there is no good" (339). By mid-February Bestuzhev became adamant:

> I am simply quite angry with you, Pavel. There have been three posts since I wrote you in request of the medicine. And you haven't even written me to let me know you received my letter. Of course you are not well, but although sickness may preclude your doing something, it does not inhibit your mouth from giving a command. And so, thanks to your scrupulousness I am still neither entirely well or ill, for I don't want to apply the local concoctions, and you concern yourself over my health so little that my five requests to perform this silly duty go unanswered. Is this because you imagine I am improved or have changed my mind, that *this* is not necessary, or at least not necessary any longer? I ask you once and for all, either refuse to perform this duty, or do it right now, upon receiving this letter, and without considering

whether or not this is a whim on my part or a dire necessity. I know my mind in this and can hardly think that every post that I have sent to you about my illness has been lost in route. . . . I am still sick; at least *you* are getting better. (340)

Four months after his initial letter, Bestuzhev received a vial with the medicine from his brother: "Dearest Pavel. On the post just preceding this one, I received a little box with the medicine. But since the stopper in the bottle was glass, half of the contents leaked out. Who was the genius who thought of sending a glass stopper by post? This post brought me a box with buttons, gloves, stockings, two pair of rubber galoshes, and one pair of suspenders which I don't need in the least, but which are surely very expensive. What can I do? I can't send them back. And why didn't you send a letter?" (ibid., 340–41). Within a week Bestuzhev could finally announce: "My hemorrhoids disappeared in three days thanks to the medicine you sent—what a miracle! No sign of relapse either" (342). The details of this episode concern us only to the extent that they demonstrate Bestuzhev's careful delineation of audience and behavior. The literary hero's image in the early nineteenth century was devoid of reference to the lower body and its functions. Transcending the base flesh, Bestuzhev usually managed to keep the necessities of the natural world beyond the vision of his audience. But man's nature requires attendance to the lower body. When necessary, therefore, Bestuzhev informed no one of his dilemma except Pavel, thus effectively reducing to one the audience privy to the body below the mask.[24]

The nature of the information was entirely different when the addressee was female. Then, under the guise of making available to her the secrets of his heart (in actuality a literary frontstage under the guise of being a backstage performance), Bestuzhev resorted to every marlinist device to insure the persona's integrity from the perspective of that addressee:

The Azov Sea rolls its shining waves; the offshore breeze harkens to me with the voice of Halcyon. Like a well-bred steed preparing to throw itself into battle and champing at the bit, the ship pulls on its anchor chain. Do you hear the reverberations of the farewell shot? . . .

24. Of necessity, the censor is excluded from this calculation.

Forgive me.

There was a time when the sea lulled me like a dream, when the wind's breath whispered sweet promises to my restless soul, when the vision of full blown sails lured me more than the shape of a young girl's buoyant breasts. Happy was this time now passed! The Azov Sea grows dark, waves like a funereal shroud; the wind moans mournfully like a funeral knell; the light brig seems a grave awaiting a lonely soul . . . does it wait for me? In truth, hasn't he died who quite alone and in total isolation sets off for the mountain's high valleys from amidst the valleys of the ocean's waves? I am told—there awaiting you is the friendship of comrades, a new life filled to overflowing with a warrior's ways and the strong effect of the battle. But when your soul no longer responds to the hearty toasts of your friends, neither to the impatient neighing of your battle steed, nor to the cry of victory, then you feel yourself full of apathy on the precipice of a life of action, you recognize that amidst the teeming crowd you are alone; and loneliness is nothing other than death itself! Could it really be that taking a breath means to live? As through the black husk of a tree struck by lightning the spring sends buds, and after them weak shoots of new growth as final signs of its life, thus, my dear lady, has my heart sent for the last time its final flower, a flower of friendship for you.

This flower will not perish; my friendship is true. It is founded on gratitude for everything good you have bestowed upon me, and on the respect I shower upon you. Believe in it! At my age you don't make confessions of this sort to just anyone. One mustn't squander his affections in vain; one must be stingy in this regard or otherwise end up with nothing.[25]

Bestuzhev would have his lady see him as a sailor, lover, tired warrior, and forsaken exile, to which he attached literary images—he is a steed, a ship, the reverberations of a cannon shot, the sea, and a dying tree. There are a host of self-images Bestuzhev manufactured to associate himself with the persona. He likened himself to a Tatar, the local inhabit-

---

25. N. P. Chulkov, ed., *Dekabristy, Letopisi Gosudarstvennogo literaturnogo muzeia* 3 (1938), 79–80. Self-description of this type occurs with ever greater frequency during Bestuzhev's final year. The addressee here is unknown.

ants of the Caucasus, and to those Russians (*kavkaztsy*) who resided there without ever returning to the homeland.[26] He continually recognized in himself a hero in battle, a superior warrior, and a competent leader of men.[27] He claimed that he was Russia's Byron, Napoleon, Ovid, Childe Harold, and Prometheus.[28] He ascribed characteristics to himself that belong to these personae—pride, hot-temper, disaffection, and bile.[29] He claimed to be a fatalist who keenly felt the isolation, persecution, and longing that come with being a victim of misdeeds and misunderstandings, suffering for a just cause, and wasting his talents.[30]

26. Letters dtd. May 14, 1831; July 12, 1833; March 15, 1834; and November 8, 1835, in "A. A. Bestuzhev (Marlinskii): 1798–1837," 5:149, 6:315, 6:342, 7:51.

27. Letters dtd. January 29, 1831; September 26, 1831; and December 16, 1831, in "Pis'ma Aleksandra Aleksandrovicha Bestuzheva k N. A. i K. A. Polevym, pisannye v 1831–1837 godakh," 3:289–93, 3:306–8, 3:309–17. Letter dtd. April 22, 1832, in "A. A. Bestuzhev (Marlinskii): 1798–1837," 5:155. Letters dtd. January 15, 1833, and February 1834, in "Aleksandr Bestuzhev na Kavkaze:1829–1837," 7:46–48, 7:57–59. Letters dtd. February 1835, and April 13, 1837, in "A. A. Bestuzhev (Marlinskii):1798–1837," 6:346–47, 7:75–76.

28. Letter dtd. December 27, 1830, in "Aleksandr Bestuzhev na Kavkaze, 1829–1837," 6:503–4. Letters dtd. February 24, 1832, and March 9, 1833, in "A. A. Bestuzhev (Marlinskii):1798–1837," 5:150–53, 5:163–64. Letters dtd. August 17, 1833, and September 7, 1833, in "Aleksandr Bestuzhev na Kavkaze, 1829–1837," 7:49–50, 7:51–52. Letters dtd. August 2, 1834, and November 8, 1835, in "Pis'ma Aleksandra Aleksandrovicha Bestuzheva k N. A. i K. A. Polevym, pisannye v 1831–1837 godakh," 4:461–63, and 4:474–75.

29. Letters dtd. April 23, 1831, and July 28, 1832, in "Pis'ma Aleksandra Aleksandrovicha Bestuzheva k N. A. i K. A. Polevym, pisannye v 1831–1837 godakh," 3:296–98, 3:329–31. Letter dtd. February 1834, in "A. A. Bestuzhev (Marlinskii):1798–1837," 6:337–38.

30. Letter dtd. September 3, 1829, in "Aleksandr Bestuzhev na Kavkaze, 1829–1837," 6:495–96. Letter dtd. January 29, 1831, in "Pis'ma Aleksandra Aleksandrovicha Bestuzheva k N. A. i K. A. Polevym, pisannye v 1831–1837 godakh," 3:289–93. Letter [nd] 1831, in "A. A. Bestuzhev (Marlinskii): 1798–1837," 5:147–48. Letters dtd. April 23, 1831; May 28, 1831; February 4, 1832; and March 15, 1832, in "Pis'ma Aleksandra Aleksandrovicha Bestuzheva k N. A. i K. A. Polevym, pisannye v 1831–1837 godakh," 3:296–98, 3:298–300, 3:321–22, 3:322–24. Letter dtd. June 23, 1832, in "Aleksandr Bestuzhev na Kavkaze, 1829–1837," 6:513–26. Letter dtd. July 28, 1832, in "Pis'ma Aleksandra Aleksandrovicha Bestuzheva k N. A. i K. A. Polevym, pisannye v 1831–1837 godakh," 3:329–31. Letters dtd. August 7, 1832; September 1, 1832; and October 5, 1832, in "Aleksandr Bestuzhev na Kavkaze, 1829–1837," 6:518–19, 6:519–20, 6:520–21. Letters dtd. March 9, 1833, and March 16, 1833, in "A. A. Bestuzhev (Marlinskii):1798–1837," 5:163–64, 5:164–65. Letters dtd. December 7, 1833, and December 21, 1833, in "Aleksandr Bestuzhev na Kavkaze, 1829–1837," 7:52–53, 7:53–55. Letter dtd. February 8, 1834, in "A. A. Bestuzhev (Marlinskii):1798–1837," 6:338–40. Letters dtd. February 21, 1834, and May 3, 1834, in "Pis'ma Aleksandra Aleksandrovicha Bestuzheva k N. A. i K. A. Polevym, pisannye v 1831–1837 godakh," 4:453–55, 4:455–57. Letters dtd. July 28, 1835, and June 19, 1836, in "Aleksandr Bestuzhev na Kavkaze, 1829–1837," 7:60–62, 7:67–69. Letter dtd. November 15, 1836, in "A. A. Bestuzhev (Marlinskii):1798–1837," 7:66–67. Letter dtd. November 23, 1836, in "Aleksandr Bestuzhev na Kavkaze, 1829–1837," 7:70–72. Letter dtd. May 12,

Bestuzhev's understanding of himself in mythological terms quickly absorbed religious ideas. In an allusion to his Caucasian exile, but with covert reference to a quasi-hagiographical self-conception, he announced to Ksenofont Polevoy, "I am not an inhabitant of this world" ("Pis'ma k Polevym," 435). Bestuzhev assumed the garb of the holy fool, donning willingly man's sinfulness (a reference to Decembrism only at a superficial level), which he gladly wore despite the "shame of bearing Adam's cloak" (433). To his mother he was no less than a martyred saint:

> What can I say about my fate? The further I go in life the darker it becomes. Eight years of suffering, of labor, battles have served me nothing. . . . Almost all my comrades of misfortune [the Decembrists] have been granted favors, almost all of them have been promoted to officer's rank, save me alone. . . . But never will my tongue grumble against Providence. Let it be so. I accept this test with an invincible spirit, I lift up my heavy cross and climb the mount. Posterity will look kindly upon me. The bosom of God is open to those who suffer on this earth. We are closer . . . to the embrace of the Father who is all love, all forgiveness. And do you know that at the turn of the New Year I was comforted by the thought that I have forgiven all mine enemies in my deepest heart, that people may be enemies and work evil deeds against me, but not I toward them even though I have suffered so much injustice at their hands! Oh, grant that this year is happier than the last unto eternity if only because I now feel that I am more worthy to receive His gifts! ("Aleksandr Bestuzhev na Kavkaze," 56–57)

Bestuzhev added to these qualities that of an ascetic: "I have received word from the spas that people recently arrived from Petersburg think and believe that I have taken to drink, I, who, when it comes to temperance, could shame any hermit, I, who only through a strict dietary regime manage to preserve myself from this pernicious climate" (ibid., 58).

It is not only to his mother that Bestuzhev wrote in this vein. In describing a long bout with tapeworm (which he claims brought him to

---

1837, in "Pis'ma Aleksandra Aleksandrovicha Bestuzheva k N. A. i K. A. Polevym, pisannye v 1831–1837 godakh," 4:485–86.

the edge of death), Bestuzhev wrote his two exiled brothers employing similar images:

> Yes, my kind friends, all misfortune suddenly and one after another fell upon me and finally managed to rend my cast-iron health. Sorrows and the force of a sorrowful military service prepared the disease, and the doctors were wise enough to allow it to develop because they simply could not make out what it was. At first I endured the disease for which there are no records in the medical journals—I would not wish such sufferings on my worst enemy even for a day! With each passing day, each hour, I wasted away, and then suddenly in one night after terrible fevers, I felt the cold hand of death upon me. My pulse disappeared, my heart felt silent, but my head remained clear. I asked my comrades to write out my last will and testament. My thoughts inclined to Russia. My final warm feelings flamed up for those whom I loved, who loved me. I shall tell you the truth: I didn't feel like dying, but I met death without the least fear, albeit with no warm greeting. I don't know if this was the apathy of the mortal flesh or the courage of my soul. Only one happy thought, one reconciling feeling did I find in myself at this fateful hour—a complete absence of hatred or enmity. I sought them out so that I might confess them, but I found none. I could not imagine how I might be against anyone, I, who had been the innocent victim of so many unknown enemies. Oh, an important lesson of salvation was given me this night! Surely I shall be a better person for it. (Ibid., 60)

The confrontations with death took on a new reality within his experience. He seemed less driven by unconscious urges toward demise than drawn toward the knowledge a consciousness of mortality brings. Somewhat like a Tolstoyan protagonist, Bestuzhev experienced revelation (and its concomitant projection of self into more idealized forms) without the benefit of a perspective from which to view it.

He attempted to relate personal experience, literature, theory, and history through that experience. Thus Bestuzhev absorbed sacred tradition within romanticism. As early as January 1833 Bestuzhev claimed that romanticism was originally "*invented* (note, not created) . . . in the era of Christianity" ("Pis'ma k Polevym," 426). In his criticism of the

1830s Bestuzhev expounded this theory, attempting to expropriate to romanticism the entire history of Western civilization, most of which he maintained to be fundamentally under the sign of Christianity.[31]

The absorption of traditional Christian categories within romance was not new. However, the projection of his persona onto heroic Christian iconography was rare in early-nineteenth-century Russia. In a letter to Nicholas Polevoy in which Bestuzhev catalogued the sins of high society, the deceit, duplicity, and image-manufacturing which disfigure mankind, Bestuzhev cast his image of the hero in transcendent terms. Having first itemized Polevoy's misfortunes in society, Bestuzhev continued, "I was happier than you in society. I knew many people whose only sin was that they considered themselves heroes. I am even happier than you at this doorway to hell where I languish, for I know people whose fall has become their resurrection. Oh what elevated souls, what angelic patience, what purity of thought and behavior [there is in them]" ("Pis'ma k Polevym," 312). Bestuzhev referred to his brother Nicholas as a case in point, but the potent self-reference can hardly be missed.

The expropriation of life and death cycles in the personage of the idealized hero indicates a traditional understanding of spiritual time, the all-consuming chronos inhering in mortality. Beneath these categories, though, there resided a pre-Christian orientation toward carnival with its own conception of spirituality, life, and death:[32] "You speak of my rebirth, about the difference between my present and former selves. I think this is more appearance than substance. Sinful Adam wore holes in me, it is true, and has yet to fall from my shoulders. My flightiness was nothing but a domino for social carnivals, in which I fell over for each transaction on the stock exchange. . . . How rare for me now are those bright thrills of love and sacred displeasure which could in a trice raise me to such heroic heights, to such feats of eloquence" (311). This mixture of minimally connected metaphors contradicts itself. Bestuzhev first claims he has not changed from the pre-Decembrist years, then goes on at more length than cited here to present the opposite case. At another level, however, the

31. See his review of Nikolai Polevoy's novel, *Kliatva pri grobe Gospodnem: Russkaia byl' XV veka*, in Bestuzhev-Marlinskii, *Sochineniia v dvukh tomakh*, 1:559–612.

32. "In our most recent battle we suffered the unhappiness of losing one [of our Decembrist group] who was known for his bravery, lieutenant Miklashevsky. He was a real Ajax and fell like a hero. Each year we lose more of the same. . . . The number of unfortunates [Decembrists] shrinks visibly. Those in the front lines always fall, and we are always in the front lines; my turn will come soon too" ("Pis'ma k Polevym," 313).

inconsistencies in Bestuzhev's argument serve as a coherent example of a carnival spirit, which is chaotic and takes pleasure in the sheer incomprehensibility of life and its cycles of death and rebirth.

Bestuzhev frequently alluded to the theme of resurrection. At Easter 1831, he wrote the Polevoys, "On this holiday which celebrates the renewal of nature, I embrace you in my mind, respected Nicholas Alekseevich. I also embrace your brother—this kiss is not from a Judas. On the second day instead of a decorated egg I received from you books and a letter. I am thankful to you for the first, and for the second four times over. Now Holy Week will be a real holiday for my mind and heart" (ibid., 296). A complex of images is proffered here that reflects a fusion of secular and religious celebrations. First Bestuzhev acknowledges the holiday in pagan terms—as the celebration of nature's renewal, the rites of spring. This is immediately transformed into a Christian concept, but not with an emphasis on the resurrection of Christ. Instead, it is on the betrayer Judas that Bestuzhev focuses, but only to claim that his kiss cannot be likened to Judas's. Secular and religious elements recombine in the discourse with a particular emphasis on the folk or pagan rites attached to the season: a play with numbers, as in divination rites of the vernal equinox; reference to Easter eggs, which represent the seed of life and rebirth; the egg's transformation into a gift more prized than the other by Bestuzhev—books and a letter. With these secular blessings the pagan holiday is suddenly transformed into Holy Week again, not as an abstraction, but as a "real holiday for my mind and heart."

The nexus of pagan and Christian images perforce develops into a carnivalesque celebration of the renewing potentials of the cycles of life and death. The metaphors of death, rebirth, and life constitute a carnivalized triad grounded in Bestuzhev's experience beginning, perhaps, as far back as his father's death and as recently as December 14, 1825. The thanatic figures of speech he utilized, therefore, represent the sincere and meaningful expressions of an authentic self.

In writing to Nicholas and Mikhail on the eve of Christmas, Bestuzhev resorted again to images he considered a logical outgrowth of his and their condition: "When I recall you, then the Yakut frost runs through my veins despite the tropic heat about me here. And what are you up to, and how are you now? I have a better idea of the shores of the Styx than I do of your Petrovsky graveyard. Are you vegetating on the earth, under the earth, fixed with only a chain, as if it were a root, to this cold earth!?

Horrors!" ("Aleksandr Bestuzhev na Kavkaze," 510). The vegetable images engender a sense of life's continuous cycles of renewal. The graveyard can be apprehended as a garden; oneself as a plant, the roots of which are the prisoners' chains. There is a potential here for resurrection, which Bestuzhev imaginatively acknowledged through what otherwise appears to be a chaotic assortment of metaphors.

On December 14, 1832, seven years after the Decembrist Revolt, Bestuzhev wrote Ksenofont Polevoy in a similar vein: "Today is the day of my death. In silence and contrition I conduct the funereal feast for the salvation of my soul. And when will I find this salvation? Recollections lay upon my heart like corpses, no, like relics" ("Pis'ma k Polevym," 335). The preservation of the saint's relics, of course, allows for a certain kind of physical immortality, and with it veneration. Bestuzhev's metaphoric death, in other words, may lead to his own form of resurrection, of perpetuity, immortality, and thus reverence.

Bestuzhev's apparently inconsistent religiosity is coherent at another level—in the transformation of the secular hero into the spiritualized (in a pagan sense) carnival king. In this guise the propensity of carnival to ascribe to itself whatever form it will, the high and the low, the religious and the irreligious, the orthodox and the pagan, is manifest in Bestuzhev's expansion of the parameters of the hero's identity. That this image began to dissolve into a kind of chaos does it no harm, apparently, for it can then be likened to all existence. The hero, in other words, becomes a rival of God much in the manner of Dostoyevsky's nihilists or one of their prototypes, Byron's Manfred. This rivalry is tested most effectively in ultimate terms, in the hero's confrontation with death, not a symbolic death, of course, but an actual biological demise. The immanence of this test was ever before Bestuzhev as a literary event, like a novel of indistinct outline:

> I am wavering about writing either a novel or a tragedy, I don't know which, but the story line is rich. In it I can illumine each [human] strength which has been torn asunder [by focusing] on those who represent those strengths, and illumine each feeling [which is manifest] in behavior. Striking myself on the forehead, I, like Chenier at the guillotine, can say, "There is something here," but this something is yet bound up, dark, or, to put it a better way, so bright that the mind is blinded and cannot make this something out. (Ibid., 430)

Citing Chenier's example, Bestuzhev focuses on the embattled, tragic, but elevated romantic hero. For Bestuzhev, that image possessed substance, for it was historically grounded in an authentic personage who lived the linkage of life and literature. The material is indeed worthy of a novel, a text to match the life-text. On April 5, 1833, again an Easter holiday, Bestuzhev concluded a letter to the Polevoys in which he recited plans he never fulfilled:

> Oh, if fate would give me but one year devoid of human enmity so that I might try my wings not constrained by a chain! But as it is, once started into an important project (a novel), fate adorns me in thunderclouds. I do not possess the clarity of spirit to pour out onto the page what boils in my soul. But this will pass and I will send you a fragment in which I depict a poet perishing from the black death . . . a poet who recognizes his gifts and sees an [approaching] death which will swallow up his unfinished poem, his titanic dreams, and the miraculous visions he sees in his delirium. So what if they do not understand me; I will be daring in these ravings. (Ibid., 439)

At this juncture death became a conscious component Bestuzhev found possible to attach to his heroic mask. No longer repelled, Bestuzhev was decidedly attracted to the literary potential inherent in death both as a reality and as a literary event. He exploited it. Bestuzhev initiated the theme of his demise well in advance of his departure from Derbent, a period of relative calm in his life. As early as December 1830, upon hearing that his brothers had been moved in Siberia from Chita to a new prison, Petrovsky Zavod, Bestuzhev wrote them: "To congratulate you on such an occasion would be like complimenting a corpse for the receipt of a new grave" ("Aleksandr Bestuzhev na Kavkaze," 503). Within a month Bestuzhev sent his mother a melancholy letter about his recollection of past Christmas holidays in the bosom of the family:

> I met, or I should better say, the New Year found me asleep. This time there were not even any dreams out of which I might have fashioned a Christmas castle. . . . There was nothing which recalled the customs of the homeland, nothing to gladden the heart in the manner to which we had grown accustomed since earliest childhood. . . . Oh, "homeland" is not an empty sound, not a

prejudice of upbringing. Were I to live in paradise I could never forget my distant homeland, where I blossomed as a child, lived as a youth, and even where I suffered and perished. It seems to me my heart is buried there far from my own self; thence fly my thoughts, my longings. (505)

The metaphoric apprehension of death gleaned from Bestuzhev's letters overwhelms any realistic assessment of his circumstances. Only on rare occasions did Bestuzhev actually present an account of the dangers to his person in the Caucasus, particularly after 1834 when he was continually on the march in the plains, the mountains, and the forests by the sea. As early as 1831 Bestuzhev noted the distinct possibility of his own demise while fighting against the mountain tribesmen. In December 1831 he wrote the Polevoys about a battle in which one of the Decembrists fell "heroically," a comment he immediately follows with a prediction: "my turn may come next" ("Pis'ma k Polevym," 313).

Within three years his tone changed dramatically from an objective description of what was a likely possibility to a manipulation of that information to serve the persona:

Well, we have just completed our truly remarkable and difficult expedition through the impenetrable thickets, across mountain passes to the Black Sea, pouring forth ours and the enemy's blood all along the way. I have stopped believing that a bullet can touch me, and the whistle of the shot has become for me nothing but the whistle of the wind, even less remarkable, for the wind at least makes me turn my head, whereas bullets make no impression on me. At first, at least, it was pleasant for me that they flew past. Then it was pleasant to listen to their wild song. Now I am indifferent whether it is there or not. . . . And so it is, we lose all our pleasures through habit, and the dangers of battle finally bore us when they cease to boil our blood. However, I am not entirely asleep, and the shouts of a skirmish beckon me like the voice of a beloved lady; they fling me into the fire and into the frenzy of oblivion. (Ibid., 465–66)

The dangers in which Bestuzhev was constantly placed are a matter of record. Whether from the perils of battle or the hazards of disease, Bestuzhev's life was indeed in jeopardy. On August 6, 1836, he wrote:

I have become distressed, dearest Ksenofont Alekseevich, for I have not received any news from you for such a very long time. I am still ill with fevers. It leaves me for a time, say a week, and then returns again. It has worn me so thin that I could be used in place of glass on a lantern. I have written to you through Sevastopol and through Kerch, but there is still no answer. . . . About Gagry [where I am now stationed] I have written you in detail, but clearly you have not received my letter containing the description. It is simply a coffin. My health is still poor. (Ibid., 481)

Toward a Fifth Act

Bidding farewell to Derbent, Bestuzhev traveled to the central and western Caucasus where he served as a frontline soldier until his end. Bestuzhev felt that this was an important move for him in order to win his release through distinguishing himself in battle. He accomplished his plan by accounting heroically for himself in numerous battles along the Black Sea, in the mountains, along the rivers and backwoods of the lowlands.[33]

During these years Bestuzhev literally walked from the central mountainous regions northward to the steppes and from there to the Black Sea. He marched several times in succession from the sea to the central mountains and back again. He suffered malaria, intestinal parasites, tapeworm, hemorrhoids, scurvy, and other diseases that often decimated the ranks of the battalions in which he served. Bestuzhev had a strong constitution, but continual sickness, a poor diet, primitive medical treatment, and damp, cold bivouacs gradually undermined his health. He was sent infrequently to the local watering holes of the Russian aristocracy to take the cure, but he was not allowed to remain long because of the sympathy he received from the civilian population. Kept under constant surveillance, his quarters were searched and his letters were read at each posting.

Late in 1835 Bestuzhev was surprised to find that he had been promoted to noncommissioned officer, a minor advancement that nonethe-

---

33. For a summary of Bestuzhev's years on the march, see Vasil'ev, 23–29.

less encouraged his diminishing hopes. When one remembers the tsar's explicit instructions that Bestuzhev not be promoted, it is clear that his hand must have remained in the matter. Later, in May 1836, Bestuzhev was promoted to ensign, the rank with which new military school graduates came to the Caucasus. Again Bestuzhev was led to believe he had reason to hope for a pardon. Feeling that he was suddenly in a position of strength, Bestuzhev solicited the aid of Count Vorontsov to intercede for him before the tsar—surely he would take pity on his sorry lot now that he was ruined in body, forgotten more and more in literature, and incapable of threatening the crown in any way. He sought a more advanced officer's status and the decorations which he so richly deserved. Word returned, however, that the tsar would not allow recognition of a criminal. Bestuzhev could no longer avoid seeing in whose hands he had been resting since December 14, 1825. He began to lose heart, although not completely, becoming more quick-tempered, serious, and brooding, as he described himself to the Polevoys ("Pis'ma k Polevym," 479–81). His body wrecked by pain and disease, hopes reduced to idle thoughts, Bestuzhev saw nothing before him but continuous, interminable marches and difficult battles until the end of his term of exile (which was still several years away). There was only one thing for him to do, and that was to make a good *show* of himself, for his own sake, for the tsar's amusement, for the sake of society, and to the delight of his audience. He would display in his best form the integrity of the romantic hero. This much was yet in his control, for he was well practiced in the art.

Behind the denial of his promotion Bestuzhev could sense the tsar's personal plan to bring him to his knees. It necessitated his transfer to two consecutive posts where disease had severely reduced the population. In one garrison alone the turnover in a year had been 150 percent. Smallpox and cholera reduced the Akhaltsy garrison by over half in the short time Bestuzhev was stationed there. It is surprising that he did not succumb to one of these deadly diseases during his exile.[34] Perhaps the tsar intended Bestuzhev to die ignominiously (from a romantic perspective) of a wasting sickness, as though in literal re-creation of Byron's sorry model. Bestuzhev went forward stoically, seemingly cognizant of the plot in which he found himself, conscious of its author and the role he was

---

34. Even in his first year in Derbent, over 10 percent of the population died from cholera (which was epidemic in the region during Bestuzhev's exile).

expected to play in it. He had to submit to this fate, but he chose to do it in his own way.

Bestuzhev received and reviewed medical books on home remedies. He modified cures, refused others (for example, blood letting), and concocted his own medicines. This attests to a strong survival instinct, the motivation for which lay not in his hope of pardon for heroism and valorous service to the state (which he had now abandoned), but in his romantic heroic imperative. A hero could no more die of disease than he could be killed in bed at the hands of thieves. It would be unthinkable. By literary design and historical example (Byron notwithstanding),[35] Bestuzhev intended his end to be a performance of lasting value.

Proving he was in control of the persona Marlinsky, if not the fate of the historical personage Bestuzhev, upon arriving in Gagry Bestuzhev struck a familiar social pose:

> In an entirely new full-dress coat, pomaded, perfumed, [Bestuzhev] arrived on that day looking more like a general than anyone else, and thus involuntarily [!] brought on himself the attention of the detachment officers against whom Bestuzhev stood out in full contrast. . . . I sat at table with the commander, Prince Shakhovskoy, with Bestuzhev and the aide-de-camp Bibikovsky; Bestuzhev said to the Prince, "Have you noticed, Prince, that in Pataniotti [the commander of the Black Sea squadron, a vice-admiral] there is something divine?" "How is that?" responded the Prince. "Because in his conversation there is neither beginning nor end." This unexpected witticism made us all laugh. (Vasil'ev, 32)

Bestuzhev eased his lot as best he could, concerning himself with family affairs, the well-being of his brothers, sisters, and mother. He immersed himself in nature, finding solace in the diverse Caucasian landscape. He discovered, too, that he found a measure of oblivion in battle. Furthermore, when Bestuzhev visited the spas, he immediately lost himself in affairs. In each instance, and without the slightest effort, he maintained the image of an integrated self. This self, of course, was Marlinsky.

On one trip to take the waters, Bestuzhev was asked to write in a young society lady's album the thing most valued by him. He wrote his own name (ibid., 34). This was no light jest. It indicated his desperate

35. Bestuzhev was not aware of the actual cause of Byron's death.

position. He could no longer write with skill and passion. The one work that remained in him to write ("Mulla Nur") was an obvious struggle. Given that his work was known in Russia only under his assumed name, Bestuzhev longed for the recognition of his authentic personage. His attempts to guide his readers within his stories and travelogues to his true identity had failed, and those who knew that Marlinsky was Bestuzhev forbore mentioning the connection lest they jeopardize his freedom to publish. Not only was he Marlinsky to many, his works under that name were being roundly attacked in the press from 1834 on for their florid style, formulaic plots, and stilted characters. His health was steadily worsening, and he saw before him nothing but endless battles, marches, bivouacs. When he wrote his name to signify the most important thing to him, he was asserting the primacy of his self in the face of his diminished circumstances. He was proclaiming his right to be recognized as a historical entity. Yet this was more than a predictable ego-gesture of a fashionable romantic of the day. By naming himself in this manner, Bestuzhev symbolically asserted the domination of his ego over his personal history. Symbols were the last shots he had to fire. They were heard.

Count Vorontsov, again taking pity on Bestuzhev, attempted to ease his lot, this time requesting of the tsar that Bestuzhev be transferred permanently to the Crimea. This would at least release Bestuzhev from the dangers of battle and disease for the remainder of his exile. The tsar refused, permitting Bestuzhev instead a temporary rest in a small town between Tiflis and the Black Sea. Then in the spring of 1837, Bestuzhev discovered that Tsar Nicholas planned to visit military units stationed on Adler Promontory where he was soon to be stationed. Barely masking his wish to see the tsar (in hopes of influencing him through a personal interview), Bestuzhev wrote, "We all await the tsar-father with love and impatience" ("Pis'ma k Polevym," 485). Bestuzhev knew that his talents, even if he were forced to remain in exile, were being wasted and that if he might assume a command suitable to his gifts, life would be better for him: "I feel that I would make a good general given a regular advancement in this business of mine; but what does my experience and bravery serve instead? Walking the front lines with an ensign just out of school, getting shot up in some stupid cross fire in some forgotten corner of some forsaken woods! What a delightful prospect! . . . I am worn out" (485–86).

When Bestuzhev arrived at Adler Promontory in early June 1837, he learned that the tsar would not visit there after all. His chances of a personal interview dashed, and with them his hope of surviving the marches for another eight years, on the morning of June 7, Bestuzhev made out his last will and testament. On this day at Adler Promontory he was to be involved in a minor battle. Fighting along the shore, in the woods, and on the bluffs was a tricky business, but Bestuzhev had learned from Caucasian natives how to escape harm if at all possible. He was admired as much by the natives for his skill in fighting as he admired them. Yet, on this day, with nothing any longer for him to await but pain and a meaningless existence, Bestuzhev may have elected to die, not as a sickly, weakened, and ordinary soldier downtrodden by circumstances, but as a romantic hero. Not only did he write his will, he penned the following words to his brother Pavel: "I embrace you my dear brother. If God does not grant that we meet again, be happy. You know that I have loved you greatly. This, however, is not an epitaph. I don't think about dying, nor do I long for it to come soon, however, in any event it is best to bid you farewell. When you show this letter to mother, do not reveal this part; why worry her needlessly?" ("Aleksandr Bestuzhev na Kavkaze," 75).

Death seems to have approached, not merely as a conclusion to life, but as a literary event that might have been staged to suit Bestuzhev's persona and to fit the expectations he had created in his audience. The end, consequently, could be viewed as Bestuzhev's final creation, the consummate fifth act that would fuse text and life-text permanently. Yet, there is no conclusive evidence that permits us to consider this assumption any more likely than a variety of other possibilities. Bestuzhev's words leave a particular stamp on his disappearance, but they cannot prove his intent to die. This battle would be as open to various possibilities as any preceding it. Death remained a possibility in each one just as much as survival. Thus, it is not any more reliable to argue that Bestuzhev purposely died at Adler Promontory than it is to finalize his life by saying that he simply disappeared either in death or through the machinations of some literary plot he had concocted with the complicity of Cherkes natives.

The truth is, we do not know what happened to Bestuzhev. The record's inconclusiveness and contradictoriness attest to an open-ended reading of his disappearance. Readers, however, have finalized his life in conformity with their reading of the persona. If Bestuzhev's texts and life coalesced at this historical juncture, it was because readers made it happen. But always, of course, with Bestuzhev's help.

10

The Mature Fiction

To tell you the truth, there is not the slightest
difference between my blood and the ink I use.
—Bestuzhev-Marlinsky

Society

In the 1820s the formula "fiction equals life" operated in large measure
under the belief that literature influenced reality. In the 1830s the causal
direction did not simply reverse. The relationship became a more complex dialogue between fiction on one side and daily life, recent history,
social mores, and ideology on the other. "The Test" suggests this reorientation. On the one hand, it is a story greatly influenced by society tales
from Europe. Victor Hugo and, to a lesser extent, Honoré de Balzac
established models for Bestuzhev's critical description of high society,
and Bestuzhev had not forgotten Scott and Byron.[1] Bestuzhev's personal

1. N. K. Kozmin, *Ocherki iz istorii russkogo romantizma* (Petersburg, 1903), 72–73; I. I.
Zamotin, *Romantizm dvadtstaykh godov XIX stoletiia v russkoi literature*, 2:83.

experiences in society constituted another resource for his Caucasus fiction. The reality of the Hay Market scene, the masked ball (with its description of social convention), and the Strelinsky and Gremin code of behavior are substantiated in Bestuzhev's letters, diaries, and in the correspondence of his contemporaries as well. Society's speech and behavioral norms entered fictional texts wholesale.[2]

During the 1830s, Bestuzhev wrote approximately thirty stories and tales, half of which describe the Caucasus. The other half represents a variety of genres: the sea stories "Lieutenant Belozor" ("Leitenant Belozor," 1831), "The Frigate 'Hope' " ("Fregat 'Nadezhda,' " 1832), and "The Sailor Nikitin" ("Morekhod Nikitin," 1834); tales of horror à la Radcliffe, "An Evening at a Caucasian Spa in 1824" ("Vecher na kavkazskikh vodakh v 1824 godu," 1830), "A Sequel to an Evening at a Caucasian Spa in 1824" ("Sledstvie vechera na kavkazskikh vodakh v 1824 godu," 1830), "A Terrible Divination: A Story" ("Strashnoe gadanie: Rasskaz," 1830), and "The Cuirassier: A Partisan Officer's Story" ("Latnik: Rasskaz partizanskogo ofitsera," 1831); one historical tale, "The Raids: A Tale of the Year 1613" ("Naezdy: Povest' 1613 goda," 1831); and the society tale "The Test." The remainder are stories of the Caucasus, which represent Bestuzhev's major achievement in fiction during his exile. What is particularly noteworthy about the historical piece, the society tale, the sea stories, and the gothic tales is the speed with which Bestuzhev wrote and published them. All appeared between 1830 and 1832 (with the exception of "The Sailor Nikitin").

The dramatic effect these texts had on the audience may be due in some measure to the frequency with which Marlinsky's name appeared in print. Virtually unknown in 1830, by 1833 Marlinsky had become a household word. A consequence of his quick delivery to the publishers, however, was uniformity. In 1834, one year after the conclusion of Bestuzhev's furious pace of writing and publishing, Vissarion Belinsky, in "Literary Reveries" ("Literaturnye mectaniia," 1834) scored Marlinsky for this aesthetic deficiency: "[Bestuzhev's] talent is entirely one-dimensional; his pretensions at creating true feeling are quite suspect; there is no depth, no philosophy, no [real] dynamics in his works, the consequence of which are the following: all the heroes of his tales are cut from the same cloth and differ one from the other only by their names."

---

2. William Mills Todd III, *Fiction and Society in the Age of Pushkin* (Cambridge, Mass., 1986), 39–44, 110–12.

He repeats himself in every work. There is more phrase-making in him than real ideas, more rhetorical bombastics than the expression of [authentic] feeling."[3]

Belinsky acknowledged Marlinsky's popularity, he could hardly do otherwise, but only as a criticism of the audience itself: "Nowadays all are on their knees before [Marlinsky], and if they are not all in one voice calling him a *Russian Balzac*, it is only because they fear to demean him thereby, and expect the French to call Balzac a *French Marlinsky*."[4] To set both the reader and the author straight, Belinsky claimed he would perform a new service for Russian letters: "While awaiting the [Bestuzhev] miracle to run its full course, we shall, with a bit more composure, examine his right to such huge authority. Of course, it is a terrible thing to go off into battle against public opinion and to make a stand against its idols. But I am decided on this course of action as much from valor as from a selfless love of the truth." Belinsky apparently satirized the hero ethic Bestuzhev's audience loved in Marlinsky by claiming it for himself—but not as a warrior-poet-hero. He is the hero–literary critic: "I am encouraged [to perform this service] by the fact that public opinion is beginning little by little to recover its senses from the blow struck by the recent publication of Mr. Marlinsky's *Russian Tales and Stories*. There are abroad of late dark thoughts about the strained nature, the dull uniformity, etc. of these tales. So, I have made up my mind to become the organ of a new public opinion. I know that this new opinion will find entirely too many opponents, but no matter what, on this earth truth is more dear than someone or other's prestige" (Belinskii, 83). Belinsky's comic aim at personally besting Bestuzhev (in mock heroic terms) does not obscure the import of his judgments: "We have very few authors who have written as much as Mr. Marlinsky; but this abundance springs not from the largess of talent, not from a surplus of creative energy, but from habit, simply from doing it over and over again.... He has talent, but not a great talent; talent weakened by the eternal compulsion to be witty" (83–85).

Belinsky, however, did not understand the circumstances in which Bestuzhev wrote. Nor did he appreciate one compelling motive for the

3. Vissarion Belinskii, *Polnoe sobranie sochinenii*, 2:83.
4. Ibid., 83; cited in Lauren Leighton, *Alexander Bestuzhev-Marlinsky*, 13. *Alexander Bestuzhev-Marlinsky* is henceforth *ABM* when cited parenthetically in text or notes.

writing "habit" Bestuzhev possessed—his need to support himself and his family. Belinsky's remarks, consequently, represent a shift in the reception of Bestuzhev's work, but only within a small circle of a burgeoning intelligentsia.[5] He did not represent, as he candidly admitted, the general reading public with its taste for the adventurous tales it associated with Marlinsky's name, for the impassioned form of his characters' and narrators' speeches, and for the witty style and metaphoric grandiloquence of the discourse. Nevertheless, Belinsky presaged, perhaps even formulated, posterity's opinion of Bestuzhev's prose. But in 1834, Bestuzhev's Marlinsky was in command of the audience. As early as 1821 his work had created expectations about the purposes of verbal art which he continued to fulfill to the letter in the 1830s.

We can understand from the perspective of over a century and a half how very accurate Belinsky's response in fact was. Whether historical tale, sea story, society tale, or Caucasian novella, Bestuzhev duplicated his prose. Doing so meant immediate renown and financial gain, both of which he sought, first to fulfill a persona project, second to support himself and his family. A full appreciation of Bestuzhev's fiction of the 1830s, then, must accommodate these disparate vantage points. We must appreciate Belinsky's opinion (as a function of literary evolution) and at the same time the reading public's response: "We all love Marlinsky frightfully for his dashing and courtly heroes, for what seemed to us a magnificent ardor of feeling, and finally for his brilliant and whirling language. . . . We dote on Marlinsky with boundless delight" (quoted in Leighton, *ABM*, 13).

Bestuzhev's prose represented popular culture, the art of a growing mass culture, the aesthetics of entertainment, and the idea that life equals literature. It was this last proposition Belinsky saw as thoroughly antiquated, myopically conventional, and unnecessarily dangerous. He prop-

---

5. Two excellent studies treat the development of a literate public in Russian culture, but neither treats the period in question in any detail: Jeffrey Brooks, *When Russia Learned to Read: Literacy and Popular Literature, 1861–1917* (Princeton, N.J., 1985), and Gary Marker, *Publishing, Printing, and the Origins of Intellectual Life in Russia, 1700–1800*. Marker briefly mentions the romantic period in the conclusion of his study and states, "Certainly from the middle of the reign of Alexander I onward, writers and journalists . . . watched with keen interest the occasional commercial success of recognized authors, such as Krylov, Pushkin, and Zagoskin, in hopes that at least someone was reaching through to the wider readership and thereby breaking down the cultural barriers between them and the common readers" (236). Brooks dates the development of "a common culture based on common literacy" from 1861 (xiii). Bestuzhev's accomplishments certainly contributed to this development.

agated a new notion of literature as a form of art that attempted not to invent the world, but to reflect it adequately.[6] For Bestuzhev, the very uniformity of his prose constituted evidence in support of the fundamental idea governing his every move in life and in letters. Wit, flashy figures of speech, impassioned declamations, and emotional tirades represented the language of art and life. Bestuzhev experienced the effectiveness of these forms of speech each day; his audience responded to them in his fiction; his family and friends harkened to his style in his letters. The artificial plots, implausible circumstances, and unnatural relationships of his fiction, which Belinsky denigrated, were no more nor less artificial, implausible, or unnatural than the conditions of his exile—caught between vastly different cultures, languages, religious beliefs, and value systems, constrained to fight an enemy with whom he sympathized and in whom he recognized the qualities he had adopted for himself. For Bestuzhev, lived experience validated his fiction. Prose did not distort reality; it was the quintessential opportunity to inscribe his idea of life and authentic selfhood onto Russian cultural history.

"The Test" is a case in point. Examining the story from a rhetorical point of view, we see that Bestuzhev successfully integrated the theme linking literature and life within his story through the figure of his alter ego, the narrator. The narrator is cast in the third person, he is dramatized and intrusive, self-conscious at times, most often reliable, and authoritative when delivering interpretive comments. There are moments, however, when his perspective is limited. As witnessed in the first period of Bestuzhev's creativity, the dramatized narrator performs a number of services. He reminds the reader he is always dealing with fiction and with the consciousness that created it:[7] "Each person has his own fantasies, and each author his own way of telling a story. However, if you are that curious, send someone to the commandant's headquarters to check the list of recent arrivals in town."

Since the narrator constitutes the bond cementing discrete elements of creative activity (generation and reception), he establishes for his readers criteria for judging the narrative in all its disparate elements. As a self-

6. "It has been pointed out that Belinskij's entire career represents a search for a definition of "reality" [deistvitel'nost']. That art was to represent the reality of life Belinskij never doubted for a moment" (Victor Terras, Belinskij and Russian Literary Criticism [Madison, Wis., 1974], 77).

7. As Abrams points out, romanticism engendered a shift in interest from the poem to the poet, a literary fact Bestuzhev continually substantiated in practice (M. H. Abrams, The Mirror and the Lamp: Romantic Theory and the Critical Tradition [New York, 1971], 21–26).

conscious narrator he is willful (as we see in the digressive second chapter on the Hay Market); he is ironic (for example, when he satirizes his protagonists and their callow understanding of the world). Readers are asked to adopt the formal distance these traits develop rhetorically, participating in the reception of the text in the spirit of its generation. When the narrator ironically describes Alina, who nonetheless represents the ideological (Decembrist) center of the tale, readers are asked to view the passage from the narrator's perspective:

> Rays of the cold morning sun had already begun to play on the diamond colors of the large window panes of the grafinya Zvezdich's bedroom, but within, behind the triple canopy, a mysterious darkness lay and the goddess of sleep flew to and fro on gentle wings. Nothing is more sweet than morning dreams. As we sleep initial duty is fulfilled toward fatigue, but as one's soul gradually overcomes the body's demands, dreams become more and more delicate. The eyes, turned inward, see more sharply, visions become illuminated clearly and the sequence of ideas, images and dream occurrences become more orderly and even real. One's memory may retain these creations intact. But this is a matter for the heart alone. . . . It beats, yet it is enthralled by the dream's sweet presence. It alone is the witness to their momentary existence. Such dreams guarded Alina's sleep, and although there was nothing quite definite in them, nothing of the stuff out of which romantic poems or historical novels are fashioned, they yet contained everything essential to enchant a youthful imagination. Her initial dreams, however, were less colorful than entertaining.[8]

The narrator unmasks the idea that Alina's dreams are literary and makes fun of the romance of the unconscious, a mainstay of the romantic canon. The narrator suggests we are to take the literary material here described with a grain of salt, effectively debunking the assumed linkage of literature and life. At once thematizing and criticizing the belief in literary plots that encompass his characters' psyches, he simultaneously preserves the theme's validity at another level—the one that links narrator and reader.

Elsewhere, too, the narrator assaults his characters' idea that litera-

---

8. Aleksandr Bestuzhev-Marlinskii, "The Test," 162.

ture equals life: "In the book of love most charming of all is the page on *faux pas:* and to each his own. Alina was now no longer the seventeen year old, attracted to every kind of social model or to the seductive logic of anxious seducers, who was swept away by her first dalliance, as by a new toy, and, imagining herself the heroine of some novel, wrote three passionate letters to Prince Gremin" (ibid., 172). The narrator suggests that the reader familiar with romantic literary archetypes join him in his critique. He beseeches the reader to engage in the task of generating the tale he refuses to narrate, at least once it has proven to conform completely to literary expectation:

> No matter how sure [Strelinsky] was that he loved and was loved in return, the wondrous words, "I love you," had died upon his lips twenty times without being uttered as if he were required for some reason to conceal them. The grafinya also, like all women it seems, was as afraid of the words, "I love you," as of a pistol shot, as if each of its letters were made of blazing silver! And no matter how prepared she was for that word from Strelinsky, no matter how sure she was that it had to happen one day, all the blood in her heart rushed to her head when Strelinsky, having seized the right moment, with trepidation began to express, but then concealed his love. . . . I leave it to the reader to complete such scenes for himself. I think that each with either a sigh or a smile may recall and then draw the details of similar moments in his youth. And, surely, each will err only slightly. (173)

Bestuzhev's narrator alternates between facetious and reliable discourse, between a judgment of man's hypocrisy and a castigation of myopic obeisance to literary model. In each instance the narrator represents the point of view of the author. The limitations the narrator feigns are subverted by the reliability of his judgments. For instance, in describing the ball at which Strelinsky and Alina meet, the narrator exposes the duplicity of high society by summarizing its actions and by peering into what might be considered its collective mind: "Skimming along the mirror-finished parquet floor, like aerial apparitions, behind their mothers and aunts who were all dolled up for the occasion, the young girls enchantingly, how enchantingly, responded with a slight nod to the courteous bows of the cavaliers whom they knew, and with smiles in response to the knowing glances of their girl friends. And the entire time lorgnettes were directed at them, and every lip was busy analyzing them. Yet, not a single heart beat with true affection for any of them . . . perhaps" (ibid., 155). The narrator shifts his perspective from person to person, from couple to couple, stepping into their minds and discovering therein mean pettiness and egocentricity, self-righteousness and false pride: "And so our admirer, having first sat with her mother, an old, successful manipulator, listens with rapt attention to her nonsense, then showers greetings upon the daughter herself, and while dancing, makes goo-goo eyes at her and licks his lips, for he is adding up her riches in his mind" (156).[9]

The complexity in narrator roles that derives from Bestuzhev's play with voices in the text is best revealed in the final chapter of the story where, because of the narrator's many guises, Bestuzhev places reliable commentary in the personage of another character introduced specifically for this task—the physician who attends the duel between Strelinsky and Gremin. Early in Bestuzhev's career Doctor Loncius played a similar role in "The Tournament at Revel." After observing the happy resolution of the conflict, the doctor states that he must return to his office to make notes for a study he is composing: " 'A dissertation, I am sure, on the passions of oysters!' Gremin said smiling. 'On the contrary,' the doctor replied, 'It's on the felicitous foolishness of man' " ("The Test," 194). Perhaps the most important element of the exchange between the doctor and Gremin is its covert representation of the author's point of view. In that exchange Gremin and Strelinsky are compared to oysters in which the precious pearl of individuality has not yet been developed. By implication, the narrator possesses the prized object.

The linkage between art and life is tenuous. Bestuzhev's narrator takes pains to show the reader that this story is not meant to encapsulate the real world. Furthermore, its characters are not meant to be fully delineated. Through the faults of character, and through the corrective perspectives of the narrator, Bestuzhev's message is made clear—the relationship between fiction and reality must be reconstituted; not dismissed altogether, but reformulated.

This new conception of fiction, of course, was not at all similar to Belinsky's. Bestuzhev's notion of art now incorporated the model "art equals life" from a dialogic perspective. His experiences during and after

---

9. The connection between balls and the carnivalesque was discussed as early as 1823 in *The Polar Star* (Todd, 38–39).

the revolt, and now in exile, suggested that a new arrangement was more appropriate for the propagation of literature as a molding force in the lives of his readers. Strelinsky's and Gremin's behavioral models are shown to be inadequate to reality, life-threatening, and consequently in desperate need of change. Through satire Bestuzhev underscores the need to transform the callow hero's code. As a consequence, the narrator takes a hierarchically superior position to the characters in the tale, effectively distancing himself from them intellectually, morally, and emotionally.[10] The narrator in "The Test" models a reconstituted version of the formula "literature equals life." This is not to say that there is a simple one-to-one correspondence between the image of the narrator and the behavioral forms a naive reader might wish to imitate. The picture is somewhat more complex. The narrator's sundry guises reaffirm a standard of behavior that links social reality and literature—the notion of the self as a series of masks prescribed by social convention. But the performances of selfhood in daily life do not present the only level on which the modeling takes place. The narrator is developed by Bestuzhev in a way that suggests the author's presence. As Alina states to Strelinsky at the masked ball, "The more you conceal your identity, the more surely I know it" (161). Bestuzhev's literature of the 1830s possessed this carnival effect.

Poetry and prose were read at this historical moment with the belief that depth was secured in the identification of author and text. Bestuzhev exploited this belief in "The Test," teasing the reader to fuse author and narrator:

> There are moments in life, hours even, of heavy ineffable sadness. . . . The mind, as though paralyzed, suddenly gets lost. But one's feelings, poisoned by a full understanding of a great disaster, like an avalanche, rushes down one's heart and smothers it in the frigid cold of despair, a mute, but deep, senseless and torturous despair! At such times the eyes have no tears, the lips no words, and even worse, a sadness takes form in the heart, more acrid than bitter tears. And the heart itself, like some subterranean being overflowing with blazing sulphur, strains to throw from itself the heavy burden which is crushing it, but it cannot. (Ibid., 197)

10. Wayne C. Booth, *The Rhetoric of Fiction* (Chicago, 1961), 149–266.

Through the narrator, then, direct association could be made with the persona that Bestuzhev, not without justification, propagated in reality. The persona projected here is completely coincident with Bestuzhev's life experience. At moments such as this, the revalued relationship of literature and life becomes concrete in the image and voice of the narrator. He constitutes the link between author and reader engaged in the mutually supportive acts of text generation and reception at a level that is apprehended as authentic, real, and substantive. It is a peculiarity of Bestuzhev's prose of the 1830s that it asserted the linkage of letters and life not through the agency of fictional plots and characters, but through the rhetorical apparatus from which fiction is built. The reality to be gleaned from Bestuzhev's new prose was the reality of his life not as it was in fact (Bestuzhev), but as he perceived it (Marlinsky).

The didactic intent of "The Test" represents one of its more radical features, suggesting again Bestuzhev's belief that fiction can indeed influence life. The society tales, sea stories, and historical tales that Bestuzhev penned in rapid succession advanced the same set of values elaborated in "The Test." Although many of these narratives represent, at a superficial glance, the same type of fiction Bestuzhev wrote in the 1820s, there are marked differences. Bestuzhev's protagonists possess those same heroic qualities which endanger their lives. Where this was an implicit, perhaps unconscious, element in the prose of the 1820s, Bestuzhev makes it an explicit theme in his post-Decembrist work. In many instances the hero is killed, a new event in the Bestuzhev canon. As the protagonist loses his ability to make the world conform to his will, the narrator takes on more of his heroic qualities. The link between protagonist and author is broken in favor of a new bond between the author and his narrator. From 1830 through 1834, Bestuzhev's readers thought they were apprehending the authentic voice of Alexander Marlinsky (and for those in the know, of Alexander Bestuzhev). In either case there was a belief, shared by reader and writer alike, that fiction embodied the writer himself, and that the man was a sensitive warrior-poet-hero straight out of his own fiction.

If there was a complete uniformity in Bestuzhev's dramatis personae, as Belinsky correctly asserted, it is for reasons that escaped the critic. They represented a monolithic conception of identity from which the narrator and his protagonists constituted a dialogic tension out of which the persona of the author grew. Their uniformity and consistency do not represent a fault in Bestuzhev's aesthetics, but the goal of his fictional program. Bestuzhev confessed this much in a letter to his brother Nicholas, who had apparently attacked Bestuzhev's fiction for its stylistic bombastics. Bestuzhev's self-defense (with specific reference to "Lieutenant Belozor") underscored how canonical indeed was his conception of the relationship between characters, narrator, and author:

> Yes, I recognize in you, brother Nicholas, my ideal of social good; [I also recognize in you] the same brother and critic who in no manner wishes to spoil his sibling, who strokes the child's head and says, "Study, Sasha! Look upward, Sasha!" Oh, how I would like to throw myself upon your shoulder and say, "Scold my stories as much as your heart desires, but behold me—do you really not see in me the same heart, even a much improved heart because it has been baptized by tears, a heart which in truth is better than all that I have written and that I will write. However, the book is the man and creation is the reflection of the Creator. This is what I think, what I believe. And this is why I should like to say a few words in defense [of my fiction]. You say that I imitate frequently, but whom? This would be as difficult for me to tell you as it would be for me to figure out. True, in a story I sometimes imitate now this author and now that author, just the same as one sometimes imitates the voice or the gait of someone whom you love, with whom you live. But a voice is not a word, and a gait is not behavior. I may have caught upon someone's script, but never [copied] his style. Proof of this comes from the fact that my style is unique and novel. I am incapable of the kind of forgery written by so many others who are quick to take up the pen but slow to produce anything of quality. . . . The main thing, my dear Nikolya, is that you miss the big picture by sticking to the small details. Can it really be, for example, that in the "botanical lecture," as you call [Lieutenant] Belozor's conversation, you have missed the point? . . . There are chapters, which should be clear, that I have placed in the tale outside the plot, as, for example, Kokorin's conversation with the physician. But who knows? Did I not wish merely to arouse the curiosity of the reader by making him impatient? This, you know, is one of the secrets of art. Besides this, my stories can be viewed as the history of my thought, for I have set a rule I follow in composing—not to restrain my pen.

And as concerns my [stylistic] flashes, my mind is sown of this cloth. To remove them from me would mean ceasing to wear my own suit of clothes, to quit being myself. Thus have I always been in society; thus I am on paper. Can it be that you really do not know me? I am not pretending when I say that I do not seek witty expressions [in my work]. They are who I am completely. [Chto zhe kasaetsia do blestok, imi vyshit moi um: striakhnut' ikh—znachilo by perestat' nosit' svoi kostium, byt' ne soboiu. Tak ia v obshchestve i vsegda, takov i na bumage: uzheli ty menia ne znaesh'? Ia ne pritvoriaius', ne ishchu ostrot—etot zhivoi ia.]"[11]

Bestuzhev viewed his style as an adequate representation of himself, arguing for a finalized definition of his self-idea (which, of course, ultimately limits it). From Bestuzhev's point of view, the composition of work and self are sufficient to each other. From Nicholas's point of view (like Belinsky's), the conception is no longer adequate—the persona and its products are repetitious, clichéd, excessive, and even dangerous. Echoing Nicholas's perspective, Senkovsky reinforced the notion of a literary evolution that was leaving Bestuzhev behind: "What do heroes do? The same as other men, except that in addition these . . . nonentities cast terrible, fiery glances at each other, engage in love affairs senselessly and irresponsibly, become inflamed, kiss, sigh, weep, fall sometimes into fits of incandescent ecstasy and sometimes into fits of wild despair, perpetuate all possible kinds of stupidity and, finally, hurl themselves ingloriously into marriage or into the grave. This is imagination!? This is what is called beautiful!?"[12]

The Sea

In the 1830s prose was evolving in ways for which Bestuzhev had less affinity. Nikolai Gogol's first stories bore little resemblance to Bestuzhev's fiction, and with Gogol's immediate success, Bestuzhev had cause

---

11. "Aleksandr Bestuzhev na Kavkaze, 1829–1837," 53–54.
12. Cited in John Mersereau Jr., *Russian Romantic Fiction*, 218–19.

to worry.[13] He was aware of new, powerful voices emerging in Russian fiction, and he attempted to respond to them. Reacting to interest in the common people, their speech, behavior, values, daily life, interests, trials, hopes, and fears, Bestuzhev began to consider using the middle class in his fiction. By 1834, when Gogol commanded more and more popularity, Bestuzhev wrote an unusual tale, "The Sailor Nikitin," which bears witness to his awareness.

"The Sailor Nikitin" is a deeply polemical work that represents Bestuzhev's attempt to secure his position in Russian prose. The story constitutes Bestuzhev's self-defense of his art in the face of a new prose. But it comprises, too, a challenge hurled at the literary world to see in his fiction a model worthy of emulation and abiding appreciation. At once defensive and aggressive, "The Sailor Nikitin" suggests the growing ambiguity of Bestuzhev's status in Russian letters.

The year 1834 was a turning point in Bestuzhev's life and art. It marked the conclusion of a prolific period of writing and the advent of his final years of life on the march in the Caucasus. Tragedy and scandal surrounded his name; both the Nestertsova affair and his brother's breakdown occurred that year. In literary circles the new prose was becoming more firmly entrenched; Vissarion Belinsky's severe and penetrating attack of Bestuzhev's prose appeared that year. In the article in which Belinsky praised Bestuzhev's language in "The Sailor Nikitin" he set Bestuzhev's work against that of Gogol, seeing the two as antipodal developments in Russian prose. Belinsky was drawn to "Nikitin" because it represented his Gogolian preference, at least in regard to the sailors' language. Belinsky missed the work's polemical intent.

"Nikitin," for all its folk pleasures,[14] is Bestuzhev's assault on the new prose. Significantly, Bestuzhev chose to cast his polemic in the characters and language of his adversaries. While Belinsky enjoyed the results of Bestuzhev's labor, it conditioned a greatly divided narrative, unique in that Bestuzhev opted to work within the emergent structure of the medium he attempted to discredit. This technique, of course, is at the heart of parody. But the polemical element dominates so thoroughly that mere

13. Although there is no text extant in which Bestuzhev comments upon the rising star of the next generation of writers, we do know that Bestuzhev had in his possession a copy of Gogol's *Arabesques*.

14. V. Bazanov, *Ocherki dekabristskoi literatury: Publitsistika, proza, kritika*, 436–49; F. Z. Kanunova, *Estetika russkoi romanticheskoi povesti (A. A. Bestuzhev-Marlinskii i romantiki-belletristy 20–30-kh godov XIX v.)*, 105, 109, 113, 152.

parody cannot be considered Bestuzhev's sole intent. Rather, Bestuzhev asserted the primacy of his manner from within the confines of the new fiction, extracting his diamond from its rough. Bestuzhev, however, validated unwittingly the "rough" in the process of denying it. The tale's self-dividedness is evident at the story's digressive outset.

From the point of view of structure, digression does not merely rival the development of plot (as it so often does in Bestuzhev's stories), it threatens to overcome it entirely. In statistical terms Bestuzhev's digressions occupy forty-four percent of the narrative. Twenty-eight percent alone account for digressive material with nothing to do with the development of the story line, and sixteen percent consists of material proximate to the plot but decidedly on its periphery. The remainder is dedicated to the story of Savely Nikitin: his commercial voyage to Solovki from Archangelsk to secure a sum required to win the hand of Katerina; his capture by a British pirate named Turnip; Nikitin's valiant arrest of the British captain and crew; and his heroic return to Archangelsk where, with the tsar's blessing, he is immediately wed to his beloved.[15] Until the final sixteen hundred words of the ten-thousand-word narrative, the text is evenly divided into digression and plot development.

Bestuzhev's narrator initiates the tale twice before he successfully avoids digression altogether and enters into the complication. The narrator's first attempt ("In 1811, in the month of July, from the mouth of the Northern Dvina a small craft set forth out to sea")[16] immediately leads to an extended digression of over seven hundred words related to four loosely connected topics: (1) tidal conditions where salt and fresh water meet; (2) sailing vessels; (3) the etymology of the Russian word for ship (*korabl'*); and (4) Russian roots, both verbal and edible: "I, as you may see, am a deep-rooted [*korennoi*] Russian, I come from Russian roots [*kornia*], and I have grown up on Russian herbs [*koren'iakh*]" (384). The digression concludes with a chauvinistic bit of braggadocio about the homeland and native Russian prose fiction.

Each of these features of Bestuzhev's initial digression refers imagistically, symbolically, and linguistically to the author's literary polemic. The tides represent the give and take of the "pure" and "impure," the

15. It is quite obvious that there is a great deal of wish-fulfillment in this tale, relating specifically to Bestuzhev's own desires to find release from his captivity through courageous service to his homeland in the Caucasian wars.

16. A. A. Bestuzhev-Marlinskii, *Povesti i rasskazy* (Moscow, 1976), 383.

fresh and salt waters, and suggest the theme of literary authenticity at a time when many non-Russians were commanding the audience's attention, from the Poles Bulgarin and Senkovsky to the newcomer, the Ukrainian Nikolai Gogol. The symbol of the ship indicates the native versus the foreign and parallels the opposition between purity and impurity. The narrator traces the etymology of *korabl'* (ship) to native roots rather than to a Greek word that, he asserts, "I do not know, I do not want to know, since it is a lot of nonsense, a lie, a calumny made up by some trader of Greek nuts or the like" (ibid.).

Having said this much, Bestuzhev, consummate ironist, presses the native Russian issue in regard to sailing vessels, claiming primacy for the simple local variety. But in his praise of the humble Russian bark, the narrator makes striking use of English naval terminology ("hot pressed" and "man-of-war"). The humble Russian bark is dramatically overtaken by Anglicisms, the pure (Russian) suddenly marked by the impure (foreign). This apparent inconsistency identifies Bestuzhev's subjectivity in matters of literary debate. In the not unnatural state of affairs in which literature argues with itself through its various practitioners, the pure and the impure meet, the native and the foreign commingle, fuse, advance, and retreat, and individual authors (ships) maintain relative integrity to their traditions, but not without influence from without. The question, therefore, is not whether or not one should be influenced from outside, but what influence might be most productive. Clearly, Bestuzhev's allegiance is to the foreign literary tradition that influenced him most directly—Sterne, Scott, and Byron—Sterne the quintessential representative of digression as structural dominant, Scott of national and historical fiction, and Byron of literary heroism. It is digression and the hero which comprise the diamond Bestuzhev would extract from the rough in which he has placed his narrative.

Having established criteria for determining the relative purity of the Russian text, Bestuzhev launches into an extensive digression about common Russians. It is cast in the language and style of an illiterate. That is, the narrator's speech shifts from its basis in marlinisms to *skaz* (the speech genre in which a narrator's utterances are illiterate). The second half of the initial digression represents a vernacular genre, boasting:

> You bet ya! Just think, a Russian ol' boy, trader, regular joe, sailor at that, on some little bitty chip of wood, on a bark, in some hide canoe, without compass, no map, nothin', nothin' but a hunk of

bread in his pocket, just sails off, what he does, yup, off to Grumant, that's what they call the New Land, to Kamchatka from Okhotsk, and on to America from Kamchatka, whatever, the heart ups n' laughs, but it makes ya just feel all buggy or somethin'. Around the world, ya say? Done.

[Да-с! Когда вздумаешь, что русский мужичок-промышленник, мореход, на какой-нибудь щепке, на шитике, на карбасе, в кожаной байдаре, без компаса, без карт, с ломтем хлеба в кармане, плывал, хаживал на Грумант,—так зовут они Новую Землю,—в Камчатку из Охотска, в Америку из Камчатки, так сердце смеется, а по коже мурашки бегают. Около света опоясать? Копейка!] (Ibid., 385)

The narrator continues in this vein, eventually turning the boast over to the direct speech of the simple wayfaring sailor himself. The narrator insists that we attend to the way the sailor speaks: "From Brazil we bumped off to Kamchatka, and thence, what say ya, to Sitka, by God, in a trice" [Iz Brazilii *peretolknulis* v Kamchatku, a ottol' ved' na Sitku-to *rukoi podat'!*] (ibid.). The narrator is infected by the vitality of the sailor's vernacular speech and begins to cast his own in like manner: "Well shiver me timbers, these lads are great—just send them off after the waters of life and see what happens! Ya say the ocean's acting up? Just bale 'er out with a cap! A sea of sand? Just snuff 'er up like tabak. Icebergs? Just chomp 'um up like hard candy" [Vot etakikh udal'tsov podavai mne,—i s nimi khot' za zhivoi vodoi posylai! Okean vstrelsia? Okean shapkami vycherpaem! Peschanoe more? Kak tavlinku, vyniukhaem! Ledianye gory? Vmesto ledentsa sgryzem!] (385).

Bazanov considers this passage representative of the story's patriotism, its song of the great gifts of the common Russian, its glorification of the folk and its vernacular forms of address (Bazanov, 436–49). He does not take the passage's function into account and, therefore, misses its irony. Not, of course, that Bestuzhev's digression is unpatriotic or condescending. On the contrary, Bestuzhev attempted here to prove himself a better patriot than those who stoop to a lowly prose manner. Bestuzhev in effect proves that he is not only capable of producing such speech but is better than those who use it in their fiction as a stock item.

Validation of this perspective can be found at the conclusion of the digression.[17] Bestuzhev's narrator directly attacks Senkovsky-Brambeus's *skaz* narratives. Addressing his reader, the narrator ironically asserts that recent Russian prose itself verifies the boast that Russians are far and away the most accomplished at whatever it is they seek to do:

> Plunge but once into our literature and make it your task to read through from beginning to end the fiery articles on one's immortal hours with a cuckoo, on the influence of native macaroni on morality, and on the cultivation of Virginian tobacco; articles so very much inflamed that it is virtually impossible to read them without wearing a fireman's asbestos vest. Just try it and you will be convinced that literary geniuses in Russia are just as common as dried mushrooms during Lent, [you will be convinced] that we are more learned than all the scientists put together, for we have come to the astute conclusion that science is nonsense. [You will be convinced] that we write with greater conscience than all of Europe, for in our compositions there is nothing killed, save common sense.

> [Окунитесь только в нашу словесность, решитесь прочесть с начала до конца пламенные статьи о бессмертных часах с кукушкою, о влиянии родимых макаронов на нравственность и о воспитании виргинского табаку, статьи столь пламенные, что их невозможно читать без пожарного камзола из асбеста,—и вы убедитесь, что литературные гении—самотесы на Руси так же обыкновенны, как сушеные грибы в великий пост, что мы ученее ученых, ибо доведались, что науки вздор; что пишем мы благонравнее всей Европы, ибо в сочинениях наших никого не убивают, кроме здравого смысла.] (*Povesti i rasskazy*, 385–86)

As Bestuzhev's narrator warms to his polemical task, as the irony of his stance opens and becomes overt, he returns to his original voice. The narrator plays with language, finds the striking metaphor, utilizes parallel constructions for symmetry, and in a final dash, seeks to make his point by addressing the reader directly. Reversion to the narrator's "nor-

---

17. Note that the story proper has yet to be initiated and still has to wait one further digression before it actually begins.

mal" voice indicates the conclusion of the digression, the end of his initial argument: one may write in the manner of the new school, even excel at it, but is it really necessary?

Bestuzhev's point, of course, is that his prose not only holds an honored place in romantic literature, but, when compared to the new prose, is superior to it. For readers and writers who might doubt this claim, Bestuzhev raises the issue of aesthetic differentiation. He has his narrator initiate the story a second time only to fall into a second extended digression (the difference between fish and fowl):

> But to the business at hand. In 1811 not a single steamship with loud paddle wheels had frightened the fish folk in the Russian rivers, and as a result the Dvina fish without the least anxiety poked their little heads out of the water to admire the bark, black as a raven, the pitch color of coal, and the people sailing it as it passed by. Here are the physiological details [of the bark] which I obtained from one of the witnesses, a certain pike. Despite the poor quality of the Archangelsk brine [in which it traveled] and the low, wide sledge which made an unusual trip for it, the pike's manner of speech was so very colorful, just as though she had swallowed up the tales of all those dark, particolored and blue fairy tales [we have read of late]. (Ibid., 386)

The specific mention of particolored tales refers to Prince Vladimir Odoyevsky (1804–65), the Russian Hoffmann,[18] specifically his "Particolored Fairy Tales, with a Pretty Little Word, Collected by Iriney Modestovich Gomozeyko, Master of Philosophy and a Member of Various Scholarly Societies, Published by V. Voiceless" ("Pestrye skazki s krasnym slovtsom, sobrannye Irineem Modestovichem Gomozeikoiu, magistrom filosofii i chlenom raznykh uchenykh obshchestv, izdannye V. Bezglasnym," 1833).[19] To discount the new prose, its language, and subject matter, Bestuzhev again utilizes its own techniques. He turns the narrative over to the aforementioned pike: "The river (fish always begin

18. Neil Cornwell, *The Life, Times and Milieu of V. F. Odoevsky: 1804–1869* (London, 1986), 38–46; Charles E. Passage, *The Russian Hoffmannists* (The Hague, 1963), 89–114.
19. The reference to Odoyevsky makes it clear that Bestuzhev's polemic is not aimed at non-Russian authors alone, but at a developing school that was, to use the image of the tides already encountered, impure (salt water) and insufficiently attuned to the literary models that affected Bestuzhev's prose.

their discourse with reference to their homeland, their native element:
prudent fish! In this wise they do not follow in the least the mammalian
composers who more and more prefer writing about whatever it is they
know the least)—the river was barely flowing" [Reka,—ryby vsegda
nachinaiut rech' s svoego otechestva, s svoei stikhii: blagorazumnye
ryby! v etom oni niskol'ko ne sleduiut sostsepitatel'nym sochiniteliam,
kotorye vsego bolee liubiat govorit' o tom, chto oni znaiut naimenee,—
reka chut' struilas'] (*Povesti i rasskazy*, 386). The narrator's parenthetical remark constitutes the center of his argument against the new school.
Its representatives write about a world from which they do not come,
which disqualifies them from any authority they might otherwise claim
for themselves. By inference, Bestuzhev claims to be with the fish: they
have the sense to stick to what they know.

Enclosed within the pike's narrative we find a fowl:

> The fish blew its nose and continued. "Only the solitary crane,
> the tsar of this wasteland, wandered there, like a scientist through
> the sundry zoological disciplines. . . . He, that is the crane, not the
> scientist, stuck his nose into the cloudy waters, into the mucky silt
> and, having pulled out some kind of worm or gudgeon, proudly
> raised its head. Looking around at the vessel, with its eye it mea-
> sured the distance to it and, seeing that he was beyond its reach,
> chased a frisky frog while bobbing its tail without a care. It found
> frogs much more absorbing than people."

> [Рыба сморкает нос и продолжает: "Только одинокий
> журавль, царь пустыни, бродил там, как ученый по части
> зоологии. . . . Он,—то есть, журавль, а не ученый,—втыкал
> нос в мутную воду, в жидкий ил и, вытащив оттуда
> какого-нибудь червячка или пескаря, гордо подымал голову.
> Оглянувшись на карбас, он рассчитал глазомерно расстояние
> и, уверившись, что находится вне выстрела, погнался за
> резвою лягушкою, безпечно кивая хвостиком. Он нашел
> лягушку гораздо занимательней людей."] (Ibid., 387)

For Bestuzhev the new prose sticks its nose not only into unknown
territory, but does so with false pride. Quoting from Senkovsky-
Brambeus (who published "The Sailor Nikitin"!) to the effect that
frogs are more absorbing than people, Bestuzhev attacks the conde-

scending and humiliating perception of human life contained in the new prose.[20]

For Bestuzhev, human beings deserve the most serious consideration and respect. To debase them, to lower their dignity through too close (and therefore too subjective) a perspective, diminishes their heroic capabilities, their romantic potential. Not that the author is disallowed by Bestuzhev from playing with the medium of prose, from digressing à la Sterne, displaying his wit and intellect to aggrandize himself (ironically or otherwise), or from experimenting with the ornamental capacities of the language for its own sake. These features are synonymous with Bestuzhev's marlinisms. Bestuzhev objects to the loss of the heroic element in fiction. Without a loyal, passionate, daredevil there is no romantic prose, much less a prose worthy of the name. In "Nikitin," therefore, Bestuzhev attempted to resurrect his hero, polemically, within the very context in which the possibility of heroism is diminished. The second digression, in which the question of the relative value of frogs and people is raised, moves quickly to the central problem. This rhetorical maneuver sets the next stage of the narrative, in which Bestuzhev's characters are introduced. Only after careful polemical preparation was Bestuzhev willing to initiate his story.

There are four men on board the humble Russian vessel: Savely Nikitin, the captain; Uncle Yakov, an experienced sailor; Ivan, an empty-headed peasant; and the novice Aleksei who, on this voyage, sails for the first time. Bestuzhev develops the differences between the first two as against the latter two in the very same terms in which he has already developed his polemical material. Savely and Yakov are handsome, witty, experienced, and possessed of common sense. Savely, the tale's protagonist, is even fashionable and eternally youthful, qualities that single him out as central: "At the rudder sat a fine lad of twenty-seven years. Hair in a ball, mustachios like parentheses, a bit of a beard curling down, red of cheek promising not to fade until age sixty, with a smile on his face, a smile that moreover could not even be removed by the ninth wave, nor even by the devil himself; in a word, a face both keen and simple, carefree and decisive. This was the physiognomy of a real northern Russian" (*Povesti i rasskazy*, 387). Bestuzhev strives here for a balanced set of qualities in signaling that his protagonist is a natural man. In

20. Bestuzhev precedes Dostoyevsky's perspective, which took shape after Bestuzhev's death and in specific response to Gogol's "Overcoat."

terms of the polemic, Savely's clothes do not merely describe his appearance, but indicate a theme encountered in the first digression—the felicitous blending of the foreign and the native: "In his dress he belongs to a transitional species. On his head an English cap, on his torso a cloth jacket with silver buttons; then a bright red blouse in Russian fashion hung down to his oriental trousers. His boots, by that fashion which has been preserved since the victory at Kulikovo, bent his sharp socks upward" (387). Reference to transitional species, contemporary fashion, and English influence call attention to the tale's polemical categories. Attention is also given to the Battle of Kulikovo (1380), at which Russians, under Dmitrii Donskoi, drove the foreigners back (in this instance, the Mongol Tatars).

If Bestuzhev was to succeed in resurrecting the common man (*qua* hero) from the grave in which he had recently been laid by the new generation of writers, it was important to Bestuzhev to have Savely represent the new order with a difference. Bestuzhev's summary remark fixes Savely in this signal role: "By virtue of the self-confident glances which our helmsman shot at the topsail newly invented by him, the topsail unfurled well above the jib, it was clear that he belonged to the school of innovators [on prinadlezhal k shkole novovvoditelei]" (ibid.).

Unlike the captain (and unlike Uncle Yakov, who represents age, wisdom, and experience, but lacks Savely's heroic features) are the callow Aleksei and the nearly mute and illiterate Ivan. If literature raises these two to center stage, the possibility of the heroic is utterly lost. Bestuzhev sees to it this does not happen:

> On the bark's prow face down with his head over the side lay a stocky shipman with a physiognomy the likes of which nature pours out by the thousands for the dime a dozen breed. You could hardly hang a feeling from off that face it was so obscure; and even if you were to nail a thought by all four legs to his forehead, it wouldn't last there a second. He spat into the water and watched transfixed as the current carried away the liquid expression of his existence, then spat again, crying, "Oh, not just one! Heh, not just one!" then spat again. He belonged to that unending order of practical philosophers who live out life in the most untroubled manner—work when necessary, sleep when possible. (Ibid., 388)

For Bestuzhev, Ivan represents the antiheroic pole, the passive and igno-rant masses who live unconsciously, without a unique thought, devoid of any potential for protest, incapable of even one theatrical gesture in life. Hence his disappearance from the text during Savely's heroic insurrec-tion on board the British captain's vessel.

If Savely represents the opposite extreme, it remains Bestuzhev's task to make of his captain a hero while maintaining Savely's humble origins and prosaic desires. If Bestuzhev elevates Savely beyond his station in life, the story loses its polemical value, its ability to attack the new school on its own terms. To avoid this pitfall, Bestuzhev maintains a constant attentiveness to two elements of the new prose which signal Savely's origins—lower-class utterance and bourgeois desires.[21]

Material desires play an important role in the new prose, and Bestuzhev sees to it that this element enters his tale at many levels—image construction, metaphor building, the development of Savely's character and psychology, and the understanding of human motives. If Savely Nikitin represents a rising bourgeoisie, he does so in the grandiose manner of all Bestuzhev's heroes. He is not presented merely as an entrepreneur, but as a member of an honorable estate: "He belonged to that truly august class of artel merchants, people of highest standards, hard-working, enterprising, honest, and wise" (*Povesti i rasskazy,* 388).

The young innovators in prose fiction introduced the bourgeoisie by design, as a representation of an ideological point of view and literary predisposition, but they often did so naively, for they were not them-selves representatives of this class. Bestuzhev came from a family that wed two classes, including the "honorable merchants" Bestuzhev de-scribes in such glowing terms. Bestuzhev's familiarity with the bourgeoi-sie was firsthand. This placed him by definition in a position superior to the innovators. Bestuzhev's interest, however, was not merely polemical. He sought the merchant class's authentic heroic potential.

To keep reader attention on the bourgeois/heroic element, and describ-ing the secret kisses stolen by the young couple in a moment of privacy, Bestuzhev's narrator states: "So it must be, dear sirs! In trade there is always contraband, in matchmaking—secret barter!" [V torgovle vsegda est' kontrabanda, v svatovstve—potaennye sdelki!] (ibid., 389).

---

21. Throughout the tale Bestuzhev utilizes substandard speech, folk sayings, "nonliterary" lexicon (from the point of view of the canon), and a high frequency of particles of speech (i.e., subunits of regular parts of speech which add emotional flavor).

In a digression on the mind's capacities, Bestuzhev begins with an extensive folk image only to conclude with a strikingly prosaic metaphor: "The old man . . . scratched the back of his head, and I say the back of the head because this is the center of human reason into which all the clamor of prejudice is dumped, all the rags of moral admonition, the buckets of wornout ideas and beliefs, broken vessels of imagination, or, to put it better, [the back of the head] is a dark backalley shop into which nice customers are drawn to unload some faded and outmoded junk" (390).

Since from Bestuzhev's perspective a literature that develops the content of this inferior storehouse is worthy of little more than contempt, it is precisely in the inclusion of bourgeois features that Bestuzhev risks his polemical strength, his power over his subject matter. By attacking the new prose within its own domain, by developing with integrity the world out of which he hopes to extract a protagonist possessing traditional heroic traits, Bestuzhev runs the risk of splitting his vision to such an extent that the two halves cannot meet. If his irony is developed too far, then the world from which he would deliver a hero is rendered so absurd that the heroic in its midst is invalidated. But if the middle class is depicted with integrity as a rightful object of literary investigation, Bestuzhev legitimizes the very thing he wishes to dismiss. The narrative must either succumb to its own criticism or fail in its polemical purpose.

This ambiguity is focused in the character of Savely. It is not always possible to determine which voice Bestuzhev has in mind when describing him. When, for instance, Savely stands at the rudder lost in thought, it is difficult to ascertain what the narrator intends—the resurrection of the heroic type from the mire in which he lives, or his debunking as a petty bourgeois: "Savely, by privilege granted all people who hear a jingle in their minds or in their pockets, constructed castles in the air" (ibid.). "Castles in the air" (*vozdushnye zamki*), a stock item in Bestuzhev's fiction from the 1820s, conditions one set of expectations in regard to the hero—dreams and aspirations centered around heroic action and the consequent attainment of the prized object (a woman). But the contrast between the jingle of coins and the ringing of an interior bell, one in the pocket and the other in the mind, debases the romantic material beyond repair.

In attempting to prove his superiority in "Nikitin," Bestuzhev enters the new school's terrain to fight on its terms (in its milieu and language).

He enters confident in the effectiveness of his own weapons—marlinisms, heroic story structure, stock characters and plot formulations, digressions by egocentric narrators, surprising metaphors, and polemical asides. The battle, however, delivers no clear victor.

Bestuzhev indicates the impossibility of reconciling the two positions of his narrative when he describes the cutter sailing to Archangelsk. The Englishmen are held below deck; but they have the food supply in their quarters. The Russians control the ship and the water supply on deck. The two parties form an uneasy truce based on a shared desire for survival:

> The cutter was a strange and unusual phenomenon in politics. This was not a *status in statu,* but a *status super statum,* a state over a state—victors without the vanquished; and the vanquished who would not acknowledge the victors: this was two pillars of the Tower of Babel set out to sea.

> [Куттер этот был забавное и небывалое явление в политике. Это не было уже status in statu, но status super statum, государством верхом на государстве,—победители без побежденных, и побежденные, не признающие победителей; это было два яруса вавилонского столпа, спущенные на воду.] (Ibid., 413)

This image incorporates precisely the stalemate into which Bestuzhev has played himself in the narrative. Although fantasy delivers a victory to Savely (the wish fulfillment typical of Bestuzhev's early prose), it is nonetheless clear that Bestuzhev cannot be sure of the real outcome of the literary polemic in which he engages. In the image of a sailing Tower of Babel Bestuzhev aptly depicts the literary debates of the 1830s—new voices commingle with his to create a polyphonic clash of great disharmony:

> "Boy!" shouted [Captain Turnip] threateningly. . . . "Boy!" he repeated with the addition of a hundred curses. But the boy did not appear, although the captain's invocations could have called forth all the devils of Hades. The poor lad, a youth of merely twelve, the captain's orderly, was deprived this time of the un-avoidable kick which served as an exclamation point to the voca-

tive case. "Boy, bring a bottle! Boy, call the boatswain!" And then a kick in the rear and the lad flies down the stairs like a hawk.

[—*Бой!*—закричал он грозно, услышав необычайную суматоху на палубе. —*Бой!*—повторил он с приложением сотни браней; но *бой* не являлся, хотя заклинания капитанские могли бы вызвать всех чертей из ада. Бедняга, мальчик лет двенадцати, вестовой капитана, был лишен на этот раз неизбежного пинка, служившего знаком восклицания звательному падежу—*бой!* Он давал ему невероятную быстроту движений. "*Бой,* принеси бутылку! *Бой,* кликни боцмана!"—и пинок в зад, и он взлетал по пестнице соколом.] (411)

If the lad holds an inferior position, he is nonetheless a hawk, a fowl of distinct heroic qualities.[22] Indeed, the hawk and the boy are to be compared with the simple Russian boat (symbol of the new prose's object), which is likened to a goldeneye (*gogol'*) at the tale's outset: "The frightened, soaked Aleksei let go the canvas from out of his hands. The sail fluttered wildly, the boat rose up and plowed headlong over the top of the wave in a trice, and burst through the watery wall. In five minutes it was sailing like a goldeneye upon the sea, which dashed upon the shore with a murmur" (*Povesti i rasskazy*, 392). If the goldeneye (Gogol) is to conquer the hawk (Bestuzhev) in Russian literature, as it seems Bestuzhev expects, then the hawk shall fight. Thus "*boi*" (battle) enters the tale as the Russian equivalent of the English word "boy," and as its consequence. In the boy/*boi* pun Bestuzhev most clearly acknowledges that his position in the new literature is tenuous. But if the new prose is to treat him like a "boy," then "Nikitin" is testimony to Bestuzhev's willingness to fight back (*boi*).[23]

Ironically, it is not only the orderly with whom Bestuzhev is identified in the story, but with Savely and Captain Turnip also. The relationship

22. Compare the images of fowl utilized by Bestuzhev earlier in the story.
23. When Captain Turnip cries "Boy!" we are to understand simultaneously that the call is to battle. It is for this reason that Bestuzhev does not give us "boy" in English, as he does "comfort," but in Russian transliteration: " '*Boi*' he shouted threateningly, hearing the unusual commotion on deck" (ibid., 411). Bestuzhev extracts from literary reality signs of the appropriateness of romantic categories. He *views* reality through a different filter from that of the next generation of authors.

between the two captains is mobile, unfixed hierarchically. Relative to each other, they sequentially hold inferior positions. In the passage immediately following the development of the "boy / *boi*" pun, Captain Turnip, the superior to the boy, is captured. He falls into an inferior status in relation to Savely and his crew (his former captives). The principle operating here is inversion. The high are rendered low, and vice versa. The tale's final ambiguity for Bestuzhev pertains to his identification with Savely and by implication with Turnip as well. In the first instance Bestuzhev's wish is fulfilled in fantasy. But the potential for inverting fantasy resides in Turnip. In the reversal of Turnip's position, Bestuzhev's dread is encountered. Even *boi* (battle) may prove insufficient in an unheroic world.

If there is any solace to be found, it is not in the triangular foci of Bestuzhev's incomplete defense—polemic, romantic posturing, and fantasy. Release is located, even if only marginally, in the laughter that celebrates inversion as a prime dictum of life. The reader first encounters this irrational form of release when the sailors face death. In the midst of a violent storm, the simpleton Ivan sings a nonsensical folk couplet that crystallizes his mates' anxieties and hopes and simultaneously vents their fears in riotous laughter: "From out of the distance along the Volga a godparent-gossip came sailing in a sieve / rowing with a spindle, a skirt for sails" [Iz-za Volgi kuma v reshete priplyla / Veretenami grebla, iubkoi parusila] (ibid., 400). Drawing the image of the crazy song and the sailor's response to it closer to himself, the narrator writes,

> Can you believe it? When the roar of the thunder quieted in the sailors' souls, they split their sides at Ivan's song and laughed long, laughed in eager rivalry, as if in a fever. Just you try to figure out the heart of man! In a moment of terrible grief or horrible fear he gives over to laughter sooner than to anything! I have seen and experienced this myself.

> [И поверите ли? когда стих гул громового удара в душах пловцов, они расхохотались песне Ивана и смеялись долго, смеялись наперерыв, будто в припадке. Разгадайте теперь сердце человеческое! Оно скорей всего дает смех в минуты самой жестокой скорби и ужаса! я это видел и испытал.] (400)

In the tale's final scene, Captain Turnip completes the carnival motif. In name and by fate he is the fool. He steps ashore in Archangelsk, hands his dirk to the governor, and under guard marches through the crowd to prison singing, "Rule Britannia the waves!" Whereupon "everyone laughs" (ibid., 44). Turnip's mock-heroic gesture and the crowd's response represent the comic context in which carnival's leveling laughter reigns. In this spirit all hierarchical structures are temporarily suspended—no superiors, no inferiors, not even in literature.

This laughter is Bestuzhev's final gesture in the face of the new literature. Experiencing diminution in literary circles in Petersburg and Moscow, Bestuzhev responded in "Nikitin" with a dramatic, witty, uncommonly honest, complex, but confused polemic that placed his romantic knight within the jaws of the dragon he sought to vanquish. The knight suddenly appears a mere man, vulnerable, limited, and if heroic, only for a moment. Neither titanic nor eternal, Savely marries and thereby turns into his counterpart, a Turnip.[24] What more is there to do but laugh?

The Mountains

Bestuzhev's fiction about the Caucasus represents the most substantial artistic contribution he made to Russian letters. It generated all manner of response, from the departure of his young readers to fight in the Caucasian wars he described to the creation of a host of literary clones, from the generation of political debate about the wisdom of the government's campaign against the mountain peoples to Lermontov's paintings of selected scenes from the most popular of these works, "Ammalat-bek" (1832),[25] and from the production of stage plays based on this work to outright negation of their aesthetic value. "Mulla Nur," the second most influential work of the period, appeared in 1836. Between these two dates several minor works of fiction appeared, "The Red Veil" ("Krasnoe pokyrvalo," 1832), "The Story of an Officer Who Was a Captive of the Mountain Tribes" ("Rasskaz ofitsera byvshego v plenu u

24. Lewis Bagby, "Bestuzev-Marlinskij's 'Morechod Nikitin': Polemics in Ambiguity," *Russian Literature* 22 (1987), 311–42.
25. William Edward Brown, *A History of Russian Literature of the Romantic Period*, 2:214.

Fig. 5. Lermontov illustration for "Ammalat-bek": Verkhovsky (seated) before his assassination, 1832–34

gortsev," 1834), and "He Was Killed" ("On byl ubit," 1836). All these works bear the stamp of the marlinism. "Do you know," Turgenev once confessed to Tolstoy, "that I used to kiss Marlinsky's name on journal covers?" (quoted in Leighton, *ABM*, 106). Tolstoy, for his part, was fond of these tales as a boy, a fact he reinforced in reverse when later in his life he attempted to debunk the romantic illusions of the Marlinsky text in order to establish his authority over them: "In Tolstoy's *The Cossacks*, the protagonist, Olenin, arrives in the Caucasus under the spell of Marlinsky's work, as Tolstoy himself perhaps did" (Mersereau, 121). Alexander Dumas was impressed by "Ammalat-bek" and translated it into French under the title "The Sultanetta." In the preface to his translation Dumas wrote, "Among the papers left in [Marlinsky's] room when he died was a manuscript. This manuscript had been read subsequently by

Fig. 6.   Lermontov illustration for "Ammalat-bek": Ammalat-bek kills
Verkhovsky, 1832–34

several persons, and, among their number, by the daughter of the officer
in command in my time, who spoke of it to me as a story full of interest.
At her recommendation I had it translated, and finding the little romance, as she had done, not only very interesting, but also remarkably
strong in local coloring, I resolved to publish it."[26] The story was also
translated into German, Danish, Czech, Polish, and English (Leighton,
ABM, 110).

Since their publication the Caucasian tales have been considered "the
most extraordinarily imaginative and incredible of Marlinsky's prose
tales, although at the same time they are the most authentic of all Russian literary works on the Caucasus" during the 1830s (ibid., 107).

26. Alexander Dumas, *Tales of the Caucasus,* trans. Alma Blakeman Jones (Boston,
1895), 1.

Fig. 7.   Lermontov illustration for "Ammalat-bek": Ammalat-bek delivers
Verkhovsky's head to the dying Khan, 1832–34

Virtually all commentators have calculated the interest these stories hold
for the ethnographer, anthropologist, folklorist, historian, and literary
critic. Bazanov notes that the story is a veritable encyclopedia of
Dagestan legends, sayings, beliefs, and vocabulary. From the epigraph,
"Slow to Offend—Quick to Avenge," to the thirty-five footnotes
Bestuzhev appends to explain the language of the natives, "Ammalat-
bek" is replete with the local color that struck Dumas.

Vano Shaduri notes that Bestuzhev "interlaced his tales and essays
with numerous historical references and ancient legends, described in
minute detail the various rituals [of the peoples], the nature and mode of
life of the Caucasus, supplied his works with a multitude of ethnographic, historical, and linguistic comments and elucidations. . . . [It] is
through these details [Bestuzhev] strove to penetrate into the dynamics

Fig. 8.   Lermontov illustration for "Ammalat-bek": Ammalat-bek in his final battle, 1832–34

of life in the Caucasus" (cited in ibid., 107). In effect, life there confirmed Bestuzhev's belief in the connection between literature and reality. Obvious in all the Caucasian tales is the interdependence of life and literature, for in the two most significant works in this genre Bestuzhev took his characters and plot from local legends and from authentic historical personages. In explaining "Ammalat-bek" to his publishers, Bestuzhev wrote that

> none of the events written [in this story] are made up. . . . As concerns the conclusion of the tale, it has been taken by [me] from local legends. . . . Many witnesses have told me that they have more than once heard Verkhovsky [Ammalat-bek's Russian guard-

ian and friend] describe Ammalat's heady passion for the Sultaneta, who was praised abroad for her beauty. . . . Legend indicates, too, that the Avar khan himself demanded Verkhovsky's head if Ammalat was to win the khan's daughter in marriage. . . . As concerns Ammalat's bestial robbery of Verkhovsky's grave, I have not departed from the original story one iota; soldiers recall the event to this day with indignation. . . . All the anecdotes about [Ammalat's] daring in riding and shooting described in chapter one circulate even now in Dagestan.[27]

Claims of this type have obscured the cardinal feature of "Ammalat-bek"—that it is fiction. The story is as follows: Ammalat-bek is the head of a village near Dagestan. He protects his people from the Russians who occupy his village while they wage war against the mountain tribes. One day the Sultan Akhmet Khan of the Avar mountain tribe comes to Ammalat's village, confronts the Russian captain in charge, incites the villagers to resist, and kills the captain. Since Ammalat is responsible for what transpires in his village, he must either face imprisonment or flee with the ruthless Sultan into the mountains. He chooses the latter.

Once in the Sultan's village, Ammalat falls in love with his daughter, the Sultaneta. Before their love can bloom fully, they are separated. Ammalat leaves to raid a Russian camp. The raid fails, many of the Avars are killed, and Ammalat is taken captive. Ermilov, the general in command of the Caucasian campaign, sentences Ammalat to death. A Colonel Verkhovsky pleads for Ammalat's life, stating that he will take responsibility for him. Ermilov agrees, and Ammalat becomes Verkhovsky's ward. The young, idealistic, and compassionate officer educates Ammalat, teaching him to read and write. Ammalat is impressed but not convinced that his way of life is any less valuable. He longs for his Sultaneta and, upon hearing that she is dying (pining away for him), receives permission from Verkhovsky to visit her.

Ammalat visits the Sultaneta and she recovers. Against her wishes, Ammalat returns to the Russians and Verkhovsky. Tormented by the

27. "Pis'ma Aleksandra Aleksandrovicha Bestuzheva k N. A. i K. A. Polevym," 305. Attesting to the influence of literature on life, Alekseev writes that legends in the twentieth-century Caucasus about "Ammalat-bek" conform to Bestuzhev's rendering of the tale in the 1830s. Alekseev concludes, "The legend has become fact" (M. P. Alekseev, *Etiudy o Marlinskom* [Irkutsk, 1928], 44).

sense of duty which draws him back to the Russian side, by his love for the Sultaneta, and by his captivity, Ammalat begins to resent his benefactor. Hearing of this, the Sultan calls Ammalat to a secret meeting in a cave. There he tells Ammalat that Verkhovsky has been ordered by Ermilov to exile him to Siberia. Were Ammalat to kill Verkhovsky, the Sultan would give his daughter to him in marriage. Ammalat vows to avenge himself. Ammalat slays Verkhovsky along the shore of the Caspian within view of the Russian army.

To prove to the Sultan that he has indeed killed Verkhovsky, Ammalat steals into the graveyard where the lieutenant's body is buried, digs into the tomb and decapitates the corpse. He carries the grim proof of his revenge to the Sultan whom he finds on his deathbed. Half-crazed, Ammalat presents the severed head to the Sultan. Horrified by this blood offering at the very moment he is trying to make peace with eternity, the Sultan curses Ammalat and promptly dies. His wife and daughter, who do not know of the Sultan's deceit, are provoked by Ammalat's insensitivity toward the dying man and blame him for the death. Ammalat is cast out of the community.

During a Russian attack on the village of Anapa, a stronghold of the tribal counterinsurgency, a Caucasian native defies Russian forces with utter daring. He rides within rifle range and challenges their skill. A young Russian officer, Verkhovsky's brother, mortally wounds him. The Russians bring him to their lines, where he dies horrified at the specter of his mentor's face.

Considering "Ammalat-bek" from the perspective of literary evolution, that is, without taking note of the myriad treatises on Bestuzhev's indebtedness to Dagestan history and legend, John Mersereau, Jr. finds the story entirely cliché-ridden:

> Regardless of rampant hyperbole and anthropomorphism, Marlinsky's descriptions of nature accorded with the accepted image of storm-shrouded, icy peaks and savage, untamed rivers.... Ethnographic information is stuffed into the narrative not for padding or retardation [to create suspense], but for its own sake, because Marlinsky, an avid student of foreign languages and cultures, found it interesting and wanted his reader to share his interest.... *Ammalat-Bek* provides numerous examples of the endless rhetoric and emotional excesses typical of Marlinskian dialogue.... The thematic and stylistic petrifaction of Mar-

linsky's art is apparent in a comparison of *Ammalat-Bek* with *Roman and Olga,* written almost a decade earlier.[28]

In contrast to Mersereau's perspective, Lauren Leighton's opinion of the tale is, on balance, favorable. He recognizes the work's deficiencies, especially from a historical perspective, stating that its "presentation of many events and plot situations strain credulity to the extreme," and that "in its manner of expression the tale is one of Marlinsky's most hyperbolic" (Leighton, *ABM,* 115).[29] "Little wonder," he concludes, "*Ammalat-bek* became a favorite point of reference for later criticisms of Russian Romantic works" (115). At the same time, Leighton views the text as one of Bestuzhev's most psychologically astute: "The themes of awakening of the consciousness of a primitive man, of the confrontation between man and nature and between man and civilization, of individual freedom, embodied in the resentment of one man in the face of another's generosity are unexpectedly sophisticated in Russian literature of the 1830s. . . . [For this reason] the tale is Marlinsky's most famous, it is his most extreme, and it stands as the finest illustration of his talents as Russia's first beloved writer of prose tales" (115–16).

Studying Bestuzhev's rough drafts to "Ammalat-bek," Kanunova compared them with the canonical text. The discrepancies between draft and text can be attributed either to the censor or to the author. The censor removed politically sensitive subject matter, for example, anti-imperialistic digressions. Expunged was a bilious tirade by Sultan Akhmed Khan that reads: "And suddenly they wanted me to allow them to build a fortress [on our territory]. But of what worth would my name have been were I to see the blood and sweat of the Avars, my brothers!? And even if I had attempted this, do you really think I could have done it? Thousands of free blades and bullets which cannot be bought would have flown at the heart of the betrayer; the cliffs themselves would have thundered down upon the head of the one who would sell his homeland" (quoted in Kanunova, 183).

The censor also removed passages the informed reader (who knew that Marlinsky was Bestuzhev) might construe as autobiographical, such

28. Mersereau, 122–24. Brown writes, "The subject is melodramatic and might be called implausible, except for Marlinsky's assurances of its historical basis which other sources confirm" (2:215).

29. Brown reinforces Leighton's perspective. "Unevenness is in fact one of Marlinsky's leading characteristics—everywhere, but particularly in *Ammalat-Bek*" (2:216).

as the following: "To exhaust a person in a stuffy prison without light and fresh air, or to send him into an eternal winter, into a night which brings forth no life, to bury him alive in the belly of the earth, and in this to torture him with penal servitude, deprive him not only of his will to act, but even the means to speak with his family about his sorrowful fate; to disallow him not only the right to register a complaint but to even shout into the wind—and you call this life? and you praise this ceaseless torture by calling it an unheard of generosity?!" (ibid., 195).

Bestuzhev's own revisions are somewhat more complex. Kanunova writes that the central problem of the story is the development of an integrated identity: "The fundamental [idea] of the tale is contained in those chapters in which Ammalat's cultural development is shown, his struggle to acquire [an identity], and the passionate attempts of the Russian man of the Enlightenment [Verkhovsky] to draw the man from out of the power of the blind primal forces of nature. The enlightened humanist Verkhovsky fights not only to secure in Ammalat someone loyal to Russia, but to make of him a real person who would combine the beauties of body, soul, spirit, and mind in harmony with one another" (ibid., 208). Ammalat-bek fails in this endeavor just as much as Bestuzhev does in pursuit of aesthetic coherence in his tale. The causes of these parallel deficiencies appear to be the same.

The drafts indicate a failed connection between writing and personal discovery. Unlike Pushkin, or secondary writers like Orest Somov and Vladimir Odoyevsky, Bestuzhev did not cut his draft to make it more efficient, compact, and economical. He added, embellished, and elaborated what he had already written. Not that Bestuzhev appended superfluous material to his text. Rather, his embellishments attempted to explain in more detail what his rough copy referred to with greater subtlety. Bestuzhev added emotionally charged descriptions to his text, each embellishment bringing a distinctly autobiographical flavor to the passages which in turn stimulated readers to draw conclusions about the author's identity (his living conditions, longings, dreams, and desires). When the rough draft reads, for example, "The serpentine trace of ennui etched onto the cheeks by tears, and the forehead's deep wrinkles carved by the years, disfigured [Ammalat's] beautiful face" (ibid., 216), the metaphoric flourish clearly identifies the marlinist style. But the published text reads quite differently: "The serpentine trace of ennui etched on the cheeks by tears, the forehead's deep wrinkles carved not by *the summers but by passion, and his bloody wounds* disfigured [Ammalat's] beautiful face, *upon which there was an expression of something more racking than any pain, something more horrible than death.*" The thanatic note was added only later.

The theme of death runs through the story from beginning to end, from the murder at the outset in Ammalat's house and his death sentence for permitting the crime under his roof to Verkhovsky's murder; from the removal of Verkhovsky's head in a scene of gothic grotesquery to the sudden death of Ammalat's nemesis, Sultan Akhmed Khan; and from the death of a faithful old steed at Ammalat's hands to Ammalat's wish-fulfilling demise in battle at the story's conclusion. This is the stuff of Bestuzhev's persona as it touches directly on the central fascination of his life both at conscious and unconscious levels. In his youth Bestuzhev had found solace from his mortality in the flamboyant, fearless persona of the folkloric hero. The lad's undaunted bravado supplied a form of behavior that flew in the face of mortal fear. Heroic action supplanted fear. It did not, however, eliminate it. Thoughts of death were banished to the unconscious. As in Bestuzhev's early poem, "Dream's Domicile," the giant, which is this fear, sleeps but lightly. The cave of sleep continued to represent symbolically Bestuzhev's relationship to the dream's content, the writing on the wall of the cave in which the dreamer and his dream slumbered.

In exile Bestuzhev discovered death at another level; it could act as a palliative. Once a frightening specter, death became a balm with mythic powers attached to it. Death turned into a conscious construct, again related to the hero (but not to a callow, folkloric one). The mythic hero's confrontation with mortality constituted a transformational ground of lasting value. The hero might die in fact, but unlike the young prince (or fool) Ivan brought back from mutilation and dismemberment through the Waters of Life and the Waters of Death, the mythic hero is reconstituted by his audience. Immortality is bestowed on authentic historical figures who die so gloriously that the community resurrects them in its lore. Ammalat-bek is a case in point. He died valiantly and defiantly only to be immortalized in the legends of the people. At this level of apprehension, death becomes an aesthetic phenomenon subject to personal control as a theme both in fiction and life.

In "Ammalat-bek" Bestuzhev purposefully informed his final draft with the mythic powers of death. Where, for example, the draft's conclusion reads: "[Ammalat] fell, the icy hand of death choked out the final breath of his chest, and the imprint of a final ennui fixed upon his brow.

It was frightful to see his eyes rolled back" (ibid., 217), the canonical version is much more extended, focusing clearly on the process of dying and heroic suffering. Death is a solution to life's problems, and disfiguration holds the potential for a wholeness that eludes the body not yet exposed to its mortality:

> *The shot had gone straight into [Ammalat's] heart. The ligature attached to the main artery broke apart from the sudden rush of blood which gushed through the bindings!* . . . With just a few twitches of the body and several wheezes from his breast, the icy hand of death choked out the final breath of *the mortally wounded man's* chest, and the imprint of a final ennui fixed upon his brow, *an ennui which had slowly gathered whole years of repentance in one sudden moment in which the soul strains to be released from the body, feels equally the tortures of life and of insignificance, feels suddenly all the pangs of the past and all the fears of the future.* It was frightful to see *the dead man's disfigured face.*[30]

Bestuzhev consigns mythic, death-dealing forces to an imagistic space lying between public and private spheres. Whereas death is associated with enclosures, the ongoing life of the community is related to open spaces. At the meeting point of the two, dramatic tension is created of a carnivalesque nature. "Ammalat-bek," in fact, begins on a festive day which Bestuzhev describes in a manner suggesting the life-death celebration of carnival:

> It was *juma* [a day of rest]. . . . The sea, eternally lapping the beach, rolls in like mankind itself come to play upon the firmament. The spring day was drawing toward evening and all the town's inhabitants, called out surely more by the freshness of the evening air than by idle curiosity, left their dwellings and gathered in crowds along both sides of the road. Women without veils, in colored scarves rolled into turbans upon their heads, in long silk gowns drawn up to the length of short *arkhaluki* (tunics), and in wide-cut pants, sat in rows as lines of children formed in front of them. The men congregated in circles. They stood, sat on their

30. Bestuzhev-Marlinskii, *Sochineniia v dvukh tomakh*, 1:546.

haunches, or sauntered around in groups of two or three. Elder men smoked tobacco from small wooden pipes. Happy chatter was heard all around, and at times the clang of horseshoes and the cry "*Kach, kach!*" (Watch out!) from riders preparing for their races rose above the throng.[31]

The sign "women without veils" [zhenshchiny bez nokryval] reinforces the break both with normal routine and the sacred code lying at carnival's heart. Mankind "come to play" reinforces this idea, as do Bestuzhev's appeals to all the senses: shouts and cries, the taste of tobacco, the scent of roses: "Millions of glowing roses just like sunsets spill in red from the cliffs" [Milliony roz oblivaiut utesy rumiantsem svoim, podobno zare].[32] Figurative embraces that equate human and plant life perform the same function: "Almond trees, resembling cupolas, stand ablaze in silver bloom; about them tall vines entwine their leaves in spirals" [Mindal'nye derev'ia, tochno kupoly pagodov, stoiat v serebre tsvetov svoikh, i mezhdu nikh vysokie rainy, to uvitye list'iami, kak vintom] (212, 1:424). An atypical mixture of discrete categories is apparent throughout the text as well, reinforcing the carnival idea. Public celebrations—"You might imagine that on this *juma* the outskirts of Buynaki are even more animated [than usual] with a picturesque mixture of folk" [Mozhno sebe voobrazit', chto v den' etoi dzhumy okrestnosti Buinakov eshche bolee ozhivleny byli zhivopisnoiu pestrotoiu naroda] (212, 1:424), are accompanied by rude speech—"a large crowd of soldiers . . . gathered to heap abuse on the [Russian] train" [mnozhestvo soldat . . . okruzhili poezd s bran'iu] (214, 1:431).

Within Ammalat-bek's house a scene unfolds distinct spatially from the *juma* scene, but related to it thematically. In public, in the open air, Sultan Akhmet Khan incites Ammalet-bek's village to revolt against the Russian forces occupying it, and while the fight is in progress he visits Ammalat's house. Within this enclosure, a Russian captain enters to arrest the Sultan, whom Ammalat defends out of obeisance to custom—

31. "Ammalat-bek: A Caucasian Tale," trans. Lewis Bagby, in *The Ardis Anthology of Russian Romanticism*, ed. Christine Rydel (Ann Arbor, Mich., 1984), 212.

32. Ibid., 212. The original Russian may be found in Bestuzhev-Marlinskii, *Sochineniia v dvukh tomakh*, 1:424. "Ammalat-bek" is henceforth cited in the text by title, if needed, and page number of the Bagby translation; and for the original, by volume and page number of Bestuzhev's *Sochineniia v dvukh tomakh*, as appropriate.

the Sultan is a guest in his domicile. The Sultan murders the captain and initiates Ammalat's life as a fugitive.

Bestuzhev alternates scenes from the public domain (war, battles, arrests, sentencings, and confrontations of various kinds) with the private world of enclosures (associated with death in almost every instance). This pattern is maintained until the end of the story. When the Sultan tricks Ammalat into killing Verkhovsky, their meeting takes place in a cave: "They inched along the steep ledge in continual danger of falling, grabbing onto sweetbriar roots for safety, and finally, after much difficulty, they landed at a narrow opening into a small cave at water level. . . . Therein, Sultan Akhmet Khan lay upon a carpet and seemed to be waiting patiently while Ammalat gazed about in the thick smoke which swirled around him" (ibid., 232).

Ammalat murders Verkhovsky in the open air, that is, in the public's eye: "An alarm went along the front lines, soldiers and Don Cossacks responded quickly to the shot. But they arrived too late. They could neither prevent the vicious crime nor catch the fleeing murderer. Within five minutes the bloody body of the treacherously killed colonel was surrounded by a crowd of soldiers and officers" (ibid., 236). Ammalat beheads Verkhovsky in a deep grave: "It seemed to him that the flame of his torch enveloped him, that hell's own spirit world, dancing and howling in laughter, wound about him. . . . With a labored groan he tore himself upward, crawled out unconsciously from the narrow grave and began to run, fearing even to look back" (237). This scene reinforces, too, the notion of sleep as it is linked with the unconscious: "Neither revenge, nor pride, nor even love—in other words, no single passion of his which had moved him to kill the man earlier—could now bestow on him the courage to perform this nameless, godless act of mutilation. Turning the head back to reveal the neck, in a dark forgetfulness reminiscent of sleep, Ammalat began to chop Verkhovsky about the neck" (237). These gruesome physiological characteristics, belonging to ancient sacrificial rites in which the "king" is dismembered, complete the carnival grotesque.

The theme of dismemberment occurs in the text on more than one occasion. The Russian soldiers cry out when they see the Sultan in their village, "Grab him! Take him! Make him pay for the Bashli massacre. The scoundrel hacked our wounded to pieces!" [Bezdel'niki v kuski izrubili nashikh ranenykh!] (ibid., 214; 1:431). On a raid against the Russian forces, a mountain leader, Jembulat, "not trusting a ritual display, had placed the settlement under guard and warned the inhabitants that whosoever might attempt to inform the Russian [of their presence] would be hacked to pieces [budet izrublen v kuski]" (221, 1:462). When Ermilov sentences Ammalat to death, he shouts, " 'No, a bullet is too decent a death for a thief . . . it's on the bullock cart shafts your neck will be bridled—this is the reward you deserve' ['arbu vverkh oglogbliami i uzdu na sheiu—vot tebe dostoinaia nagrada']" (226, 1:475).

Associated with the theme of dismemberment, and consistent with carnival cycles, rebirth enters the text as its mythological pair, sometimes clearly linked to Promethean images of eternal suffering: " 'Leave me, Sultan Akhmet Khan,' [Ammalat] said decisively. 'Leave an unfortunate to his own fate. The road is long and I am done in. Remain with me and you shall perish for naught. Look at the eagle flying above us; it senses that my heart is soon to die within its claws [on chuet, chto moe serdtse skoro zamret v kogtiakh ego] . . . thank God. It is better to find the aerial grave of a great bird's nest than to lay down my dust for a Christian foot to tread upon" (ibid., 218). The Promethean image of suffering and immortality is associated with the mountain tribesmen: "The khan rode next to the bek, a falcon on his arm. To the left, along the steep slope, an Avarian was clinging, throwing a hooked pole into a cleft and then, hanging from this attachment, climbing higher and higher. On his waist was tied a bag which held seeds; a long rifle hung from his shoulders" (231). The seeds underscore the theme of rebirth; the precipice indicates the Promethean locus of suffering; and the falcon symbolizes the bird of prey taken from the myth. In these images Bestuzhev associates dismemberment with immortality.

The Sultan chastises Ammalat for his wish to die at the mountain top, calling him back to the sacred cycle of death and rebirth in terms directly related to the tale's images: " 'Sacred duty is to avenge ourselves on the Russians. Return to life if only for that' " (ibid., 219). Ammalat responds to the Sultan's call and, later in the text, projects the Promethean idea onto himself in no uncertain terms: "My soul is like a bare precipice where birds of prey fly in consort with evil spirits, dividing their prey and readying themselves for the next kill" [Dusha moia podobna teper' goloi skale, na kotoruiu sletaiutsia odni khishchnye ptitsy i zlye dukhi delit' dobychu ili gotovit' gibel'] (235, 1:528). When Ammalat brings Verkhovsky's head to the dying Sultan, the tragic element inherent in any mortal's quest for immortality is sounded in Ammalat's sorrowful mention of rebirth: "Greetings, khan! I have brought you the gift you sought

of me, a gift fit to drive death from your door and to bring the dead back
to life. Prepare the wedding!" (238). Ammalat's misreading of the situation affects his fate for the worse, consigning him to perpetual suffering.
But it is not only a mythic anguish—as his final remark to the Sultan
makes clear, it is framed by the ironic forces of the ritual carnivalesque:
"Prepare the wedding!"

The drama unfolds between two spheres, the public and private, between life and death. Bestuzhev underscores this intermediate ground,
this threshold, as central to the tragic moral to the tale. In the graveyard
scene, the distinction is made quite clear: "No stars in the sky; clouds
upon the mountains; a wind from the high ridges, like a nocturnal fowl,
was striking the forest with its wings; an involuntary shudder coursed
through Ammalat at the very threshold of the dead [posredi mertvetsov],
whom he was daring to disturb" (ibid., 236; 1:537). Later, when
Ammalat delivers Verkhovsky's head to the Sultan, the threshold is un-
derlined: "Surkhay silently pointed to the door, and in utter confusion
Ammalat crossed a decisive threshold [perestupil za reshitel'nyi porog]"
(237, 1:539).

Although the blending of these carnival images may suggest Bestuzhev's apprehension of the cave's dark secret at a conscious level, at the
tale's conclusion there is a suggestion that the fear of death has not been
entirely assuaged. The conscious thematization of death, in other words,
may not deliver release from mortal dread. As the Sultan dies, Ammalat
reads the following on the warrior's face: "The khan lay upon a mattress
in the middle of the room, disfigured by a ravaging disease. Invisibly, but
unmistakably, death hovered over him. The slowly extinguishing gaze of
the dying man showed clearly that he was facing death in utter terror"
(ibid., 237). The hero is not exempt; heroism is no cure. Ammalat's
death monologue reflects the same ultimate anxiety even when death has
been sought consciously as a solution to life's problems. But, as
Verkhovsky's brother observes, there is something to be read in the dead
man's face that transcends mortal fear, something more horrible than
death itself: "A reptilian trace of anguish, well-marked grooves upon the
cheeks, deep wrinkles on the forehead, earned not by time but by ex-
hausted passion, and bloody scars disfigured a handsome face whereon
some unknowable, torturous pain, something surely more horrible than
death, had etched itself" (239). Ammalat gives voice in his last moment
to the content of that something "more horrible than death": "It was so
stifling on this earth . . . and so cold in that grave! . . . How horrible to

be a corpse! . . . I am a fool. I have sought death. . . . Oh, let me return to the good earth! . . . Let me live, even if only for one more day, if only one more short hour! . . . Find out for yourself how it is to die! . . ." (239). Worse than death, it appears, is the longing for life in the face of certain demise.

If only momentarily, Bestuzhev arrests this anguish in a public space that stands on the threshold of art and life. Ammalat-bek was a historical personage who in reality became a legendary figure for his people. Bestuzhev's story extends the legend to a larger audience (widened yet again by Dumas). Immortality may indeed be accessible to the one who dies dramatically enough to stimulate an audience to generate the myth.[33]

The necessity of destruction as a component of identity is apparent in Bestuzhev's final piece of fiction, the second most popular tale of the Caucasian fiction, "Mulla Nur." Self-destruction applies to the dramatis personae in "Ammalat-bek," but in "Mulla Nur" it applies at a higher level of abstraction, to the fictional enterprise itself. This story is an extensive work, like "Ammalat-bek," of incongruent principles and diverse thematic elements: a recreation of a Dagestan myth, an extended meditation on the evils of civilized man, and a florid tale about the bandit Mulla Nur. The most striking feature of the tale is its failure to synthesize its disparate parts. It may well be that Bestuzhev's awkward treatment of his subject matter reflects a dramatic turn away from the canon, a swerve conditioned not only by literary evolution, but also by the uncontrolled and deeply tragic development of his own life. Bestuzhev's uncharacteristic mishandling of the plot, confusion concerning the story's protagonist, and the abrupt alteration in the narrator's image and his role in the narrative, all reveal the romantic period's most popular author of prose in the throes of an unexpected, unwanted, and uncomfortable transformation that was as much psychological as it was aesthetic and intellectual.

"Mulla Nur" is a story about the hypocrisy of the powerful. It is typical romance. Derbent is suffering a terrible drought. A religious leader shames the people for their sins, then recounts to them a legend

---

33. This confirms Mikhail Bakhtin's opinion that others complete our identity. See his "Avtor i geroi v esteticheskoi deiatel'nosti," in *Estetika slovesnogo tvorchestva,* ed. S. G. Bocharov (Moscow, 1979), 15, 22–48. This essay also appears in *Art and Answerability: Early Philosophical Essays by M. M. Bakhtin,* ed. Michael Holquist and Vadim Liapunov (Austin, Tex., 1990), 14, 22–52.

about another drought for which a solution was found: A youth, good and pure, was selected from among the people. He went up into the mountains and gathered snow from the highest peak and brought it back to the Caspian, whereupon the drought ended. This is the mythic portion of Bestuzhev's tale, and it relates directly to the social questions raised in it.

A wealthy, powerful, and hypocritical man, Fetkhali, goes to his rival Iskander-bek and requests that he go to the mountain for the snow by which Derbent's drought might be ended. Iskander agrees if he will receive in return Fetkhali's niece, Kichkene, in marriage. Fetkhali had formerly refused Iskander her hand. If Fetkhali fails to obtain Iskander's aid he will be humiliated. Fetkhali agrees to the betrothal. Iskander leaves for the mountain with his companion, Yusuf, a comic character who displays distinctly unheroic qualities à la Sancho Panza. Iskander is angry with the people of Derbent, for they have ruined his father and made him an outsider. He nevertheless goes to the mountain, but not out of moral obligation. He wants Kichkene.

As Iskander-bek and Yusuf begin their ascent, Yusuf is captured by Mulla Nur's wife while Iskander and Mulla Nur battle at the edge of a great precipice. Iskander has the opportunity to slay his opponent, but spares him instead. For this act the bandit Mulla Nur pledges his life to him, proceeds to free Yusuf, and aids the pair in obtaining the snow. At the mountain's peak Iskander experiences a profound change. He rides solemnly back to Derbent and pours the snow into the sea. Clouds immediately form and the drought is ended.

Iskander looks forward to his marriage, but Fetkhali has conspired in his absence to marry her to another. Iskander steals into Kichkene's compound and, having learned of her devotion to him (she has seen him only once before), plans their elopement. Iskander is arrested and falsely accused of robbing a number of homes in Derbent. The city commandant knows that someone as upright as Iskander could not have performed these criminal acts. He meets with the city elders, shames them for their deceit, and frees Iskander. Mulla Nur, in the meantime, has crept secretly into Derbent, captured the real thief, and absolved Iskander of any wrongdoing. It is clear that Fetkhali arranged the arrest in order to marry Kichkene to another. Mulla Nur returns to the mountains and there captures the father of Kichkene's newly intended, forces him to cancel the wedding and compels him to convince Fetkhali that Kichkene marry Iskander. At the wedding Mulla Nur arrives incognito to celebrate the feast. The populace discovers the brigand and drives him into the Caspian Sea, in which, it appears, he drowns.

In the epilogue, set several years after the events of the story, the narrator describes his own journey into the mountains and a private meeting with Mulla Nur who tells the narrator why he originally had to flee Derbent. He had killed his uncle for reasons the narrator refuses to pass on to his reader. The tale ends with Mulla Nur's secret intact.

One's first impression is that Iskander is the protagonist of "Mulla Nur." Mulla Nur himself does not appear in the narrative until the tale is half told. And yet, from the title, one would assume that this is Mulla Nur's story. This opposition between Iskander and Mulla Nur reveals a core flaw in the work—Bestuzhev cannot decide which character to make its protagonist.

Bestuzhev based his story on a Dagestan legend, which at its deepest levels answers to the variously described tasks of myth—the quest of the hero; his maturation through the establishment of a concrete heroic identity; the temporary suspension of a cultural antimony (that is, dearth versus plenty); and the fabulistic treatment of an intellectual problem (that is, how there came to be water on the earth). Typically, Bestuzhev ignored the intellectual levels of the material with which he worked and focused only on that feature of the Dagestan myth which appealed to him personally—the hero and his quest for truth and justice. Essential to this portrait of the hero is the motif of purity, for in the myth only the righteous youth attains the highest earthly plane, and there is delivered the gift of the heavens—purity (in the form of snow). Only the chaste youth obtains thereon God's gift, brings it back to the city, pours it into the unclean, earthly waters (the Caspian), and thereby cleanses the lowly, terrestrial world. By mixing the heavenly and earthly waters, the hero cleanses the earth. The lowlands are then rewarded by great abundance. The archetypal movement from dearth to plenty based on the actions of a questing hero can be recorded schematically. The column on the left identifies narrative loci of the myth, the other depicts the narrative movement the story realizes:

Loci	*The Myth*
Initial condition	Drought
Spiritual place	Mountain Top
Representative substance / act	Snow
Earthly dwelling	Derbent

Representative substance / act   Caspian Sea
Final condition   Rain (drought ended)

In order that the narrative advance from its initial condition to its final one, the hero must move between the high and the low, the pure and the impure, the sky and the earth, the gods and society, and bring them together in symbolic integration. Without the hero there can be neither a myth nor a solution to the problems posited in it.

Bestuzhev reconceived the mythic hero as a romantic hero, and thus distorted the mediating principle that organizes the myth. Apparently unable, or perhaps merely unwilling, to appreciate fully the complexities of balancing the high and the low, the pure and the impure, Bestuzhev moved away from the delicately suspended oppositions of mythology. He located the ancient tale within the relatively new romantic genre, which focuses almost exclusively on the low, the human, and the earthly. Bestuzhev, therefore, infused his myth with themes and motifs taken from the society tale. In the course of the narrative this contemporary material replaces the mythic content. It is as though the original impulse behind the story, the condition that sends Iskander on his mission, dissolves in profane intrigue.

Bestuzhev transformed the image of his hero in the process of unleashing his romantic formula onto the mythic material. Although Iskander is initially cast in the role of the good youth, he is not quite that. He does not go to the mountain to fulfill the selfless quest of the epic hero. He goes for selfish motives. This diminution in Iskander's stature is made through Bestuzhev's investigation of the hero's motivation. Iskander states unequivocally, "They're fools, they are, thinking that I'd give my sweat so that they can have some rain! But for such a beauty as Kichkene I'd not spare my own blood" (*Sochineniia*, 2:356). The purifying task of the mythic hero gives way to the symbolic romantic quest for identity inherent in the Marlinsky text (in which marriage equals personal fulfillment, the acquisition of an identity with possession of a woman, a theme that harkens back to 1823 and "Roman and Olga"). In giving voice to Iskander's selfish motives, Bestuzhev qualified his protagonist's fitness for fulfilling the mythic task required of him. He is, in the end, not that good and pure. Iskander's mythic status qua hero is reduced, and myth slips into the formulas of the society tale.

This muddling of the myth is reflected not only in the image of the protagonist, but in the image of the narrator as well. In the first four chapters the narrator is omniscient and given to sententious remarks of a serious nature. It is his function to present the social, interpersonal, psychological, and historical conditions of the story. When because of these very conditions the purity of the hero is thrown into doubt, the narrator is transformed into an intrusive, unreliable, and comic voice. This shift in the narrator's persona occurs as Bestuzhev's anxieties about the hero grow in the process of writing the tale. This type of inconsistency is usually explained by the exigencies of Bestuzhev's life as a common soldier. It is argued that he did not have time to edit his work, for he was much too busy surviving the physical and emotional dangers of battle, forced marches, and tropical disease. But the reason for the shift in the narrator's identity lies at a much deeper level, not separated from Bestuzhev's life, but embedded in it.

The society tale of romance inclined toward a metonymic understanding and representation of reality, and it directly influenced the style of the next generation of writers, both the naturalists (Gogol and his imitators) and the realists (Tolstoy in particular).[34] By dint of this genre's movement toward greater metonymy, that is, toward an investigation of the protagonist within a social, cultural, and physical environment, Bestuzhev was forced deeper into his hero's psyche than ever before. With the discovery, in the more realistic context he explored in "Mulla Nur," that the hero in his pristine and purely romantic form was an impossibility, a product of fantasy and desire, his narrative altered radically. The shift that takes place in the narrator's role occurs precisely at that point in the narrative when Bestuzhev had completed his investigation of the hero's motivation and found it to be wanting. Once Bestuzhev saw the world contained no real heroic ideal, he altered drastically the narrative scheme.

In his life and in his stories Bestuzhev had always required a hero of epic proportions, a hero with few human faults. In "Mulla Nur" he fled from a new (metonymically inspired) knowledge of the hero and sought refuge in the well-established formulas of his own ubiquitous romantic hero, in this instance, Mulla Nur. It is logical, therefore, that the story veers from its inherent conflicting tendencies (mythic import versus metonymic investigation), toward a new hero and a new story line, both of which are in keeping with Bestuzhev's rigorously defined canon.

The hero's quest in the society tale is usually representative of the fate

---

34. Todd reveals indirectly just how significant this shift was (see Todd, 142 and 151).

of the society to which he belongs. As Iskander fulfills his duty, he discharges the moral obligations of the city and its people. When he is purified (by attaining the mountain top and its gift of snow), so is the city—Iskander finds happiness at his wedding in rain-drenched Derbent. Thus, Iskander's and Derbent's movement from complication to denouement may be coded on the pattern of myth:

Loci	Iskander	Derbent
Initial condition	Outsider	Sin
Spiritual place	Mountain top	Mountain top
Representative substance / act	Obtains snow	Receives snow
Earthly dwelling	Derbent	(Itself)
Representative substance / act	Pours snow into Caspian	Caspian Sea
Final condition	Insider	Forgiven, purified

As the Dagestan legend is demythologized through the application of society-tale themes, motifs, and character types, it is simultaneously remythologized through the figure of Mulla Nur. In this instance Bestuzhev inverts the direction of the initial story about Iskander and Derbent. Rather than beginning with myth only to reduce it to a romantic formula, Bestuzhev begins with romance in Mulla Nur's story and raises him to mythological proportions.

Mulla Nur is more than the typical romantic outsider we see in Iskander, living at the edge of society, but longing to be a part of it. He is truly an outcast who lives in complete physical and mental exile. He has killed his uncle. It is significant that the reader is not told why. Bestuzhev does not supply motivation for Mulla's murderous act, placing him outside the society-tale genre's impulse in the 1830s toward a psychological understanding of the hero. By removing Mulla from the metonymic sphere, Bestuzhev insists on a canonical perception of the good villain, a perception based upon the reader's understanding of the Robin Hood archetype in literature.[35]

Since Bestuzhev does not raise the question of how people like Mulla Nur become villains or saints, he turns his gaze onto the hero's milieu.

35. Recall the villain Berkut in "Roman and Olga" who turns out to be a folkloric helper and misunderstood outsider.

Through the genre features of this story we learn that unjust, cruel, materialistic, and despiritualized societies make villains out of the just and the good, a thesis with a remarkably self-serving autobiographical element in it. This is Mulla's lot. From this perspective, Mulla Nur is not a villain, but a traditional romantic hero. Understanding his behavior is not necessary—he does what he must, and he must do what is right.

Remythologizing the text, Bestuzhev puts Mulla Nur through a series of tests that conform to mythic structures. By having Mulla experience an archetypal rebirth, Bestuzhev restores his narrative to the elevated position he had initially intended for it. Mulla Nur's portrait is thus set in opposition to that of Iskander, who is ultimately removed from the text as he is circumscribed by society. Mulla Nur's condition is permanent—genuine exile. Unlike Iskander who must journey to the mountain in order to obtain the purifying snow, Mulla Nur inhabits the mountain itself. This is a signal of his immense purity of heart. Furthermore, on the quest for snow Iskander acquires Mulla as folkloric helper. Without the snow neither Iskander nor Derbent can be saved, and without Mulla Nur the snow cannot be safely and successfully obtained, Iskander married, Derbent saved from drought, and the true villains of the story unmasked. The snow and Mulla Nur are equated on spatial and functional levels: they both reside on the highest mountain and they serve as agents of transformation. In addition, in Derbent (the lowly, earthly domain) Mulla Nur is transformed much as the snow. The snow becomes the Water of Life that cleanses the impure Caspian and brings healing rains. Mulla Nur, rather than acting the villain, captures the real thief and sets things right. Then, at the wedding, like the snow before him, Mulla Nur enters the Caspian Sea. He survives his confrontation with death and is reborn, returning to the mountain just as the snow returns through evaporation and precipitation. Unlike Iskander and Derbent, Mulla Nur's final condition is his initial one—he remains an outcast to the end, and thus true to his natural condition. This effectively proves his authenticity:

Loci	Mulla Nur	Snow
Initial condition	Outcast, exile	Purity (Itself)
Spiritual place	Mountains	Mountains
Representative substance / act	Snow equivalent	(Itself)
Earthly dwelling	Comes to Derbent	Comes to Derbent

| Representative substance / act | Enters Caspian | Enters Caspian |
| Final condition | Outcast, exile | Purity (Itself) |

It is in the return to Mulla Nur's initial condition that the romantic structure of the happy ending is inverted and the story's mythic proportions are restored. Mulla Nur repairs to the mountains, to the purified sphere where goodness of necessity resides, far from corrupt and deceitful social man. Aiding Iskander and Derbent represents only a temporary relief from the more permanent condition of sin that Mulla Nur suffers. He accepts the consequences of his misdeed silently, heroically. One can hardly say this about Iskander or those with whom he now lives in harmony in Derbent.

In Bestuzhev's deformation of genre expectations, in the tale's shift from one hero to another (with its consequent demythologization and remythologization cycle), the aesthetic deficiencies of the work are most deeply felt. Not that "Mulla Nur" is such an imperfect story that the pleasures of reading it are severely reduced. On the contrary, it is as exciting and complex a piece of fiction as any he produced in the 1830s. Nevertheless, these flaws, entirely unique in Bestuzhev's prose, underscore Bestuzhev's insistence on romance against the psychological complexities and banalities of everyday life that were arising in the new fiction.

The implications of Bestuzhev's choices in penning "Mulla Nur" are not only aesthetic. The structural confusion of the story reflects the emotional condition of Bestuzhev's psyche in the final year of his life. Like Mulla Nur, Bestuzhev himself was living in an inhospitable land, a harsh environment, and a cruel exile, fighting Caucasian natives in the mountains by the Caspian and Black seas. Bestuzhev was destined, as was Mulla Nur, to remain in exile for his entire life. Bestuzhev found, too, that he had to accept the consequences of his own actions—his active participation in the Decembrist Revolt; the responsibility he may have felt for Olga Nestertsova's death; his inability to effect a change in his brother Peter's mental health; his mother's loneliness and her longing for her sons; and his separation from his siblings and his friends.

Bestuzhev's own story, therefore, may be coded after Mulla Nur's. The most significant point of contact between their respective fates is the final condition they achieve, the state of being that sets them apart from all others and focuses their tragic lot:

Loci	Marlinsky
Initial condition	Outcast, exile
Spiritual place	Mountains
Representative substance / act	Snow equivalent
Earthly dwelling	Derbent and elsewhere
Representative substance / act	Heroic military deeds
Final condition	Outcast, exile

"Mulla Nur" encapsulates many of Bestuzhev's deepest concerns about life. The impact of these anxieties rendered him incapable of unifying his story aesthetically. Bestuzhev was trapped in the narrow corner of romantic art into which he had painted himself from the beginning of his career. In "Mulla Nur" he attempted to fashion a window through which he might leap to a new freedom, to a literary medium (equally romantic from our vantage point) with new basic assumptions. This window was myth, the archetypal narrative of transition and flux, of the hero's quest and its resolution. Yet myth ran counter to the kind of tale Bestuzhev was wont to tell in his grandiose, carefree, often careless, periphrastic, and marlinist style. Where myth impels narrative toward profundity, Bestuzhev's canonical tales of adventure cling to superficiality. A conflict between myth's dynamic force and Marlinsky's redundant formulas arose, preventing a synthesis that might have been of import to the evolution of Russian prose.

In personal terms, too, Bestuzhev's concerns explain his inclination toward myth, the fictional paradigm of personal transformation, the hero's quest for meaning and identity in life, the balancing of irreconcilable positions. It is as though Bestuzhev had asked himself whether romantic heroism were actually attainable in the real world. Iskander's metonymic world represents a negative response to this question. As if in alarm, Bestuzhev overthrew his new narrative structure to ask the same question within the literary vacuum his metaphoric approach to art had created. Within this vacuum he found the affirmative answer in which he unwaveringly believed. The shift from one hero to another constituted a wish fulfillment (similar to "Roman and Olga") and simultaneously a recognition of the tenuous position of the hero in both the real and the fictional worlds.

Bestuzhev needed to rekindle the fire of romance. As with any monolithic cultural system, romance supplied ultimate solutions in life and in art. Bestuzhev left it to his readers to unmuddle his myth, to reaffirm the romance he represented and wrote. And this was accomplished rather quickly in legend, poem, song, and drama.[36]

Bestuzhev did a great deal to inscribe his Marlinsky mask on the consciousness of his reading public, most particularly when under assault by the next generation. He was assisted at each step by the evolution of romanticism on Russian soil. Even the decline of romanticism supplied his public self with a theme of cultural death consonant with audience expectations. After the tragedies of Nestertsova and his young brother Peter, a third assault on him in 1834 took an entirely unexpected form. Literary circles in Russia were in the process of change without him. He found himself in the position of a literary "conservative," representative of an older generation whose time had come to step aside. In 1834 Bestuzhev's art came under resounding pressure. Vissarion Belinsky took Bestuzhev (as Marlinsky) apart in the press. Furthermore, Nikolai Gogol, a new face on the scene only a few years earlier, began to command the popular attention that Bestuzhev felt he alone should have been accorded. In the face of these changes, Bestuzhev clung tenaciously to romantic aesthetics, for it supplied him with the equipment necessary to combat this fresh assault. Romanticism represented a large enough receptacle to hold the mystery of life's joys and torments. His stories comprised a central portion of its aesthetics. Bestuzhev, therefore, would withstand this pressure and fight for preeminence. Unfortunately, Bestuzhev had no medium for propagating his side of the issue except through literature—he could not argue his case before his peers in the literary circles in the capital, he could not engage in personal debate with literati. In this context his stories became less oriented toward pure storytelling; he began to write much less, and extremely little fiction. What he did write was self-defensive and argumentative. His stories became parodies of themselves, their narrator a combative intruder who foisted his opinion on the public at each turn. His work began to suffer, justifying all the more the criticism he received.

When Bestuzhev's fiction came under attack for its limitations, Bestuzhev made a clever polemical move. He turned from fiction, removed the presence of fictional heroes, and focused his narratives (travelogues) not only on the ostensible object of the writing (Caucasian nature, natives, villages, roads, and chance meetings) but also on the narrator.

36. M. P. Alekseev, "Legendy o Marlinskom," in *Etiudy o Marlinskom*, 3–32.

Bestuzhev did everything he could to dramatize the narrator in terms of his own life. For the informed reader, the narrator's voice represented Bestuzhev. A knowledge of his character and life found complete reinforcement in his writing. The parallels between Bestuzhev and his narrator were not subject to debate—the two were cut from the same cloth. For the uninformed, however, the narrator represented Marlinsky, who was assumed to be an authentic historical personage living in the circumstances described by Bestuzhev. The images of Bestuzhev and Marlinsky coincided, the personage and the persona were effectively presented as one. He removed from his writing the ambiguities caused by fiction. If he was to be criticized for creating literature without the least pretense toward representing reality (as the new generation understood reality),[37] he would argue the continuity between life and letters by creating a literature of fact—travelogues, ethnographic studies, nature descriptions, casual dialogues on literature and life, philosophical digressions, social criticism, and a body of personal letters—all predicated on the idea that *his* life and *his* letters were synonymous. One important example here should suffice to animate this point.

Byronism

As early as 1831, in a letter to his publishers, Bestuzhev casually insisted on the linkage of art and life, writing, "My inner world has become miraculous: read *The Darkness* [*sic*] by Byron and you will understand something of what it is like; it is an ocean, 'beset by a heavy gloom, immobile, dark and silent' . . . [zadavlennyi tiazheloiu mgloi, nedvizhnyi, mrachnyi i nemoi] over which glimmer some unclear forms."[38] To appreciate what significance the reference to "Darkness" may have had for Bestuzhev's project of self-creation (and the importance of Byron as a model in Bestuzhev's life), it is necessary to examine the poem as it passes through the filter of Bestuzhev's consciousness.

"Darkness" was penned in the period July–August 1816 during a time of personal crisis and concomitant literary activity in Byron's life.

37. See Lidiia Ginzburg, *On Psychological Prose*, trans. Judson Rosengrant (Princeton, N.J., 1991).
38. "Pis'ma k Polevym," 291. Bestuzhev misnames Byron's poem, which lacks an article.

He was in some financial difficulties associated with his marriage obligations and his rather profligate way of life. Byron and his wife had recently separated (after only one year together), and after signing papers formalizing their legal affairs, he left for Switzerland where he spent the summer before moving on to Italy.[39] In Geneva he met the Shelleys who were also traveling under a cloud of scandal. This was Byron's first meeting with Shelley, which came about thanks to the efforts of the latter's sister-in-law, Claire Clairmont, stepsister of Mary Shelley, author of *Frankenstein; or the Modern Prometheus*.[40] The apocalyptic genre, in which "Darkness" is cast, was rarely used by Byron, but on several occasions this small group of literati engaged in gothic speculations that might have stimulated the verse's imagery. Jerome McGann suggests that the brief presence among them of M. G. ("Monk") Lewis, with his preference for dark musings, may have impelled Byron in this direction.[41] The poem is bleak, as one would expect, in its vision of "man's last days in a dying universe."[42] If it is a poem rather uncharacteristic of Byron's creativity, it nevertheless shares a dramatic sense of isolation, death, and longing with other poems of the four months in Switzerland, particularly "The Dream," "Prometheus," and ["A Fragment"].[43]

Since for Bestuzhev this was the beginning of a period of great pro-

39. Byron also suffered rumors about incestuous relations with his half-sister, Augusta. His poem "Epistle to Augusta" (Diodati, 1816) could only fuel those rumors.

40. For details concerning Byron's and Shelley's relationship, see John Buxton, *Byron and Shelley: The History of a Friendship* (New York, 1968). Buxton overstates Shelley's influence on "Darkness" and the other poems of 1816 (262). The intellectual and physical atmosphere that produced "Darkness" may have influenced the creation of *Frankenstein* as well; see John Clubbe, "The Tempest-toss'd Summer of 1816: Mary Shelley's *Frankenstein*," *The Byron Journal* 19 (1991):26–40. On the basis of her acquaintance with Byron for the three months she and her husband lived adjacent to him on Lake Geneva, Mary Shelley portrayed Byron in the character Raymond in *The Last Man* (Buxton, 267).

41. *Lord Byron: The Complete Poetic Works*, ed. Jerome J. McGann (Oxford, 1986), 4:459n.

42. Leslie A. Marchand, *Byron: A Biography* (New York, 1957), 2:637.

43. Clubbe emphasizes the Promethean theme. Note Bestuzhev mentions Prometheus in his letter to the Polevoys. Clubbe's description of the mythological figure's importance to Byron might easily apply to Bestuzhev as well: "In [1816] Byron came to understand better the essential character of the myth: that while Prometheus' fate was symbolic of the general human lot, it was still a fate ennobled by suffering and by a tremendous effort to maintain his mind's independence" (" 'The New Prometheus of New Men': Byron's 1816 Poems and *Manfred*," in *Nineteenth Century Literary Perspectives: Essays in Honor of Lionel Stevenson* [Durham, N.C., 1974], 17).

ductivity coupled with a hope of eventual release, Bestuzhev's reference to "Darkness" might seem a bit puzzling. But as the letter makes amply clear, Bestuzhev was frustrated by the conditions in which he lived and attempted to write. The fullness of life and its new promises were matched by a contrary feeling of emptiness and misery in which his potentials as a human being were being thwarted and his talents as a writer wasted on trifles. These elements become matters of significance in Bestuzhev's citation of the Byron poem, which begins "I had a dream, which was not all a dream" (*Lord Byron*, 4:40–43). This prefatory line encapsulates several facets of Bestuzhev's relationship to the poem. First, through it he likens poetry to experience, or meaning to sense (to cite a distinction Ricoeur makes),[44] and thereby claims the relevance of Byron's verse to his life. Second, he operates within the dialectic embodied in the relationship of dreams and waking advanced by Byron and romantic aesthetics in general. These factors taken together prompt the reader, specifically the Polevoy brothers, to comprehend the text at two levels—as Bestuzhev's experience of life (somehow unreal to him yet concretely experienced) and as a mode of assessing Bestuzhev's discourse (through the simile Bestuzhev proffers: " 'Darkness' is like my life").

Within this dream world, with equal emphasis on both "dream" and "world," elements pertaining to the end of time take on special signifying value for Bestuzhev:[45]

> The bright sun was extinguish'd, and the stars
> Did wander darkling in the eternal space,
> Rayless, and pathless, and the icy earth
> Swung blind and blackening in the moonless air;
> Morn came and went—and came, and brought no day,
> And men forgot their passions in the dread
> Of this their desolation; and all hearts
> Were chill'd into a selfish prayer for light.
> (Byron, "Darkness," lines 2–9)

44. Paul Ricoeur, *Interpretation Theory: Discourse and the Surplus of Meaning* (Fort Worth, Tex., 1976), 19–22.

45. Bestuzhev's argument, in effect, is that his life is a representation of a representation, a blending of verbal discourses that, and this is the key moment in his rhetoric, refer to a substantive reality. The literariness of identity and lived experience is highlighted here (as elsewhere) in Bestuzhev's letter.

These lines possess double referential value—they signify Byronic themes (which implies an interpretation of Byron's texts) and Bestuzhev's status in exile (which requires another, structurally similar act of interpretation of Bestuzhev's letter). At yet another level, each of the interpretative centers of Bestuzhev's rhetoric are "validated" by the assumption that Bestuzhev and Bestuzhev's readers were likely to make, that Byron's poetry equaled Byron's life. The distance separating Byron and Bestuzhev, as tenor and vehicle in metaphoric utterance, is thus nullified, at least if the Polevoy brothers read Bestuzhev as Bestuzhev read Byron.

The reader familiar with either the original or one of the several translations of "Darkness" is asked to equate poem and life-text through the intermediacy of Byron's descriptive language:

> And they did live by watch fires—and the thrones,
> The palaces of crowned kings—the huts,
> The habitations of all things which dwell,
> Were burnt for beacons; cities were consumed,
> And men were gather'd round their blazing homes
> To look once more into each other's face.
>
> (Lines 10–15)

The apocalyptic destruction of habitations, cities, and relationships is reminiscent of the war in which Bestuzhev participated. In the letter's postscript Bestuzhev's description of his part in the war indicates the degree to which the borrowed poetic text and the self-text Bestuzhev generated can be viewed by a willing reader as equivalent.[46] The impact of ultimate demise on individuals who, like Bestuzhev, experience personally the waste of war (apocalypse), and others who *read* about it, becomes a point of contact for addressers (Byron and Bestuzhev) and addressees (Bestuzhev and the Polevoy brothers):

> The brows of men by the despairing light
> Wore an unearthly aspect, as by fits
> The flashes fell upon them; some lay down

---

46. "Communication has been cut off, our mounts starve . . . Kazi-Mulla . . . threatens all the local cities and towns with a new siege. . . . The battle of Agach-Kale cost us four hundred men. . . . Eight of our excellent officers went down" ("Pis'ma k Polevym," 316).

And hid their eyes and wept; and some did rest
Their chins upon their clenched hands, and smiled;
And others hurried to and fro, and fed
Their funeral piles with fuel, and look'd up
With mad disquietude on the dull sky,
The pall of a past world; and then again
With curses cast them down upon the dust,
And gnash'd their teeth and howl'd.

(Lines 22–32)

The distance that separates people within the poem reiterates the theme of Bestuzhev's letter. Yet there is a difference. In the poem death separates people in ultimate terms. That is, within the self-referential world of "Darkness" human beings die alone; there is no reversal possible when "Darkness . . . [is] the Universe." Bestuzhev, however, works two themes at one time, separation and union, distance and communion. In his letter he refers to the inevitability of the soldier's death on the front lines and makes specific reference to himself:

> Your brother asks that I guard my life: that's a bit tough for a soldier. Nature has not bestowed upon me an animal daring which is extolled as bravery; but I am less impulsive in my actions than I used to be. Glory cannot shield me from danger with its azure wings and hope does not gild the smoky dust. I throw myself forward [in battle], but this is more out of duty than from inspiration. Labor and fatigue and the ill weather I bear with patience: no one has heard me mumble in complaint, "the beard is not bemoaned once the head is severed." ("Pis'ma k Polevym," 316)

In the parallels Bestuzhev suggests between the specific content of "Darkness" and his life (as he describes it), he draws down the explicit content of "Darkness" onto the surface description of his own experience. At the same time, he works at nullifying the ultimate separation inhering in "Darkness" and draws his reader into close personal proximity:

> And War, which for a moment was no more,
> Did glut himself again;—a meal was bought
> With blood, and each sate sullenly apart

> Gorging himself in gloom. No love was left;
> All earth was but one thought—and that was death,
> Immediate and inglorious; and the pang
> Of famine fed upon all entrails—men
> Died, and their bones were tombless as their flesh.
>
> (Lines 38–45)

These stark images are meant to activate parallel structures in the reader's perception of three texts—Bestuzhev's letter with its citation, the full text of the poem itself, and the life-texts of the two authors, Byron and Bestuzhev. The separation across cultures, individuals, languages, codes, genres, and messages is vitiated, but, again, only if the addressee is willing to perform the part scripted for him in Bestuzhev's text. The model for proximity, rather than distance, is supplied in "Darkness" with its famous reference to faithfulness:

> The meagre by the meagre were devour'd,
> Even dogs assail'd their masters, all save one,
> And he was faithful to a corse, and kept
> The birds and beasts and famish'd men at bay,
> Till hunger clung them, or the dropping dead
> Lured their lank jaws. Himself sought out no food,
> But with a piteous and perpetual moan,
> And a quick desolate cry, licking the hand
> Which answer'd not with a caress—he died.
>
> (Lines 46–54)

Byron's ironic reference to friendship is not matched by Bestuzhev's rhetoric. Bestuzhev would not have dogs, but humans (the Polevoy brothers, his Decembrist confreres) be friends of the type idealized in the literary and Masonic circles of the late eighteenth and early nineteenth centuries. Reference to his brothers, Nicholas and Mikhail, and to Kondraty Ryleyev occur elsewhere in the letter and set up cross-references that reinforce the theme of personal relations (that is, Byron's man/dog, Bestuzhev's man/man) as distinct from the failed relations catalogued in "Darkness" in its allegorical depiction of society. From this perspective Bestuzhev utilizes Byron's poem as a negative example, one that his readers were asked covertly to supersede in an act of understanding and sympathy (but not pity).

There is no ontologically necessary tie between Byron's imagery and Bestuzhev's or, for that matter, between Bestuzhev's argument and its reception. Rather, emphasis is placed on Bestuzhev's utilization of the poem to activate readers' associations available to them in the symmetry of the texts (poem and letter). To this end Bestuzhev presents the Polevoy brothers with some guidance, but it is they who are to draw overt parallels. It is in this form that Bestuzhev's rhetoric is most effective, for it involves suggestion, not declaration, persuasion, not command. By supplying the reader the opportunity to invest meaning in the reading experience, to make explicit connections where Bestuzhev himself has only made suggestions, Bestuzhev signifies the condition in which the normal and necessary distance that separates authors and readers can be surmounted and emotional proximity established. This was the goal of the word for Bestuzhev in exile.

Within the nexus of associations available to Bestuzhev as a reader of Byron, to Bestuzhev as writer of self-texts, and to the Polevoy brothers as readers of Byron and Bestuzhev, perhaps most compelling is Byron's use of images of water and ships. For the Russian reader they came to symbolize the plight of the Decembrist and of post-Decembrist society:

> The world was void,
> The populous and the powerful was a lump,
> Seasonless, herbless, treeless, manless, lifeless—
> A lump of death—a chaos of hard clay.
> The rivers, lakes, and ocean all stood still,
> And nothing stirr'd within their silent depths;
> Ships sailorless lay rotting on the sea,
> And their masts fell down piecemeal; as they dropp'd
> They slept on the abyss without a surge—
> The waves were dead; and tides were in their grave,
> The Moon, their mistress, had expired before;
> The winds were wither'd in the stagnant air,
> And the clouds perish'd; Darkness had no need
> Of aid from them—She was the Universe.
>
> (Lines 69–82)

This imagery of the boat at the conclusion of the poem signals a relationship between the cosmic and the earthly domains, both ruined, static, and lifeless. As elsewhere in the poem, Byron reinforces the emptiness of the universe in the repetition of the suffix -less. It is this absence that apparently prompts Bestuzhev's interest in referencing the poem, replacing the emptiness to which the poem refers with the substance of verbal encounter. Again distance is overcome as separation yields to proximity through the shared word.

Bestuzhev feels no need to cite the poem in his letter to the Polevoys. They could have known the poem in the original, but probably knew one of its translated variants. Bestuzhev chooses to highlight only one part of the poem (interestingly, not its dense third and fourth stanzas).[47] On the basis of the lines Bestuzhev quotes it is difficult to ascertain with any precision its relation to the original. Of the myriad images available to him, Bestuzhev refers only to part of the sixth "stanza": "[an ocean] beset by heavy gloom, motionless, dark and silent" [(okean,) zadavlennyi tiazheloiu mgloi, nedvizhnyi, mrachnyi i nemoi]. These lines seem to refer inexactly, but conceptually and imagistically, to Byron's lines: "The rivers, lakes, and ocean all stood still [*nedvizhnyi*] / And nothing stirr'd within their silent [*nemoi*] depths."[48]

Whether Bestuzhev, at the time of his writing, was recalling from memory the lines he cites, referring to a Russian or French translation of the poem, or simply engaging poetic license,[49] the changes he makes in the

47. The third "stanza" ("The brows of men by the despairing light") stands out from the rest of "Darkness." It contains a higher frequency of enjambment than the rest of the poem, which gives the verse a particular drive during its initial stark descriptive passages. It also contains a fairly regular caesura, which reinforces rhythmically the description of man's persistent degradation. It also contains the poem's sole truncated foot, which occurs when flame and the heavens are linked in something of an inverted Promethean image. It also contains a high frequency of spondees, which makes more powerful the epithets "dull sky," "past worlds," "wild birds shriek'd." And finally, the stanza contains rhymed elements otherwise missing from the poem and consequently deserving of attention as a coherent lexical series: "brutes / multitude / food." These prosodic features reinforce the poem's focus on a death that is rendered in individual, group, and cosmic terms. The fourth stanza contains similar features, but not in the density of the third. Bestuzhev is clearly more moved by imagery than prosodic elements, which is not unexpected in someone who was a prose writer first and a poet only fourth (after literary criticism and epistolary writing).

48. This passage also enticed British readers contemporary to Byron, excluding Scott and other literati (R. J. Dingley, " 'I Had a Dream': Byron's 'Darkness,' " *The Byron Journal* 9 [1981], 20). Rotchev translated these lines as follows: "Ozera, reki / I more—vse zatikhlo. Nichego / ne shevelilos' v bezdne molchalivoi" (Dzhordzh Gordon Bairon, *Izbrannaia lirika* [Moscow, 1988], 249). In Bestuzhev's rendering, "okean" replaces "more," "nemoi" displaces "zatikhlo," "nedvizhnyi" supplants "ne shevelilos'," and "mrachnyi" substitutes for "molchalivaia." This suggests that Bestuzhev was either quoting from memory or citing a different translation.

49. The lines in Russian may have been of Bestuzhev's own composition from memory.

original are suggestive. First, Bestuzhev excludes the rivers and lakes. Whether conscious or not, the elimination of these images may be the result of a desire to have the poem correspond to his actual circumstances: he was living at the time in Derbent, which is located on the Caspian Sea. The sea, of course, is a standard romantic image utilized to suggest a dualism inherent in personality, a dualism, moreover, which Bestuzhev keenly felt, if we can, in some measure, believe his remarks to the Polevoy brothers.[50] Second, Bestuzhev includes the qualifiers "dark / gloomy" (*mrachnyi*) and the epithet "heavy gloom" [*tiazhelaia mgla*], evaluative addenda that suggest Bestuzhev's reading of the original, not its specific content. In effect, Bestuzhev makes an interpretation of the poem's mood (which is not too difficult to do), and encapsulates it in his rhythmic rendering of the lines. In sum, Bestuzhev's reference to "Darkness" and his translation of two of its lines indicate both biographical and aesthetic information associated with him. He is a remaker of myths in order to create his own.

These two categories (biography and aesthetics) form the center of any rendering of texts by Bestuzhev, whether his own or others': they incline in two directions beyond the text toward Bestuzhev's life and the persona he develops in society through his writing, and internally toward the dialogical transformation of the text from within (as though from a prior pre-utterance code to another that emerges secondarily as a response to the first).[51] These two simultaneous events underscore the cross-cultural transformation Bestuzhev makes for his readers—through verbal art as well as in his letters he attempts to render a literary image of

---

Concordances of Byron, Pushkin, and Shakespeare, authors with whose work Bestuzhev was familiar, do not deliver the images of the ocean he here cites. Note, too, Bestuzhev incorrectly cites the poem's title: there is no article in Byron's "Darkness," an interesting translinguistic addition on Bestuzhev's part and perhaps an indication of his finely tuned, if here misguided, understanding of English. If Bestuzhev was referring to the French translation, "Les Ténèbres," this could have supplied the article he inserted in English in his letter. I am indebted to Professor Khama Basili Tolo for his assistance on this matter. See "Les Ténèbres," in *Oeuvres Completes de Lord Byron*, trans. M. Benjamin Laroche (Paris, 1841), 286–87. This is a prose translation that was available to Russian readers in the 1830s.

50. The dualism is isomorphic to Bestuzhev's utilization of Byron's poem.

51. This process is most apparent in translations from one language to another, but less so at the surface level within the same language. Bakhtin's descriptions of this process are most enlightening: "An element of response and anticipation penetrates deeply inside intensely dialogic discourse. Such discourse draws in, as it were, sucks in to itself the other's replies, intensely reworking them." See Mikhail Bakhtin, *Problems of Dostoevsky's Poetics*, 197.

self both as author and hero. It is a self-making not unlike Byron's, at least structurally if not in terms of the details or the image's complexity. For the Polevoys, and through the reference to Byron, Bestuzhev demonstrates his affinity to literary texts that equate with his life and at the same time provides proof of his sensitivity to the aesthetic word—not an insignificant act for a writer to perform in his correspondence with his publishers, particularly those in direct contact with the literary milieu from which Bestuzhev was excluded and through whom he could be reintroduced qua hero and "poet."

Bestuzhev's brief mention of "Darkness" is significant for what it indicates more or less overtly. But it is perhaps more dramatic for what it leaves out—eighty lines of verse, that is, most of the poem. Bestuzhev's reference to two lines supplies the Polevoys (and any they would privilege to read Bestuzhev's private correspondence) with a way to interpret Bestuzhev's relationship to Byron's poem, not the poem itself. In effect, through Bestuzhev's allusion to Byron's text, he instructs his publishers how to read the image of his life he wishes to project (and in which he sincerely believed). The transformation inherent here is significant not for what it does aesthetically with Byron's poem, but for what it imposes on a reader sensitive to Bestuzhev's life circumstances. It asks the reader (the Polevoys, their circle of intimates) to place Bestuzhev in a mental landscape adjacent to a vast and powerful body of water, the dualism of which can be inferred by poetic canon, and the political nature of which can be read by reference to other post-Decembrist texts, for example, Pushkin's "Arion" (1827).[52] It asks the reader to understand the qualifiers Bestuzhev uses, particularly those he adds to the original, as they pertain to his life.

Bestuzhev equates his isolation with immobility and stasis ("nedvizhnyi") and he views himself as silenced ("nemoi") because of the censorship of his work under the name Bestuzhev. This brings up a crucial issue—Bestuzhev's identity before the public, his self-making, which is the central, albeit unstated (and perhaps even unconscious), concern of his letter to the Polevoy brothers. Its heart is conditioned by the very real distance that separates him from his family, friends, publishers, the literary world, and social scene in the north. It is the source of his

52. For a discussion of "Arion" and of the relations between Pushkin and Marlinskii, see Lauren Leighton, "Puškin and Marlinskij: Decembrist Allusions," *Russian Literature* 14 (1983), 351–82.

desire, the font of his "dream . . . not all a dream," to remove the distance, to overcome the isolation, and feel (if not be) proximate to a world that is alive and responsive to him.

Bestuzhev would like to be seen in a tragic, romantic guise. To foster the image of self as martyred hero, for which he had no small claim, he emphasizes literary antecedents. He is the Byronic "I" of "Darkness," which views the microcosm (for Bestuzhev, Petersburg and Moscow) from the macrocosmic vantage of the end of time. This is at one and the same time a witty condemnation of vacuous society and a longing for its ambiguous and varied pleasures. It is grand society, after all, that has driven him, at least indirectly, into exile, but that same society which once held him in high esteem as a writer, publisher, and promising young officer. These are clear Byronic themes. Interestingly enough, there is sufficient truth to them in Bestuzhev's life to make the rendering relatively accurate. Bestuzhev saw to that.

Bestuzhev projects an image of himself that is "of" the world and "above" the world, much like the images of Prometheus the romantics valorized in their lives and texts, and like the image of Christ Bestuzhev also invokes in his letter. With the aid of these man-god images, Bestuzhev places "Darkness" in the self-mythologizing context toward which his rhetoric works:

> In place of harmony I find within myself a desert wind whispering in the ruins. Beneath my cross, my burdensome cross (which is more spiritual than material), I fall for a moment, and not just once. My spirit is strong; but this is more a [physical] numbness than firmness [of character]. Only two jewels have I extracted from the flood: the soul's pride and peace before everything that is beautiful. My inner world has become incredible: read Byron's *The Darkness* [sic] and you will get a sense of something of which I speak.

In Bestuzhev's use of Byron's stark poem we observe a collision of cultures in which the extreme romanticist, Bestuzhev, suggests a manner by which he is to be understood as a cultural monument; condemns the society that supports him even as it exiles him; and mythologizes himself on the order of the cosmic "I" of Byron's poem. Bestuzhev ensures these readings by topographical allusion (his location on the Caspian Sea); meaningful subtractions from the original poem; significant biographical additions to the original; reference to Lord Byron as a pancultural phenomenon (whose biographical and literary texts lionized the poet for Russian and world culture); and subtle insistence on an isomorphism that relies on reader sensitivities to the biographical and literary details of his and Byron's personae. Bestuzhev's literal absorption of Byron into his life and texts indicates dramatically his desire to achieve a specific form of selfhood. Paraphrasing Ricoeur, it is the Bryonic text (life-text and aesthetic texts), with its power of world disclosure, that gives a self here to Bestuzhev's ego. It is not inappropriate that he should be called Russia's Byron, not because of the accuracy of the description at the surface level, but because of its conformity to Bestuzhev's deepest wish and his brief success at realizing it.

In "The Road to the Town of Kuba" ("Put' do goroda Kuby," 1834) Bestuzhev, speaking in his own voice in one of several travelogues, does not attempt to deny the connection between text and life-text, but asserts it in bold, direct language: "I have made it a rule to go nowhere in Asia without a trustworthy rifle and I have had no occasion to regret the decision. In Russia we say, 'Hide not poorly, invite no thief into sin' [Ne kladi plokho, ne vvodi vora v grekh]; but in the Caucasus one should say 'Ride not poorly' [Ne ezdi plokho]" (*Sochineniia*, 2:183). With pen in hand, Bestuzhev inscribes his poet-warrior identity (with gun in hand) as it is necessitated by the dangerous circumstances of his life. Texts of these types, both travelogue and private letter, constituted Bestuzhev's comprehensive effort to stimulate an interpretation of his person through the ideal of the heroic persona. In his fiction he drew analogies between the thanatic forces operative in the lives of his heroes and in the life of the implied author. In his literature of fact, the narrator focused reader attention on the authentic romantic circumstances of his life—he was isolated, exiled, lonely, sensitive to the call of nature, dramatically self-conscious, and confident in his ability to withstand the onslaughts of an unjust fate. In the semi-fictional, semi-factual "The Story of an Officer Who Was a Captive of the Mountain Peoples," Bestuzhev's narrator extols the simple pleasures a Russian exile derives from living amid isolated mountain peoples who exist in a Rousseau-like pristine state.

Escape into nature represented one type of solution to the narrator's dilemma. As in "Darkness," death was yet another solution: "In both his literary works and his correspondence of the last years he took a great interest in 'Byronic' deaths, and he expressed envy of the English poet's 'glamorous' death in the Greek revolution. Two of his works written in the years just prior to his death—*On byl ubit* ('He Was Killed') and the chapter titled 'Zhurnal Vadimova' ('Vadimov's Journal') of the uncompleted novel *Vadimov*—are based on the thoughts of men preparing for their own deaths" (Leighton, *ABM*, 34). In his correspondence with the Polevoys and with his brothers, Bestuzhev directly mentioned the inevitability of his death. Brother Mikhail comments that in the final year of his life, Bestuzhev seemed determined to die.[53] In a letter to his brother Pavel written three months before his disappearance, Bestuzhev discussed the violent deaths of two of his fellow writers, Alexander Pushkin and Alexander Griboyedov: "I cried then as I am crying now [writing this letter to you], with hot tears, cried for a friend [Pushkin] and a comrade in arms [Griboyedov, a Decembrist sympathizer], and cried for myself. When the priest chanted, 'For the immortal souls Alexander and Alexander,' my sobs tore at my breast. The phrase seemed to me to be not only a remembrance, but also a premonition. . . . Yes, I feel that my death will be just as violent and unexpected and that it is close at hand."[54] The themes of demise and escape conditioned Bestuzhev's audience for his fifth act. It has been the most durable and the most impressive aesthetic accomplishment of Bestuzhev's creativity.

53. M. K. Azadovskii, *Vospominaniia Bestuzhevykh*, 223.
54. Cited, with emendation, from Leighton, *Alexander Bestuzhev-Marlinsky*, 34–35.

Conclusion

The heart would like to write with such
wide, bold strokes, but the page is so
cramped.

—Bestuzhev-Marlinsky

Bestuzhev's mature fiction of the 1830s was written with great passion
in obeisance to the willful, spontaneous, and incautious aesthetics of a
grandiose romantic persona. He attempted to fix the identity of the hero
into a context that appeared "real," that is, recognizable for its representation of incoherent contemporary society. The hero's quest for identity
was the primary focus of all his fiction. From the manners of early-
nineteenth-century high society in "The Test" to the primal impulses of
"Ammalat-bek," Bestuzhev depicted human nature at its most compelling and self-destructive. Like Tolstoy later in the century, Bestuzhev
juxtaposed the recurring themes of purity and primitivism, but infused
with a spirit of both Byronic and carnivalesque proportions.

In the tension between the extremes of annihilation and incorruptibility, large forces ruled beyond the reckoning of the characters, their narrators, and at times even the author. These forces found artistic expression in the ritual forms preserved in Russian culture by the folk in their carnival celebrations as well as in the art of writers like Bestuzhev. The fusion of life and death in carnival action, speech, gesture, and behavior underscores a mythic principle operative in Bestuzhev's many texts— that new life comes into being mysteriously and is destroyed dramatically and violently, only to initiate a new cycle. The perception of life and death that Bestuzhev encountered in the practices and legends of the peoples of Siberia and the Caucasus appealed to him. In his work the carnivalesque took shape in chaotic form, probably at an unconscious level. It gave direction, however, to the final structure that Bestuzhev brought to his life-text and with which he informed his fifth act, giving substance to the myriad, topsy-turvy events of his public life—from the literary club debates, games, and battles to the debauches of the officers' group, from the escapades of a gay blade to the deadly dueling of the gentleman, from the Decembrists' idealism to the execution of Ryleyev, from the folk festivities of the Siberian natives to the dismemberment of Alexander Griboyedov in Persia, from the hero's reanimation in the Caucasus to Olga Nestertsova's tragic death. Carnival was the stuff of Bestuzhev's life and animated his last day. Its power can be measured by the reception of his texts and his life in society.

Bestuzhev was one of the first to push ashore on Adler Promontory along the Black Sea on June 7, 1837. He was in the vanguard that crossed the beach into the trees under enemy fire. The Russian advance was not well coordinated, and Bestuzhev's detachment moved into the woods too quickly to be supported by those still at the shoreline. They found themselves overextended and were suddenly assaulted on three sides by Cherkes natives. In the vicious cross fire, Russian soldiers began to fall all around Bestuzhev. His captain, lacking the requisite independence of thought to take control of the situation and save his men, sent Bestuzhev back to the beach for new orders. Luckily, Bestuzhev made his way without sustaining injury. When the general commanded a retreat, Bestuzhev had to fight his way through the intense battle back to the young captain to deliver the order. As the vanguard began to withdraw, the Cherkes sensed their advantage and charged, shooting wildly. Bestuzhev apparently remained behind to cover the retreat. According to the testimony of several soldiers who managed to witness the event while running for their lives, the natives overran the line of defense and apparently killed Bestuzhev.

After the battle's conclusion, when the Russians went out to recover their dead and wounded, Bestuzhev's comrades looked for his body. It was gone, perhaps removed by the enemy or perhaps hacked to pieces and scattered throughout the woods. Because of the chaos, no one was able to recreate accurately what had occurred that day. Witnesses presented conflicting testimony, some saying that Bestuzhev had been shot (once or twice) during the retreat, and others insisting that he had not been wounded at all but had escaped with the natives to freedom. In a brief description of Bestuzhev's death, one of his most reliable comrades, V. A. Sheliga-Pototsky, testified that Bestuzhev was definitely shot and then dismembered by the Cherkes warriors.

The facts of Bestuzhev's disappearance are not known, but Russian society's response to his end is. Announcements of Bestuzhev's death in the press represented the first time his name had been mentioned officially since the Decembrist Revolt. For many, then, his death also constituted his symbolic rebirth. Lost to the public for twelve years, he was suddenly found. Marlinsky became Bestuzhev, fulfilling a covert goal of Bestuzhev's fiction during his exile.

The identification of Bestuzhev's person with the work of Marlinsky solved a series of puzzles, such as Marlinsky's allusions to exile, his being misunderstood and unappreciated by society, and the mysterious crime he had committed. His fiction was read as representational art, not fantasy; and the once separate phenomena "Marlinsky" and "Bestuzhev" were given the unity he had sought for them throughout his life. The union of mask and man represented a major cultural event. Stage productions of Bestuzhev's tales of the Caucasus were presented to large, sympathetic audiences moved to tears by the coincidence of persona and historical personage. His poems about the natives were sung on stage and in drawing rooms. By appearing in print media, the drama of his final act, with its romantic inconclusiveness, was given the air of legitimacy.

With the word that Bestuzhev's body had not been retrieved from the forest at Adler Promontory, his audience began to circulate wild rumors in the capital, in Moscow, and in the provinces. His readers' projections attest to the efficacy of his persona in finding concrete existence in their minds. Some considered the great spiritual and military leader of the Caucasian peoples, Shamil (whom Tolstoy immortalized in his story

"Hadji Murat," 1904) to be Bestuzhev in disguise. They saw in Bestuzhev a trickster who had outwitted the authorities by staging his death to
find freedom among the Cherkes peoples he had extolled in his Caucasian tales. Others believed that Bestuzhev had retired into the wilderness
of the Caucasus, taken a native wife, and lived a peaceful life tending
sheep, the garden, and his new home. Evidence could be adduced from
the ethnographic tale, "The Story of an Officer Who Was a Captive of
the Mountain Peoples." In the provinces stories were further embellished. It was thought that Bestuzhev had drowned. These readers saw
Bestuzhev as a Wertherian hero who had thrown himself in despair into
the Terek, the torrential river with which many a romantic identified
himself. Radishchev's suicide and Bestuzhev's gloomy letters in exile
supported this variant. Some told of Bestuzhev being killed in a duel by a
jealous husband. The text for this reading of the persona was real life,
for Bestuzhev lost himself in affairs during his brief stays at the fashionable spas where he played the consummate Byronic outsider with no
small degree of conviction and success.

Each of these readings was undergirded by a linkage of literature and
life, no less evident and passionate an expression of faith than we find
in Bestuzhev himself. It was a belief that characterized an entire generation of readers and writers. This shared cultural "ideology" engendered
deeply personal responses to Bestuzhev's life and death. The image of
the romantic hero he projected was received as biographical fact. The
rumors, consequently, carried Bestuzhev's existence qua persona forward in time, conferring on him the laurel he had always sought—
immortality. Paradoxically, death proved to be the solution to the problem of mortality.

Bestuzhev's readers included private citizens and literati, men and
women, government officials and the tsar. And it was as difficult for the
tsar to accept the death of the hero as it was for the general public. The
government took it upon itself to test these rumors. It is highly probable
that Nicholas I was behind this bit of official intrigue. A Cherkes native
conscripted by the Russian side was dispatched to find Bestuzhev or his
grave. The agent discovered neither one nor the other but reported from
interviews with the Cherkes that Bestuzhev had indeed been killed. One
piece of evidence, although inconclusive, did turn up—Bestuzhev's ring
appeared in a marketplace stall. The tsar called off further investiga-
tions; but he refused to allow the publication of Bestuzhev's picture in a
volume of Russian fiction two years after the disappearance. This cul-

tural web captured everyone capable of sharing the romantic word and its mythological telos.

Whether or not Bestuzhev went out to die on June 7 (either masking his intent in heroism or realizing it in the extreme à la Dostoyevsky's nihilists), doubts about his death elevated the Marlinsky persona to the stature of social text. Somewhere within this cultural narrative it did not actually matter whether he was alive or dead. Although his person was now lost to Russian culture, his Marlinsky persona was firmly attached to his name and has remained, albeit often with prejudice, in the public's collective mind through the twentieth century.

The fusion of text and life-text enacted a life tale in which Bestuzhev believed wholeheartedly. As in fiction, his life was a narrative conceived with a demarcated beginning, middle, and end. From his childhood reading, a personal immersion in European romanticism, a longing for fame and glory, and the death of his father, Bestuzhev was drawn to modern literature's heroic persona as a solution to life's ultimate mystery. The specter of his mortality reached consciousness during the Decembrist Revolt and informed his psyche during his years of exile. With pen in hand, Bestuzhev's Caucasus years allowed him to thematize death from the perspective that his youthful unconscious had recognized intuitively. The dread of death gave way to thanatic drive, for in the hero's glorious end a victory could be won.

To lift the hero's literary plot out of fiction and place it into life, an entire career was required which could encompass life and letters in a manner that proved their coincidence both to the writer and to his readers. Lord Byron, of course, was Bestuzhev's primary model. Byron had achieved immortality through the identification of fiction with reality, at once sacrificing himself to the romantic ideal of freedom and self-will and bestowing upon world culture a body of work that has withstood the test of time. It is under this last criterion that Bestuzhev's quest for immortality failed. The quality of Bestuzhev's texts represents the fatal flaw in his life-text, for literati attain immortality only as long as their work is valued. Bestuzhev's ultimate heroic gesture was not as effective as Byron's, because future generations have dismissed his art. Even substantive assaults in the press in 1834 were not sufficient to convince Bestuzhev that his romantic ideas were on the verge of collapse. Perhaps he had been cut off from Russia's intellectual life too long to recognize the conceptual inadequacy of romanticism in the face of new historical conditions, a new social reality, and an altered literary world.

If the cultural context shifted around Bestuzhev, effectively nullifying the synchronic conditions that had fostered his beliefs, the psychological framework inherent in the romantic ideology also proved inadequate. Bestuzhev apparently did not understand that what he attempted to achieve for himself belonged only to one facet of his identity, to his Marlinsky persona, which he had generalized to encompass his whole notion of self. Recognizing at some level that one cannot bestow immortality on oneself (history performs this function), Bestuzhev selected from historical and literary artifacts the material he thought decisive in solving the ultimate problem of life. In the heroic persona he located an *idea* that, he felt, secured immortality. Following his generation's assessment of texts as behavioral codes, Bestuzhev resolved to become the hero. He tried to control his image in society and in letters so that the two reinforced each other. The coalescence of personality and persona could be proved, empirically, by the consistency Bestuzhev brought to the mutually reinforcing productions of texts and life. Even if his work, overshadowed thoroughly by the next generation of authors, has been largely forgotten by the public (save the young) and preserved only by scholars, it is testimony to Bestuzhev's skill that his life-text has always been understood in terms of his persona.

Bestuzhev's aim, as for many a romantic, was to subsume all reality under romanticism. This aim represents an impulse toward complete integration through the aggrandizement of the persona, but it confesses to deep-seated insecurities. Bestuzhev had to explain all of reality in terms of his idea; if he had not been able to, he would have been left with nothing but an invalid persona and a vacant self. In the 1830s he was forced to feel, if not confront, the restrictive contours that enclosed his idea of self. This was particularly true for him as the cultural context evolved into another set of propositions about life, art, and language. Bestuzhev projected the deficiencies of his notion onto objects that traditional romance had already absorbed into its canon. He saw society, the government, and the tsar in a conspiracy to limit his growth as a citizen, soldier, and writer. He transformed the necessity of personal and intellectual reassessment into a critique of the world.

The psychological projection inherent in Bestuzhev's romantic persona underscores an essential feature of his self-idea that bothered his brother

Nicholas—its utter subjectivism. In "The Sailor Nikitin," "Ammalat-bek," and "Mulla Nur," Bestuzhev found the consequences of analytic thought and introspection detrimental to the image of the heroic persona, so he rejected his brother's advice. He used what analytic skills he had to justify himself and his art. At this juncture Bestuzhev—not Marlinsky, but the creator of Marlinsky—is clearly visible. For reflection represents a function of the personality that may be marshaled toward the difficult task of altering one's idea of self. Bestuzhev did not call forth this feature of his personality. He consigned self-examination to regions outside the boundaries of the hero's identity. Anything that might damage the persona's character was by definition excluded. But what Marlinsky gained by this maneuver, Bestuzhev lost to selfhood. By dismissing introspection and discursive logic Marlinsky banished fear, self-doubt, and anxiety, but Bestuzhev lost the possibility of development and growth.

What Bestuzhev could not or would not see is that the persona, as the root indicates, is no more than a mask. Sincerely donned in his youth and worn with rigid constancy throughout his life, the mask remained entirely opaque to him. He did not see through it to his more complex nature. The persona functioned originally to incorporate his identity. Eventually it became censorial, not admitting to less heroic, more human features. When it came to his final experiment in asserting the equivalence of mask to identity, Bestuzhev could not conceive that a measure of immortality could be achieved only for his heroic projection. In attempting to win a victory for the persona, Bestuzhev had to lose his whole being.

Against this cultural and psychological information, Bestuzhev's death becomes multivalent. When in St. Petersburg the canonical fusion of literature and life was criticized in essential ways by an emerging intelligentsia made up of classes Bestuzhev's fiction did not address, and as his work was attacked for its narrow conception of art, personality, and life, he was confronted by the unimaginable. His ultraromanticism began to collapse under the weight of its own theoretical deficiencies. It could not encompass a more inclusive vision of social reality or place an evolved heroic psyche within that configuration. Where others (Pushkin, Gogol, Lermontov) were capable of casting aside or modifying the narrow categories of romantic ego philosophy, Bestuzhev could not. As he confessed to brother Nicholas, he had only a Marlinsky language, a Marlinsky ideology, a Marlinsky idea of plot. Without them he had nothing.

Romantic will, however, was predicated on a good measure of personal well-being, on strength and health, as well as on the sanction of society. When Bestuzhev's physical health changed for the worse after 1834, he was less capable of asserting that will. As time passed his spirits flagged, for he recognized that without his health he had little will left him. Surely Bestuzhev experienced this loss as symbolic death. Trapped in these conditions, unwilling or perhaps merely unable to break out of them by altering his ideas and language, Bestuzhev fell back on the theatrical literary program that constituted his conscious identity. He began to envisage death as an elevation of the romantic will. It flowed logically and naturally from the persona of the hero, not so much as an end to entrapment, but as the fulfillment of being. As with Dostoyevsky's postromantic nihilists, the completion of heroism, its ultimate proof, was death by choice. Bestuzhev's final and tragic insistence on the unity of mask and man raised the stature of his Marlinsky persona to overwhelming proportions.

Rather than submit to the materialist and empirical notion that Bestuzhev's life and death are the inevitable products of a social determinism inherent in any description of early-nineteenth-century Russia (a determinism in which writers, their texts, and their reception are encompassed by a shared ideology and the language which embodies it), a more elusive, though liberating and inclusive, idea can be used to encompass his life-text. In the pancultural celebration of the fundamental mysteries of life and death, of self and persona, of subject and object, of realism and subjectivism, the comprehensive spirit of death-dealing and life-celebrating carnival offers an interpretive angle that encompasses mystery even as it subsumes empirical description with its inevitable determinism. From the perspective of a ritual enactment of life's incomprehensibility, the carnival can be observed in Bestuzhev's life. When Bestuzhev selected his pen name, Marlinsky, he performed an act of self-crowning by which he meant to elevate himself to a high station. The Decembrist Revolt, furthermore, animated the carnival spirit in Bestuzhev and presented him with an opportunity to establish his place in Russian culture. In the tragicomic farce of the insurrection and its aftermath, Bestuzhev suffered symbolic death in several ways—the loss of family status; the loss of noble station; the loss of contact with his family; and the loss of active participation in literary society. Literally alive, but figuratively dead, Bestuzhev again entered the magic sphere of the carnival's public pageants.

Life and death lie at the heart of carnival. Bestuzhev, the self-proclaimed carnival king of Marli, experienced their interplay in his own life. He may have suffered dismemberment, the traditional fate of the sacrificial ruler, the Fool King of antiquity. No matter how he died, however, his disappearance on Adler Promontory fulfilled the secret aim of a lifelong fascination. Through the passionate and extreme embodiment of romanticism that Bestuzhev bestowed as his Marlinsky legacy, the tragicomic mask of carnival has been donned by successive generations. Whenever Marlinsky is taken for Bestuzhev or Bestuzhev for Marlinsky, the call of carnival is again fulfilled, eliciting a symbolic roar of delight from the forest at Adler Promontory. The carnival laughter proclaims that there is little behind a mask but the unfulfillable longing for a finalized self, the riveting eye of death, and the unruly hope of rebirth.

Bibliography

Primary Sources

"A. A. Bestuzhev." *Russkaia starina* 21 (1889): 375–78.

"A. A. Bestuzhev (Marlinskii): 1798–1837." *Otechestvennye zapiski* 5 (1860): 122–66; 6 (1860): 299–350; 7 (1860): 43–100.

"A. A. Bestuzhev v Piatigorske." *Russkaia starina* 29 (1880): 417–22.

"Aleksandr Bestuzhev na Kavkaze, 1829–1837: Neizdannye pis'ma ego k materi, sestram i brat'iam." *Russkii vestnik* 6 (1870): 485–524; 7 (1870): 46–85.

"Aleksandr Bestuzhev v Iakutske: neizdannye pis'ma ego k rodnym, 1827–1829." *Russkii vestnik* 6 (1870): 213–64.

Arkhipov, V. A. *Poliarnaia zvezda A. A. Bestuzheva i K. F. Ryleeva.* Moscow, 1960.

Azadovskii, M. K., ed. *Pamiati dekabristov.* 12 vols. Leningrad, 1926.

———. *Vospominaniia Bestuzhevykh.* Moscow, 1951.

Bestuzhev, A. F. "O vospitanii." In *Russkie prosvetiteli (ot Radishcheva do dekabristov)* vol 1. Moscow, 1966.

Bestuzhev-Marlinsky, Aleksandr. "Ammalat-bek: A Caucasian Tale." Trans. Lewis Bagby. In Rydel, 212–41.

———. "An Evening on Bivouac." Trans. Lauren Leighton. In Proffer, 138–44.

———. *Fregat "Nadezhda": Povesti.* Ed. V. I. Sakharov. Odessa, 1983.

———. *Izbrannye povesti.* Ed. N. L. Stepanov. Leningrad, 1937.

———. *Polnoe sobranie stikhotvorenii.* Ed. M. A. Briskman. Leningrad, 1961.

———. *Povesti i rasskazy.* Ed. A. L. Ospovat. Moscow, 1976.

———. *Revel'skii turnir: Istoricheskie povesti.* Ed. V. I. Sakharov. Odessa, 1984.

———. *Romanticheskie povesti.* Ed. V. V. Dement'iev et al. Sverdlovsk, 1984.

———. *Sobranie stikhotvorenii.* Leningrad, 1948.

———. *Sochineniia v dvukh tomakh.* Ed. V. I. Kuleshov. Moscow, 1981.

———. *Sochineniia v dvukh tomakh.* Ed. N. N. Maslin. Moscow, 1958.

———. "The Test." Trans. Lewis Bagby. In Proffer, 145–95.

Bestuzhev, Nikolai. *Stat'i i pis'ma.* Ed. I. M. Trotskii. Moscow, 1933.

Dumas, Alexandre. *The Snow on Shah-Dagh and Ammalat-Bey: Posthumous Romances by Alexandre Dumas.* Trans. Gordon Home. London, 1889.

———. *Tales of the Caucasus.* Trans. Alma Blakeman Jones. Boston, 1895.

Fedosevaia, E. I. "Stikhotvorenie, posviashchennoe pamiati Aleksandra Bestuzheva." In *Dekabristy i ikh vremia*, ed. M. P. Alekseev and B. S. Meilakh. Moscow, 1951.

Griboedov, A. S. *Sochineniia v dvukh tomakh*. Moscow, 1971.

Izmailov, N. V., ed. "A. A. Bestuzhev do 14 dekabria 1825 g." In *Pamiati dekabristov: Sbornik materialov*, vol. 1. Leningrad, 1926.

"Iz zapisok dekabrista Iakushkina." *Russkii arkhiv* 8–9 (1871): 1566–86.

"Iz zapisok Nikolaia Ivanovicha Grecha." *Russkii vestnik* 6 (1868): 371–421.

"Iz zapisok Nikolaia I v 14 dekabria 1825 g." *Krasnyi arkhiv* (1924): 222–34.

"K istorii pokoreniia na Kavkaze." *Russkii arkhiv* 3 (1877): 106–9.

Kostenetskii, Ia. I. "Aleksandr Aleksandrovich Bestuzhev (Marlinskii)." *Russkaia starina* 11 (1900): 441–57.

Lebedovaia, L. A. "Pis'mo Pavla Bestuzheva k A. Bestuzhevu (Marlinskomu) o smerti Pushkina." In *Dekabristy i ikh vremia*, ed. M. P. Alekseev and B. S. Meilakh. Moscow, 1951.

"Neizdannye pis'ma A. A. Bestuzheva k Polevym." *Russkoe obozrenie* 10 (1894): 819–34.

Nevelev, G. "Neopublikovannye vospominaniia ob A. A. Bestuzheve-Marlinskom." *Voprosy literatury* 2 (1976): 207–17.

"Pis'ma A. A. Bestuzheva iz ssylki." *Byloe* 5 (1925): 114–20.

"Pis'ma A. Bestuzheva—F. V. Bulgarinu." *Russkaia starina* 2 (1901): 392–404.

"Pis'ma Aleksandra Aleksandrovicha Bestuzheva k N. A. i K. A. Polevym, pisannye v 1831–1837 godakh." *Russkii vestnik* 3 (1861): 285–335; 4 (1861): 425–87.

"Pis'ma Aleksandra Bestuzheva k P. A. Viazemskomu (1823–1825)." In Vinogradov, 60:191–230.

"Pis'mo A. A. Bestuzheva (Marlinskogo) k A. S. Pushkinu." *Russkii arkhiv* 1 (1881): 425–27.

"Pis'mo Aleksandra Bestuzheva—grafu Dibichu." *Russkaia starina* 11 (1881): 886–87.

"Pis'mo Bestuzheva (Marlinskogo) k A. M. Andreevu." *Russkii arkhiv* (1869): 606–8.

"Posledniaia popytka 'oblegcheniia uchasti' A. A. Bestuzheva." In *Dekabristy: Neizdannye materialy i stat'i*, ed. B. L. Modzalevskii and Iu. G. Oksman. Moscow, 1925.

Pushkin, Aleksandr S. *Sobranie sochinenii*. Ed. D. D. Blagoi et al. 10 vols. Moscow, 1959.

Rydel, Christine, ed. *The Ardis Anthology of Russian Romanticism*. Ann Arbor, Mich., 1984.

Shtraikh, S. Ia., ed. *Zapiski, stat'i, pis'ma dekabrista I. D. Iakushkina*. Moscow, 1951.

Turgenev, I. S. *Perepiska I. S. Turgeneva*. Ed. K. I. Tiun'kin. 2 vols. Moscow, 1986.

"Zapiski A. A. Bestuzheva, predstavlennaia Nikolaiu I." In *Iz pisem i pokazanii dekabristov*, ed. A. K. Borozdin. St. Petersburg, 1906.

Secondary Sources

Abaza, G. B. *Metod i stil' istoricheskoi prozy dekabristov*. Kalinin, 1973.

Abrams, M. H. *The Mirror and the Lamp: Romantic Theory and the Critical Tradition*. New York, 1971.

Afanas'ev, B., ed. *Russkaia romanticheskaia poema pervoi poloviny XIX v.: Antologiia.* Moscow, 1985.

Akutin, Iu. M., ed. *Aleksandr Vel'tman: Povesti i rasskazy.* Moscow, 1979.

Alekseev, M. P. *Etuidy o Marlinskom.* Irkutsk, 1928.

———, ed. *Ot romantizma k realizmu.* Leningrad, 1978.

Alexander, Alex E. *Bylina and Fairy Tale: The Origins of Russian Heroic Poetry.* The Hague, 1973.

Arkhipova, A. V. *Literaturnoe delo dekabristov.* Leningrad, 1987.

Aronson, M. I., and S. A. Reiser, eds. *Literaturnye kruzhki i salony.* Leningrad, 1929.

Babbitt, Irving. *Rousseau and Romanticism.* New York, 1935.

Bagby, Lewis. "Bestuzev-Marlinskij's 'Morechod Nikitin': Polemics in Ambiguity." *Russian Literature* 22 (1987): 311–42.

———. "Bestuzev-Marlinskij's 'Mulla Nur': A Muddled Myth to Rekindle Romance." *Russian Literature* 11 (1982): 117–28.

———. "Bestuzev-Marlinskij: Personality-Persona." *Russian Literature* 22 (1987): 247–310.

———. "Notes on Sentimental and Romantic Prose (and Literary Evolution)." *Russian Literature* 14 (1983): 103–48.

Bairon, Dzhordzh Gordon. *Izbrannaia lirika.* Moscow, 1988.

Bakhtin, Mikhail. "Avtor i geroi v esteticheskoi deiatel'nosti." In *Estetika slovesnogo tvorchestva,* ed. S. G. Bocharov. Moscow, 1979. Published in English as "Author and Hero in Esthetic Activity," in *Art and Answerability: Early Philosophical Essays by M. M. Bakhtin,* ed. Michael Holquist and Vadim Liapunov (Austin, Tex., 1990).

———. "The *Bildungsroman* and Its Significance in the History of Realism." Trans. Vern W. McGee. In *Speech Genres and Other Late Essays,* ed. Caryl Emerson and Michael Holquist. Austin, Tex., 1986.

———. *Problems of Dostoevsky's Poetics.* Ed. and trans. Caryl Emerson. Minneapolis, Minn., 1984.

———. *Tvorchestvo Fransua Rable i narodnaia kul'tura srednevekov'ia i Renessansa.* Moscow, 1990. Published in English as *Rabelais and His World,* trans. Helene Iswolsky (Bloomington, Ind., 1984).

Baranovskaia, M. Iu. *Dekabrist Nikolai Bestuzhev.* Moscow, 1954.

Barber, Richard. *The Knight of Chivalry.* New York, 1970.

Barlesi, Dominique. "Fonction et langue de personnages dans les nouvelles historiques de Bestuzev-Marlinskij." *Revue des Etudes Slaves* 49 (1973): 7–26.

Barratt, Glynn. *The Rebel on the Bridge.* Athens, Ohio, 1975.

———. *Voices in Exile: The Decembrist Memoirs.* Montreal, 1974.

Bashnin, Iu. N. *Literaturno-esteticheskie vzgliady dekabristov.* Petrozavodsk, 1969.

Bazanov, V. *Ocherki dekabristskoi literatury: Poeziia.* Moscow, 1957.

———. *Ocherki dekabristskoi literatury: Publitsistika, proza, kritika.* Moscow, 1953.

Belinskii, Vissarion. *Polnoe sobranie sochinenii.* 13 vols. Moscow, 1953–55.

Bethea, David M. *Pushkin Today.* Bloomington, Ind., 1993.

Bok, Sissela. "Secret Societies." In *Secrets.* New York, 1983.

Booth, Wayne C. *The Rhetoric of Fiction.* Chicago, 1961.

Borovkova-Maikova, M. S., ed. *"Arzamas i "arzamaskie" protokoly.* Leningrad, 1933.

Borozdin, A. K., ed. *Iz pisem i pokazanii dekabristov.* St. Petersburg, 1906.
Bortnevskii, V. G., ed. *Dnevnik Pavla Pushchina: 1812–1814.* Leningrad, 1987.
Bowra, C. M. *The Romantic Imagination.* New York, 1961.
Briggs, A.D.P. "Fallibility and Perfection in the Works of Alexander Pushkin." In Reid, 25–48.
Briskman, M. A., ed. *Dekabristy i russkaia kul'tura.* Leningrad, 1975.
Brombert, Victor. *Victor Hugo and the Visionary Novel.* Cambridge, Mass., 1984.
Brooks, Jeffrey. *When Russia Learned to Read.* Princeton, N.J., 1985.
Brown, William Edward. *A History of Russian Literature of the Romantic Period.* 4 vols. Ann Arbor, Mich., 1986.
Bulakhovskii, L. A. *Russkii literaturnyi iazyk pervoi poloviny XIX veka.* Kiev, 1957.
Buxton, John. *Byron and Shelley: The History of a Friendship.* New York, 1968.
Lord Byron: The Complete Poetic Works. Ed. Jerome J. McGann. 4 vols. Oxford, 1986.
Oeuvres Completes de Lord Byron. Trans. M. Benjamin Laroche. Paris, 1841.
Cawelti, John G. *Adventure, Mystery, and Romance: Formula Stories as Art and Popular Culture.* Chicago, 1976.
Chamokova, E. A. *Proza A. A. Bestuzheva-Marlinskogo 30-kh godov XIX veka.* Leningrad, 1968.
Chmielewski, H. V. *Aleksandr Bestuzev-Marlinskii.* Munich, 1966.
Chudakov, M. O., ed. *Proza russkikh poetov XIX v.* Moscow, 1982.
Chulkov, N. P., ed. *Dekabristy.* Letopisi Gosudarstvennogo literaturnogo muzeia 3 (1938).
Cizevskij, Dmitrij. *The Romantic Period.* Vol. 1 of *History of Nineteenth-Century Russian Literature.* Trans. Richard Noel Porter. Nashville, Tenn., 1974.
Clubbe, John. " 'The New Prometheus of New Men': Byron's 1816 Poems and *Manfred.*" In *Nineteenth Century Literary Perspectives: Essays in Honor of Lionel Stevenson.* Durham, N.C., 1974.
———. "The Tempest-toss'd Summer of 1816: Mary Shelley's *Frankenstein.*" *The Byron Journal* 19 (1991): 26–40.
Conrad, Peter. *Shandyism: The Character of Romantic Irony.* New York, 1978.
Cornwell, Neil. *The Life, Times and Milieu of V. F. Odoevsky: 1804–1869.* London, 1986.
Cross, A. G. *N. M. Karamzin: A Study of His Literary Career, 1783–1803.* Carbondale, Ill., 1971.
Debreczeny, Paul. *The Other Pushkin: A Study of Alexander Pushkin's Prose Fiction.* Stanford, Calif., 1983.
Dekabristy M. i N. Bestuzhevy: Pis'ma iz Sibiri. Irkutsk, 1929.
Diaconova, Nina, and Vadim Vatsuro. "Byron and Russia." In Trueblood, 143–59.
Dingley, R. J. " 'I Had a Dream': Byron's 'Darkness.' " *The Byron Journal* 9 (1981): 20–33.
Dovnar-Zapolskii, M. V. *Memuary dekabristov.* Kiev, 1906.
Dumezil, Georges. *The Stakes of the Warrior.* Trans. David Weeks. Berkeley, Calif., 1983.
Egolin, A. M., ed. *Literaturnoe nasledstvo: Dekabristy-literatory.* Vol. 59. Moscow, 1954.
Ermolaeva, I. I. *Problema romantizma v estetike i tvorchestve dekabristov.* Moscow, 1966.
Fanger, Donald. *The Creation of Nikolai Gogol.* Cambridge, Mass., 1984.
Fokht, U. R. *Problemy romantizma.* Moscow, 1967.

Frizman, L. G., ed. *Literaturno-kriticheskie raboty dekabristov.* Moscow, 1978.
Frye, Northrop, ed. *Romanticism Reconsidered.* New York, 1963.
———. *The Secular Scripture: A Study of the Structure of Romance.* Cambridge, Mass., 1976.
Gasparov, B. M. "Ustnaia rech'kak semioticheskii ob"ekt." *Uchenye zapiski Tartuskogo Gosudarstvennogo Universiteta: Semantika nominatsii i semiotika ustnoi rechi—lingvisticheskaia semantika i semiotika I* 442 (1978): 63–111.
Garrard, John G. *The Eighteenth Century in Russia.* Oxford, 1973.
———. "Karamzin, Mme de Stael, and the Russian Romantics." In *American Contributors to the Seventh International Congress of Slavists,* ed. Victor Terras. Mouton, 1973.
Gliukh, D. I. *Evoliutsiia ritmicheskoi organizatsii prozaicheskikh khudozhestvennykh proizvendenii v russkoi literature 20–30kh godov XIX veka.* Moscow, 1977.
Ginzburg, Lidiia. *O psikhologicheskoi proze.* Leningrad, 1971. Published in English as *On Psychological Prose,* trans. Judson Rosengrant (Princeton, N.J., 1991).
———, ed. *Poety 1820 i 30ikh godov.* Leningrad, 1972.
Girard, Rene. *The Scapegoat.* Baltimore, 1986.
———. *Violence and the Sacred.* Baltimore, 1977.
Gleckner, Robert F., and Gerald E. Enscoe, eds. *Romanticism: Points of View.* Detroit, Mich., 1975.
Goffman, Erving. *The Presentation of Self in Everyday Life.* Woodstock, N.Y., 1973.
Golubov, S. *Bestuzhev-Marlinskii.* Moscow, 1960.
Gordin, Ia. *Sobytiia i liudi 14 dekabria.* Moscow, 1985.
Goriushkin, L. M. *Ssyl'nye dekabristy v Sibiri.* Novosibirsk, 1985.
Goscilo, Helena. "The First Pechorin en route to *A Hero:* Lermontov's *Princess Ligovskaja.*" *Russian Literature* 11 (1982): 129–62.
Grigor'ian, K. N., ed. *Russkii romantizm.* Leningrad, 1978.
Grikhin, V. A., ed. *Russkaia fantasticheskaia povest' epokhi romantizma.* Moscow, 1987.
———, ed. *Russkaia romanticheskaia povest' (pervaia tret' XIX veka).* Moscow, 1983.
Gukovskii, G. *Pushkin i russkie romantiki.* Moscow, 1965.
Henzel, Janusz. *Proza Aleksandra Biestużewa-Marlinskiego w okresie Petersburgskim.* Warsaw, 1967.
Hirsch, E. D., Jr. *The Validity of Interpretation.* New Haven, Conn., 1967.
Hoffer, Eric. *The True Believer.* New York, 1966.
Ignatov, I. N. *Teatr i zriteli: Pervaia polovina XIX veka.* Moscow, 1916.
Isakov, S. G. "O 'livonskikh' povestiakh dekabristov." *Uchenye zapiski Tartuskogo Gosudarstvennogo Universiteta: Trudy po russkoi i slavianskoi filologii: Literaturovedenie* 8 (1965): 33–80.
———. "O livonskoi teme v russkoi literature 1820–1830-kh godov." *Uchenye zapiski Tartuskogo Gosudarstvennogo Universiteta: Trudy po russkoi i slavianskoi filologii III* 98 (1960): 144–93.
Iser, Wolfgang. *The Act of Reading: A Theory of Aesthetic Response.* Baltimore, Md., 1978.
Iusufov, R. Iu. "Degestansaia tema v tvorchestve A. A. Bestuzeva-Marlinskogo." *Degestan i russkaia literatura kontsa XVIII i pervoi poloviny XIX vv.* Moscow, 1964.
Ivanov, Via. Vs. "K semioticheskoi teorii karnavala kak inversii dvoichnykh pro-

tivopostavlenii." *Uchenye zapiski Tartuskogo Gosudarstvennogo Universiteta: Trudy po znakovym sistemam* 8 (1977): 45–64.

Jenkins, Michael. *Arakcheev, Grand Vizier of the New Russian Empire.* New York, 1969.

Kanunova, F. Z. *Estetika russkoi romanticheskoi povesti (A. A. Bestuzhev-Marlinskii i romantiki-belletristy 20–30-kh godov XIX v).* Tomsk, 1973.

———. *Iz istorii russkoi povesti kontsa XVIII–pervoi treti XIX v.* Tomsk, 1969.

Karlinsky, Simon. "Bestuzev-Marlinskij's *Journey to Revel'* and Puskin." In Bethea, 59–72.

Katz, Michael R. *Dreams and the Unconscious in Nineteenth-Century Russian Fiction.* London, 1984.

———. *The Literary Ballad in Early 19th Century Russian Literature.* London, 1976.

Knox, Bernard M. W. *The Heroic Temper.* Berkeley, Calif., 1964.

Kotliarevskii, N. *Dekabristy Kn. V. F. Odoevskii i A. A. Bestuzhev-Marlinskii: Ikh zhizn' i literaturnaia deiatel'nost'.* St. Petersburg, 1907.

Kovalevskii, M. O. "Melochi proshlogo: Satiricheskie kuplety na dekabristov." *Katorga i ssylka: Istoriko-revoliutsionnyi vestnik* 34 (1927): 78–82.

Kovarskii, N. "Rannii Marlinskii." In Tynianov and Eikhenbaum, 135–58.

Kozmin, N. K. *Ocherki iz istorii russkogo romantizma.* St. Petersburg, 1903.

Kroeber, Karl. *Romantic Narrative Art.* Madison, Wis., 1966.

Kupreianova, E. N., ed. *Istoriia russkoi Literatury.* 2 vols. Leningrad, 1981.

Ladurie, LeRoy. *Carnival in Romans.* Trans. Mary Feeney. New York, 1980.

Lampert, Eugene. *Studies in Rebellion.* London, 1957.

Landsman, Neil B. "Decembrist Romanticism: A. A. Bestuzhev-Marlinsky." In Reid, 64–95.

Leemets, Kh. D. "K voprosu o semanticheskoi strukture metaforicheskogo epiteta v russkoi proze nachala XIX v. (na materiale proizvedenii A. Marlinskogo)." *Uchenye zapiski Tartuskogo Gosudarstvennogo Universiteta: Trudy po russkoi i slavianskoi filologii* 17 (1971): 190–99.

———. "Metafora v russkoi romanticheskoi proze 30-kh godov XIX veka." Ph.D. diss., University of Tartu, 1974.

Leighton, Lauren. *Alexander Bestuzhev-Marlinsky.* New York, 1976.

———. "Bestuzhev-Marlinskii's 'The Frigate *Hope*': A Decembrist Puzzle." *Canadian Slavonic Papers* (1980): 171–86.

———. "Bestuzhev-Marlinsky as a Lyric Poet." *Slavonic and East European Review* 47 (July 1969): 308–22.

———. "The Great Soviet Debate over Romanticism: 1957–1964." *Studies in Romanticism* 22 (1983): 41–64.

———. "Marlinism: istoriia odnoi stilistiki." *Russian Literature* 12 (1975): 29–60.

———. "Marlinskij's 'Ispytanie': A Romantic Rejoinder to *Evgenij Onegin*." *Slavic and East European Journal* 13, no. 2 (1969): 200–216.

———. "Marlinsky." *Russian Literature Triquarterly* 3 (1972): 249–68.

———. "Puskin and Marlinskij: Decembrist Allusions." *Russian Literature* 14 (1983): 351–82.

———. "Romanticism, Marxism-Leninism, Literary Movement." *Russian Literature* 14 (1983): 183–220.

———. *Russian Romanticism: Two Essays.* The Hague, 1975.

Lemke, Mikhail. *Nikolaevskie zhandarmy i literatura 1826–1855 gg.* St. Petersburg, 1908.

Levin, Iu. "Ob obstoiatel'stvakh smerti A. A. Bestuzhev-Marlinskogo." *Russkaia literatura* 2 (1962): 219–22.

Lezhnev, A. Z. *Proza Pushkina*. Moscow, 1937. Published in English as *Pushkin's Prose*, trans. Roberta Reeder (Ann Arbor, Mich., 1983).

Likhachev, D. M., and A. M. Panchenko. *Smekhovoi mir drevnei Rusi*. Leningrad, 1976.

Lincoln, W. Bruce. *Nicholas I: Emperor and Autocrat of All the Russias*. Bloomington, Ind., 1978.

Lotman, Iu. M. *Aleksandr Sergeevich Pushkin*. Leningrad, 1983.

———. "Dekabrist v povsednevnoi zhizni (Bytovoe povedenie kak istoriko-psikhologicheskaia kategoriia)." In *Literaturnoe nasledie dekabristov*. Leningrad, 1975. Translated by C. R. Pike as "The Decembrist in Everyday Life," in Shukman, 71–124.

———. *Kul'tura i vzryv*. Moscow, 1992.

———. "Ob odnom chitatel'skom vospriiatii 'Bednoi Lizy' N. M. Karamzina (K strukture massovogo soznaniia XVIII v)." In *Rol' i znachenie literatury XVIII veka v istorii russkoi kul'tury*. Moscow, 1966.

———. "P. A. Viazemskii i dvizhenie dekabristov." *Uchenye zapiski Tartuskogo Gosudarstvennogo Universiteta: Trudy po russkoi i slavianskoi filologii III* 98 (1960): 24–142.

———. "Poetika bytovogo povedeniia v russkoi kul'ture XVIII veka." *Uchenye zapiski Tartuskogo Gosudarstvennogo Universiteta: Trudy po znakovym sistemam VIII* 411 (1977): 65–89.

———, ed. *Poety nachala XIX veka*. Leningrad, 1961.

———, ed. *Poety 1790–1820*. Leningrad, 1971.

———. "Puti razvitiia russkoi prozy 1800-kh–1810-kh godov." *Uchenye zapiski Tartuskogo Gosudarstvennogo Universiteta: Trudy po russkoi i slavianskoi filolologii IV* 104 (1961): 3–57.

———. "The Theater and Theatricality as Components of Early Nineteenth-Century Culture." In Shukman, 125–42.

———. "Ustnaia rech'v istoriko-kul'turnoi perspektive." *Uchenye zapiski Tartuskogo Gosudarstvennogo Universiteta: Semantika nominatsii i semiotika ustnoi rechi—lingvisticheskaia semantika i semiotika I* 442 (1978): 113–21.

Lotman, Iu. M., and B. Uspenskii. "Spory o iazyke v nachale XIX v. kak fakt russkoi kul'tury ('Proisshestvie v tsarstve tenei, ili sud'bina russiiskogo iazyka'— neizvestnoe sochinenie Semena Bobrova)." *Uchenye zapiski Tartuskogo Gosudarstvennogo Universiteta: Trudy po russkoi i slavianskoi filologii XXIV—literaturovedenie* 358 (1975): 168–322.

Lukacs, Georg. *The Historical Novel*. London, 1978.

Mann, Iu. V. *K istorii russkogo romantizma*. Moscow, 1973.

———. *Poetika russkogo romantizma*. Moscow, 1978.

Marchand, Leslie A. *Byron: A Biography*. 3 vols. New York, 1957.

———. *Byron: A Portrait*. Chicago, 1970.

———. *Byron's Poetry: A Critical Introduction*. Boston, 1965.

Marker, Gary. *Publishing, Printing, and the Origins of Intellectual Life in Russia, 1700–1800*. Princeton, N.J., 1985.

Maslin, N. "O romantizme A. Marlinskogo." *Voprosy literatury* 78 (1958): 141–69.

Massie, Robert K. *Peter the Great*. New York, 1981.

Mazour, Anatole G. *The First Russian Revolution, 1825*. Stanford, Calif., 1961.

McConnell, Frank D., ed. *Byron's Poetry*. New York, 1978.
McGann, Jerome J. *Fiery Dust: Byron's Poetic Development*. Chicago, 1968.
Meijer, M. "Vjazemskij and Romanticism." In *Dutch Contributions to the Seventh International Congress of Slavists,* ed. Andre VanHolk. The Hague, 1973.
Meilakh, V. "Literaturno-esteticheskaia programma dekabristov." In *Voprosy literatury i estetiki*. Leningrad, 1958.
Mersereau, John, Jr. *Baron Delvig's "Northern Flowers," 1825–1831: Literary Almanac of the Pushkin Pleiad*. Carbondale, Ill., 1967.
———. "The Nineteenth Century: Romanticism, 1820–1840." In Moser, 136–88.
———. *Orest Somov: Russian Fiction between Romanticism and Realism*. Ann Arbor, Mich., 1989.
———. "Pushkin's Concept of Romanticism." *Studies in Romanticism* 3, no. 1 (1963): 24–41.
———. *Russian Romantic Fiction*. Ann Arbor, Mich., 1983.
Mikhaleva, T. I. *Dekabristskaia proza (do 1826 goda)*. Moscow, 1969.
Modzalevskii, B. L. "Dostoevskii o dekabristakh." In *Dekabristy: Neizdannye materialy i stat'i,* ed. Modzalevskii and Iu. G. Oksman. Moscow, 1925.
Monas, Sidney. *The Third Section: Police and Society in Russia under Nicholas I*. Cambridge, Mass., 1961.
Mordovchenko, N. I. *Russkaia kritika pervoi chertverti XIX veka*. Moscow, 1959.
Morozov, V. D. *Ocherki po istorii russkoi kritiki vtoroi poloviny 20–30-kh godov XIX veka*. Tomsk, 1979.
Moser, Charles A., ed. *The Cambridge History of Russian Literature*. Cambridge, 1989.
———. *The Russian Short Story: A Critical History*. Boston, 1986.
Murav'ev, Vl., ed. *Mar'ina roshcha: Moskovskaia romanticheskaia povest'*. Moscow, 1984.
Nechkina, M. V. *Dvizhenie dekabristov*. 2 vols. Moscow, 1955.
———. *Vosstanie 14 dekabria 1825*. Moscow, 1951.
Nersisian, M. G. *Dekabristy v Armenii*. Erevan, 1975.
Neuhauser, R. *Towards the Romantic Age: Essays on Sentimental and Preromantic Literatures*. The Hague, 1974.
Oksman, Iu. G., ed. *Dekabristy: Otryvki iz istochnikov*. Moscow, 1926.
———. "The Politically Inflammatory Song 'Our Tsar is a German Russian.' " In Egolin, 69–84.
O'Meara, Patrick. *K. F. Ryleev*. Princeton, N.J., 1984.
Orlov, P. A., ed. *Russkaia sentimental'naia povest'*. Moscow, 1979.
Orlov, Vl. *Dekabristy*. 2 vols. Leningrad, 1975.
Ovsianiko-Kulikovskii, D. N., ed. *Istoriia russkoi literatury XIX veka*. 5 vols. Moscow, 1910.
Ovsiannikova, S. A. "A. A. Betzuhev-Marlinskii i ego rol' v dvizhenii dekabristov." In *Ocherki iz istorii dvizheniia dekabristov*. Moscow, 1954.
Paperno, I. A. "O dvuiazychnoi perepiske pushkinskoi epokhi." *Uchenye zapiski Tartuskogo Gosudarstvennogo Universiteta: Trudy po russkoi i slavianskoi filologii: Literaturovedenie* 24 (1975): 148–56.
———. "O rekonstruktsii ustnoi rechi iz pis'mennykh istochnikov (kruzhkovaia rech' i domashniaia literatura v pushkinskuiu epokhu)." *Uchenye zapiski Tartuskogo Gosudarstvennogo Universiteta: Semantika nominatsii i semiotika ustnoi rechi—lingvisticheskaia semantika i semiotika I* 442 (1978): 122–34.
———. "Perepiska Pushkina kak tselostnyi tekst: Mai–Oktiabr' 1831 g." *Uchenye*

zapiski Tartuskogo Gosudarstvennogo Universiteta: Studia Metrica et Poetica II 420 (nd): 71–81.

Passage, Charles E. *The Russian Hoffmannists.* The Hague, 1963.

Paushkin, M., ed. *Staryi russkii vodevil': 1819–1849.* Moscow, 1936.

Payne, Robert. *The Fortress.* London, 1967.

Peckham, Morse. *The Triumph of Romanticism.* Columbia, S.C., 1970.

Pedrotti, Louis. *Jozef-Julian Sekowski.* Berkeley, Calif., 1965.

Petrunina, N. N. "Dekabristskaia proza i puti razvitiia povestvovatel'nykh zhanrov." In *Russkaia literatura.* Leningard, 1978.

———. "Proza dekabristov (romanticheskaia povest' pervoi poloviny 1820-kh gg." In Kupreianova, 2:179–88.

———. *Proza Pushkina.* Leningrad, 1987.

———. "Proza vtoroi poloviny 1820-kh–1830-kh gg." In Kupreianova, 2:501–29.

Pigarev, K. *Zhizn' Ryleeva.* Moscow, 1947.

Pokrovskii, A. A., ed. *Materialy po istorii vosstaniia dekabristov.* 25 vols. Moscow, 1925.

———, ed. *Vosstanie dekabristov: Materialy.* Vol. 1. Moscow, 1925.

Popov, A. V. *Dekabristy-literatory na Kavkaze.* Stavropol', 1963.

———. *Russkie pisateli na Kavkaze.* Baku, 1949.

"Popytka brat'ev A. A. i M. A. Bestuzhevykh izdavat' zhurnal, 1818–1823." *Russkaia starina* 8 (1900): 391–95.

Postnov, Iu. S. *Sibir' v poezii dekabristov.* Novosibirsk, 1976.

Praz, M. *The Romantic Agony.* New York, 1965.

Presniakov, A. E. *14 dekabria 1825.* Moscow, 1926.

Proffer, Carl, ed. *The Critical Prose of Alexander Pushkin with Critical Essays by Four Russian Romantic Poets.* Bloomington, Ind., 1969.

———, ed. *Russian Romantic Prose: An Anthology.* Ann Arbor, Mich., 1979.

———. "Washington Irving in Russia: Pushkin, Gogol, Marlinsky." *Comparative Literature* 20 (1967): 329–42.

Prokhorov, G. V. "A. A. Bestuzhev v Iakutske." In Azadovskii, *Pamiati dekabristov,* 1:189–226.

Propp, Vladimir. *The Morphology of the Folktale.* Austin, Tex., 1968.

Pul'khritudova, E. M. "Literaturnaia teroiia dekabristskogo romantizma v 30-e gody XIX veka." In *Problemy romantizma.* Moscow, 1968.

———. *Razvitie dekabristskogo romantizma v 30-kh gody XIX veka.* Moscow, 1966.

Pypin, A. N. "Sverstnik Pushkina: A. Bestuzhev-Marlinskii." In *Istoriia Russkoi literatury,* vol. 4, ed. M. M. Stasiulevich. St. Petersburg, 1907.

Raeff, Marc. *Imperial Russia, 1682–1825: The Coming of Age of Modern Russia.* New York, 1971.

Raglan, Lord. *The Hero.* New York and London, 1979.

Reid, Robert, ed. *Problems of Russian Romanticism.* Hants, 1986.

Reviakin, A. I., and I. A. Reviakina. "Aleksandr Aleksandrovich Bestuzhev-Marlinskii: 1797–1837." In *Istoriia russkoi literatury XIX veka.* Moscow, 1977.

Riasanovsky, Nicholas. *Nicholas I and Official Nationality in Russia, 1825–1855.* Berkeley, Calif., 1969.

Ricoeur, Paul. *Interpretation Theory: Discourse and the Surplus of Meaning.* Fort Worth, Tex., 1976.

Ridenour, George M. "Byron in 1816: Four Poems from Diodati." In *George Gordon, Lord Byron.* New York, 1986.

Riha, Thomas, ed. *Readings in Russian Civilization*. 2 vols. Chicago, 1969.

Rozen, A. E. *Zapiski dekabrista*. Ed. M. D. Sergeev. Irkutsk, 1984.

Russkie povesti XIX veka 20–30-kh godov. 2 vols. Moscow, 1950.

Sadykhov, M. *Pisateli-dekabristy i Azerbaidzhan*. Baku, 1967.

Sakharov, V. I., ed. *Russkaia romanticheskaia povest'*. Moscow, 1980.

Shaduri, Vano. *Dekabristskaia literatura i gruzinskaia obshchestvennost'*. Tbilisi, 1958.

Shantarenkov, N., ed. *Russkii vodevil'*. Moscow, 1970.

Sharupich, A. P. *Dekabrist Aleksandr Bestuzhev: Voprosy mirovozzreniia i tvorchestva*. Minsk, 1962.

———. *Romantizm Aleksandra Bestuzheva*. Minsk, 1964.

Shatalov, S. E., and S. V. Turaev, eds. *Istoriia romantizma v russkoi literature. Romantizm v russkoi literature 20–30-kh godov XIX v (1825–1840)*. Moscow, 1979.

Shaw, J. Thomas. "Puskin's 'The Shot.' " *Indiana Slavic Studies* 3 (1963): 113–29.

———, ed. *The Letters of Pushkin*. Madison, Wis., 1967.

Shchegolev, P. E. *Nikolai I i dekabristy*. St. Petersburg, 1919.

Shchukin, P. S. "A. Bestuzhev-Marlinskii v Iakutske." In Vatsuro et al., 2:140–47.

Shraikha, S. Ia., ed. "Nikolai I i dekabristy: Tsar' sishchik." *Dekabristy: 1825–1925*. Moscow, 1925.

Shteingel', V. I. *Sochineniia i pis'ma*. 2 vols. Irkutsk, 1985.

Shukman, Ann, ed. *The Semiotics of Russian Culture*. Ann Arbor, Mich., 1984.

Simpson, Mark S. *The Russian Gothic Novel and Its British Antecedents*. Columbus, Ohio, 1986.

Sipovskii, V. V. *Ocherki iz istorii russkogo romantizma*. St. Petersburg, 1909.

Smirnov, I. I. *Drevnerusskii smekh i logika komicheskogo. Trudy otdela drevnerusskoi literatury* 33 (1977): 305–18.

Stepanov, N. L. "Pisatel'-dekabrist (A. Bestuzhev-Marlinskii)." In *Poety i prozaiki*. Moscow, 1966.

———. *Proza Pushkina*. Moscow, 1962.

Sutherland, Christine. *The Princess of Siberia: The Story of Maria Volkonsky and the Decembrist Exiles*. New York, 1984.

Syrochkovskii, B. E. *Mezhdutsarstvie 1825 goda i vosstanie dekabristov v perepiske i memuarakh chlenov tsarskoi sem'i*. Moscow, 1926.

Tarasov, E. "Iakutskaia ssylka Bestuzheva-Marlinskogo." In *Dekabristy na katorge i v ssylke*. Vols. 8–9. Moscow, 1925.

Terras, Victor. *Belinskij and Russian Literary Criticism*. Madison, Wis., 1974.

———. "The Russian Short Story 1830–1850." In Moser, 1–49.

Titov, A. "Aleksandr Bestuzhev—geroi zabytogo romana." *Russkaia literatura* 1 (1959): 133–38.

Tiun'kin, K. I., ed. *Perepiska I. S. Turgeneva*. 2 vols. Moscow, 1980.

Todd, William Mills, III. *The Familiar Letter as a Literary Genre in the Age of Pushkin*. Princeton, N.J., 1976.

———. *Fiction and Society in the Age of Pushkin*. Cambridge, 1986.

———. "Institutions of Literature in Early-Nineteenth-Century Russia: Boundaries and Transgressions." In *Literature and History*, ed. Gary Saul Morson. Stanford, Calif., 1986.

Tolstoy, Leo. *The Cossacks and the Raid*. Trans. Andrew MacAndrew. New York, 1961.

Todorov, Tzvetan. *The Poetics of Prose*. Trans. Richard Howard. Ithaca, N.Y., 1977.

————. *Theories of the Symbol*. Trans. Catherine Porter. Ithaca, N.Y., 1982.

Troitskii, V. Iu. *Khudozhestvennye otkrytiia russkoi romanticheskoi prozy 20–30-kh godov XIX v.* Moscow, 1985.

Troyat, Henri. *Alexander of Russia: Napoleon's Conqueror*. Trans. Joan Pinkham. New York, 1982.

Trueblood, Paul Graham. *Byron's Cultural and Political Influence in Nineteenth-Century Europe*. Atlantic Highlands, N.J., 1981.

Tseitlin, A. G. *Russkaia literatura pervoi poloviny XIX veka*. Moscow, 1940.

Tsetlin, M. *Dekabristy: Sud'ba odnogo pokoleniia*. Paris, 1933.

Turgenev, I. S. *Polnoe sobranie sochinenii i pisem v 30 tomakh*. Moscow, 1978.

Tynianov, Iu. *Arkhaisty i novatory*. Ed. Dmitrij Tschizewskii. Leningrad, 1929.

————. "Arkhaisty i Pushkin." In *Arkhaisty i novatory*. Munich, 1967.

————. *Pushkin i ego sovremenniki*. Moscow, 1960.

Tynianov, Iu., and Boris Eikhenbaum, eds. *Russkaia proza*. The Hague, 1963. Published in English as *Russian Prose*, ed. Ray Parrott (Ann Arbor, Mich., 1985).

Vasil'ev, V. *Bestuzhev-Marlinskii na Kavkaze*. Krasnodar, 1939.

————. "Dekabrist A. A. Bestuzhev-Marlinskii kak pisatel'-etnograf." *Nauchno-pedagogicheskii sbornik Vostochnogo Pedagogicheskogo Instituta v Kazani* (1926): 56–76.

Vatsuro, V. "A. A. Bestuzhev." In Vatsuro et al., 2:119–73.

————. "Lermontov i Marlinskii." In *Tvorchestvo M. Iu. Lermontova*. Moscow, 1964.

Vatsuro, V., et al., eds. *Pisateli-dekabristy v vospominaniiakh sovremennikov*. 2 vols. Moscow, 1980.

Vinogradov, B. S. *Kavkaz v russkoi literature 30-kh godov XIX veka: Ocherki*. Grozny, 1966.

Vinogradov, V. V. *Iazyk Pushkina*. Moscow, 1935.

————. *Literaturnoe nasledstvo: Dekabristy-Literatory*. Vol. 60. Moscow, 1956.

————. *Ocherki po istorii russkogo literaturnogo iazyka XVII–XIX vv.* Moscow, 1938.

————. "Stil' prozy Lermontova." In *Literaturnoe nasledstvo*, 44:517–71. Moscow, 1941.

"Vospominaniia Matveia Ivanovicha Murav'eva-Apostola, zapissanye Aleksandrom Petrovichem Beliaevym v 1883." *Russkaia starina* (1886): 519–30.

Walicki, Andrzej. *A History of Russian Thought from the Enlightenment to Marxism*. Stanford, Calif., 1979.

Woodring, Carl. *Politics in English Romantic Poetry*. Cambridge, 1970.

Zamotin, I. I. *Romantizm dvadtsatykh godov XIX stoletiia v russkoi literature*. St. Petersburg, 1911.

Zhirmunskii, V. M. *Bairon i Pushkin*. Leningrad, 1978.

————. "O ritmicheskoi proze." *Russkaia literatura* 4 (1966): 103–14.

————. *Voprosy teorii literatury*. The Hague, 1962.

Zhivov, V. M., and B. A. Uspenskii. "Tsar' i bog: Semioticheskie aspekty sakralizatsii monarkha v Rossii." In *Iazyki kul'tury i problemy perevodimosti*. Moscow, 1987.

Zisserman, A. L. "Otryvki iz moikh vospominanii." *Russkii vestnik* 5 (1876): 50–103.

Zyzykin, M. V. *Imperator Nikolai I i voennyi zagovor 14 dekabria 1825 goda*. Buenos Aires, 1958.

Index

73; German obsession of, 141–43; last will and testament of, 147; uprising against, 139, 181
Catherine the Great, 20, 21, 25, 140, 147
Constantine, Grand Prince, 22, 23, 146–48, 155–56, 159–61, 163, 173, 182
Nicholas I: Decembrist attitude toward, 176; Decembrist Revolt and, 23, 150, 153, 155–62, 165–69, 212 n. 2; interregnum and, 146–48; reign of, 23, 143; relationship with Bestuzhev-Marlinsky, 24, 137, 170–71, 189, 228, 233, 278, 347
Pavlovich, Grand Prince Mikhail, 159, 185
Peter the Great, 19, 137, 175, 224
Peter III, 140, 146
Rousseau, Jean-Jacques, 187, 342
Ryleyev, Kondraty, 191 n. 13, 336
death of, 168, 345
Decembrist activities of, 134–36, 139–40, 148–50, 157, 162–63
Decembrist poetry of, 46, 140–45
"The Exile," 65
interrogation of, 176–82, 187–88
Nalivaiko, 139
The Polar Star and, 38, 45, 45–46 n. 8, 72–73, 128–29
relationship with Bestuzhev-Marlinsky, 40, 68, 134–38, 171, 184, 187–88
relationship with Pushkin, 225 n. 21
"Voinarovsky," 135–38, 169

Schiller, Friedrich, 37, 107, 217
Scott, Sir Walter, 10, 80, 102 n. 20, 104, 107, 111, 280, 294, 338 n. 48
Secret Society. See Decembrism
Semevsky, Mikhail, 27, 216, 247–48
Senkovsky, Osip (Brambeus), 6, 67 n. 7, 291, 294, 296, 298
Sentimentalism, 89, 91
sentimental: canon, 96; cliché, 97, 101; epithets, 96; figures of speech, 96,

251; formulae, 97; images, 51; point of view, 62; school, 100; style, 85, 87, 122, 128; tale, 67 n. 7, 88, 97–98
Serafim (Metropolitan), 158–59
Shakespeare, William, 37, 217
Shelley, Percy Bysshe, 332
Shelley, Mary, 332
Frankenstein; or the Modern Prometheus, 332
Shishkov, Admiral Alexander, 58–59, 80, 85
Shteingel, Vladimir, 177
Smirdin, Alexander, 239, 263
Society of Lovers of Russian Literature, 63–66, 134, 179
Somov, Orest, 4, 43, 44, 45, 60, 129, 314
The Son of the Fatherland, 60
Sterne, Laurence, 86, 129, 294, 299

thanatos, 97
thanatic figures of speech, 271
theme: in life, 204, 234, 342; in poetry, 55; in prose, 93, 133, 240. See also death
Tolstoy, Count Leo, 2, 8–9, 17, 38, 240, 247, 269
The Cossacks, 307
"Hadji Murat," 346–47
"The Raid," 9
War and Peace, 38, 199, 206 n. 19
Trubetskoy, Prince Sergei, 23, 40, 149–50, 154, 165
Turgenev, Ivan, 1, 2 n. 1, 8
Turgenev, Nicholas, 134

Vasil'ev, V., 12, 258
Voyeikov, Alexander, 43, 44, 64, 68 n. 8
Vyazemsky, Prince Peter, 37, 42
aesthetics of, 80
attitude toward romanticism, 59
Decembrist leanings of, 138
relationship with Bestuzhev-Marlinsky, 38, 77, 81